Lloyd Hamilton

LLOYD HAMILTON

*Poor Boy Comedian
of Silent Cinema*

Anthony Balducci

McFarland & Company, Inc., Publishers
Jefferson, North Carolina, and London

FRONTISPIECE: Lloyd Hamilton, courtesy of
the Museum of Modern Art Film Stills Archive.

LIBRARY OF CONGRESS CATALOGUING-IN-PUBLICATION DATA

Balducci, Anthony, 1958–
Lloyd Hamilton : poor boy comedian of silent cinema / Anthony Balducci.
p. cm.
Includes bibliographical references and index.

ISBN 978-0-7864-4159-4
softcover : 50# alkaline paper ∞

1. Hamilton, Lloyd.
2. Motion picture actors and actresses — United States — Biography.
I. Title.
PN2287.H1783B35   2009   791.4302'8092 — dc22 [B]   2009021385

British Library cataloguing data are available

©2009 Anthony Balducci. All rights reserved

*No part of this book may be reproduced or transmitted in any form
or by any means, electronic or mechanical, including photocopying
or recording, or by any information storage and retrieval system,
without permission in writing from the publisher.*

On the cover: Lloyd Hamilton
(courtesy of the Museum of Modern Art Film Stills Archive)

Manufactured in the United States of America

*McFarland & Company, Inc., Publishers
Box 611, Jefferson, North Carolina 28640
www.mcfarlandpub.com*

To my son, Griffin

Acknowledgments

My research put me in contact with many people devoted to silent film comedy. This includes collectors, researchers, authors, archivists, film festival organizers, and people who simply enjoy watching a funny film. These individuals, in helping me to put this book together, were generous with their time, knowledge and materials. I was grateful to receive information from them, but I was even more grateful to receive their sincere encouragement, advice and friendship.

I include in this category Robert Farr, Cole Johnson, Steve Massa, Kevin Brownlow, Steve Rydzewski, Merrill T. McCord, Tom Reeder, Joe Moore, Robert Adkins, William Thomas Sherman, and Marilyn Slater. I must also give special thanks to Ned Comstock, MGM Collection/University of Southern California; Stuart Ng, Warner Bros Archive/University of Southern California; Kathy Ledech, Turner Entertainment Clips and Stills Library; Nancy Kauffman, George Eastman House; Vandalia Cemetery; Jules White; Charles Lamont; Virginia Hawksley; Richard Bishop; Sally and Stuart McKenzie; Dee Monroe; Ron Magliozzi, Museum of Modern Art; Faye Thompson, Academy of Motion Picture Arts and Sciences; Glenn Bradie, Everett Collection; Steven Lavoie, the Oakland Public Library; Barbara Hall and Jenny Romero the Margaret Herrick Library; and the staff at the Lincoln Center Library of Performing Arts.

I have to thank family members who supported this project. My cousin, Tom Balducci, came into New York's Performing Arts library with a camera and copystand to photograph material in the library's archives. He was so intent on getting the sharpest images that he pressed his eye closely to the viewer and scratched the lens of his eyeglasses. When I needed additional information on my references sources to complete my endnotes, my sister, Joanne DeFeo, spent an afternoon tearing apart our mother's garage looking for my tattered old notebooks. My son, Griffin Balducci, helped me to select and scan many of the photos found in this book.

Table of Contents

Acknowledgments   vi
Preface   1

1. An Oakland Boy   5
2. Stage to Screen   16
3. The Rapid Advancement of an Earnest and Inventive Player   23
4. Part of a New Wave   37
5. New Vision   45
6. Business Suicide   52
7. The New Mentor   58
8. Dances with Lions   66
9. Further Adventures on an Ostrich Farm   77
10. A Fresh Start   80
11. Lloyd on His Own   89
12. The Man in Blackface   102
13. The Manageable Chaplin   111
14. Tumbling Back to Shorts   125
15. Erratic Behavior   132
16. Ain't It a Crime?   137
17. "Drank Himself Out"   142
18. The Vagrant   146
19. The Comeback   152
20. The Final Fade   155
21. In Reference to Relics   182

Appendix I: Profiles of Select Sunshine Personnel	187
Appendix II: Profiles of Select Hamilton's Associates	194
Appendix III: Filmography	201
Chapter Notes	243
Bibliography	247
Index	249

Preface

I was introduced to Lloyd Hamilton through a *TV Guide* listing. It was January 2, 1974, and I was still in high school. This day, I had come back to school after a long holiday recess and I was finding it a strain to get going again. Everything was turning out to be a major chore to me. I returned home wanting nothing more than to stretch out on the couch and watch television. I browsed through the *TV Guide* to see what was on and I found a listing for *Silent Comedy Film Festival*, a five-part series ending its run on the local PBS station. I had watched other episodes of the series during my week off. By turns, these episodes spotlighted Charles Chaplin, Buster Keaton, Harold Lloyd and Harry Langdon, the bygone stars once declared by writer James Agee to be the comic masters of silent film. This had established the group as the "Big Four," an exclusive fraternity that film scholars have maintained for decades. *TV Guide* provided the following description of this final episode: "Lloyd Hamilton, known for his pancake hat and ducklike walk, is discussed by Walter Kerr, *New York Times* critic."

Based on previous installments, I expected to be treated to an amusing and informative half hour. What I finally viewed on that program was an impressive ten-minute clip from a film entitled *Move Along*. I readily identified with the main character, an introverted man coping in a frenzied city. This man was timid, sober, delicate, methodical, and mannerly. Also, it impressed me how Hamilton's gags were carefully built one on top of the other. Then, abruptly, the film ended. Graff explained that the second half of *Move Along* was not known to exist. He reported that little of Hamilton's work was available.

The subsequent discussion centered on one significant question: Would the discovery of Hamilton's missing films justify the comic's presence in the company of Chaplin, Keaton, Lloyd and Langdon? Graff contended that Hamilton should be added to this pantheon, expanding the collection to the "Big Five."

The program left me wanting more. It would be a long time before I would learn details about Hamilton's life and get to see other films he made, but the image of the waddling comedian would not leave my mind.

The next year, I found a discussion about Hamilton in *Silent Clowns*, an insightful and in-depth four-pound tome written by Walter Kerr. Kerr expressed regret that few of Hamilton's films were available and he couldn't do a more extensive analysis of his work. His discussion of Hamilton was limited, his evaluation of the old comedy star compacted into a simple caption: "Much admired, still a mystery."[1] This goaded me into action. I decided to investigate Hamilton's background and try to decrease, if not resolve, this enigma.

I did my initial research for this book in 1977. I spent a lot of time at the library, writing away for public records, and trying to find people who knew Hamilton. The efforts to find people proved the most frustrating. Those people who could have offered me the most intimate details about Hamilton's life had long ago passed away. I was most determined to locate Hamilton's first wife, Ethel, but I learned after much investigation that Ethel had died in Glendale, California, on January 21, 1965. I spent time looking for Ruth Hiatt, who was perhaps Hamilton's favorite leading lady. I looked though Los Angeles phone directories and checked if Hiatt was still registered with the Screen Actors Guild. The whole time, Ruth was right under my nose, living just 14 miles outside of Hollywood. I was still working to find her when I read an obituary for the woman, who had died of congestive heart failure. I found two of Hamilton's directors, Alfred Santell and Jack White, but both men were very ill and unable to talk with me. I began to worry that I was twenty years too late in writing this book.

I soon went back to work doing research and was able to turn up further material. I sought the help of several film historians, who loved Hamilton and were glad to help me. I kept digging away, letting nothing deter me. It occurred to me that historians haven't needed to talk to royal wife Ankhesenamen to write about King Tut. I ignored, as best I could, the unpleasant mildew smell that got up inside my nose from old magazines, pressbooks, scripts, production stills, court filings, and interview transcripts. I remained determined and was, in the end, exhaustive in my research.

My search for interview subjects extended to making contact with Hamilton's family. In 1992, I located Hamilton's great niece, Claudia Owen, in Newport Beach, California. I tried hard to get the woman to talk to me, writing to her three times. I made sure, in my correspondence, to include a self-addressed, stamped envelope. I gave her my phone number and told her that she could call me collect.

In playing hard-to-get, Claudia had managed to arouse my courtship skills. So, I had a costly bouquet of flowers delivered to her home. That night, Claudia phoned me. She opened the conversation by announcing, "Mr. Balducci, you have worn me out." Claudia politely thanked me for the flowers, which she said were gorgeous, but she maintained strict control of the conversation and seemed to have prepared what she had to say. She promised that, after the holidays, she would help me with my book. She explained that she would see many relatives at a Christmas gathering. She said that some of them knew "Uncle Lloyd" and might want to contribute their recollections. By February, I had not heard from Claudia. As a friendly gesture, I sent her a video collection of her uncle's comedies.

In the meantime, I located Hamilton's niece Virginia. As it worked out, we talked first in 1992 and a second time in 2008. Following the second conversation, Virginia told me that, if I wanted help from other family members, it was best that I go through her niece, Sally McKenzie. I drafted a letter to Sally and got it into the mail. Two months later, I got a call from Hamilton's nephew, Richard Bishop. I had been trying to contact Richard for years and was surprised to hear from him suddenly. Sally had passed my letter onto him and Richard, who admired my doggedness in tracking down members of his family, decided that I deserved whatever help he could provide.

As we talked Richard admitted that his family was extremely private and they had some embarrassment about Uncle Lloyd, who did not end his days "in good form."

Richard said his family had "stood back" from this story for many years and they preferred to keep it that way.

Richard told me that his sister Claudia had a trunk filled with personal effects that Hamilton had left behind when he died. He said that he was willing to travel 400 miles to his sister's home in Los Angeles and get this material out so that I could take a look at it. He also mentioned that he personally had a handsome portrait of his uncle as well as the slapshoes his uncle wore while playing the slapstick tramp "Ham." He offered to box up the items in the trunk, which included theatre posters, movie stills and personal photographs, and ship them out to me within the next week. Richard informed me that the trunk had once included one of Lloyd's outfits, but some kids in the family had borrowed the outfit and never returned it. He talked briefly about the photos in the trunk. He spoke of photos which showed his uncle with a series of beautiful girlfriends. He said that he had photos of his uncle with his second wife, Irene. "She was very beautiful, too," he said. He mentioned a theatre poster for the "Ham and Bud" series and a movie still featuring his uncle in drag.

Richard said that, years ago, his sister had called to say she was cleaning out her garage and didn't know what they should do with the old trunk. They discussed throwing it in the trash. After all, the trunk had been sitting in storage for sixty years.

He promised to at least get these items to me. I asked him a question about something that had come up while I was working on revisions. It was a simple, harmless question, nothing that he should have had a problem answering, but he responded that he was unable to get into this area with me. He explained that he wanted to do more to help me with the book, but he would be going against the wishes of his mother and his aunt to "tell all." "Believe me," he said, "I am caught between a rock and a hard place." He said that, maybe, he could talk to other people in his family and get their permission to talk about these things with me. I explained that the book was respectful of his uncle and I wouldn't have written the book if I didn't have true admiration and affection for the man. It was my ultimate goal for people to rediscover this very special artist. The last thing I wanted to do, I said, was to tear down the person. "I know that," he said quietly.

When Richard's offer fell through, I contacted Sally, who happened to be taking care of her mother's home. She was able to locate the trunk. It was a portmanteau, a traveling trunk that opens out into multiple compartments. She informed me, with regret, that the trunk was "100 percent empty." Yet more traces of Lloyd Hamilton lost to the mists of time.

In talking to family members about Lloyd Hamilton, I could occasionally sense their pride in the man. Virginia described being a little girl and attending a public ceremony where Oakland officials named her movie star uncle "Mayor for a Day." Sally told me that, one day, she had lunch with her mother and aunt in Sherman Oaks and they decided to visit the comedian's star outside of Grauman's Chinese Theatre. She said that, for the first time, she saw an outpouring of pride from these women, who evidently did appreciate the accomplishments of their uncle.

I spent more than two years holed up in various libraries. When I would tell people what I was working on, they usually had no idea who this silent comic Lloyd Hamilton was. Some people would confuse Lloyd Hamilton with Harold Lloyd and tell me they liked that movie where he hung off the clock.

One day, though, I met a man who knew exactly who Lloyd Hamilton was. I got on an elevator in the New York City Public Library. A bleary-eyed old man joined me on the elevator. He told me that he got tired looking through a large assortment of art etchings. He said that I looked tired, too, and he asked me what I had been up to in the library. We were leaving the elevator and stepping into an atrium when I told the man I was researching a book on a silent film comedian named Lloyd Hamilton.

As if by magic, the man's sore eyes instantly brightened. "Do you know what my favorite Hamilton bit is?" he asked.

The man commenced to relax his facial muscles and widen his eyes, assuming a look of innocence and bewilderment that Hamilton had perpetually exhibited on screen. Suddenly possessed by this character, the man glanced about the quiet, cavernous atrium. While providing narration, he proceeded to re-enact one of Hamilton's routines. This dealer in art prints had readily, vividly and fondly recalled not only a bygone comic but a bit of business that, 50 years earlier, he had seen that comedian perform.

I worked hard to bring this impressive comedian out of the realm of mystery and revive his story for historians and fans. This book is a product of the author's passion, curiosity and doggedness. I expect readers to learn about the devotion and hard work of an ambitious artist who staked a claim in a newly flourishing and fiercely competitive field and, in the process, met with both great success and great failure. In the process, they may gain a new insight into the origins of film comedy.

1

An Oakland Boy

Lloyd Hamilton's sound, conservative middle-class background set him apart from most of the early slapstick comedy stars, who had come from broken families, theatrical families and poor immigrant families. Charlie Chaplin was raised for a time solely by his mother, who made her living singing in British music halls. He made his own show business debut on the music hall stage at the age of five. After his mother was committed to an asylum and his alcoholic father died, he spent time in a workhouse and a school for orphans and destitute children. When he became a star in Hollywood, he was praised as an immigrant who had used his comedy talents to escape poverty. Buster Keaton had a checkered past as a child star in vaudeville. His reputation for performing dangerous stunts on stage got his parents in trouble with the Gerry Society, whose job it was to enforce child labor laws. Harold Lloyd's father, Foxy, had trouble holding onto a job and dragged his family from state to state looking for work. This nomadic existence caused marital strife and eventually led to divorce. Harold grew up in the custody of his father and helped out in his spare time at his father's pool hall. Roscoe Arbuckle found himself on his own at twelve years old, after his mother died and his father abandoned him. He performed as a singer to help support himself. At the age of twelve, Harry Langdon ran away from home to join a traveling medicine show.

Lloyd Hamilton's childhood experiences were not marked by poverty, divorce, deceased parents, workhouses, asylums, vaudeville, pool halls, the Gerry Society, immigration, or children running away from home. He grew up in a stable, prosperous home under the watchful eyes of his mother and father, who had been committed to their marriage for decades.

It was in the middle of the 1870's that William C. Hamilton and Mary Edith McEntee married in a ceremony in Detroit, Michigan.

The McEntees were immigrants from Ireland who ran a family farm. Mary, a hardworking daughter, had been born in 1859. Richard Bishop, who knew Mary for the first twenty-one years of his life, said that she was "a charming woman with mid–Victorian manners."

The Hamiltons were an affluent group in their homeland of England. William's grandfather was a judge and several other relations were lawyers. The Hamiltons, descendants of the Pilgrims, were members of a Protestant denomination known as the Congregational Christian Church. These were thinking and methodical people who strictly regulated their lives and behaved in a reserved manner. They were sturdy, resourceful and hard-working. They were an aloof people who strove to maintain an image of respectability. To borrow a phrase from Robert Louis Stevenson, they "wore a more than commonly grave countenance before the public."[2]

William was born in 1847, the second child of William and Donna Hamilton. He was English on his father's side and Scottish on his mother's side. His father's profession, according to the 1860 census, was farmer. Farming was, in fact, the predominant occupation in the area during this period. Census takers at the time recorded sixteen men with the name William Hamilton living in Michigan and every one of those men reported being farm laborers. In 1860, according to the census records, William had an older brother, Charles; two younger brothers, Frank and Thomas; and a younger sister, Edda.

In the 1870s, Michigan was a land of farmers, lumbermen, copper-miners and fur-traders. The state was largely agricultural, comprised of many lonely farms. An author wrote that Detroit, its only municipality of any significance, was "a quiet, tree-shaded city, unobtrusively going about its business of brewing beer and making carriages and stoves."[3]

During the 1820s and 1830s, Michigan had attracted a considerable share of pioneers moving westward, mostly from New England. By 1840, this group constituted two-thirds of Michigan's population. Various members of the Hamilton and McEntee families had come from New York and Connecticut.

William and Mary were not married long before they moved away from Michigan. The couple came to a prosperous place that lay far beyond their roots, a city fast becoming a world center of trade and finance. Author Richard Koszarski called this place "a gold rush boom town masquerading as a graceful European capital."[4] The Hamiltons' new home was San Francisco.

San Francisco, despite its wealth, was not the most sound or still place to live. It was, according to newspaper editor Samuel Bowles, "audacious and original."[5] It was an unkempt metropolis that was widely taken by observers to be "the wickedest city in the world."[6] Rudyard Kipling, after visiting San Francisco in 1889, called it "a mad city — a city inhabited for the most part by perfectly insane people."[7]

San Francisco's most notorious quarters were Chinatown and the Barbary Coast. Stories of Chinatown revolved around brothels, opium dens, mysterious underground passages, and the bloody Tong wars. The neighboring Barbary Coast was almost exclusively inhabited by rough sailors, coarse gold prospectors, bawdy dancehall girls, and a wide variety of criminals. The regulars of the Barbary Coast were, according to author Benjamin Lloyd, known mostly for their "drunken carousals and broils."[8]

The city's five Congregational Churches had, according to Mr. Lloyd, "large memberships and thriving conditions."[9] William and Mary Hamilton attended service at the largest of these churches, the First Congregational Church, which was located at California and Dupont Streets. Some of the wealthiest citizens in town gathered inside this building on Sunday mornings.

Nearby were other majestic churches, including Grace Church and St. Mary's Cathedral, but the churchgoers found scant refuge in this place as the wicked and the dissolute of the town were never far away. Mr. Lloyd wrote, "Devout Christians assemble at these churches and engage in the solemn service of the sanctuary.... [They] thither repair upon the Sabbath day, and unite their voices in praise and thanksgiving for the goodness and mercy of the Lord ... [while] a block away the streets are lined with houses of prostitution; and a stone's throw beyond, is the Barbary Coast reeking in infamous filth."[10] Pacific Street, which led directly from the wharf at the Barbary Coast to the center of town, near Portsmouth Plaza, was the town's major thoroughfare, but it was a street that had deteriorated into "the haunt of the low and the vile of every kind."[11] Reporter Albert S. Evans wrote, "The whole street, for a half dozen blocks, is literally swarming with the scum of creation."[12]

Mary Hamilton may have kept to the tamer streets, but these streets, whether Market Street or Montgomery Street, could not have been tame enough for a religious Midwestern farm girl. Mr. Lloyd wrote of "a constant stream of restless life pour[ing] through these thoroughfares."[13] A New Zealand tourist, who walked down Montgomery Street one Saturday morning in 1880, spoke of "pass[ing] with difficulty through hundreds of seedy looking men and women."[14] She wrote, "[A]ll is bustle and confusion, for ... no one ever keeps to their own side of the street as in other Christian countries, but they walk anyhow, pushing one way or the other, and the only chance on a Saturday is to elbow your way as best you can."[15] Guillermo Prieto, who visited the city in 1877, described an army of peddlers "laying insolent sieges to pocketbooks." He wrote, "They have trays of flowers; handcarts filled with peanuts and oranges; pen-knives, buttons, neckties, lemonade and soda-pop in boxes on tripods."[16] Some peddlers sold second-hand hats, shoes and garments. "[T]he homeliest of artifacts of private life are gathered in a heap," sniped Prieto.[17]

Sharing the sidewalks with Mary was a wide assortment of odd and disconnected characters. Bowles wrote, "[San Francisco] holds in chaos ... all sorts of elements; the very best and very worst, and all between."[18] The city was largely divided between the extremely rich and the extremely poor, a point consistently emphasized by the observers of the period. Mr. Lloyd noted, "In no part of the world are poverty and affluence so nearly mingled in the same cup."[19]

French engineer Louis Laurent Simonin wrote, "In the mixture of luxury and decay, ... appear the most disparate and unusual costumes."[20] Rich women shopping on Market Street displayed extravagancies of dress. They wore flowered hats, satin dresses, and sable coats. They had themselves covered in diamonds and powder. But they were not alone on Market Street. Passing through the richest streets, said Prieto, were "liquory, tattered men."[21] The flashy costumes of the rich, which displayed "an artistic blending of colors,"[22] contrasted sharply with the faded rags of the beggars. The beggars, as grubby and foul-smelling as they were, made it their business to entertain passersby, maybe juggling balls or playing a fiddle.

The city was, by all accounts, a noisy place. Kipling wrote, "[T]he streets [were] clanging with traffic and the restless roar of a great city [was] in my ears."[23] Mary, walking along the streets and promenades, could likely hear the cries of ragmen, newsboys, fruit sellers, and street preachers. Mr. Lloyd wrote that, often, "frequent outbursts of profanity and ribaldry startle[d] the quiet passerby."[24]

Gangs of boys dawdled in the streets unsupervised. They were called, by reporters, "the little wanderers"[25] and "the street boys."[26] Samuel Williams wrote, "Nowhere else are the restraints of parental authority so lax as here."[27] Allowed to run wild on the streets, these boys grew bold in their activities. Boys, including the newsboys, collected on street corners to smoke cigarettes or two-bit cigars. A visitor described being appalled by the sight of a street urchin smoking a grand stogie.

It is quite possible that Mary also encountered a notably outrageous sideshow man who called himself Oofty Goofty. Goofty was a familiar figure on Market Street and other parts of the city. Herbert Ashbury wrote of him, "From crown to heel he was covered in road tar, into which was stuck great quantities of horsehair, lending him a savage and ferocious appearance."[28] Dressed in either his horsehair outfit or an alternate outfit made of fur and feathers, Goofty paraded the town emitting weird animal cries. He would permit anyone to kick him for ten cents or to hit him with a cane for twenty-five cents. The sight of Goofty and his ilk surely compelled a passerby to wonder who could have reared such individuals. Mr. Lloyd noted, "The most excitable and unsettled people have been attracted hither from all parts of the world, bringing with them a temperament favorable to the development of insanity."[29] In general, these many sights and sounds combined to produce a gross effect for a newcomer.

William Hamilton got a job selling pianos for Bancroft Brothers. Bancroft Brothers, headed by Hubert Howe Bancroft, had established a good reputation in San Francisco for publishing books and retailing musical instruments. The company owned a two-story brick building on lower Market Street.

At the summer's peak in 1881, William and Mary blessed their marriage with their first child, a daughter whom they christened Mabel Claudia.

It was soon after Mabel's birth that the Hamiltons moved to Oakland, a picturesque city situated directly across the San Francisco Bay. Oakland, known as the "All-American City," was highly regarded as a decent and genuine community. It was clean, orderly and affordable and the ideal place for family residence.

Oakland's immaculate image, however, was not absolute. The Hamiltons settled in the city at a time when its population contained a strange case named Robert Louis Stevenson. Stevenson was, according to San Francisco historian Doris Muscatine, "a long-haired maverick, often barefoot, eccentric in his soiled, rumbled clothes, with no intention to do proper work."[30] Stevenson, who wrote popular stories about pirates, dual personalities, drug addiction and psychopathic killers, was a dark and bulky speck within this thin and clear soup.

Other creative types were around, too. At the time, Oakland's young natives included Jack London and Gertrude Stein. In 1878, the London family had fled San Francisco to escape a diphtheria epidemic. Within the next few years, London and Stein would acquire worldwide fame for their radically unconventional novels.

Hamilton signed this early 1920's portrait for his mother and father (courtesy of the family of Lloyd Hamilton).

It is possible that Oakland's standards were so stringent that those wishing to reject them had to act in a forcible manner. Years later, the city would become a hotbed of rebellion and anti-establishment heroes. The Black Panthers originated in Oakland. Sonny Barger, a living icon of the Hell's Angels, founded one of the foremost chapters of the Hell's Angels in Oakland.

Still, in the late 1800s, Oakland was generally dull and homogenized. In a short story, London referred to Oakland as a "little world." Stein said, "The thing about Oakland is that when you get there, there's no *there* there."

Regardless of its alleged triviality, the Hamiltons were quick to embrace Oakland as their home. Mary became a devout member of the local Congregational church. For the typical Congregationalist, the basic unit of life and organization was the autonomical local church. Soon after the family settled in Oakland, Mary had a second child, a daughter named Hazel.

Mabel was extremely ill as a child. Virginia Hawksley, Mabel's daughter, wasn't able to say what disease Mabel had contracted, but she believed it was one of the many respiratory infections that were epidemic in the nineteenth century. Hazel fell ill during the same general period. This little girl, who had contracted the measles, died soon after at the age of three. Mary was devastated by the loss and never fully recovered.

William and Mary's next child was born more than five years later. This progeny, a pretty and blue-eyed baby boy, was welcomed into the family on August 19, 1891. He was named Lloyd Vernon Hamilton. Lloyd was born into modest circumstances, but this situation changed when William achieved success in the real estate trade.

Mary was, by every indication, a dedicated mother. Was she anything like the overly attentive mothers of Lloyd's later fiction? If this were true, it would mean she made sure that Lloyd ate enough, that his clothing was always clean, and that he didn't ever leave the house with a runny nose. It would also be likely that she demanded her son always work hard, be useful, and maintain strict control of his actions. These, after all, were Protestants edicts. After losing one child and nearly losing a second, Mary would have had every reason to be protective of her young boy.

Lloyd was still a child when his sister Mabel and her new husband, Pierce Morehouse, moved to the neighboring community Piedmont. The departure of her firstborn likely increased Mary's attention on her younger offspring.

The Hamiltons remained dedicated to their religion. The Congregational Christian Church, of which they were members, was known for its strictness and formality. The church was located downtown, two blocks from Broadway, which was the main thoroughfare. Charles Reynolds Brown, a thirty-four-year-old minister trained at Boston University, took charge of the church in 1896. Brown, though committed to traditional doctrine, believed in applying the lessons of the Bible to modern life, making them useful to daily activities and deriving real effects from their application. Brown, to his disappointment, found this modern view of Scripture to be unwelcome at the church. He was cautioned, on his arrival, to be patient with his congregation and not force these views on them so quickly. "These people," he was told, "were rather conservative."[31]

Brown found no one more conservative than church deacon Edward C. Williams. Williams was proud to tell people that he was a direct descendant of Jonathan Edwards, a Congregational preacher well-known in Colonial America for his fire-and-brimstone sermons. The deacon, intolerant of vice in San Francisco, had one time joined a vigilante committee to round up rowdies and roughs suspected of criminal activity. The committee, according to Brown, "hung some of the rascals."[32]

The congregation, in general, included many lawyers, judges, politicians, and business owners. Lawyers, the most important figures in the church, occupied powerful positions in the community. These men included Guy C. Earl, who was a regent at the University of California, and Frederick S. Stratton, who was the Collector of the Port of San Francisco. Warren Olney, Jr., one of the most prosperous lawyers in the area, was destined to serve as a California Supreme Court Justice. Brown was proud to say that, in the fifteen years he presided as pastor, the congregation included three Oakland mayors.

Despite the presence of these rich and important people, Brown insisted that the members of the congregation "were not all rich by any means."[33] He claimed that he himself was not rich and that three-fourths of the congregation were no more affluent than he was.

Brown preached in his Sunday sermons that people should develop inner strength by setting high expectations for themselves, being guided by right thinking and clear purpose, and demonstrating firm resolve and active self-control. "Christian life is not easy," he admitted. "It is the most difficult life there is."[34] Still, he insisted, a life devoted to Christian values was the most rewarding life. He wrote, "There is an upper level of spiritual privilege which towers above the common grind as the Matterhorn towers above the valley of the Rhone. But to reach it involves a stiff climb. You can do it if you will."

Heaven was promised as the eventual reward for rightdoing, but the doctrine of the church also dictated that no one could ascend to Heaven unless they were favored by God. A person was incapable of influencing God's favor or recognizing their own state of grace, but they must consider themselves chosen, combating all doubts as temptations of the devil and crucial tests of their faith. This manner of self-confidence was vital, regarded as an absolute duty. Its absence signified insufficient faith and certain damnation. Above all else, it was success in a calling, the strenuous and exacting life-task imposed upon a man by his position in the world, that could disperse the fear of damnation and provide a person with the certainty of grace. Brown also preached social responsibility. He believed that it was important for Christians to be altruistic, making it a priority in life to help others in need—feeding the poor, caring for the infirm and comforting the broken-hearted.

Brown put young charges though a long and arduous process of Protestant education. He acknowledged that children may find it disagreeable to be administered the higher criticism of Biblical scholarship. He compared these lessons to castor oil. "But," he wrote, "it will be good for you, and it may remove certain things from your system which you are better off without."[35]

Lloyd, one of Pastor Brown's young charges, was a pleasant boy. He was cute, charming, good-natured, mannerly, imaginative, and clever. In 1917, a reporter with *The Oakland Tribune* talked to people who knew Lloyd as a child. He concluded, "His chums and school companions, many of them living in Oakland today, knew him as a quiet lad, with little to say and much to do."[36] For the most part, Lloyd indulged in placid and lonesome hobbies, his favorite of which was reading. He was especially fascinated and excited by books which introduced him to intrepid characters and dangerous places. When he wasn't reading, he fished and swam in nearby lakes. He often would remove a horse from the barn behind their home and ride on the quiet bridle paths that wound through the local hills. He sometimes stalked the hills with his trusty squirrel rifle.

At an early age, Lloyd developed an ardent interest in the theatre. When he was nearly twelve, he viewed a legendary stage version of *Dr. Jekyll and Mr. Hyde*, based on the 1885 novel by Robert Louis Stevenson. The story concerned a distinguished doctor who challenges his community's strict moral restraints. It is interesting to note that Stevenson wrote the novel while living in Oakland. The restrained community was likely to have had some influence on the book, although greater influences were evident earlier in Stevenson's background. Stevenson was born in Edinburgh, Scotland, in 1850. The Old Town and New Town districts of Edinburgh were starkly different from each other, even more so than San Francisco and Oakland. New Town was well-kept, orderly, elegant and respectable, while Old Town was filthy, rundown, crowded and lawless. In 1828, Edinburgh received international attention when Old Town criminal William Burke was prosecuted for murdering 17 people and selling their bodies to Dr. Robert Knox, a respected surgeon who operated an anatomy school. Stevenson wrote about this case in his short story "The Body Snatcher." Many believe that this dark, corrupt association between doctor and serial killer was the inspiration for the Jekyll and Hyde story. Other believe Jekyll and Hyde was inspired by Edinburgh resident Deacon Brody, who was a gentleman councilor by day and a brutal burglar by night. One way or another, Stevenson was aware that people and places could be sharply divided by good and evil forces.

Richard Mansfield, a popular stage actor, first played the Jekyll-Hyde role in 1887 and had been touring in the role for nearly two decades. A mystifying attraction of the show was Mansfield's full-view transformation from the meek-looking Jekyll to the hideously apelike Hyde. Lloyd was greatly impressed by Mansfield's performance.

At the time, more than one youngster sought excitement and popularity by organizing a makeshift theatre. For a nominal fee, these children would perform for neighborhood peers. This scaled-down entertainment form may sound especially familiar because Hal Roach would later exploit the concept for an occasional *Our Gang* comedy. Two of Roach's most renowned stars, Harold Lloyd and Stan Laurel, could have provided input for these films as both comics staged shows as youngsters. These boys were constantly encouraged by their fathers. Over the life of his son's amateur dramatic society,

A charming boy at age five (courtesy of the family of Lloyd Hamilton).

Harold's father constructed multiple stages.[37] Stan's father employed his professional playhouse staff to transform an attic into his son's miniature theatre.[38]

Lloyd, unlike Harold and Stan, acted in secret when he organized his own stock company and prepared their premier presentation. Directing two friends as his assistants, he converted his family's barn into a temporary theatre. To make room, the boys dismantled the stalls and relocated the horses. They sneaked a few chairs out of their homes and set them up in the barn. Possessing an inadequate number of chairs, they completed the audience section with soap boxes. Once set up in their makeshift theatre, the youngsters presented Lloyd as the star of *Dr. Jekyll and Mr. Hyde*. Pins, marbles, gunnysacks and bottles were accepted as the price of "admishun."

According to more than one account, a woman interrupted Lloyd's brutish performance as Hyde to save her son from a melodramatic strangling. A couple of versions of the story ended with Lloyd getting beaten by his father. In one version, his father was angry at Lloyd for upsetting the barn. In another version, his father was intent on disciplining his son for choking the other boy. Lloyd said that this discipline session was "one of my most painful memories."[39]

Undiscouraged, Lloyd and his company proceeded to produce *The Cattle Rustler's Daugh-*

ter. As this was a western thriller, Lloyd was able to leave the barn intact and employ the horses as extras.

Lloyd's acting endeavors may have brought this quiet boy out of his shell, but they failed to garner the favor of his parents, who preferred sober utility much more than artistic tendencies. Lloyd explained that his mother "was a member of the church and not very strong for theatres."[40] This was a time when acting was largely regarded as a disreputable profession and certainly not an appropriate pursuit for this "scion of rigid respectability," as Lloyd was described by writer Frank Capron.[41] Mary, who highly valued education, had planned for her boy to attend college. She could imagine her son becoming nothing other than a technical engineer. His father wanted him to join him in the real estate business.[42]

Lloyd was near the end of his tenure at the local elementary school, the Franklin Grammar School, when his parents enrolled him at the Oakland Polytechnic High School; located at Twelfth and Market Streets, it was one of two high schools in Oakland at that time. The school was not big by modern standards. At the time of Lloyd's freshman year, 16 teachers were responsible for 347 students. The school was in operation for a short time, from 1902 to 1910, and not much information is available on its history. A few details about the school's curriculum are provided in an *Oakland Tribune* article about a reunion held in 1954. At the time, a ceremony was held to honor Mary Teel, who had taught the girls cooking and sewing, and Walter Tenney, who had taught the boys pattern-making and bench work. Other subjects taught at the school include woodwork, mechanical drawing, commercial law, stenography, typing, and bookkeeping. For the next four years, Lloyd was engaged in manual training as part of a college preparatory program. The school yearbook, called Class Scribe, indicated that Lloyd was known at the school for his sense of humor. He was said to have had "an enlarged joshuary gland."

It was while preparing for graduation that Lloyd resolved he did not want to be a pattern-maker or a technical engineer. He was more interested in applying for work at a local playhouse, The Ye Liberty Theatre, where extras were being hired for the mob scenes of a Shakespearean production. By this time, Lloyd weighed more than 200 pounds. In the last few years, he had grown to six-foot-one and had developed a broad and sturdy build. However, contradicting the vast expansion of his physique, he still had his boyish looks. His face had retained "baby fat" and his eyes exuded a childlike innocence.

Anxious to answer the extra call, Lloyd threw on some clothes and rushed to Ye Liberty. Once there, he joined a crowd of prospective extras. The director, on the lookout for strong-looking males to appear in soldier dress, was quick to notice Lloyd. He beckoned the large youth aside and revealed to him a special offer. Following a brief dialogue, the two apparently reached an agreement. In one hand, Lloyd took firm hold of a prop spear; in the other, he took firm hold of a broom. He had agreed that he would appear as a soldier on stage and, as a supplement to these duties, he would function as one of the theatre's supers. His weekly salary, as arranged, was $3.25.

Lloyd did not dare to let his mother know about his new job. Each evening, he would quietly slip out of his house and rush to the theatre.

It wasn't difficult being an extra. Laden with a heavy, clunky outfit (boots, helmet, breastplate, spear and shield), he stiffly marched on stage in a procession of soldiers. But Lloyd took his job seriously. His enthusiasm attracted the attention of Orral Humphrey, an eminent Pacific Coast thespian who had been Ye Liberty's leading man for several years. Humphrey made Lloyd's acquaintance and, soon after, was tutoring the young man on the fundamentals of stage acting.

Lloyd became ambitious. Lyndon Baines Johnson described ambition as "an uncomfortable companion."[43] He said of this associate, "He creates a discontent with present surroundings and achievements; he is never satisfied but always pressing forward to better things in the future."

For at least one performance, Lloyd was reportedly allocated the line "The carriage waits." But it was even more than this that the young man wanted. This is reminiscent of a scene in *To Be or Not to Be* (1942), the classic Ernst Lubitsch movie comedy centered on a stage production of *Hamlet*. Two soldier extras complain about their lowly positions. One says, "That's all we do: carry a spear in the first act." His companion adds that, even worse, they must carry off the dead king in the last act. Lloyd also grew weary of being a soldier extra. He was simply helping to dress a production, comparable to his horses' contribution to *The Cattle Rustler's Daughter*.

The theatre had already seduced Lloyd. He resolved that, after completing his studies at Polytechnic, he would work hard to distinguish himself as an actor. Lloyd had not yet disclosed his decision when Mary Hamilton learned of his private life. The inevitable confrontation occurred. Different accounts of this scene were provided in magazine articles and promotional materials throughout Lloyd's career. A particularly funny account had Mary Hamilton showing up at the theatre and breaking up a performance to drag her boy home.[44] Lloyd, himself, had fun lampooning the situation in *The Simp*. Before sneaking into his home late at night, Lloyd ties pillows to his feet to muffle his footsteps. When his father hears him and comes into the room, Lloyd drops to his knees behind a chair and bellows out a loud meow to pretend he's the family cat. But the account most often, and most credibly, described by Lloyd is that he came home late one night and found an angry mother waiting up for him. Lloyd, mustering up courage, announced that he planned to become an actor. Charleson Gray, describing this scene for *Motion Picture Classic*, spoke of "a mother crying."[45] "Her Lloyd must have gone crazy or something," wrote Gray. "Wanting to be an actor. An actor! And the Hamiltons always had been such respectable, God-fearing people. An actor! Really, it was a terrible strain on mother love." It made sense, considering that Lloyd's family was private and reserved, for the confrontation to have happened as simply as this. It was certainly bound to be more serious and subdued than Lloyd being dragged off a stage or Lloyd wearing pillows on his feet.

Soon after graduation, Lloyd secured himself work in a major Oakland playhouse known as the Broadway Theatre. He was engaged for a speaking role in a production of *The Count of Monte Cristo*.

Two local favorites, Lander Stevens and Georgia Cooper, starred as ill-fated lovers Edmond Dantès and Mercédès Mondego. Lloyd played Monsieur Morrel, an honest and kindhearted shipowner who befriends Dantès.

It was going to take talent, work, nerve and luck for Lloyd to succeed in his undertaking.

Oakland's audiences were notoriously demanding. Lloyd knew he had better be good. Opening night found him jittery and nauseous. This experience was to be a sure test. When the show finally started, he braced himself as he left the backstage wings, traveling into the bright lights. He had nearly made it to center stage when he looked up and saw a group of young ladies in a theatre box. The sight so horrified him that his every muscle froze.

His problem was familiar to Georgia Cooper, who concealed the predicament by prompting the nervous novice with improvised lines. She soon eased Lloyd out of his paralysis and guided him back into his role. Once having collected himself, he was able to present a complete performance for the evening.

Evidence of his effectiveness in *The Count of Monte Cristo*, Lloyd was assigned a larger role in the Broadway Theatre's next undertaking. He played Coach Farley in an adaptation of *Strongheart*, a college drama. The promotion succeeded in encouraging Lloyd on his theatrical campaign.

In the summer, the insides of theatre houses became sweltering and stuffy. Unable to compensate for this condition, producers would discharge their stock companies and temporarily shut the playhouses. This meant that, during the year's hottest quarter, the staff of the Broadway Theatre would be unemployed.

In the summer of 1909, Lloyd was left to carefully contemplate his professional alternatives. San Francisco was predominant in his thoughts. For the last two years, he had met a number of refugees from the 1906 San Francisco Earthquake-Fire, a legendary disaster which had caused 700 deaths and brought about $800,000,000 dollars in property damage. The earthquake, in contrast, had barely rumbled the serene city of Oakland. Lloyd was looking for change and excitement and the stories he heard about San Francisco certainly made life across the Bay sound different and exciting.

Over the last two decades, San Francisco had remained startlingly insane and perilous. As always, the city was a flamboyant and vital haven for misfits. Robin Williams, a modern-day comic whose family also migrated from Michigan to San Francisco, has said of the place: "I love this city. It's a human game preserve. It's filled with strange and wonderful people."[46] San Francisco was also a purlieu of international society and a fast-paced "world of business" center. Most important, the city was a place where fame and fortune could be won.

San Francisco was an ideal town for a large-scale dreamer like Lloyd, especially one with ambitions to be a famous actor. This was the place where an actor could prove himself. Benjamin Lloyd wrote, "[T]here is no city where the general public is more fault-finding with their actors and actresses than San Francisco."[47] An actor who had been accepted by a San Francisco audience could feel that he had proven his worth. He could, according to Mr. Lloyd, "tread the stage with the firm steps of a conqueror"[48] and be encouraged to challenge greater venues to advance himself.

Oakland lacked the same promise. The All-American City had long been overshadowed by its colorful and lively neighbor. To cope with San Francisco's grandness, Oakland's residents had developed a sense of humor similar to that of Newark and Brooklyn residents, who have to live in the shadow of Manhattan. Jack London had only faint feelings about his hometown. He once wrote, "Oakland's just a place to start from, I guess."[49] Oakland could be perceived as a stepping stone to San Francisco, which offered a threshold to the world.

Before the 1906 calamity, San Francisco had contained numerous theatres of both the elegant and rowdy sort. Its finer playhouses had presented the greatest actors of the period, including members of the famous Booth and Barrymore families. Only one of the town's theatres had survived the furious fire, but many theatres were currently being rebuilt. Lloyd decided that, in the fall, he would get a job at one of the new playhouses.

By the fall, San Francisco had recovered, an achievement marked recently by the Portola Festival. During the recovery, the city's theatre district had not received as much support as its fellow districts, but it was managing to make a comeback nonetheless.

Though the frantic crowds generated plenty of heat, the temperature of San Francisco was consistently ten degrees lower than that of Oakland. Lloyd would have had to dress more warmly than usual before starting for the wharf, where a ferry steamer named *The Oakland* regularly crossed the East Bay to deliver Oakland laborers to their peculiar but prosperous neighbor. The young man was daring to take a major step. He would be regularly venturing into a strange, wild land beyond the amity of the working class and the clarity of daylight. It was the perception of many respectable, hard-working people that the darkness had no purpose other than to hide evil deeds. Benjamin Lloyd claimed that good citizens, who "have had enough of earth's follies for one day," were "glad when the thickening gloom of darkness warn[ed] them to their beds," but the "rowdies and dissolute ... grow boisterous at twilight, and when night has enveloped the city, are emboldened and do not hesitate to commit the most fiendish crimes."[50]

If he was real careful, Lloyd might only get himself shanghaied.

2

Stage to Screen

Charles Augustus Keeler, a naturalist and poet, described what it was like to visit San Francisco during this time. He wrote, "To be dropped off the ferry into the very center of the maelstrom of life, where every mortal is bent upon his own task.... After the repose of the country, the wide serenity of the hill-encircled bay, to grapple with the noise and stir of the city! But what a sensation of exhilaration, this elbowing with the eager crowd, this trotting with the pack after the quarry, this pressing on with the tumult of men in the rush for place! Here life and effort are focused."[1]

Once in San Francisco, Lloyd applied for a job at the Alcazar, a popular theatre located on O'Farrell Street. Frank Butler, the theatre's director, was a kindly man receptive to young actors. He was quick to welcome Lloyd into his stock company as a minor player.

While a member of Butler's stock company, Lloyd befriended two other juvenile thespians, Lloyd Bacon and Edmund Lowe. Bacon and Lowe shared many characteristics, including good looks, cleverness, charm, flamboyance, and playfulness. They were only a year older than Lloyd and their experience on stage was not greater than his own, yet Lloyd accepted them as his guides through the theatre's strange and rocky channels.

Lloyd, Bacon and Lowe became an inseparable trio. Lloyd had come to believe that, until he had mastered his skills, eradicated his defects and widened his range, he would not move on to leading roles. He now wanted to bear down and do good work. However, Bacon and Lowe were able to coax the ambitious young actor to join them in some adolescent foolishness.

Performing in San Francisco, Lloyd would have found that audiences expected to be entertained with broad humor, sentimentality and inventiveness.[2] He was eager to learn what it took to be a good performer and make an audience happy. He eventually joined the Great Actors' Training School, where he was able to study elocution, makeup, fencing and dancing. The school tested Lloyd's skills in various plays, including "Hamlet" and "East Lynne."

Lloyd decided that he had enough experience and training to apply for a position with W.J. Elleford, one of the West Coast's most popular repertory men. Elleford ended up assigning Lloyd double duty as a minor player and prop boy.

The Elleford troupe toured up the Pacific Coast and across into Nevada. These travels would take Lloyd away from his family, friends and hometown. He was now following in the footsteps of his ancestors, religious radicals and bold pioneers who had deserted their homes in search of autonomy. They wanted to realize their own identity and achieve great success. Ready or not, Lloyd was going forth into the wide world.

The young actor starts his film career in 1913 (author's collection).

Elleford said that his actors had a calm and comfortable experience traveling on the road compared to what he had to endure when he started touring more than thirty years earlier. He said that modern hotels offered actors more conveniences and it was less taxing riding in a Pullman than riding in a stagecoach as he had done. Still, this was a rougher and more adventurous life than Lloyd had known. Much of it was new to him and many of the people were different. He was, in his travels, introduced to less than genteel characters who acted in discord to his parents' moral instructions. But migration can be a strong solvent of convention. Adapting to his new life, Lloyd assumed some of his fellows' loose and lively habits. He drank. He smoked. Most evenings, he and his friends topped off the night with a visit to a bar. The private, unassuming and serious man that Lloyd presented in the workplace differed much from the carefree and outgoing fellow who emerged in these idle hours.

Lloyd, who was a cooperative, kind and generous companion, easily won the fondness of his fellow strolling players. They gave him the double-edged nickname "Ham," which referred to both his surname and his theatrical nature.

With Elleford, Lloyd appeared in six different plays a week. The Elleford productions were not unlike the productions of most other repertoire companies of the time. Elleford staged either rough-action versions of popular dramatic novels or impromptu one-night-only thrillers. The latter commanded attention with titles like "The Convict's Sweetheart," "Sold Into Slavery" and "The Opium Smugglers of Frisco."

At first, Lloyd appeared in Elleford's dramas in character roles, his physically imposing size making it easy for him to play a heavy. The young actor, submerged beneath greasepaint, putty and wigs, was uninhibited on stage and played these roles with exceptional vigor. Months after joining Elleford, Lloyd was promoted from character player to juvenile lead. In his new position, he was featured in presentations of "Faust," "Secret Service" and "Hearts of Gold."

Elleford, presumably due to failing health, decided in late in 1910 to take a year off from the theatre. Lloyd approached eminent impresario James K. Hackett, who welcomed the young actor into his dramatic company. Hackett made Lloyd a swashbuckler, putting him to use in "The Prisoner of Zenda" and "Monsieur Beaucaire." These shows allowed Lloyd to work in superior houses and cover a wider area of the West Coast. He toured California, Oregon, Washington, Montana, and British Columbia. According to the *Anaconda Standard*, the Hackett company visited Butte, Montana, in November, 1910, to perform "The Prisoner of Zenda." The cast included several notable actors, including Charles Trowbridge as Capt. Fritz von Tarlenheim and Arthur Hoops as Rupert of Hentzau. Lloyd appeared as Josef, a servant who is killed defending the crown prince against kidnappers.

Lloyd could, at times, become playful between scenes. Once, he got people laughing backstage by parodying a stage manager. A Hackett official who had witnessed the performance advised Lloyd to pursue a career as a comic. At the time, Lloyd said, he shrank from the suggestion.

It was after appearing in his third Hackett opus, "Don Caesar's Return," that Lloyd resigned from Hackett's company and returned home.

In late 1911, Lloyd decided to try his hand at comedy after all. He went to San Francisco, where he joined a musical-comedy ensemble at the America Theatre. He never indicated having trouble making the transition from drama to comedy. Still, it couldn't have been easy. Comedy tends to put more strain on a performer. The laughs, that constant, open and affectionate response from an audience, can make comedy highly rewarding, but that is only when the laughs are coming. A performer can become filled with desperation and dread waiting for the next laugh and he can be crushed when that next laugh doesn't come. In the end, though, Lloyd must have seen it as worthwhile to accept that risk.

During this period, the *Oakland Tribune* regularly listed Lloyd's name on the guest list for young adult society parties, mainly debutante balls. It is unknown if Lloyd's entrance into these parties had to do with his family's status, the associations he had made, or the prestige he had earned in the theatre.

Lloyd next joined a traveling act called The Frank Cooley Show. Cooley, a middle-aged comic actor, employed Lloyd as a performer and advance man. The duties of an advance man required Lloyd to precede the rest of the troupe into a town, at which time he would post bills, rent furniture for stage sets, engage extras, and check that the house in which they had been booked had not recently burned to the ground.

In 1912, the entire motion picture industry was in the midst of moving to California. Filmmakers were attracted to California because, as writer Rudi Blesh observed, the state provided "unmetered sunshine" and "rent-free plains."[3] And what better to do with expansive, unspoiled land and consistently fine climate than to embark on the year-round production of outdoor dramas. This certainly offered more secure employment than the legitimate theatre, which subjected actors to summer layoffs.

Lloyd was performing in musical comedy when he met Albert Edward Duncan, a versatile entertainer more commonly known by the nickname "Bud." Bud, though eight years older than Lloyd, was not one to inspire a younger actor's veneration. He was, to start, a harmless-looking fellow. His height, the first thing a person noticed, was by no means imposing. "Bud was a little man," said director Alfred Santell, "as a matter of fact, he wasn't much taller than a midget."[4] The man, in fact, barely reached a height of 4'11". He also did not, by his attitude, give anyone a reason to be intimidated. A genial smile, suggesting a good and uncomplicated nature, was impressed prominently on his face. Bud, though, had acted in motion pictures and this made him special to actors who had never worked outside a theatre. Bud was eager to talk about his recent movie experiences and Lloyd, based on his ambition to work in motion pictures, no doubt made an avid listener. Lloyd knew that he would in time work in film, but he had no way of knowing that Bud would play a key role in his motion picture career.

Bud was born in Brooklyn, New York, on October 31, 1883. He was the first child of Albert Odell and Lillian Duncan. Albert was a traveling salesman at the time; he later went on stage as a ventriloquist. Bud joined his father's act at age six. Later, when Bud was a teenager, his father enrolled him in Berkley, a boarding school that prepared boys for military service. Bud claimed that, although he was an eager student, his stunted growth ruined his ambitions to become a military officer.

On graduating from Berkley, Bud acquired a clerical job at the Grand Opera House. He was promoted to assistant treasurer soon after, but he was bored by box office ledgers and left the job to join a dramatic stock company. Later, he played in tents as part of a touring repertory show. He had his most long-standing success in vaudeville. At first, he worked alongside vaudeville legend Lew Fields. Afterwards, he appeared in "A Night in a Music Hall" on the U.B.O. (United Booking Offices) circuit and appeared with the comedy team of Kolb and Dill in "The Delicatessen Shop" on the Orpheum circuit. For two years, he teamed with a tall comic named Lee Moran and, together, they performed a sketch called "The Long and Short of It."

Al Christie, a director at the Nestor Film Company, noticed the small, exuberant performer in a stage production of "Peck's Bad Boy." Christie was turning out "Mutt and Jeff Fotofarces," a series based on Bud Fisher's widely syndicated comic strip. His "Jeff," Gus Alexander, was leaving the series and Christie was seeking a replacement. Bud, he thought, was just the person he needed.

Nestor promoted the *Mutt and Jeff* series as "talking pictures" in that dialogue was conveyed via subtitles. The gimmick proved to have limited appeal as the series did not earn nearly as much money as the westerns the studio produced. The western genre, which exploited the beauty of California's abundant mountains and ranges, had proven overwhelmingly popular with theatergoers. At least one third of the films made in 1912 were westerns.

The "Mutt and Jeff Fotofarces" ended after Bud starred in only two installments. It was at this point that Bud returned to the stage and first encountered Lloyd.

From talking to Bud and others, Lloyd saw definite prospects in motion pictures. He set out in 1913 to thoroughly investigate those prospects. He would later claim that he was being driven by the swiftly spreading malady called "motion picture fever." It was, as with comparable fevers, brought on by the promise of riches and glory.

Spurred by the public's willingness to spend endless coins in its passion to be entertained, the motion picture industry had greatly expanded within the last few years. Before 1909, the industry was controlled by the nine companies that had pioneered filmmaking: Edison, Biograph, Vitagraph, Lubin, Essanay, Selig, Kalem, Méliés, and Pathé. The pioneers, claiming to have a patent on the motion picture camera and projection equipment, organized into "The Trust." During 1909 and 1910, there arose numerous film companies challenging The Trust. These independents, led by the Fox Film Corporation, contended that The Trust represented an illegal monopoly. To insure their survival, most of the independents united under the umbrella of two distribution organizations. These distributors, Universal and Mutual, quickly drained the pioneers of considerable revenue. The pioneers formed their own distribution company, simply named General Film.

By 1913, the motion picture had developed into a vastly popular form of entertainment. Compared to the greatest play producer, the average film distributor was embracing a much vaster audience. The infant industry was offering a promising performer the opportunity to execute a dazzling rise to greatness. Even the typical salary of a screen extra, a daily wage of four dollars, was enticing to most stage actors. This innovative entertainment form was also appealing to those with a pioneer spirit, the artist who was brave and resourceful.

Many performers had been seized by motion picture fever. The American Film Company had employed Lloyd's early acting teacher, Orral Humphrey, as a director and leading man. James K. Hackett had recently starred in a successful screen version of *The Prisoner of Zenda*. It could have encouraged Lloyd to know that Max Asher, one of the day's leading film comics, was another Oakland son.

A stage engagement brought Lloyd to Los Angeles, the new heart of the film industry. At this time, a talented actor visiting the town could easily be absorbed by a flourishing film company.

Lloyd, with the same fate in mind, abandoned his touring act in early 1913 to obtain employment at Lubin. He explained, "My first experience [with the motion picture industry] wasn't a very encouraging one. In the first place, the man in charge of the studio where I applied for a position refused to give me a job until I had told him the story of my life."[5]

In trying to persuade the film producer, he injected ample doses of humor and pathos into his life story. When the man asked him if he could ride a horse, he rendered a vivid account of his pleasant horseback rides in the Oakland hills.

Lloyd was put to work on the next day. He said, "When I showed up bright and early the following morning, they gave me a horse that was camera-wise and knew more about pictures than I could learn in a week. Well, after staying on his back through thirty scenes, I decided to go back to the stage."[6]

This is not the whole story.

Certainly, it wasn't a fun job. Lubin's open-air players performed vigorous action scenes on sun-scorched plains. At the end of a day's work, they were usually hot, tired, dusty, and sore. Lloyd typically worked as a heavy. His size made a formidable-looking menace in the wide shots, but his boyish face failed to sustain his ominous appearance in tighter shots. Consequently, he was required to cover his face with a coarse and unruly beard.[7]

Contrary to Lloyd's expectations, his stay at Lubin proved to be short. If one of his early profiles can be trusted, his departure was assured when a bookkeeper embezzled his unit's funds.

The Oakland Tribune reported, on April 30, 1913, that Lloyd V. Hamilton, 21, and Ethel Anderson, 18, both of Oakland, were issued a marriage license. The couple married days later in an Oakland ceremony. Soon after his marriage, Lloyd acquired work at Frontier, a

Hamilton is a border guard with a big cannon in *Pretzel Captures the Smugglers* (1914) (courtesy of Cole Johnson — Slapstick Archive).

new film company releasing its product through Universal. Originally, the company had been located in Albuquerque, New Mexico. *The Goat Girl of Bear Canyon*, a likely charmer, introduced the company on December 12, 1912. Other films followed in quick succession. The reviews suggested that, although the plots were not always good, the action scenes were generally rousing, the photography was consistently sharp, and the acting was always brisk.

At this early stage, audiences easily overlooked flimsy story lines. Sufficient in a film's success was the union of beautiful exteriors and superior cinematography. *Across Swiftcurrent Pass*, a 1913 Edison release, would receive a brief description that summarized the situation: "A short film with good views of mountains. The audience was plainly interested."

Though Frontier was initially devoted to rugged western melodramas, the company eventually extended into farce. This expansion was made possible by Dot Farley, an actress with comic rhythms and funny looks. Most dominant in her appearance was an outrageous set of buckteeth.

In the summer of 1913, the St. Louis Motion Picture Company purchased Frontier and relocated the company to Santa Paula. The company operated out of a facility previously owned by Meliés. It was immediately following the move that Lloyd joined Frontier. At first, he starred opposite Farley as a country bumpkin.

The ownership change created discord within Frontier. Gilbert P. Hamilton, the company's general manager, argued regularly with his new bosses and, on October 3, 1913, he left Frontier to form the Albuquerque Film Manufacturing Company.[8] Farley and other actors followed the studio chief.

On Farley's departure, Lloyd was assigned dramatic roles. He played Mexican bandits, gray-haired old fathers, and juvenile leads. The studio's comedy output became the responsibility of J. Arthur Nelson, who also starred in a series called *Slim*.

In 1913, the Keystone company produced a phenomenally successful series of comedies which challenged the domination of the Hollywood western. The Keystone comedies were broad, rapid, violent, and ultimately pointless. The company's principal comic, Ford Sterling, played Teheezal, the deranged chief of an inept police squad. The prominence of Sterling and the Keystone Cops instantly influenced the rest of the film industry, stimulating flagrant and widespread imitation.

At the end of the year, Frontier returned Lloyd to comedy roles, having him succeed Nelson as their chief funnyman. Frontier prominently displayed Lloyd in a full-page ad. The ad, published in *The Pictureplayer*, carried the following message: "A Genuine Western Greeting to the World from Three Frontiers Men." Amidst this text appeared portraits of Lloyd and two co-stars, Joseph J. Franz and Walter L. Rodgers. Lloyd, whose likeness occupied the center of the page, had a straw hat coolly set off his brow. The caption read: "Lloyd V. Hamilton/Character Comedian."

Over the next three months, Lloyd starred in thirteen comedies. In most of these films, he depicted a character named "Pretzel." Pretzel looked and acted very much like Ford Sterling's Police Chief Teheezal. He was a warped figure of authority, whose alternating titles included Colonel, Captain and Chief of Police. His home was in the rural town of Cuckooville. Lloyd maintained high rank in his other roles. In a spoof on the Battle of Little Big Horn, he was Colonel Custard. He peddled Kentucky moonshine as Colonel Bourbon. He did slum on two occasions to play a more lowly Cuckooville resident, a rube simply named Hiram. But he made his most distinct departure playing an urbane, middle-aged businessman. It was a role for which he devoted much attention to makeup, burying his face in bushy eyebrows, a beard, and a long putty nose. Maybe Lloyd relished this role more than the others. Maybe he wanted to do more than imitate Ford Sterling.

This may explain why, on May 30, 1914, the *Universal Weekly* carried the following news item: "Lloyd V. Hamilton, who for some time has been principal comedian with the Frontier company, has left that company."

3

The Rapid Advancement of an Earnest and Inventive Player

The Kalem Company opened in June, 1907. Three New York businessmen, George Kleine, Samuel Long and Frank Marion, established the company with a meager investment of $400.

The company soon rose to major status with a screen version of *Ben-Hur*, Lew Wallace's bestseller. This outstanding moneymaker resulted from cleverly compacting Wallace's sweeping adventure story into sixteen scenes. But *Ben-Hur* did not prove to be a perfect success. Since Kalem had failed to obtain legal access to the source material, a lawsuit was brought by the publisher of the novel and the producer of a related stage play. It was contended in the suit that literary rights have a bearing on material produced for the screen. In a good-natured response, Kalem contended that their picture was acting as an effective advertisement for the book and play. The final court order, which established a far-reaching legal precedent, required the Kalem Company to pay the plaintiffs $25,000 in damages.

Following a course charted by rival film companies, Kalem's production people eventually migrated from New York to the West Coast. California's spacious landscapes and resplendent skies had proven far more captivating than New York's shoddy and unconvincing indoor sets. Many of California's first motion picture bases were established on ranches in disuse. In photos, Kalem's first West Coast settlement resembles a poor tobacco farm. Amid these new surroundings, the studio relied heavily on the western genre. Two genuine Indians, Red Wing and Mona Darkfeather, were soon among the studio's leading players.

In 1912, Alice Joyce and Carlyle Blackwell were the Kalem Corporation's foremost stars. Joyce arrived at Kalem in 1909 as a 22-year-old model. Her grace and beauty so endeared her to audiences that she quickly displaced "Kalem Girl" Gene Gauntier as the studio's star actress.

As their largest undertaking of the year, Kalem dramatized the life of Christ in a film entitled *From Manger to Cross*. The film was directed by Sidney Olcott, who had also helmed *Ben-Hur*.

The studio, which recognized that they risked embarrassment and charges of sacrilege if they had their messiah preach on obvious Los Angeles tracts, transported the production to historical locations in Egypt and Palestine. Contrary to the studio's standard policy, the film was designed as a five-reel presentation. *From Manger to Cross* was such a substantial success that it became a traditional holiday release.

A lesser production on Kalem's 1912 program was a western-comedy series featuring Ruth

Roland. Roland, a pretty nineteen-year-old, had starred earlier in Kalem melodramas. The entries of Roland's new series were "split-reelers." This meant that each episode ran for the majority of a ten-minute projector reel, leaving the reel's remaining minutes to be filled out with documentary footage. It might be nature scenes or a travelogue. One documentary was *Ruth Roland, the Kalem Girl*, which simply featured footage of the actress riding, swimming and diving.

Kalem had produced little comedy in prior years. Before 1912, their most notable step into the comedy area had been to briefly engaged Mr. and Mrs. Sidney Drew, a team that had achieved popularity through a series of stage sketches.

Roland proved to be a superior comedienne. Her series, which premiered with a May release entitled *Hypnotic Nell*, was Kalem's first comedy hit.

By the following year, John E. Brennan and Marshall Neilan had joined Ruth as principals of Kalem's lone comedy unit. Brennan was a bald and stocky actor with unremarkable credentials. Neilan was the more promising leading man. He had been born in San Bernadino, California, on April 11, 1891. Prior to joining Kalem, he had worked as a stage actor and had been employed by two film companies, American and Biograph. This handsome, charming man was, in his efforts, intelligent, ambitious, and uncompromising. All the qualities that made him a dynamic actor also made him a popular ladies' man. Gloria Swanson, who dated Neilan for a time, described the man, at alternate times, as "wild," "animated," "mischievous" and "irresistible." She wrote, "Everybody adored dashing, brilliant, madcap Mickey Neilan.... The omnipresent playboy, Mickey always knew where the good gin was hidden, where the best party was going on, where the best band was playing."[1] She called him "the most bewitching man in Hollywood."[2]

The combination of Roland, Neilan and Brennan succeeded in expanding the audience of Kalem's fotofarces. Neilan and Roland usually played conventional sweethearts while Brennan handled a more offbeat role. The series, no longer limited to western-type comedies, allowed many variations on this formula.

The Hash-House Count was one of the trio's definitive films. Brennan portrayed the title role, a waiter pretending to be royalty. The waiter courts a rich woman while Roland, cast as the rich woman's daughter, is romantically pursued by Neilan. A problem with this arrangement was that Brennan lacked the talent to counterbalance his more charming and talented co-stars. In doing his part, he primarily relied on his unaesthetic appearance. When called upon to play a rube, he implied his character's idiocy by simply twisting his face into an odd grin.

It was the summer of 1913 when Neilan, dissatisfied with Kalem's management philosophies, left the company to join the Flying A Studio.

Following Neilan's departure, the Kalem comedies continued with Roland and Brennan. Writers experienced difficulty in regularly crossing the chasm between the pretty young lady and uncomely leading man. George Larkin, enlisted as a supporting player, was meant to bridge the gap by playing Roland's love interest as well as Brennan's best friend. Larkin's unassuming presence did little to improve the situation.

For several months, Kalem's officials worked to induce Neilan to return. In late 1913, Neilan signed a one-year contract giving him full creative control of his own series. His return to the company was marked by a special one-reel comedy about a dedicated smalltown doctor. Neilan produced the comedy, wrote it, directed it, and starred. The action was sedate compared to the chaotic nonsense that Keystone was turning out. An ad for the comedy carried the headline "Comedies with Real Plots."

3. The Rapid Advancement of an Earnest and Inventive Player

Kalem's comedies, despite their success, were still not shown the greatest respect by the studio. Its executives were unwilling to permanently expand the length of the comedies to one reel. They reserved the longer length for special occasions, such as a time when dramatic star Carlyle Blackwell decided to trifle with less serious material as a novelty. In Kalem's weekly program ads, spacious announcements for "multi-part" and one-reel dramas crowded Kalem's comedy bill into a small corner square.

Neilan spent more time directing than acting. From his new perspective, he could see that the cast was lacking a performer who could play broad comedy. In trying to correct the problem, he recruited a rough and ready actor, Victor Rottman.

In the meantime, the popularity of Keystone's wild and crazy comedies was increasing. On the insistence of his bosses, even a light-handed director like Neilan engaged in Keystone's indelicate brand of humor. Neilan went as far as copying the Keystone Cops. Packaged in ill-fitting police uniforms and tons of makeup, minor players acted foolishly frenetic. They mugged, sprung off the ground, ran into one another, and fell down. As the cops of Keystone's exercises in unruliness, this comic blue line would bolt into a film at the eleventh hour. While their intrusion guaranteed a lively finish, these characters appeared misplaced in a Neilan film. A discordant dissimilarity existed between the wild, abnormal-looking cops and Neilan's more conventional characters. By thrusting the rude cops into one of his comedies, the director annoyed at least one critic, who reported that the cops' last-minute appearance "spoiled an otherwise pleasant film."

The Bingville Fire Department, probably the most flagrant of Neilan's Keystone imitations, featured Rottman as Police Chief Schnitzel. Schnitzel vigorously participates in a race because its outcome will determine if he can wed the mayor's daughter. This comedy had

Hamilton is burly Roman bad guy Villainus in *The Slavery of Foxicus* (1914). His costars, from left to right, are Victor Rottmon, Ruth Roland and Marshall Neilan (courtesy of Cole Johnson — Slapstick Archive).

obviously been fashioned after the exploits of Police Chief Teheezal, who regularly courted the mayor's daughter. Rottman presented no threat to Ford Sterling.

In the spring of 1914, Neilan found his broad comic. While Schnitzel and his fellows raced about and submitted pop-eyed stares to the camera, a large, baby-faced actor delicately entered the picture. The actor, whom Neilan had hired as a minor player, was named Lloyd Hamilton.

On the set, Lloyd was taken aside by his new director, who instructed him simply to dress as a rube. Then, as the director and his crew attended to more immediate business, Lloyd snooped through a supply of costumes and makeup and managed to gather together some interesting odds and ends. It wasn't until after he reviewed himself dressed in a variety of disguises that he settled on wearing dusty shoes and frayed pants. Afterwards, he summoned his makeup proficiency to camouflage his face. He managed calculated applications of greasepaint to his face and pasted a scraggly strip of hair over his upper lip. He then returned to the set.

The sudden appearance of the big, ragged rube triggered an outburst of laughter. Neilan was amused and amazed by the radical change in Lloyd. His timid, tentative actor had become a swaggering brute. In a review of *McBride's Bride*, the comedy Neilan produced that day, a *Moving Picture World* critic would note: "Some unnamed Kalem actor contributes a good 'bit' with his characterization of a tramp."

Following his premier performance at Kalem, Lloyd was hired at a weekly rate of $40 and placed in the front line of Neilan's misfit lawmen.

In June, 1914, Kalem executives extended the length of the Friday comedies to one reel. Promoted as the first expanded "rib-tickler" was *The Deadly Battle of Hicksville*. The film, set during the Civil War, wasn't as much deadly as it was silly. Brennan starred as a general. Lloyd, the earnest and inventive newcomer, was promoted to the role of Brennan's rival.

On the heels of his *Hicksville* assignment, Lloyd acted opposite Neilan in *A Substitute for Pants*. It was with little affectation that Neilan enacted the role of a charming rural politician. This sharply contrasted Lloyd, who made himself up to look crude and grotesque as Neilan's corrupt opponent. Lloyd pulled a wig over his head, attached an uncomely putty nose, and adopted a hunch. By debating on a platform strewn with campaign banners, Neilan and Lloyd created a juxtaposition that humorously anticipated the presidential contest of John F. Kennedy and Richard Nixon.

Neilan's next production, which utilized a cops-and-robbers story, firmly established Lloyd as Kalem's rough-and-tumble comedy star. Occupying the fringes of the film's plot, Brennan and Lloyd supported Roland as bungling law enforcement rivals. As police officer Sherlock Bonehead, Lloyd failed to apprehend the criminal but still managed to command the action. In acknowledgment of Lloyd's dominance, the comedy was released under the title *Sherlock Bonehead*.

The effects of *Sherlock Bonehead* were immediate. Overshadowed by Lloyd, Brennan was reassigned to a new unit.

Neilan worked to create a film that would draw forth more of Lloyd's skills. In his first vehicle, Lloyd played a slow-witted telephone lineman whose habitual flirting got him into trouble. Since Lloyd would have husbands and boyfriends chasing him in the film, and he knew the fact he was bigger than them diminished their threat, he stooped over to make himself look smaller. He worked carefully in establishing a look for the character. He noted in press material that he wore a battered derby he purchased from a plumber. The film, *Ham the Lineman*, was, by critics' estimates, brisk and delightful.

3. The Rapid Advancement of an Earnest and Inventive Player

Hamilton plays a flirtatious iceman who fails to melt housewives' hearts in *Ham the Iceman* (1914). The actress prepared to strike him with a pot is Ruth Roland (courtesy of Cole Johnson — Slapstick Archive).

Lloyd's next film was *The Slavery of Foxicus*, a farce set in ancient Rome. This costume comedy was especially interesting as it allowed Lloyd to burlesque his dramatic heavy roles. He played a fierce antagonist named Villainous. He created the character by discarding his timid hunch, instead unfolding his broad shoulders.

Encouraged by the talents of his new star, Neilan figured to improve on an earlier comedy. He remade *The Hash-house Count* with Lloyd in the role originated by Brennan. The new reel was titled *The Tattered Duke*.

Neilan and Lloyd were similar in that they didn't thrive on pressure. Both men felt hindered by the urgent pace at which they were required to work and resented the interference of management. Being perfectionists, the pair did not like being hurried and would have preferred to explore a variety of options. They were inclined to ponder their problems and experiment. Comedian Joe E. Brown noted, "Neilan was the kind to sit around and play the piano half the morning getting himself in the mood to work."[3] Kalem executives, who were primarily concerned with meeting their weekly deadlines, wanted Neilan to proceed briskly. They expected their directors to avoid delays with snap decisions and strict adherence to proven devices. This one difference led to repeated clashes between Neilan and the executives.

Hard-working individuals often use liquor as the great unwinder. Lloyd and Neilan tended to complete a day of hard work with a bit of carousing. Lloyd said that, as long as it was used properly, "liquor [was] all right."[4] Charleson Gray, who interviewed Lloyd on the subject years later, explained the comedy star's belief that "[h]e deserved some relaxation for grinding out laughs in one of the most tiring professions."[5]

Top: Hamilton, with putty nose and soup-bowl bangs, attempts to develop an innocent and endearing rube character in *Ham and the Villain Factory* (1914). The factory boss terrorizing Hamilton is actor Victor Rottman. *Bottom:* Ham reports a problem to Neilan's faux Keystone Kops in *Ham the Lineman* (1914). The detective leading the police officers is portrayed by Chance Word (both photographs courtesy of Cole Johnson — Slapstick Archive).

Neilan decided to take more advantage of the comic's extraordinary form. Lloyd's burly physique differentiated him from those many comics who were small, slightly built, or rotund. This distinction, originally hidden, was now to be maximized. For *The Reformation of Ham*, the comedymaker had Lloyd play a sailor who was strong, aggressive and hard-drinking. He emphasized the gob's physical magnitude by providing him with a sidekick appropriately named Shorty.

Neilan's faith in Lloyd was rewarded when exhibitors reported that "Ham" was a big hit with patrons. In November, Kalem showed their appreciation of Lloyd in at least three ways. First, they featured Lloyd in a full-page ad headlined "The Best Comedies Exhibited in America." The ad displayed a formal portrait of Neilan alongside a photo of Lloyd concealed in one of his heavy disguises. Second, Lloyd was the subject of a cover story in Kalem's monthly exhibitor book. Third, Kalem introduced Lloyd's new sidekick, Bud Duncan.

Since Lloyd had last seen him working in musical comedy, Bud had been writing and appearing in Biograph films. He also worked at Apollo, where he was a foil to Fred Mace. Prior to joining Kalem, he visited Mexico to appear in a travelogue film. The engagement, according to *Motion Picture Magazine*, had been disrupted by the outbreak of a revolution.[6]

Set beside Bud, Lloyd looked like A.O. Duncan must have looked when paired with one of his knee-figures. Lloyd was over a foot taller than Bud and possessed a much vaster build. Nothing similar would exist until seventy-five years later, when Arnold Schwarzenegger would be matched with Danny DeVito for *Twins*. Neilan was certain that, apart from showcasing the pair's expertise with broad physical comedy, he needed to exploit the obvious humor in their physical contrast.

A script entitled *Lizzie the Lifesaver* cast Lloyd and Bud as a couple of ragged janitors. As the boss janitor, Lloyd was to depict a brash and belligerent behemoth. He adorned his upper lip with a dark, heavy moustache. To make himself look fierce and powerful, he swelled his chest and assumed a pompous physical attitude. The new team was dubbed "Ham and Bud." *Lizzie the Lifesaver* revolved around a romance between Roland and Neilan. In every other scene, Lloyd and Bud engaged in knockabout exploits independent from the love story. Ham and Bud, easily the reel's livelier couple, were apportioned the film's climax, a scene involving a motorboat. The plot had Bud trying to use the motorboat to outdistance his infuriated partner. Lloyd was supposed to grab a mooring line trailing from the moving vessel and be pulled across a river.

Neilan had one end of a fifteen-foot rope attached to a motorboat and the other end secured around Lloyd's waist. Lloyd settled back. He later said, "I expected a gentle jerk followed by a pleasant ride into the cooling water and a pleasing imitation of a surf-board ride. What I actually received was a violent yank, a cannonball flight through the air, ending as the whole Pacific Ocean rose to meet me. I sank immediately and after an eternity, or so it seemed, I was hauled out of the water."[7]

Marion directed Neilan to increase his output. The Brennan comedies had been temporarily removed from Kalem's program and this vacated slot needed to be filled. As one of his many December releases, Neilan produced a polite and romantic comedy that featured himself and Roland. In flashbacks to prehistoric times, Lloyd appeared briefly as a caveman.

Kalem recognized the "Ham and Bud" characters as a valuable property. The call for slapstick was on the rise. Exhibitors let the studio know that their audiences favored Ham and Bud's slapstick antics over Neilan's more subdued comedy. *Lizzie the Lifesaver* made a definite impact. Two years after its release, Stanley Todd, writing an article about Ham and Bud for *Motion Picture Magazine*, plainly recalled how the team "first excited interest of photoplay fans ... [playing] two janitors slid[ing] around the wet floors in an office building."[8] To give the paying customers what they wanted, the slipping and sliding comedy team returned in *Ham the Piano Mover*.

Mary Hamilton could not have been among the many people who enjoyed Ham's antics. A Protestant mother, who had taught her son to be clean, orderly, rational and dignified, could not have been pleased that her son had adopted this impetuous character, a character who was in every way the antithesis of the ideal Protestant. Ham lacked self-control and reason; he was unwilling to work; he lived principally for impulsive enjoyment. Lloyd could be perceived as a rebellious and derisive child to have taken on such an image.

Following the formula of *Lizzie the Lifesaver*, Neilan constructed a pleasant comedy aptly entitled *Love, Oil and Grease*. The film opens with a garage owner and his girlfriend having a lovers' quarrel. Afterwards, the garage owner hires two destructive and inept mechanics. Neilan and Roland, who acted as the garage owner and the girlfriend, endowed the reel with the love. Ham and Bud, cast as the mechanics, generously dispensed the oil and grease.

Ham and Bud are humorously introduced in the film. Bud points to a "Help Wanted" sign and calls to a companion concealed behind a building. Bud takes hold of the person's long arm and tugs, but he encounters fierce resistance. By pulling harder, Bud finally drags Ham into view. Ham, his knees shaking, appears to be thoroughly terrified at the prospect of a job.

Neilan's alternating plots crammed too much information into the tight space of a reel. Ham and Bud's less complicated scenes dominated.

In December, three leading men departed Kalem. First, Brennan left the company to join the Sterling Motion Picture Company, where he was featured in short comedies as a character named Snitz. The Sterling Motion Picture Company closed the following month, at which time Brennan's short-lived career ended.

Next, Neilan declined to renew his contract. He left Kalem to direct Selig's *Chronicles of Bloom Center*, a series of rural-based two-reel comedies. Once away from Kalem, Neilan rapidly rose beyond the realm of short films. Within a matter of months, he would be contracted to star opposite Mary Pickford in a big-budget feature version of *Madame Butterfly*. At the film's completion, the Lasky company would sign Neilan to direct features.

Finally, Carlyle Blackwell left the studio to join Lasky. For Kalem, this last departure was the most devastating.

Marion presented attractive offers to Roland and Lloyd. Roland agreed to star in *The Girl Detective*, a new mystery-adventure series. Marion, with a contract in hand, also proposed featuring Lloyd in his own series. Lloyd embarked on a two-week vacation to consider the contract. He accepted the contract on his return.

Love, Oil and Grease was Kalem's last comedy release of 1914.

At the start of 1915, Alice Joyce was Kalem's biggest star. The film organization's second most precious property was *The Hazards of Helen*, a railroad-adventure series starring Helen Holmes. Kalem executives, who saw Lloyd as their next big star, devoted a large amount of their January promotion to their comedy releases.

Upon his return to Kalem, Lloyd was reunited with Bud. From this team, Kalem intended to draw their latest Tuesday series. Chance E. Ward, Neilan's bull-necked assistant, was made the series' producer-director. Charles Inslee was assigned a regular role as the team's chief adversary. Marin Sais became the unit's leading lady. Lloyd and Bud, besides playing the lead characters, would write the new series.

Kalem's *Ham* series officially debuted in the middle of March.

A Pause for Analysis I

Ham and Bud occupy a remote recess of movie history. Being nearly a century removed from the team, a contemporary audience might perceive them as curious creatures. They could react to ancient footage of the duo not much differently than they would to a magical video tape of an actual brontosaurus and triceratops.

Despite their great age, Ham and Bud were not the movies' earliest comedy team. Notable predecessors existed as early as 1910, during which time Augustus Carney and Victor Potel cavorted as "Hank and Lank." In the *All Movie Guide,* Hal Erickson wrote that Carney and Potel, "one short and one tall," were "evidently hired on the basis of their resemblance to comic-strip characters Mutt and Jeff."[9] The team did well for their studio, Essanay, but Carney and Potel split up after a few months to star in individual series.

In 1913, Vitagraph and Selig both tried to launch a series starring a tramp pair. Vitagraph unveiled a try-out vehicle for Sandy and Shorty, alias Robert Thornby and George Stanley. The two actors had provided effective comedy relief in more than one of Vitagraph's western adventures. Nonetheless, a series did not stem from their test release. Selig's tramp pair, Bump and Willie, also did not last beyond their series' debut. Thanks to Ham and Bud, Kalem succeeded where Vitagraph and Selig had irrefutably failed.

Ham and Bud were baseborn. They were part of the lowest level of civilization, completely detached from mankind's awesome accomplishments and wider concerns. The two, seeking to satisfy their basic needs, regularly crawled out of a filthy gutter. An author of Kalem's press releases would refer to the pair as "hardened men of the road," a polite way to describe the hopeless bums.

Ham's face was heavily embellished. Greasepaint triangles widely broadened the inner ends of his eyebrows. His bangs settled on his forehead in a curled and oily clump. Dominating his comic mask was a monstrous moustache. At the time, a big prop moustache was the comedy star's signature. Comics used wax to fix their moustaches into a wide assortment of bizarre and flamboyant shapes.

The principal pieces of Ham's outfit included an undersized derby, a worn black vest, and dusty pants upheld by unraveling suspender straps. His tall and sturdy legs ended in tattered cuffs and a gargantuan pair of slapshoes. The comic bluchers were thick, wide, and four inches longer than the feet they contained. But the shoes seemed aptly sized for Ham, who was perceived to be a giant. Walter Kerr described Ham as "ferociously muscular and given to bending iron bars with his bare hands."[10] Lloyd actually looked so big in comparison to Bud that some observers assumed he was as much as seven feet tall. Audiences did not believe that attached to the end of Ham's legs were oversized shoes — some foot prostheses — but what one critic called "seven-league feet."

Bud, simply enclosed by several roomy rags and an oversized bowler, was much less conspicuous in dress.

Ham and Bud were obvious reprobates. Their appearance was not as shabby as their behavior. The pair, lustful and aggressive, was the embodiment of a rampaging id. They were indifferent to everything except their own immediate needs and interests. Being amoral, they broke the rules of convention. They were frightfully ill-mannered, recklessly violent, grossly self-centered, unduly envious, and completely untrustworthy. They would readily cheat or rob in order to get what they wanted. By radiating a childish innocence and charm, this iconoclastic pair were seen by their fans as lovable bad boys.

Ham and Bud were rugged brawlers. They would unhesitatingly and brutally dispose of

Ham (right) understands that a good detective searches for clues, talks to witnesses, and shoots off a lot of bullets. His devoted assistant is played by Bud Duncan. *Ham the Detective* (1915) (courtesy of Cole Johnson — Slapstick Archive).

opponents. A big, bad westerner stomps into their diner, blasting a pair of revolvers. After the wildman ends his exhibition, Ham and Bud casually remove baseball bats from under the counter and proceed to beat the rowdy patron senseless.

When not trouncing a mutual adversary, Ham and Bud battled each other. In fact, the major portion of the combat in a *Ham* comedy stemmed from a fierce and ceaseless rivalry between the pair. During a typical row, they would throw at each other every heavy and unattached object available. The end of their battle would never be reached until the immediate surroundings had been exhausted and devastated.

Decided by brawn rather than brain, Ham was the senior member of the knockabout *farceurs*. As team leader, he was the pair's absolute strategist. He regularly concocted crude courses of action, usually moneymaking schemes. To protect his unsteady leadership, he would kick Bud for any independent thought.

Ham, a wild and irrepressible colossus, was more immoderate than Bud. He was crasser, bolder, probably more dishonest, and certainly more amorous. An attractive woman could not get near without him flashing an immodest leer. Women took priority over anything else going on in his life. One time, he commanded Bud to watch for a pursuing cop so that he and a pretty young lady could chat. For the most part, though, Ham's leering amounted to nothing more than boyish flirtation. In *Ham and the Harem*, Ham seeks to meet harem girls for their alleged "hip-hurling" dancing abilities. Once he forces his way into the harem, his interest remains limited to showing the girls his purported mastery of the latest dance steps.

In his relations with Bud, Ham constantly took advantage of his physical superiority.

3. The Rapid Advancement of an Earnest and Inventive Player

He tyrannically exploited his sturdy build along with the terrible might this build contained. On a piano-moving assignment, he looked on and arrogantly delivered orders as his much smaller partner carried a grand piano on his back.

In his abuse, Ham would kick Bud for a wide variety of reasons. He automatically blamed his partner for any and all misfortune. To him, Bud was an ideal target of hostile feelings. By kicking Bud, he could easily vent his anger over a failed scheme. An example of this behavior occurred while Ham was operating a photography studio. An alluring actress, preparing to be featured in a provocative photo, partially disrobed before Ham. Ham was greatly stimulated by the sight, but he was determined to maintain professional poise. The frustrated photographer directly located Bud and kicked him hard. The strong kick, which disposed of considerable outrage, allowed Ham to calmly return to his camera.

This is not to imply that Bud was never at fault. Bud, an unreliable co-conspirator and possessor of a mischievous streak, would often cause difficulty for Ham. Rarely did he properly or fully carry out his part in one of Ham's arrangements. He occasionally provoked Ham to chase him for fun. Once, while Ham tried to maintain a pose for an artist, he playfully poked his friend with a sharp stick.

Bud didn't necessarily resist Ham's malicious treatment. After all, he revered his mighty, fearless leader, whom he could rely on for care and protection. According to author Kalton C. Lahue, Bud often accepted Ham's bullying and general abuse "in stride with a zany nonchalance."[11] While Ham prepared to strike him, he might surrender his jaw and brace himself for the worst blow.

It was in dire circumstances that Ham and Bud would reveal great affection for one another. Their relationship basically resembled a troublous father-son or husband-wife relationship. Supporting the latter association, Bud would act as cook and housekeeper in a domestic situation.

Walter Kerr aptly stated that silent comedy began as though theatre never existed. The new form brought its players back to the dawn of man. In the early days of film, comics resembled lawless primitives whose actions continually tested physical limits and social tolerability. Their behavior was pre-moral.

The requirements of a weekly one-reel slapstick series dictated Ham and Bud's basic tendencies. Both plots and characters were solely designed to justify the new comedy form. The action was random, broad, violent, and fast-paced.

Due to the brevity of a *Ham* comedy, the plots had to be quickly established and quickly ended. All the connective action had to be straightforward. For this reason, the *Ham* company generally pursued plots that were simple and familiar. Rivalry stimulated by money or a girl was a perfect basis for one of their exploits.

To disguise the lack of variety, slapstick players would often be moved around to different locations. They would improvise with whatever props became available in the new setting, especially attracted to objects they could use as weapons. The casts knew to swiftly milk the setting before the audience had a chance to lose interest.

Lloyd was no different in this regard. For *Ham in the Harem*, he raced frantically around a palace set grabbing up whatever props he could use to get a laugh. He performed an impromptu sword-swallowing routine with a decorative cutlass and pretended to get dizzy from a passing drag on a hookah. The Ham and Bud characters rarely remained long in a single place, commonly switching surroundings and objectives in mid-reel. The comedians were liable, without warning, to be shipped off for renewed entanglements elsewhere.

As time did not permit the development of sophisticated characters, the population of

Ham and Bud greet the sultan in *Ham in a Harem* (1915). The actress at the sultan's side is Marin Sais (courtesy of Cole Johnson — Slapstick Archive).

a one-reel comedy consisted of expedient "types," many of whom were distinguishable by a gag name. In the course of a reel, Ham and Bud could encounter a rich woman named Lotta Coin and an inebriated man named I.C. Double.

It was necessary that the lead characters, in charge of creating slapstick comedy, be irresponsible, brash and rowdy. Since these were not qualities of the sociable and conservative bourgeois, slapstick dispensers frequently selected misfits as their lead subjects. Best fitting the bill was the tramp, who existed below social standards and whose needs, desires and problems were invariably basic. The slapstick tramps were free of middle-class attitudes. In their bumptious and anarchic activity, these individuals thumbed their nose at the middle class.

Most of the time, Ham and Bud appeared to be doing nothing more than enthusiastically playing. The pair, often referred to as "the adventurers," regularly involved themselves in occupations that promised new and exciting experiences. At various times, they became burglars, Indian-fighters, treasure hunters, and detectives. Stanley Todd, a writer for *Motion Picture Magazine*, found that the team's formula simply amounted to "Ham attempting to imitate [a new profession] and failing miserably, with Bud getting the worst of the bargain and a pretty girl thrown in for good measure."[12] If disappointed or bored by an undertaking, the fun-seekers would desert their duties. Unimpressed by the mover's life, they nonchalantly park their furniture-laden truck and depart to visit a circus.

3. The Rapid Advancement of an Earnest and Inventive Player

Ham and Bud expected everyone to join them in treating life as play. It didn't matter that most people were reluctant to participate in their wild games. This was evident in *Ham and the Jitney Bus*. By dressing in drag, Ham endeavored to attract passersby to his cab. He initially enjoyed the challenge of luring customers, but his glee and patience faded when his feminine disguise failed to draw a single customer. In the end, he simply intimidated people into becoming his fares. In another short, Ham prepared to blow a safe. To insure that the safe would stay put during the explosion, he seated Bud on top of it. When the homeowner interrupted the burglary, Ham indignantly demanded that the homeowner stay away until his safe had been destroyed.

Ham and Bud coaxed conflict, sportily running afoul of people. Playing his part in the game, Ham would merrily take flight from people whom he could obviously overpower. The chase would almost inevitably cap the comedy. Whenever they managed to best their opponents, Ham and Bud chuckled in delight and celebrated their cleverness. Otherwise, the mischief-makers accepted jail or even death as punishment for their improper deeds. More than one *Ham* reel closed with the pair surrendering themselves to an icy river's eternal embrace.

Ham and Bud, one of the silent screen's most popular comedy teams, were able to maintain their success during a time when Hollywood churned out a variety of comedy teams. Throughout this period, the most common requirement for two men to work together as a comedy team was that the men had to have some extreme contrast in their physical forms. Mutual came up with the characters "Oscar and Conrad" for a one-reel series. Oscar and Conrad were both middle-aged, had heavy beards, and were fairly homely. But, otherwise, they looked very much opposite. Oscar was, essentially, a small round head on a fat little body. Conrad, a lanky, slack-jawed fellow looming head and shoulders above buddy Oscar, looked like Abraham Lincoln might have looked if he had survived his assassination with significant brain damage.

The name said it all with the series *Plump and Runt*. The *Plump and Runt* comedies starred a plump man who would one day be comedy royalty, Oliver Hardy. Cast as Hardy's "runt" sidekick was the less noble Billy Ruge. Plump and Runt, despite their contrasting sizes and slapstick style, were very different from Kalem's comedy tramps. These characters were well-meaning boobs with wives and steady jobs.[13] They were never allowed to be downright bad, which was a serious shortcoming for this type of series. Middle-class repressions and responsibilities are dull in the context of a slapstick comedy. The storylines, though, were not their greatest problem as no real chemistry or collaboration developed between Hardy and Ruge.

Many comedy teams introduced during this period did not bond and they didn't stay together for long. Jimmy Aubrey and Walter Kendig, the principals of the *Starlight Comedies*, appeared on screen as "Heinie and Louie." Aubrey, a graduate of the renowned Karno story-pantomime troupe, drew considerably more attention than Kendig, which prompted Aubrey to dissolve the team and establish himself as a solo star.

Ham and Bud, a secure and solid team that offered more than contrasting physiques, were able to earn a dominant position in the field of slapstick comedy, but other teams managed varying success with less robust styles of comedy.

William Wadsworth and Arthur Houseman, as Waddy and Arty, were sluggish and unmotivated compared to Ham and Bud. Waddy had to squint through small wire-rimmed spectacles to see. His head was topped with tousled white hair. He looked like he had just climbed out of bed and was barely awake yet. Arty, with his deadpan expression, seemed too lazy to come up with the most meager thought. Wadsworth and Houseman performed together briefly in a few Edison comedies during 1914.

The most successful comedy team of the period had the least in common with Ham and Bud. Eddie Lyons and Lee Moran, members of Al Christie's Nestor unit, lacked any strong physical contrast. Dubbed "The Nestor Twins," they were two average, clean-shaven Midwestern men undistinguished by either height or weight. Their classy, polite situation comedy, a style decidedly different than that of Ham and Bud, was never dull despite the relative calm and restraint. Lyons and Moran still knew to keep the action moving at a lively pace and managed to use a sparing amount of slapstick to great effect. The men would maintain a partnership successfully until 1920, by which time they would be starring in features for Universal.

Ham and Bud remain a memorable part of movie history. Though their excessive behavior might be bizarre by today's standards, the escapades of Kalem's spirited team delighted many theatregoers of their day.

4

Part of a New Wave

The first releases in the *Ham* series proudly bore the name of their leading character. *Ham at the Garbage Gentleman's Ball. Ham Among the Redskins. Ham in the Harem. Ham's Harrowing Duel.* Full-page magazine advertisements promoted their release. One ad, widely released in the trades, showed Bud posed on his hands and knees, gleefully smiling at the camera, while a belligerent-looking Ham was seated on his back.

The early *Ham* comedies earned widespread acclaim. Asked his series' immediate success, Lloyd replied, "Simply this: Bud and I have originated a style of our own, and we do our best to keep our work free from anything that might be deemed offensive."[1] Lloyd was referring to a controversy over the vulgar content of some slapstick comedies. The industry's growth into different communities required producers to correspond to varying standards of taste. To be accepted by this broad audience, a dilution of material was necessary.

Sydney Chaplin, Charles' half-brother, was the Howard Stern of 1915. By relying on risqué material, he offended a large number of theatergoers. His outlook and designs in regards to comedy certainly set him apart from Lloyd.

Sydney Chaplin, in creating the character Gussle, stuffed ample padding down the back of his pants to give himself an absurdly full and prominent backside, which he was able to employ as an all-purpose prop. Gussle wiggles the backside in defiance of a jealous husband. He turns it towards a foe to let it absorb the brunt of blows. He gets it stuck in a chair. The camera often comes in for a tight shot on the padded posterior, such as when Gussle gets a dollar bill stuck to the seat of his pants. In another scene, in the same comedy, Gussle is knocked over and sits down forcibly in a puddle. When he gets back on his feet, he turns his backside to the camera and shakes it hard to dispel the excess water.

Much of what Gussle does looks suggestive. This is certainly the case when Gussle, approached by a train conductor, sticks his hand down the front of his pants and unspools a streaming train ticket. The comedian, in this way, was fairly distinctive. Many silent film comedians expressed amorous feeling towards pretty young ladies, but Gussle is unusually blatant in the way he cranes his head back to check out a young lady's derriere. Slapstick comedians are known to fling a variety of objects at a romantic rival, a police officer or a random passerby, but Gussle seems uniquely indecent and irreverent when he flings around a corset and accidentally hits a pastor's wife in the face with it. Gussle could do things that might even offend some modern viewers. Gussle, as a philandering husband, is attracted to a woman seated on a park bench with her husband. He sidles alongside her with a newspaper. He opens the newspaper, which has a small hole cut in the middle, and coaxes the woman to raise her lips

Ham (driving) and Bud look for fares in *Ham and the Jitney Bus* (1915) (courtesy of Cole Johnson — Slapstick Archive).

to the hole so he can kiss her without her husband seeing. The husband, who catches what's going on, pulls his wife away and takes her place. Gussle, unaware of the change, plants a couple of lingering kisses on the husband's waiting lips.

Lloyd was more innocent and modest in his comedy. By comparison, Ham and Bud's roughhouse antics were regarded as wholesome fun and readily welcomed into most communities.

Lloyd modestly failed to mention that the principal reason for his series' success was his amusing and singular alter ego. In reviewing *Ham* comedies, critics singled out for praise those moments that solely relied on Lloyd's efforts. An exhibitor summarized the view of many fellows in reporting: "Mr. Lloyd V. Hamilton is a great favorite with our patrons."

Lloyd had, in 1915, become a celebrity. He was part of a major new wave of comedy stars which mostly included performers from the Keystone and Christie fun-factories — Charles Chaplin, Roscoe Arbuckle, Mabel Normand, Mack Swain, Charles Murray, Neal Burns, Slim Summerville, and Hank Mann.

Along with his celebrity, Lloyd was prospering financially. The cheeks on the comedian's porcelain piggy had turned a rosy red. With the persistent growth of the film industry, the salary of the slapstick comedian was increasing steadily. In 1914, the leading comedians of the field had earned an average weekly wage of $200. Within the next year, the salary of these same performers had swelled by fourfold. That works out, in current dollars, to an annual salary of more than $800,000. For all his similar work, being slapped with canes and kicked sharply, Oofty Goofty had never seen as many quarters.

4. Part of a New Wave

As the "Ham" character was becoming increasingly attractive to theatregoers, Kalem's exhibitors were clamoring for promotional material. In response, the image of Ham was placed on posters, color-tinted stills, cuts for newspaper ads, glass transparencies, and life-size cut-outs.

The escapades of Ham and Bud had catapulted Lloyd and Bud to the ranks of the noteworthy. To satisfy the press' interest in the team, Kalem's publicity crew released biographical data concocted from half-truths and outright lies. In summary, their version of "The Ham and Bud Story" was as follows:

> It was twenty-two years earlier that Lloyd and Bud originally met on a Brooklyn sandlot. At the time, Lloyd was the leader of a juvenile gang and Bud was a new kid in the neighborhood. The two boys remained close companions. During their school years, they played hookey together and fought each other's playground battles. Prior to joining Kalem, they worked in vaudeville and burlesque as a "brother act."

The story pleasantly depicted Lloyd and Bud as loyal, durable and proficient partners. In ways, it conformed to the team's screen image. However, it did not demonstrate a respect for the facts. Kalem even exaggerated Lloyd's age by more than a decade.

Lloyd didn't seem inclined to support this fiction when a magazine writer came to interview him and Bud. The writer looked at him and asked, "Could you tell about the time that Bud's father gave you and Bud passes to see *Dr. Jekyll and Mr. Hyde?*" The writer waited for Lloyd to reminisce how he and Bud were inspired to recreate the show. Instead, Lloyd forced out a light chuckle and replied, meekly, "Let Bud tell it."[2]

Kalem's competition tried to lure Ham and Bud. Mack Sennett, president of Keystone, expressed a special interest in Lloyd. But no one, including Sennett, made a good enough offer to draw the pair from their home at Kalem.

Hollywood, though, is the great land of illusion and, in such a place, a movie producer who cannot woo a star into his ranks has the option of producing an adequate forgery. And that was what happened with Ham and Bud. In the wake of their success, more than a few slapstick comedies bore enough similarity to their act — the "Mutt and Jeff" contrast, the bullying larger partner — to justify a degree of suspicion.

No one is more deserving of such suspicion than Sennett, who launched a series starring Mack Swain as an overstuffed, imperious boss and Chester Conklin as his stunted assistant.

In March, 1915, Kalem's five Friday comedies demonstrated that Marion was working hardest to reproduce Ham and Bud's success. These productions, which revolved around crude and mayhem-creating rivals, had been clearly manufactured in the Ham and Bud mold. Three of the five reels starred Charles Dudley as a character named "Desperate Dud" and featured Ethel Teare, William Wolbert and Phil Dunham in supporting roles. Another reel was a Stone Age farce that starred Charles Inslee and Martin Kinney. The remaining reel was an extremely fast-paced comedy that featured Walter H. Stull and Robert Burns. Months later, Stull and Burns would move to Lubin, where they would achieve success as "Pokes and Jabs."

Kalem, which had allowed Stull and Burns to slip through their fingers, failed to expand upon the success of Ham and Bud. Their recent Friday comedy series fizzled out. After March, Kalem began to gradually eliminate the series. They released two Friday comedies in April ... one in May ... a "split-reel" finale in June.

The *Ham* company was obligated to manufacture a comedy within four or five days. This was a demanding schedule, requiring Lloyd to be urgent and strenuous in his efforts. Years later, an interviewer asked Lloyd if comedy work ever became tiresome. He replied, "If you refer to the days of the single reels, I must answer "yes," for it was just a

Ham is wary of his new friend in *The Hypnotic Monkey* (1915) (courtesy of Cole Johnson — Slapstick Archive).

question of going through a certain formula week after week — of getting a certain amount of footage."[3]

The *Ham* comedies were slapdash productions. They were basically formless films in which actors labored hastily to do funny, impromptu deeds. The *Ham* company, operating on a hit-or-miss basis, accomplished intermittently good work.

Explaining how he and Bud operated, Lloyd told a magazine writer: "Our director, giving us a general idea of the business which takes place in the scene, orders us to go ahead and make him laugh.... [Bud and I] can safely introduce funny business not contained in the original script, knowing the other will play to it."[4]

It more than helped the team that, in their early days, Bud totally submitted himself to Lloyd's leadership. It was mainly due to Bud's steadfast cooperation that the team could arrive spontaneously at an extraordinary number of gags.

A mild albeit uneasy friendship sprung from this professional association. Lloyd and Bud went out on the town together for a time, but the two men eventually had their differences and drifted apart. The major irritation for Lloyd was that, in his view, Bud possessed egotistical tendencies.

Dee Monroe, who befriended Bud in the 1950s, remembered that Bud liked to boast about himself.[5] He described his rugged outdoor adventures as a hunter and fisherman. He talked, too, about his glory days as a movie star and his extensive military training. Bud, in fact, served as First Sergeant in California's 51st Gun Company from 1917 to 1919. Monroe felt that Bud's bravado was his way to counter the inferiority he felt about his short stature. She thought that it was also out of this insecurity that he was quick-tempered and had the occasional outburst.

A class distinction may have also formed a barrier between the men. The contrast is evident in a candid photo of the pair. The photo, which a magazine captioned "A couple of dudes go to Los," features Lloyd and Bud attired in street-wear.[6] Lloyd's growing reputation as a sharp dresser is not contradicted by the picture. By comparison, Bud appears slovenly. His suit is baggy, his pants are falling down, his shirt tail is hanging out, and his shoes are covered in dust.

Greater differences were evident in their professional objectives. In explaining his work, Lloyd would express serious and high-minded ideas. He spoke of "art." In contrast, his uncomplicated partner would consider doing whatever it took to get the most and loudest laughs.

For leisure-time diversions, this odd couple would visit the Los Angeles Athletic Club. Chaplin would later describe the place as a "headquarters of bachelors and businessmen."[7] The club's main attraction was furious amateur fights staged in an expansive loft over the club's saloon. Many were drawn to the battles because they were independent from recent legislation lessening the severity of professional boxing. The action of these bouts would be crammed into four rounds. That was a raw and violent concentration of power.

Among the club's fight enthusiasts were numerous comedy stars. Regularly present at ringside, invariably obscured by thick tobacco smoke, were Charles Chaplin, Mack Sennett, Mabel Normand, Roscoe Arbuckle, Charlie Murray and Slim Summerville.

The bouts were exceptionally entertaining because the comics contributed to the action. On one typical evening, Arbuckle acted as a fighter's attendant and Chaplin presided as a guest referee. In 1914, Arbuckle and Chaplin re-created their antics in *The Knockout*. Chaplin, who appears as a referee, pretends to take a wild blow. He collapses against a ring post and then, in retreat, groggily pulls himself along the ropes.

Rough boxing matches only represented one side of life at the Athletic Club. In sharp contrast to the popular boxing matches, the club hosted a highly publicized chess exhibition. This year, a seven-year-old chess champion concurrently played twenty men, including a distinguished doctor with a statewide title. The match drew an equally large crowd.

Lounge rooms and a large dining room were located on the first floor of the establishment. This area would be opened to ladies during the evening hours. The local elite would sip cocktails in the club's barroom while, in an elaborate gym, the more athletically inclined guests would exert muscles and sweat glands.

Lloyd, who had embraced the club as his principal retreat, could usually be found there in his off-hours. The club granted him membership for a monthly charge of twelve dollars. Under the arrangement, the actor received a room and the privilege of using the club's assorted facilities.

Lloyd regularly utilized the gym. He refrained from mild calisthenics in favor of strenuous gymnastics. He believed that, due to the physical demands of slapstick, he needed to keep his body in peak condition via a rigorous daily routine. He would toss a medicine ball, box with the club trainer, and swim at length in one of the gym's two large pools. He approached this routine as if he was on a Protestant crusade. Protestantism accepted sport if, Max Weber wrote, "it served a rational purpose, that of recreation necessary for physical efficiency. But as a means for the spontaneous expression of undisciplined impulses, it was under suspicion."[8] This gym routine must have done more than build a body. Boxing has been known as a way to relieve tension and release hostility. And swimming, the other activity that Lloyd pursued, is relaxing and exhilarating. Submerged in a pool, gliding through a silent and weightless world, the swimmer feels isolated, serene, and free. Every part of his body becomes liberated. His limbs carelessly drift from the rest of his body. Tense muscles loosen up.

While residing at the club, Lloyd socialized with other prominent film actors, none more prominent than Chaplin. It was impossible not to notice Chaplin. After taking a relaxing bath, Chaplin, wearing nothing but a towel wrapped around his waist, would wander thoughtfully around the building playing the violin. The club would later inspire one of Chaplin's best comedies, *The Cure*.

Kalem was having difficulty holding onto their leading ladies. After accepting an offer to star in Pathé serials, Ruth Roland left the studio in March, 1915. Kalem filled the vacancy that Roland left in the *Girl Detective* series by moving up Cleo Ridgely from the supporting cast. But then Ridgely defected, followed soon after by Alice Joyce. The Kalem brass kept shuffling around actresses as fast as they could. Marin Sais, Ham and Bud's leading lady, was hastily transformed into the third Girl Detective. Ethel Teare replaced Sais in the "Ham and Bud" series.

Sais didn't prove commanding as Kalem's favorite female sleuth. In August, Kalem debuted a revamped version of *The Girl Detective*, which they called *Mysteries of the Grand Hotel*. True Boardman, a handsome 32-year-old actor, assumed the lead role while Sais was kept around to lend support.

For unknown reasons, Chance Ward left the *Ham* company in April. Kalem's search for Ward's replacement ended the following month, at which time Rube Miller became the *Ham* series' new producer. Miller possessed experience as a circus clown and Keystone Cop. He had recently gained experience directing comedies while working for producer Henry Lehrman.

Miller was given an assistant, William Beaudine. Beaudine, an energetic young man from New York City, had learned the basics of filmmaking while working as an assistant director at Biograph. He was brought into Kalem by Neilan, who had Beaudine working as his assistant for a short time before he left Kalem. Beaudine was then assigned to assist Chance Ward, but Beaudine maintained that Ward had him do most of the work. "I practically directed."[9] Beaudine claimed that he also had to do much of the work for Miller, who was unfamiliar with how the series was produced: "I nursed [Rube] through about 10 or 12 pictures."[10]

Within weeks of Miller's appointment, Lloyd was injured in the line of duty. Slapstick players exposed themselves to danger by constantly trying to surpass their previous accomplishments and outdo their competitors. Based on an escalating trend, dangling a carload of comics off a cliff edge was becoming a trite trick.

Miller was willing to assure the safety of his stars. "[Rube] was an ex-stunt man and actor," explained Beaudine, "so when Lloyd Hamilton wouldn't do a stunt, Rube would put on the pants and do the stunt himself."[11] But Miller was unable to protect Lloyd this time. On this day, Lloyd felt fit when it came time to begin shooting and was prepared to rough it up in the scene ahead. It was at that moment, as he was turning to take a step, that the extended toes of his slapshoes became tangled. He tripped, tumbling down a steep embankment.[12] People awkwardly descended the slope to reach Lloyd, who had rolled all the way to the bottom. When they got near, they got a clear look of the bone sticking out of his leg. That one wrong step had left Lloyd's leg with a compound fracture.

Kalem's publicity staff, who may not have wanted their exhibitors to become alarmed, refrained from making the proverbial mountain out of the slippery hill. They avoided any dramatic exaggeration and, instead, reported that Lloyd was recovering well as an in-patient of St. Catherine's Hospital. Lloyd tried to take the opportunity to rest, but it was not long before he propped himself against his pillows and began scribbling ideas in a notepad.

Though lacking its main attraction, the *Ham* company continued to fulfill their weekly obligation. In honor of Lloyd, the troupe adopted a new mascot, a piglet named "Ham."

Despite hard work, the *Ham* company failed to compensate for Lloyd's absence. At first, Miller featured Bud and Ethel in Keystone-style comedies. When these comedies turned out to be less than appealing, Lloyd recommend that Miller hire some of his former stage associates to liven up the action. These new cast members, including Charles Mulgro, Owen Evans, Dave Morris, and John Rand, were not the type of performers to stand out and take charge of the action. They were loyal, durable support, serving more as water-bearers than soldiers. Morris, the most experienced as a film actor, was coming off a three-year stint at Biograph, where he tended to show up briefly as an incidental character. In dozens of films, he played a wide range of utility roles, from boxer to flutist, from policeman to thief, from physician to tramp. These performers were not stars and they did not enjoy long, distinguished careers, but they served a purpose when they got before the cameras. Thoughout his career, Lloyd gave Morris and Evans work whenever he could. Rand remains the best known of the group for his appearances in classic Chaplin comedies. He is the shop assistant who tussles with Chaplin in *The Pawnshop* and the sanitarium attendant trapped in a revolving door in *The Cure*.

Miller directed these players through a number of vigorous, fast-paced scenes, but the ensemble failed to offer an adequate alternative to the series' missing star. It was Miller's final plan to create a competent imitation of Ham and Bud. At first, Miller, himself teamed up with Bud. This new team of mischievous tramps was billed as "Bud and Dud." Dud, like Ham, violently abused Bud. This was best illustrated when, at the close of one adventure, Dud angrily throws Bud into a lake. However, there must have been something special about Ham's brand of violence. Dud, for all his efforts, was unable to fill Ham's oversized slapshoes. Miller, possibly out of desperation, tested his assistant, Beaudine, as Bud's next hungry and footsore traveling companion. This latest team, Bill and Bud, didn't work out well either.

Soon after, Miller announced to trade journals that he had found a suitable partner for Bud. He cast Charles Inslee in the role of Spike. Inslee, as a stock player in D.W. Griffith's Biograph company, had starred in some of the earliest American comedies. Recently, he had worked in a few Chaplin comedies, including playing the bank president in *The Bank*. His Spike character borrowed traces of Ham's temperament, particularly in an angry moment when he throws Bud down a flight of stairs. The Bud and Spike team did little better than the previous teams. On a visit to St. Catherine's Hospital, Bud reportedly joked to Lloyd, "Since you've been laid up, we haven't had anyone who could kick me as artistically as you can."[13]

In the meantime, Kalem suffered another major loss. Helen Holmes switched tracks to make "train dramas" for Thomas H. Ince's Bison Company. Kalem promptly announced that future installments of *The Hazards of Helen* would star Helen Gibson, the daughter of a railroad engineer. Helen Gibson was, in fact, Rose Gibson, a rodeo performer and the wife of cowboy star Hoot Gibson. She was not the daughter of a railroad engineer. Despite the fraudulence of its new Helen, Kalem's railroad series managed to continue without losing steam.

At this time, Kalem's weekly program was completed by "three-act modern dramas"; Blackwell and Joyce reissues; *The Ventures of Marqueritte* starring Marqueritte Courtot; and, most notably, a twelve-part series called *Stingaree*, which featured the Australia-based adventures of a mysterious outlaw bushranger. It was an adaptation of a book by E.W. Hornung, who remains best known for writing short stories and novels about Raffles, a gentleman thief with a fondness for diamonds. *Stingaree* told a more melodramatic story. The lead character,

Irving Randolph, is framed for murder by his brother, who wants to take control of the family fortune. After fleeing into the Australian outback to avoid arrest, Randolph assumes a disguise and devotes himself to stealing from corrupt and greedy rich people. *Stingaree*, which represented a new assignment for the unit that had produced *The Mysteries of the Grand Hotel*, was directed by James W. Horne and starred True Boardman and Marin Sais. Intending to improve their diminishing profits, Kalem bolstered the series with their biggest publicity campaign to date. According to the promotional blitz, *Stingaree* was no less than "The Greatest of All Series."

Lloyd was retained at St. Catherine's Hospital for six weeks. Upon his release, he continued his recovery in Oakland. For several weeks, he visited his family and appeared as management's guest at local theaters. In his public appearances, he described the production of his comedies.

Lloyd was still hobbling on crutches when he returned to Los Angeles. By this time, the *Ham* company had a new director. The New York executives weren't happy with Miller's work and fired him after six weeks. They agreed to hire Beaudine if he took $60 per week, which was less than half the money Miller had been receiving. Beaudine quickly reorganized the *Ham* company. Jack MacDermott, one of the troupe's supporting players, was made Beaudine's assistant.

For his first assignment, Beaudine was given a script that Lloyd had written: *Minnie the Tiger*, which recalled the ancient fable "Androcles and the Lion." A sweet-natured man is facing defeat against an unscrupulous romantic rival when he befriends escaped tiger Minnie. Minnie, who possesses a ferocity lacking in the hero, delivers the villain's well-deserved comeuppance.

Lloyd watched the film being made from the sidelines.[14] He offered ideas and opinions to Beaudine, who welcomed the help. The finished comedy, which featured an actor outfitted in a cartoonish tiger costume, was enjoyably silly.

By all indication, Lloyd and Beaudine got along well. For the following weeks, Lloyd participated in the direction of his company's sure-footed players. The series' latest lead characters were violent and amoral tramps Bud and Mac, Mac being Jack MacDermott. By combining their talents, Lloyd and Beaudine were able to recapture some of the series' unique charm and fun.

"[A]ll the decisions were made in New York," said Beaudine. "The film was not even developed here, we didn't know what the hell we got. We would shoot the picture and box it up and send it to New York and they'd develop it and cut it and print it, and the only time we'd see it is we'd go downtown to the theatre when it was running."[15]

Late in the year, the *Ham* troupe added a new character player: Gus Leonard. Leonard, a former Orpheum circuit star, had recently toured the U.S. and Europe with a drunken waiter routine. He better complemented Bud than MacDermott, who was now relegated to the sort of straight role that Neilan had once played. So now, in a typical plot, Bud and Leonard were detectives involved in the divorce efforts of a husband-and-wife divorce team played by Ethel and MacDermott. This new quartet, pleasant and efficient, helped to further lift the series out of the dumps.

Still, no matter how much the series improved, Marion remained anxious for Lloyd's recovery.

5

New Vision

Lloyd returned to work at the start of 1916. Despite a publicized vow, the comic loaded his feet into another pair of floppy shoes.

Kalem executives were pleased that their star was again off and running. Ham's first adventure in several months was *Ham Takes a Chance*. A gala celebration was held to honor the comeback. Hamilton Smith, the recently appointed Kalem western representative, presented Lloyd with a 300-page album filled with letters that exhibitors had submitted to express their wishes for Ham's prompt return.[1]

Kalem vigorously promoted the February release of *Ham Takes a Chance* and *Ham the Diver*. Their publicity crew launched a "Back-and-Better-than-Ever" campaign.

Marion was confident that, within his *Ham* company, he had accumulated the makings of a second comedy unit. On this basis, he initiated a Wednesday series. Ethel Teare starred in the series; Jack MacDermott and Gus Leonard acted as Ethel's main support; and Harry Millarde, a longtime Kalem leading man, presided over the trio as the series' producer-director.

Kalem began the new year with some triumph. With its latest offerings, the *Ham* series was able to surpass its previous popularity. The *Stingaree* serial was a big success and elevated Boardman to superstar status. However, the studio was unsettled by yet another defection. Marqueritte Courtot went to Famous Players. The replacement for *The Ventures of Marqueritte* was *Sis Hopkins*, a rural-set comedy based on a popular play. Rose Melville, the writer and star of the play, acted as the homespun "Sis." Kalem now entered March with three comedy series on its six-title program. Their ads proclaimed: "KALEM MEETS COMEDY DEMAND."

Beaudine left Kalem on April 23, 1916. "After doing about 26 of them," said Beaudine, "they found out I didn't know what it was all about and they fired me."[2] Lloyd and Beaudine, who had recently extended their association to the golf course, would remain good friends in the coming years.

Undeterred by Beaudine's departure, studio officials invested an extraordinary amount of money in a war burlesque entitled *Ham Agrees with Sherman*. Kalem reported that, to stage the production, they utilized artillery equipment, airplanes, and hundreds of extras.

Within the next couple of months, three noteworthy additions were welcomed to the *Ham* company. The first acquisition was Sam Taylor, a recent graduate of Fordham University, who joined the unit's scenario staff. Years later, Taylor would gain prestige writing and directing features.

Ham is an unlikely general in *Ham Agrees with Sherman* (1916). Bud Duncan (saluting) and an unidentified guard stand by as the general questions the spy played by Norma Nichols (courtesy of the family of Lloyd Hamilton).

The second addition was Lloyd Bacon. Bacon had been one of Lloyd's good friends since the Alcazar Theatre's 1909 season. It was his role in the *Ham* series to alternately enhance dramatic threat and diminish physical threat. This meant acting as a heavy until Lloyd's role became hazardous, at which point he would step forth as a double.

The final addition was Harry Edwards, a tenacious Keystone director and one of Lloyd's Athletic Club acquaintances, to handle the series. The next four *Ham* comedies proved that Edwards possessed a weak understanding of Kalem's comical duo. After a month of service, Edwards left the *Ham* company and Lloyd took control.

Preston Sturges said that, as a novice director, he worried how to get what he needed from his cast and crew without making enemies, but then he remembered the advice of director William Wyler, who told him, "The hardest part of directing is resisting the impulse to be a good fellow."[3] Lloyd admitted to having a similar problem as a director. He could, as Ham, display endless bravado and wild impulsiveness, but this was not the person he was in real life. He preferred to be the good fellow, kidding around with cast and crew members, and he shunned the bold pragmatism that a director needed to make quick decisions. His history shows that he worked best under the guidance of a parental director, through whom he could filter his whims.

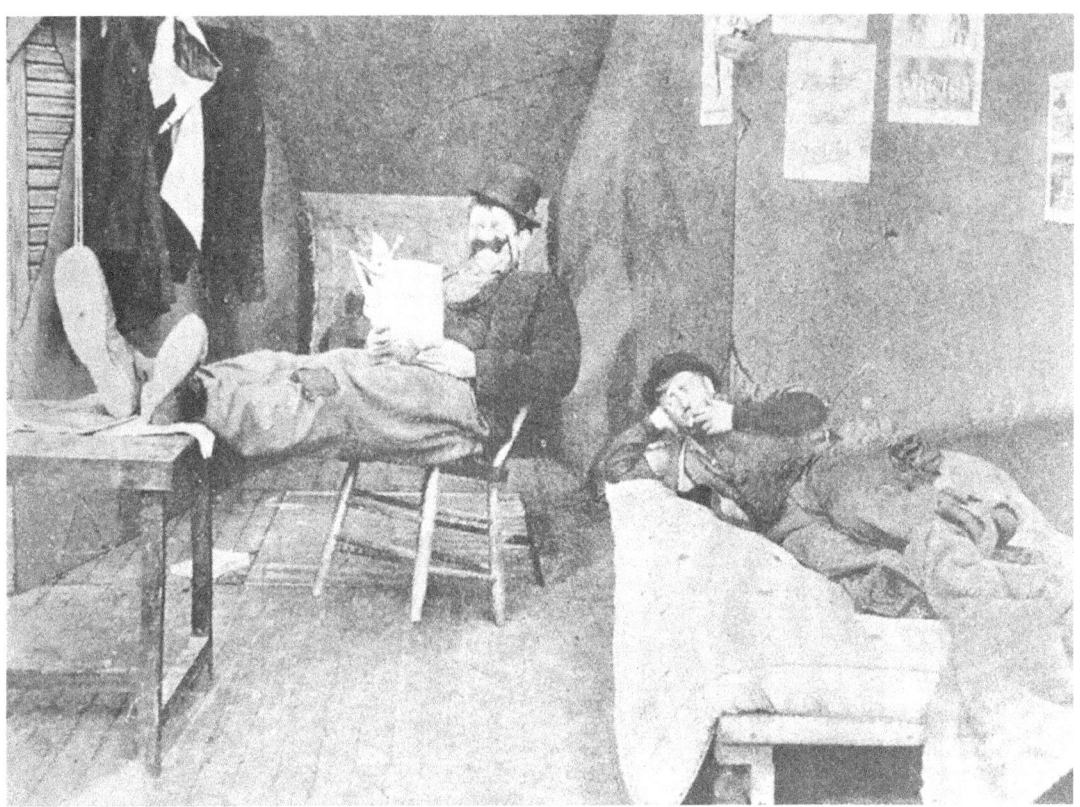

Ham and Bud live a life of luxury (courtesy of Cole Johnson — Slapstick Archive).

By this time, Lloyd and Bud's relationship had become less than congenial. Jack White, one of Lloyd's later associates, alleged that fame had driven Bud to egomania. White said, "Bud got so that he thought he knew more than Ham. He used to tell Lloyd off on the set, and Lloyd didn't like it."[4]

Lloyd's greatest problem, though, did not relate to his particular personality. It centered on his series' style and form, which could not readily welcome his new concepts. The type of material that he wanted to introduce didn't suit Ham and Bud. Nevertheless, Lloyd resolved to abandon the old format. It wasn't only that it didn't relate to his current views. It was plain that the format's limited possibilities had already been exhausted. Lloyd needed to strike out in a new direction and boldly move toward realizing his vision of the ideal comedy. Something better was possible, but it wouldn't come along by accident. It had to be scientifically planned and ambitiously constructed.

Lloyd engaged in much rumination during this period. Typically putting aside pleasure for business, he had become a professional theatergoer. He was taking full advantage of the screen actor's ability to study his own performance. He observed the *Ham* comedies with a highly analytical mind.

Years later, Lloyd would publicly describe his dissatisfaction with the Kalem reels. He was rankled by their "hokum comedy."[5] He also expressed disapproval of the "absurd makeup," which included his "hideous" Ham mask, and the "poor sets."[6]

Lloyd was also keeping abreast of the latest comedies of Chaplin, the most popular of the screen comedians. Chaplin was an ever-looming specter. Lloyd could not help but fall

Ham catches up on the news and gets some rays as Bud strains a muscle (courtesy of Cole Johnson — Slapstick Archive).

under the harsh glare of this great luminary and this was something that aggravated him even more.

By the spring of 1916, Chaplin had earned the privilege of producing a big-budget series of two-reel comedies. These films, released on a monthly basis, allowed a less strained production schedule. The extra care and dollars that Chaplin was able to devote to his work was apparent. Possessing the time and space, he could make sense of his characters' actions. He had recently halted the random running and hitting, and he had concentrated instead on characterization. By effectively incorporating pathos into his cinematic experiences, he was getting his audience to laugh while arousing their sympathy. He was developing something more profound and sophisticated than his past work. For his latest achievements, Chaplin was being hailed as a genius, a magnificent artist who was single-handedly advancing the state of slapstick.

This year, Mutual paid Chaplin an annual salary of $670,000, plus a hefty bonus. This made the comic the highest paid entertainer in history. Chaplin, who was entering a vintage period, was worth every last penny. In the next year, he would turn out his best short comedies, including *Easy Street*, *The Cure*, *The Immigrant* and *The Adventurer*. Desiring the kind of praise that Chaplin was receiving, Lloyd felt compelled to also go beyond the impulsive rough stuff and craft comedies of artistic value. He needed to fit his skills into a more structured and analytic style.

Lloyd had several ideas on how he might reach "maturity." He believed that fast action was vital in screen comedy, but he saw wisdom in forsaking liveliness for the sake of liveliness and decreasing slapstick in favor of pantomime. Also, he wanted to focus more on character and to adopt and refine a character that was less broad and less brash. In his mind, he was pursuing a more natural and substantial image.

Possessed by a strong urge to be the best, many film comics were unable to ignore the acclaim lavished upon Chaplin. Ford Sterling became obsessed with proving he could be more artistic and poignant than Chaplin.[7] He pressured his boss, Mack Sennett, to give him the creative freedom to deviate from their normal fare. Sennett became so exhausted by Sterling's badgering that he felt he had no choice but to relent. Following the production of a few horribly forced and clumsy scenes, which included Sterling performing what looked to Sennett to be some ghastly ballet, the producer insisted that the aesthetic venture be abandoned.

During the next several weeks, Lloyd shuttled between Kalem and the Athletic Club. At the time, he was seeking inspiration from everything with which he came into contact. He did not read a newspaper or walk down a street without being receptive to new material. He was, in his own words, "constantly snooping around in search of ideas."[8]

The translation of these ideas became difficult since, within the breadth of a reel and the span of a week, development was limited.

Good Evening, Judge, a comedy that survives from this period, is burdened by an overly complicated storyline. In simpler times, no set-up was necessary for a Ham and Bud adventure. Ham and Bud could show up in Egypt and the fact that these Los Angeles tramps had to find a way to travel 7,600 miles to get there didn't seem to warrant an explanation. Now, a series of events is delineated to justify the tramps helping Slippery Steve rob a home. The convolutions of the plot not only make it is hard to follow what is happening from one scene to the next but they leave little room for the comedians to be funny. Lloyd seeks laughs by making a couple of silly faces, getting his finger caught in a mousetrap, and hurling dishes across a room. The climax, the tramps' violent showdown with police, is played surprisingly without pratfalls or double-takes. It is simply two fleeing criminals trying to shoot down police officers in order to avoid capture. The only moment of comedy comes when Ham stops to take steady aim at his pursuers. He plants his free hand behind his head and spreads his legs far apart before he opens fire. It is left to this absurdly flamboyant shooting stance to remind viewers that this is a comedy situation and these childishly spirited tramps take this battle as seriously as two kids playing cops and robbers with cap pistols. Lloyd, who later insisted that a plot should never get in the way of comedy scenes, may have learned to limit storylines from his experience making comedies like *Good Morning, Judge*.

Before long, Lloyd delivered his work and frustration to his home. Ethel rarely saw her husband in those days and, when she did, she found him to be poor company.

A magazine article written by Lloyd acknowledged his bad behavior as a husband. The article, entitled "Why Comedians Don't Marry," was published by *The Cleveland Leader* on December 10, 1916. Lloyd claimed that it was the pressures of his job that made him unsettled and unhappy. He insisted that that comedymaking took "plenty of time and preliminary thought, preparation and study."[9] He agonized in preparing a film to the point that it was difficult for him to eat or sleep. He wrote, "A comedian is too eternally worried to have an appetite and, even if he does manage to scare one up, that is no assurance to wifey that they are going to have a peaceful, home-cooked meal together."[10] He described often startling awake in the middle of the night with idea of something funny he could do. He expressed sympathy for his wife having to live with such a "cranky, mournful fellow."[11]

Ham and Bud show they know how to take care of a lady in *Winning a Widow* (1916). Portraying the lady is actress Adoni Fovieri. The man confronting Ham is actor Gus Leonard (courtesy of Cole Johnson — Slapstick Archive).

Lloyd, who was trying to run a race at top speed, likely saw his marriage as binding and distracting. Ethel later admitted that she resented Lloyd for his distance and moodiness.

Lloyd's recent comedies received mixed reaction. Getting the strongest notices was *Ham the Explorer*, in which Lloyd reused plot elements and routines from *Ham in the Harem* and *Wurra Wurra*. Critics praised recent cinematic moments in which Lloyd performed pantomime. Ham, as a fortune teller, prophesized misfortune with extravagant flair. The camera remained within an intimate distance of Lloyd. The tight shot excluded his tall, sturdy legs and notorious slapshoes, without which he was unable to engage in chases and kick opponents. It focused, instead, on his physical attitude, gestures and expressions. The result was a more restrained version of Ham. It was Ham more as a character than a mayhem machine.

One critic commended the *Ham* series' latest entries for their sparing use of slapstick. Another, a critic of *Moving Picture World*, cheered Lloyd's *The Beggar and His Child* for being "muscular but unforced." However, this work was lost on the general audience. Most people were not prepared for this new type of *Ham* comedy. Perhaps it was because the transitional *Ham* vehicles were poor in the slapstick department and not much in the area of emotion.

Reflecting the more common reaction to the new comedies was this critical summarization of *The Merry Motor Menders*: "Not quite up to standard — the action is rather slow."

By this time, such words did not matter. Lloyd had already returned to his series' more reliable brand of comedy.

In its July program, Kalem offered five series, among them three continuing series: *Ham*, *The Hazards of Helen* and *The Girl from Frisco* (a western starring Sais and Boardman). Kalem had quietly terminated the Teare and *Sis Hopkins* series. Ethel was reassigned to the *Ham* company. Just two years later, the Goldwyn Corporation would turn the story of Sis Hopkins into a popular feature vehicle for Mabel Normand.

Two new series debuted. Ivy Close, a pretty English actress, inherited both *Sis Hopkins*'s program space and supporting cast. The program was completed by *Grant, Police Reporter*.

The *Close* series lasted less than three months. Henry Murdock, an actor who had been outstanding in the failed series, was immediately absorbed by the *Ham* company. The combination of Lloyd, Bud, Murdock and Ethel, which recalled Ham and Bud's original partnership with Neilan and Roland, received praise from critics.

In the fall of 1916, Kalem press releases cried "Business Suicide." Marion was stubbornly resisting a trend towards feature attractions. Theatres were centering their programs on a film at least five reels in length. Marion warned exhibitors that, if they continued to comply with the back-breaking rentals of the "feature-mad studios," the industry would fall to ruin. He argued that, by concentrating its resources on an occasional big-budget production, a company would be in constant risk of bankruptcy.

The "feature-mad" creatures of Marion's nightmares were, in fact, a number of bold and determined independent companies which had stolen the picture show from the pioneers' grasp. The early independents, through various mergings, would evolve into Warner Brothers, MGM, 20th Century–Fox, Paramount, Universal and Columbia.

General Film had been poorly managed. The company was distributing Kalem's releases to an insufficient number of theatregoers. Ham and Bud's popularity was drastically suffering. Numerous exhibitors reported to Kalem that they were having difficulty receiving installments of *The Girl from Frisco*. General's distribution became so unreliable that Kalem was forced to abandon their practice of announcing release dates.

Vitagraph and Pathé were the only pioneers who were managing to endure. Vitagraph had recently joined forces with Kleine and Essanay, establishing KESA. Pathé was substantially profiting from its two serial stars, Pearl White and Ruth Roland.

6

Business Suicide

In November, 1916, Kalem's employees gathered at a popular Los Angeles restaurant. According to the studio, the gathering represented a celebration of the *Ham* series' hundredth title. In fact, Kalem had most recently produced their sixty-seventh official *Ham* release. The exaggeration was an obvious publicity ploy.

E.M.E. Gibsone, manager of Kalem's Hollywood studios, served as hostess of the formal dinner party; Lloyd acted humble as the master of ceremonies. One by one, the Kalem officials in attendance praised Lloyd. This was not surprising as Lloyd and Boardman had been Kalem's main attractions of 1916 and held in their hands the company's hope for the upcoming year. Under a recent agreement, Boardman would reprise the role of Stingaree. It was reported that, throughout the evening, Lloyd seemed embarrassed by the acclaim.

The Kalem organization proclaimed as its leading policy of 1917: NO FILM OVER TWO REELS. Considering that Edison, Essanay and Selig had not survived to greet the new year, Marion was obviously whistling past the graveyard.

Kalem's first notable acquisition of the year was Fred R. Bechdolt, a prominent short story writer who had been hired to script a sequel to *The Girl from Frisco*.

In January, Kalem underwent a showy expansion. The studio transplanted the *Ham* company from their Hollywood lot onto a new ten-acre site in Glendale. Co-workers must not have sensed that Lloyd was excited to be working at these new facilities, for rumors were soon circulating around town that Lloyd was leaving Kalem.

Lloyd was apathetic if his work is any indication. His latest *Ham* comedies had nothing bold or original to offer. He followed a new trend of "gizmo" comedy, which required zany mechanical devices to be introduced into the action. In one reel, Ham and Bud are arrested by a sheriff whose squad car easily converts into a mobile jail. Otherwise, this was the same stuff that Ham and Bud had been doing for awhile.

Lloyd had radically reversed his position in recent months. He had begun overloading the *Ham* series with mindless, unrestrained slapstick. Due to the combination of poor distribution and dull comedies, the popularity of the *Ham* series was diminishing. In reviewing *The Safety Pin Smugglers*, a *Motion Picture News* critic wrote: "Entirely too much slapstick and no real humor.... Surely the originators of the team are running dry of material." This assessment was typical. In addition, exhibitors were complaining to Kalem that the one-reel comedy form had seen its day.

In order to improve their shabby state, Kalem's executives moved to renovate their properties. As one step in this direction, they hired a writer-director named Al Santell to relieve Lloyd as director.

Hamilton wrote on the back of the photo, "Kalem studio and my car." The comedian was known to be proud of his automobiles. He featured this particular vehicle in a 1916 comedy entitled *Patented by Ham*. What model car is it? One antique car expert reported that the unique angle at which the fender meets the running board makes it likely that the automobile is a Metz. Another expert pointed to the high radiator fill neck as an indication that the automobile is a Model N Hupmobile (courtesy of the family of Lloyd Hamilton).

Santell was a wavy-haired, intellectual lad from San Francisco. His most recent accomplishment had been writing and directing the Kolb and Dill feature film *Beloved Rogues*.

The new director's background merits examination. Santell was still a teenager when he worked to establish himself as an architect. He held down a fulltime job in an architect's office, but he managed to find extra time to moonlight as scriptwriter. His scripts got the attention of film executive Harry Rivier, who persuaded Santell to join his staff at Gaumont Pictures. Over the next year, Santell developed films and wrote continuity for Gaumont. In exchange, Rivier had paid him fifty dollars a week and taught him everything he knew about filmmaking. Following this apprenticeship, Santell worked as the director of a low-budget western series, the star of which was an energetic Indian named Jimmy Youngdeer. In this position, Santell had his limited cast triple as settlers, Indians and cavalry. In effect, he had his actors chase themselves back and forth over the course of two reels. Santell later wrote scenarios for Lubin. More recently, he directed at Keystone and Pathé.

Santell wanted to continue making features, but he was talked out of it by his agents. He said, "[My agents] did not believe the feature was a stable thing.... They said that the business eventually would have to go back to one- and two-reelers and no one would sit in a theatre for an hour, an hour and a half, two hours and look at motion pictures...."[1] Santell was

Ham tries out different outfits in a portrait session (1917) (both photographs courtesy of the family of Lloyd Hamilton).

enthusiastic to be working with a popular, established act like Ham and Bud, who he understood were big moneymakers. "Ham and Bud," said Santell, "were virtually the Laurel and Hardy of their day."[2]

Kalem's promoters assured their exhibitors that, with Santell's appointment, Ham and Bud was receiving a second lease on life. It was declared in full-page ads that this pair, who had stood the test of time, would prove that they were as reliable as ever.

Santell's improvements were immediately evident. First, Santell lessened the participation of Henry Murdock and Ethel Teare. The change inspired Ethel to take a job at the Sennett studio. Santell provided Ham and Bud's escapades with considerably more plot than usual and delivered more logic and order into the pair's conduct. Utilizing his technical expertise, Santell introduced marvelous photographic effects into Ham and Bud's world. He also used sophisticated moving shots and crane views. He employed close-ups, which was notable at the time.

Santell vigorously pursued Lloyd's character modifications. He obliterated Ham and Bud's more animalistic and asocial tendencies and permitted the pair's humane qualities to blossom. The original Ham and Bud blew Mr. Gottrox's safe for fun and profit. Lloyd's Ham and Bud poached eggs for a meal. Santell's Ham and Bud, endowed with sympathetic and even heroic qualities, behaved much differently. They begged a farmer for food and, though chased away for their effort, later returned to rescue the farmer and his daughter from a band of angry hobos. Previously, Ham was a crude and recklessly bold womanizer. But, now, he was demure. As the operator of a bootblack stand, he becomes embarrassed at seeing the ankles of one of his female patrons. Most importantly, Santell totally extinguished the boisterous rivalry between Ham and Bud. (Ham's physical outline also softened. Over the last year, Lloyd had grown rotund, his awesome brawniness replaced by a cuddly portliness.)

The critics observed Santell's work and smiled. One critic recorded: "Much improvement is seen." Aroused by the recent activity of the *Ham* company, a *Moving Picture World* critic praised Lloyd in a special article. He wrote:

The earliest examples of Hamilton's "shabby gentleman" (courtesy of the family of Lloyd Hamilton.)

> No one has ever questioned the mirth-provoking ability of Hamilton.... I do not know of a single comedian past or present, stage or screen, whose very appearance is more inducive to a hearty guffaw.... He is, beyond a doubt, the most talented of all screen people and you realize it more with each succeeding picture.

In March, 1917, Lloyd, Bud and Marion renewed their alliance with a long-term contract. In announcing this agreement, Marion sought to squelch rumors of the team's intended defection. On this occasion, Marion also announced that he would satisfy Kalem's exhibitors by arranging for a series of two-reel *Ham* comedies. He revealed that the first two-reel *Ham* comedy would be accompanied by an animated trailer featuring a new mascot, the Kalem Spider.

For the premier production of the new *Ham* series, Marion presented Santell with control over much of Kalem's enclosed Glendale facilities.

During March, Kalem unveiled renovated versions of *The Hazards of Helen* and *The Girl from Frisco*. *A Daughter of Daring* was a new series that matched Helen Gibson with numerous iron horses; *The American Girl* was the product of the Bechdolt scripts.

Stanley Todd, a writer for *Motion Picture Magazine*, visited Ham and Bud at Glendale in March, 1917. Todd reported that Lloyd and Bud got to the facility early, "before the carpenters have had time to put up the set,"[3] and worked out what they were going to do that day. Todd described them as "the busiest persons about a place that teems with activity."[4] They spent the time either "discussing how to get something that has never been done before"[5] or bruising themselves up to get a stunt exactly right.

Santell remained reticent regarding the plot of his latest picture. In the studio's press releases, it was alleged that Santell had not even revealed the story line to Marion.

Lloyd, who was excited by Santell's changes, was making changes of his own. He added glimmers of intelligence, style and dignity to Ham's appearance. For promotional stills, he dressed in a high starched collar, bowtie, frock coat, white socks, and a pair of black pants. The actor, standing fully erect and holding his chin up high, is seen in one still trying his best to look proud. He holds to one side a highly unusual prop: a book. At the same time, this character's clothing looks worn and ill-fitting. The formal coat is too tight around the waist and the pants are not long enough to cover his ankles. This individual is, as clearly indicated, a gentleman on hard times.

The *Ham* company began to shoot their first two-reeler in early April, intending to have the comedy ready for a June release. During production, ads promised "TWO REELS FULL OF LAUGHS." Soon after, Kalem reported that Santell had been suddenly sidelined with ptomaine poisoning. Rather that let the *Ham* troupe remain idle until their director's recovery, Marion called for Lloyd to direct a one-reel comedy.

No two-reel *Ham* comedy materialized in June. Kalem instead publicized the release of "a one-part fun fest." It was due to severe financial difficulty that Marion had balked on his decision to proceed with the new series. Despite all the hype, the Kalem Spider would not be getting his big break.

Marion had recently laid off many of his employees. By June, the *Grant* and *Daughter of Daring* companies were no longer in existence. The Horne crew, which had recently completed *American Girl* series, was finally working on *The Further Adventures of Stingaree*.

As if cramming full a final lifeboat, Marion channeled a good amount of Kalem's remaining resources into a pair of *Ham* comedies. Both contained sensational climaxes and, oddly, featured several of Kalem's dramatic actors in the supporting cast. To mask the company's desperate state, publicity people tried to justify the unusual support. They noted that the dramatic players' latest assignment demonstrated the Kalem actors' great versatility. It was noted that, in performing as one of Ham's latest leading ladies, Marin Sais was "recalling her comedy days." Presumably to color his screen image, Lloyd appeared in his new films wearing a checkered bow tie and matching pair of pants.

In late June, following a few setbacks, *The Further Adventures of Stingaree* debuted. Based on the quality of the series' initial chapters, the critics saluted the return of the outlaw bushranger.

The Kalem Company ceased production in August. For first run, Marion was left with several installments of the new *Stingaree* series and five *Ham* reels. While attention was focused on the balance of the *Stingaree* series, the *Ham* comedies were held in reserve.

According to Kalem, the sequel to *Stingaree* broke the box office records held by its predecessor. However, this success came too late to matter. By now, the Kalem Company had permanently closed shop. Their prop department had already shipped its large arsenal of guns to a municipality in New Jersey, where the secondhand pieces were placed into the hands of the community's home guard.

Kalem's talent remained viable. Other studios were quick to sign the actors and directors whom Kalem had released.

Upon his layoff, Lloyd agreed to be a principal of the Fox Corporation's new Sunshine series. Universal hired Alfred Santell and Helen Gibson. The studio assigned Santell to direct short comedies and starred Gibson in the *Gold Seal* series, a new string of railroad dramas.

Lois Weber, a renowned independent producer and actress, approached Boardman at the completion of the *Stingaree* sequel. The actor became her leading man in *The Doctor and the Woman*. Through Weber's influence, Boardman was also cast in the first screen version of Edgar Rice Burroughs' *Tarzan of the Apes*. Boardman was prominent in the prologue as the apeman's father, Lord Greystoke. His status rose when *Tarzan of the Apes* became one of the year's bit hits.

The American Film Company signed Boardman to a long-term contract, but the actor failed to benefit from the agreement. It was only two months later that he fell victim to nervous prostration. He was moving towards a recovery when, during a stroll, he suffered a relapse. He died on September 28, 1918.

That same year, National Films featured Bud in a one-reel series called the *Clover Comedies*. The *Clover* reels, which clearly imitated the *Ham* series, co-starred Kewpie Morgan as Bud's large rival and partner.

A more curious "Ham and Bud" revival occurred a quarter of a century later courtesy of True Boardman's son, True Boardman, Jr., who resurrected Ham and Bud routines for the Abbott & Costello feature *Pardon My Sarong*. The situations, which were barely altered, could easily be traced to their origins. Abbott and Costello get shipwrecked on an island and have to contend with savage natives (*Ham the Explorer*). Abbott and Costello try to distract a native warrior by blowing a whistle (*Ham Among the Redskins*). Abbott and Costello try to fool a person by posing as statues but give away the ruse by repeatedly changing poses (*The Toilers*). Boardman, Jr., who hung around the Kalem lot as a child, was five years old when he played "Boy at Throttle" in a *Hazards of Helen* episode. He is sure to have met Lloyd and Bud and he is likely to have developed affection for these childish comedians who worked with his dad.

In late September, as *The Further Adventures of Stingaree* finished its run, Kalem announced, "Ham and Bud will appear again in five comedy subjects, which will find favor with former friends." This limited series ran from October to November. The series was filled with simple, direct and fast-paced comedy, what one critic referred to as "Ham and Bud's special kind of fun." The team, which had become tiresome through weekly exposure, was greatly appreciated after its brief absence.

The final *Ham* comedy, *The Bathtub Bandit*, featured an appropriate conclusion — a spectacular blast of cannonfire blows Ham and Bud to bits. In the end, Kalem reissued old material in re-edited form: They released revised versions of *Grant* and *Hazards of Helen*.

Before the close of 1917, Marion sold Kalem's resources to Vitagraph. By then, *Moving Picture World* was indirectly revealing the demise of Kalem. In the magazine, a prominent page that had long been reserved for Kalem promotion now featured a relocated index.

Fellow pioneers Lubin and Biograph folded during the same year. Vitagraph and Pathé had a few years left. In 1925, Vitagraph would sell its remaining assets to Warner Brothers. Though without considerable success, Pathé would be the only pioneer to survive through the next decade. It was appropriate to see the industry's final pioneer fade out at the close of the silent era.

In an ad published on August 11, 1917, the Fox Film Corporation invited theatergoers to "Laugh with Lehrman, the Wizard of Wit." The ad included a sizable portrait of Henry Lehrman, the producer of the Sunshine series. The photo displayed a balding man dressed in fine new clothing. His manicured moustache complemented his haughty expression. Underneath the large photo was a small caption. It read, simply: "Henry Lehrman, comedy genius."

7

The New Mentor

In the chronicles of screen comedy, the most infamous of the pioneers is Henry Lehrman. Lehrman managed, in the early years of Hollywood, to produce many highly successful comedies. But the man's overbearing personality and ruthless methods, in retrospect, tarnished his reputation.

Mack Sennett hired Lehrman as a director when he opened the Keystone company in 1912. Sennett and Lehrman took turns directing, keeping production going nonstop, and it was through their dogged efforts that the studio delivered an abundant output in its first year and secured a prominent place on exhibitor programs. Later, when the Keystone comedies were getting attention, Lehrman found it intolerable that the success of the studio was largely attributed to Sennett. He blamed Sennett entirely for his anonymity and obtained financing from Universal chief Carl Laemmle to produce his own series of comedies.

Lehrman's comedies for Laemmle, including the *Lehrman Knock-Out Comedies* (L-KO), had little to distinguish them from the Keystone comedies. Kalton C. Lahue referred to them as "blatant forgeries."[1] Lehrman went as far as replicating Keystone's most popular actors. Billie Ritchie, L-KO's biggest star, dressed and acted like Chaplin. Ritchie, although not as charming, sensitive or graceful as the Little Tramp, was a talented performer who knew how to get laughs. Rotund comedian Frank Voss, who did his best to act like Fatty Arbuckle, aided and abetted Ritchie in a number of L-KO comedies, including *Hello, Bill!*, *Love and Surgery* and *Partners in Crime*.

Lehrman became a great self-promoter while producing the L-KO series. In interviews and promotional releases, he credited himself with originating the Keystone Cops and discovering Chaplin. He boasted that, in order to devise a good comedy, he had no need for "personalities," the term he used for actors. He portrayed himself as a genius innovator, from whom others took ideas.

The veracity of Lehrman's claims has been disputed over the years by different authors, including Lahue, Gene Fowler and David A. Yallop. The grandstanding producer told so many outright lies and behaved so poorly that it became difficult to believe anything he said or to concede to him the respect that, in all likelihood, he deserved.

It is no doubt true that the Keystone Cops and Chaplin both made their earliest appearances in films directed by Lehrman. The question arises, then, as to whether it is valid to say Lehrman originated the Keystone Cops and discovered Chaplin.

Lehrman was an important creative force at Keystone. Sennett was quick to recognize Lehrman's ability to come up with ideas. Not long after the two men met, Sennett encouraged Lehrman to write scripts, which he was able to sell to movie producers for a commission. In this budding relationship, Lehrman was the author and Sennett was the salesman. Sennett maintained his respect for Lehrman's creative abilities. For all their bitter disagreements, he was able to say about Lehrman years later, "[He] knew how to make a picture."[2] Regardless if Lehrman himself came up with the concept of the Keystone Cops, it is almost certain that he helped to work out the formula by which the incompetent police squad became successful. But this is where Lehrman's strong personality gets in the way of the story. Lehrman became spiteful towards Sennett, going as far as dating Sennett's girlfriend just to hurt his old friend. In the end, Sennett's great collaborator became, in the minds of film historians, a dastardly villain and Sennett's great betrayer.

It was comedies directed by Lehrman that introduced the "little tramp" character and first brought Chaplin to the attention of the public. Lehrman may have been justified to see himself as one of the people who discovered Chaplin. It is safe to say, though, that Chaplin didn't feel the slightest gratitude towards Lehrman for his success. The story began with Sennett hiring Chaplin after seeing him perform with the Karno stage troupe. He handed the newcomer over to Lehrman, thinking the director might be able to figure out what to do with him. But this turned out to be a problem. By all accounts, Lehrman didn't like Chaplin and argued with him constantly. Lehrman himself admitted that he resented this inexperienced film actor wanting to take control and do scenes his way. He could not fathom Chaplin's humor, including Chaplin picking a violet while a cop dragged him off by the heels. The director revealed, years later, that he disliked Chaplin so much that he tried to sabotage his performance in editing. Chaplin said that he became so frustrated with Lehrman that he almost quit movies and went back to the stage. All in all, Lehrman and Chaplin became embroiled in a succession of history-making rows that have permanently cast Lehrman as Chaplin's great enemy. It hardly seems right for a man infamous for nearly driving Chaplin out of the movie business to be able to take credit for discovering Chaplin.

One film historian, Richard M. Roberts, has taken to defending Lehrman, claiming that the filmmaker has been treated unfairly in the history books.[3] Roberts disputes those who would say that Lehrman was crude, unoriginal and sloppy as a director. He contends that Lehrman's comedies were wilder and more creative than anything that Sennett did. He praises Lehrman for expert pacing and clever camerawork.

The bottom line, when it came to L-KO, was that Lehrman was no longer going to be an anonymous lackey. He was determined to dominate the limelight. Press releases spoke of Lehrman's prestige and fame as if the words were to be self-fulfilling. Lehrman made it clear that he was fully in charge at Universal. Not even sickness could diminish his authority, as *Moving Picture World* suggested on January 6, 1917. "During a brief illness a few months ago," it was reported, "Lehrman had a projection machine erected above his bed, and every night the work his directors had done that day would be shown to him."[4] His promotional efforts helped to make L-KO successful, situating the company as Sennett's #1 rival.

Lehrman's growing conflict with Abe Stern, Laemmle's nephew, caused Lehrman to break from Laemmle in 1916. Soon after, Lehrman met with William Fox, who owned and operated the Fox Film Corporation.

William Fox had organized the Fox Film Corporation in 1914; it took him less than a year to guide it to prominence. The studio primarily produced feature versions of popular novels and plays. Its top star, Theda Bara, was an alluring, dark-eyed actress who had risen to fame as Hollywood's first sex symbol. At Fox, Bara played eminent females from history and fiction, her roles ranging from Cleopatra to Juliet.

For two years, Fox features had been presented with short subjects supplied by Sennett and other independent producers. At the time, feature films were dependent on short subjects, two-reel comedies in particular, to provide support and balance out an exhibitor's program. Fox was now looking for greater autonomy and wanted to discontinue his reliance on independent producers. He called for Lehrman to produce a high-quality series of two-reel comedies and agreed, for this purpose, to build Lehrman a special set based on his Los Angeles lot.

At first, Lehrman established two units. He personally handled the operation of the first unit, the leading players of which included Ritchie and Dot Farley. Charles Parrott, better known today by his later moniker Charley Chase, took charge as the director of the second unit, the principals of which included Hank Mann and Lee Morris.

Fox's comedy company quickly swelled. Walter C. Reed and Harry Edwards were hired as directors. The series showcased several new players as well as special guest stars, including Ford Sterling, Mae Busch, Paddy McGuire and Raymond Griffith. Lehrman added his girlfriend, Virginia Rappe, to the acting company. He promised the aspiring actress, whose only previous experience was extra work at Keystone, that he would make her a star.

It was announced that, throughout 1917, Fox would release a weekly series of two-reel comedies. The series, which arrived under the banner of *Foxfilm Comedies*, debuted on January 1, 1917. The immediate response from critics and exhibitors was favorable. The earliest highlight of the series was a Theda Bara spoof from Parrott and Mann. Within months, the series was also getting strong notices for comedy-westerns starring Tom Mix.

Lehrman was assigned a special project in the spring. Encouraged by the success of the recent *Foxfilm Comedies*, Fox wanted Lehrman to produce a new series with a bigger budget. The pilot film, a racing-and-romance comedy entitled *His Smashing Career*, wasn't anything that Lehrman hadn't done before. It was, in fact, highly formulaic. Still, Fox was pleased with Lehrman's test offering and scheduled the new comedy series for a fall premiere. The series, eventually named Sunshine, placed abundant resources at Lehrman's disposal.

Lehrman was at work mounting his new series when he lost his two biggest stars. Fox had promoted Mix to action-adventure features. The U.S. government had summoned Mann to serve the Allies' cause in Europe. To fill these holes in his ranks, Lehrman hired Jimmie Adams, a slightly built comic from Paterson, New Jersey. Adams, whose experience was in musical comedy, vaudeville, minstrel acts and legitimate drama, had never before appeared in motion pictures. Acting on the demise of the Kalem Company, Lehrman also hired the funnyman known widely as "Ham."

Lehrman proved, with the Sunshine series, that his creative scope was narrow. Previously, his L-KO series featured an automobile taking a long drive down a short pier. It was a mishap that turned up in many L-KO comedies as Lehrman, who used multiple cameras to capture the stunt, was able to show the action repeatedly from new angles. For the Sunshine series, Lehrman reused this same old stunt except, now, he had the money to magnify the scale and multiply the elements. Now, instead of one comic driving a car off a pier, he had a wagon packed with comics driving off a pier. He, in fact, remained compulsive about sending cars speeding through buildings and sailing over cliffs.

Lehrman adhered to rough slapstick and implausible action. He churned a chaotic and comical whirlwind around shallow and ridiculous heroes and villains. The flimsiness of the characters did not matter as the characters became lost in the action and, in the end, received minimal attention. One time, Lehrman used trick photography to show the force of an explosion blasting a comic out of a chimney. This did not depend on the comic's timing or characterization to get a laugh.

A Sunshine comedy would contain grand-scale havoc, massive demolition, spectacular stunts, and fantastic action. However, the enlargement of Lehrman's activity did not inspire the director to show more regard for his crew. To create thrilling comedies, he continued to recklessly force his players into perilous situations. Early on, he received press attention when, for *His Smashing Career*, he collapsed a grandstand filled with unsuspecting extras.

In ancient Roman pageants, the emperor required actors to sacrifice their lives for the pleasure of the masses. In depicting the death of Prometheus, an actor would lie chained to a rock while a trained eagle tore out his liver. Another actor, in the role of Daedalus, would have wings strapped to his shoulders and be thrown from the top of the arena. Lehrman approached moviemaking in much the same way, commanding cast and crew to perform dangerous acts in hope of getting a crowd-pleasing scene. It was just a matter of time before he fed his cast and crew to the lions.

Ritchie, who was willing to risk his personal safety for a laugh, was the perfect comic for Lehrman. In 1915, while making the L-KO comedy *Silk Hose and High Pressure*, Ritchie grabbed hold of a high-pressure water hose and got catapulted 30 feet into the air. He severely hurt his back and suffered internal injuries. Other mishaps followed. At New York's Library for the Performing Arts, a clippings folder on Ritchie contains news stories describing a number of injuries the performer suffered while making comedies for Lehrman. Typical is a story dated September 10, 1916, "Billie Ritchie Stuck in the Mud." The item read as follows:

> Ritchie got a signal from the director. Without hesitancy he dove headfirst off a high elevation into shallow water. A full minute passed before the assembled players realized that something was wrong. Several of the men dove into the water, and the diminutive comic was brought to the surface, his eyes, ears and mouth filled with mud. Although mostly exhausted, the little fellow insisted on finishing the scene.[5]

A Bold, Bad Breeze, a comedy in which Ritchie got caught in a tornado, had Ritchie blasted around the set by wind machines. According to *Moving Picture Weekly*, Ritchie "got a bad case of the bends caused by wind bubbles getting caught in his system."[6] The injury put him temporarily out of action. Ritchie's other daring vehicles at the time included *Scars and Stripes Forever*, *Bill's Narrow Escape*, *Bill's Waterloo*, and *Live Wires and Love Sparks*.

More recently, at Fox, Ritchie continued taking risks for Lehrman. An existing still from an early Foxfilm comedy, *The House of Terrible Scandals*, shows Ritchie clinging to a ladder that hangs off a high-rise balcony.

Ritchie was certainly the wild man on screen. Aggressively angry and rude, his comic character was more in the mold of Ford Sterling than Charlie Chaplin. Chaplin had shown that, if he was suddenly confronted by a violet, he would be so mesmerized by its beauty that he would seek to possess it. Ritchie, in the same situation, was more likely to stomp on the violet, chew off its petals, and draw a gun to shoot its stamen to bits.

Lehrman intended to construct the Sunshine comedies on tried-and-true gimmicks. The grounds of his production facility were inhabited by a group of comical cops and bathing beauties. Bathing beauties, shapely ingenues garbed in swimsuits, were Mack Sennett's latest innovation. Sunshine's bathing beauties would alternatively be called "The Rainbow Girls" and "The Sunshine Beauty Brigade."

At the start of the summer, Lehrman followed *His Smashing Career* with *A Milk-fed Vamp*, a goofy comedy starring Dot Farley and Jimmie Adams. Despite the efforts of the comics, it was a delightful chimpanzee who captured the most attention. The animal's achievement would not be lost on Lehrman.

For his first Fox comedy, Lloyd reworked the plot of *Minnie the Tiger*. The result was a script called *Wedding Bells and Roaring Lions*. Lehrman considerably changed Lloyd's story. He insisted on shifting the major emphasis to the lions, a decision causing an inversion of the title. At Kalem, "Minnie" had been portrayed by a man in a tiger suit; Lehrman's production would feature flesh-and-blood lions provided by trainer Curley Stecker. For lighter moments, Lehrman acquired ostriches and ducks.

Lloyd had proposed that his new employers engage Ethel Teare as his leading lady. Teare, though, was contractually bound to Sennett. Instead, Lehrman chose Mildred Lee as the heroine. He headed the supporting cast with Jimmie Adams and Charles Conklin. He assigned William Campbell to direct.

Before commencing production, Lloyd committed a few days to relaxing and reflecting. He rode horseback through secluded mountains. He swam regularly in the cool mountain rivers. It was reported in Fox promotional material that Lloyd was swimming when he slammed his right foot into a log and fractured bones in his heel and ankle. The injury was severe enough that a metal pin had to be permanently inserted into his foot to hold the bones together. Lloyd, informed that he would be limping for months while the bones knitted, decided to make the limp part of a funny walk. Later variations of this story indicated that Lloyd had the metal pin inserted earlier, possibly after he fell down the hill at Kalem. Lloyd in fact exhibits a variation of his funny walk in a 1916 Kalem comedy, *Good Evening, Judge*. The bones would properly knit, but the metal pin would bother Lloyd for the rest of his life.

Lloyd found his first Sunshine production to be unlike any of his past filmmaking experiences. A minimum of three weeks was allocated as the production time, which was much longer than the time he had on previous comedies, and the budget was ten times greater than the highest budget on a *Ham* comedy. More than the time and dollars, Lehrman's leadership was different. Lehrman thrived on pressure and was only happy when his work was vigorous and fast-paced. Tranquil environments frustrated and bored him. The thought of contemplation had little attraction for the producer's active nature. He exercised control through command rather than inspiration.

For all that was new, it was "something old" that Lloyd wore at his cinematic wedding. He appeared in his shabby "Ham" habit and familiar monster moustache.

Roaring Lions and Wedding Bells did not turn out solid enough to obtain management approval. Lehrman was hopeful that, though re-shooting and re-editing, the production could be satisfactorily improved. For the alterations, he presented the film to a promising assistant director named Jack White. Though only seventeen years old, White had been in the film business for eight years. He had, over time, earned Lehrman's trust.

White, whose actual name was Jacob Weiss, was an Orthodox Jew whose parents had emigrated from Hungary. He had grown up in tough neighborhoods of New York City and Chicago. When White was nine years old, his father developed breathing problems from working in a poorly ventilated factory and getting his lungs saturated with battery acid fumes. White's father consulted a physician, who told him the best chance he had to improve his health was to leave the city behind and find a place to live with some clean, open spaces. Accepting that advice, the White family traveled cross-country and settled in the scenic California town of Edendale, which was soon to be the cradle of Hollywood.

White recalled, "Mack Sennett, Tom Ince, all those big names came out here, and my brothers and I got in the business that way."[7]

White joined Keystone in 1913. When he met Lehrman for the first time, he was working as one of Sennett's office boys. It could be based on the fact that both men came from Vienna that Lehrman took an instant liking to the young man. He brought him along with

Hamilton and Costar Jimmie Adams finds the funny side of lions in his Sunshine comedy debut *Roaring Lions and Wedding Bells* (1917) (courtesy of Billy Rose Theatre Division, New York Public Library for the Performing Arts, Astor, Lenox and Tilden Foundations).

him when he left Keystone. White developed and printed still pictures for Lehrman, he ran the projection machine when Lehrman had to see dailies, and he assisted in the cutting room. When Lehrman moved to Fox, he promoted White to editor.

Within a few months, White thought that he had learned enough from cutting to try his hand at directing. An opportunity arose with a troubled film called *Damaged—No Goods*.

"[T]hey had put it on the shelf because it was bad," said White. "I had a dream one night that gave me an idea of how to salvage the picture. I talked about it to Lehrman, who said, 'Go ahead. We've spent $19,500 on it. Another $1,500 isn't going to break us.' I made a releasable film out of it that made $65,000. From that time on, my stock went up. When there was any extraneous shooting to be done, Jack would do it. They gave me a scene to co-direct with Bill Campbell, who was like a father to me. He let me direct while he sat back and observed."[8]

This scene, which depicted a wedding reception, was the climax of *Roaring Lions and Wedding Bells*. Lehrman's main objective was to inflate the scene's scale. First, he added an elephant, which was guaranteed to make the scene bigger. Next, he opened his stages to numerous "dress extras." Dress extras were largely separate from the dollar-a-day extras. They were members of the local upper class who, purely for fun and vanity, would dress in their own elegant threads and lend themselves to studios for fancy party scenes. Many dress extras answered the call to the phony wedding reception. The finely wrapped group were merrily chatting and sipping cocktails when, without warning, three lions were released into their midst. The extras fearfully dispersed. Lloyd's comic wedding gained "something borrowed" and "something blue" when funny cops rushed to the rescue. Having the dress extras run for safer spaces gave the ailing comedy an extremely effective wind-up.

Roaring Lions and Wedding Bells was completed by mid–October. It was strong enough to be selected as Sunshine's premiere release.

Lloyd and White worked well together during the reshoots and they decided to stay together as a team on future productions. White thought highly of Lloyd's abilities. "He had an excellent sense of humor and a terrific sense of comedy," said White. "With the right material and direction, I knew that he would be a funny man with or without gags. That proved to be the case. He'd come on the set and everybody would roar laughing at him, at the way he'd walk in, swishing. 'Good morning, little sweetheart.' He had a way about him; he was a funny man. He knew his capacity for being funny."[9] White, when asked if Lloyd was a good gag man, replied: "Very good, in any department. In fact, he inspired me to a lot of the good work I did."[10]

Their creative partnership, as strong as it was, never led to a relationship off the set. "We never became real close friends," said White. "Lloyd was a very heavy drinker and I didn't drink, except for an occasional highball."[11]

By now, animals had given Lehrman's new series its most sensational sequences. Lehrman, who had never valued his human subjects, committed fully to the use of animal acts. It was not, in essence, a revolutionary idea. In the nineteenth century, circuses, sideshows, vaudeville shows and traveling menageries commonly entertained audiences with animal acts. Audiences enjoyed seeing a monkey on roller skates, a bear riding a bicycle, and a dog jumping rope. Some acts kept it simple. "Miss Laura Comstock's Bag Punching Dog" featured a dog trained to hit a punching bag for several minutes. He poked it with his paws, he bumped it with his head, and he leapt into the air to throw his whole body into it. Other acts put animal stunts into an elaborate context. Miley Pleasanton Crawford's Star Dog Company, "a troupe of educated dogs," performed a one-act play called "The Lone Hand Four Aces." During the course of the play, the dogs gambled in a card game and barked out "The Chimes of Normandy." Individually, the dogs took turns performing a variety of tricks (swinging on a trapeze, jumping through a hoop, riding on a horse, and performing a waltz). Patrons reacted most enthusiastically, often roaring with laughter, when one of the dogs got up on its hind legs to push a baby carriage. Other animal acts went totally for thrills. A lion tamer built up tension using whips and chairs to fend off a roaring lion. The death-defying act reached its climax when the lion tamer put his head into the lion's mouth. Lehrman now used his extraordinary resources and creative skills to combine this wide range of animal talent into one grand new spectacle. He did, in this way, manage to create a revolution in film comedy. The animals, instrumental in the creation of disorder and wackiness, were a unique concept comparable to the Keystone Cops. The beasts, as a complement to the Sunshine company's beauties, clowns and acrobats, helped to create an unusual circus maximus.

By the fall of 1917, the Fox Corporation boasted a large assemblage of stars, including Theda Bara, Tom Mix, Gladys Brockwell, June Caprice, Dustin Farnum, George Walsh, Evelyn Nesbit and William Farnum. Fox bragged that William Farnum, who drew an annual salary of $780,000, was the highest paid of any dramatic actor.

Fox had more notable talent behind the scenes. George Walsh's younger brother, Raoul, worked there as a fledgling director. Already showing considerable promise, he was destined to become one of Hollywood's greatest filmmakers. Fox also had in their ranks one of the most popular screenwriters, Zane Grey. Grey was a New York City dentist prior to earning renown as a western novelist. Fox was indebted to Grey for many successful films, including *Riders of the Purple Sage*, *The Light of the Western Stars* and *The Last of the Duanes*.

Fox promoted the Sunshine series with a deluge of pre-release ads and press notices. They promised that, with Lehrman's supervision, they would supply audiences with "26 sidesplitting screams a year." Fox publicists called Lehrman himself a "laugh producing wizard." In other press material, they defined the habits of the big cats and bragged that their new series included life-risking sequences that could "almost raise hair on a bald man." Related ads promised theatergoers and exhibitors "Gorgeous girls! Mile-a-minute action! Uproarious fun! Amazing animals!"

Fox instructed their exhibitors to angle their exploitation towards the girls and animals. No mention was made of the Sunshine players, who were generally regarded as tiny pieces in a grand and crowded picture. Sunshine comedians frequently became UFOs — Unidentifiable Fleeing Oddballs. A typical publicity still was a wide shot featuring a lion chasing an indistinguishable comic. In another publicity still, a comic was almost entirely concealed by a swarm of bathing beauties. No more than the comic's hat and forehead was visible over a barrier of smooth shoulders.

For an acid test, three Sunshine comedies were previewed in New York City. The comedies were well-received. Critics, exhibitors and theatregoers extended warm greetings to the new series. The *Motion Picture News* critic said that the three comedies were "the best I have ever seen." The *New York Times* critic called them "the cleverest comedies ever issued." Many reviewers expressed appreciation for the series' adult slant. One critic specifically expressed pleasure over a "carefully-done" bit of business involving a pretty young lady disrobing by a backyard pool.

Upon its general release, *Roaring Lions and Wedding Bells*—which the press commonly referred to as "Fox's animal comedy"—became a tremendous success. Fox's next few "Sunshine" comedies also triumphed at the box office. Lehrman had, with some funny animals and some serious dollars, reached a high point in his career.

8

Dances with Lions

The Sunshine stages became notoriously crowded, hectic, and dangerous. The film crew was wary of their large and carnivorous associates. The large cats were tense about being in such a strange environment. Putting the actors and technicians even more on edge was. Lehrman, who by demanding that his subordinates heedlessly risk their lives, had earned the nickname "Mr. Suicide." Extras tended to avoid the Sunshine stages. A Fox executive needed to mediate when a cameraman refused to work inside a cage occupied by one of Stecker's lions.

On Hollywood's sets, the unpredictable behavior of animals was a common cause of mishap and delay. At Universal, comedienne Wanda Wiley was riding a horse when a wind machine was activated on a neighboring set. The horse, upset by the machine's roar, became violent and threw the actress to the ground. Another comedy unit tried to create a thrills-and-tickles scene by dragging a crocodile into the Los Angeles River. The crocodile hid in a tangle of bank brush and, from what could be seen of him, he came across more as confused and frightened than ravenous and fierce.

Before long, many buildings rose on the Sunshine lot. One building was a menagerie housing lions, ducks, chickens and skunks. Lehrman, in his bluster, claimed that his menagerie was exhaustive and even included trained flies. The lushest building was constructed to contain Lehrman and his staff. From his fine new quarters, Lehrman looked to please his audience by transplanting lions into a variety of unlikely places. Under this formula, the Sunshine company churned out *Hungry Lions in the Hospital*, *Roaring Lions on the Midnight Express* and *Wild Women and Tame Lions* (lions in a boudoir).

Lehrman remained bound to his office, busy with administrative decisions. He was often involved in hiring talent. He negotiated to acquire guest stars, including Tom Mix and Ford Sterling. He secured champion cowgirls for a comedy-western. It received extensive publicity when Lehrman signed Slim Summerville to a long-term contract. For *Roaring Lions on the Midnight Express*, Lehrman finagled to buy discarded railroad cars at a low rate. He supervised some of the series' more elaborate scenes, such the collapse of a burning building.

It came to be that Lehrman was rarely seen on a set. The few times he personally took charge of a production, he would carelessly stage a couple of scenes and have an assistant finish the film. Regardless, he would receive the sole director's credit. According to his acquaintances, he had simply become lazy.[1]

One day, Lehrman found that rain was leaking into his swank offices. Some would call a repair man, but Lehrman had a better idea. He had an assistant grab a cast and crew and brought them to the soggy setting. Once a camera was in place, he had his actors run around the office and pretend to be contending with the leak. When he had a few minutes of footage, he dismissed everyone. Later, William Campbell used the footage in a hotel comedy in which the drip was attributed to a pipe break and led to a mammoth flood.

To accomplish the flood, Campbell purchased British water tanks from a war exposition. Once triggered, the tanks dumped 37,000 gallons of water onto the hotel set. Hugh Fay, a supporting player, was placed in the path of the torrent, which swept him off his feet and carried him through the set.

Lehrman, not known for being civil to his actors, was more than civil to Lloyd. He liked Lloyd and he had a special appreciation of his talent. In November, Lehrman allowed Lloyd and White to have their own unit. The team's debut, *Hungry Lions in a Hospital*, was based on a Lehrman script. The script had one of Lehrman's typically silly plots — hospital patients find their lives endangered by bloodthirsty surgeons with sharp knives and bloodthirsty lions with even sharper claws. The portion of the film that still exists features Lloyd in a derby and a hospital gown. He still has the moustache he wore as Ham, but he is no longer as harsh and violent as Ham had been.

Months before, Harold Lloyd had made significant changes in his career. In favor of a more human persona, he had discarded his rowdy, pint-sized sidekick, Snub Pollard, and abandoned his off-center "Luke" character. He now blended slapstick with a genteel sort of humor. To produce work of which he could be proud, Lloyd Hamilton was prepared to take similar steps. He explained that these measures were based on "the rapid change and constant advancement in people's taste for comedy, and the constant demand for something new."[2] Just as good views of mountains were no longer sufficient, audiences now demanded that comics do more than chase each other, fall down frequently, and hit one another violently.

At this time, Lloyd observed, "It isn't like in the old days — and by this I mean only a year or two ago, which we call the old days, because a comedy taken from during that time seems decidedly old-fashioned now, due to the rapid rise in comedy prosecution since then ... [A year or two ago,] an audience would scream if someone was hit with a pie, but today the kids are the only ones who seem to enjoy it."[3]

Because of the demand for something new and more sophisticated, the motion pictures' immutable comics were quickly becoming extinct. For the sake of his survival and the satisfaction of personal ambition, Lloyd decided to make his own radical transition.

Lloyd sought a role that was more credible, more reserved, and more distinctive. He worked to invent a character that was thinking, deeply motivated, and entirely sympathetic. Rather than dressing up as a brash and brutish Hyde, he would become as restrained and respectable as Dr. Jekyll. The character's respectability was important to him. Lloyd said, in a 1927 interview for *Motion Picture Classic*, that his main idea was to portray "a shabby gentleman who keeps the semblance of immaculate respectability thru all poverty and adversity of experiences."[4] With morality and intellect, he would endeavor to be an honorable member of society. He said that, in his films, he would let "the minor actors portray the so-called types with their queer appearances." Lloyd, comedy scientist, reasoned that he "must think out [his new] character by careful experiment."[5]

Lloyd, although he had become strongly identified with Ham, was willing to forsake this familiar character. He was sure it would benefit in the long run. In shedding his old disguise, Lloyd removed the heavy moustache and mopped his brow clean of greasepaint. His boyish and empathetic face was now revealed. Lloyd became less of a clown and more of a man. Walter Kerr wrote that facial nakedness made the silent film comic "vulnerable, immediate [and] dimensional enough to stand still for a moment and interest us in his thoughtful occupation of space."[6] In reference to working in this new state, Lloyd would explain:

> There is all the difference in the world. When you wear makeup, you can rely largely on that to make you funny, but without adornments, your own facial expressions and postures must make up for that.[7]

In his ongoing struggle for laughs, Lloyd wanted to succeed with bare comic muscles. He would abandon Ham's brutish behavior and establish a distinctive character.

Lloyd claimed that, in order to create compatible comedy for his new character, he needed "a large amount of time and money, and a great deal of thought and hard work."[8] While Fox was offering the time and money, he was prepared to furnish the thought and hard work. His routine was more exacting than ever. He confessed that he rankled himself, endlessly, with one simple question: "What can I do to make people laugh?"

Lloyd spoke many times about the anxiety he felt as a comedian, not knowing whether a gag would get a laugh or fall flat. He addressed the subject in an article entitled "Harder to Get a Laugh," which was published on February 2, 1918. He wrote, "There is no state of joy in the life of a comedian."[9]

Lloyd, who became known for being deadpan as he delivered gags, was very much deadpan off-screen in creating gags. Echoing remarks he had made in 1916, he referred to himself as "a cranky old grouch forever snooping around for something that would get a laugh."[10] Articles about Lloyd often pointed out how serious-minded he was about his craft. A publicity item, published in the exhibitor book for *The Greenhorn*, read, "Hamilton is serious, a student of his art, quiet and unassuming. He is the comedian who never laughs at himself."[11] James W. Dean wrote, "Hamilton is intensely serious about his comedy. He spends hours studying comic situations. He is his own sternest critic." A journalist with the *Fort Worth Star-Telegram* wrote," Lloyd Hamilton ... is called the 'serious comedian' by his friends and coworkers in Los Angeles. This is not only because the comedian keeps a straight face through his pictures ... but because he is so deadly earnest with his work." Lloyd saw this as a reasonable attitude. He pointed out that a performers willing to go to extremes for a simple laugh — "tumble into a well and nearly drown," "fall off a roof" and "be slammed about and otherwise injured"— had to be seriously committed to what they did.

At this time, Lloyd repeated how anxiety over his job put a great strain on his marriage. He noted, "And wouldn't it send any women off to the divorce court to look up from her cup of tea and find hubby staring at her and contorting his face into the most horrible grimace under the mistaken impression that he has found a new way to make people laugh."[12]

It deeply disturbed Lloyd that, due to the scarcity of good comedy scripts, he was forced to write most of his own material.[13] He complained that, though war-sore audiences were eager for laughter, his studio's scriptwriters were busy developing melodramas. The submissions of outside writers, as he saw it, exhibited a poor understanding of screen comedy. And it made him grumble more than anything that, as a comedy writer, he had no fund of literature on which to fall back. He could not, like other Fox writers, rely on novel adaptations.

Lloyd and White, concerned with the structure and mechanics of their films, used their additional production time to carefully work out scenes. Through all his efforts, Lloyd tried to develop new and interesting concepts, what he called "real ideas."

Lloyd and Chaplin shared similar work habits and handled unexpected difficulties in much the same manner. Whenever a problem developed, Chaplin would suspend production and then strain his mind for a solution. He would spend hours either pensively sitting on the set

Hamilton has to worry about letting animals crowd him out in *A Tight Squeeze* (1918). The actress is Ethel Teare (courtesy of Billy Rose Theatre Division, New York Public Library for the Performing Arts, Astor, Lenox and Tilden Foundations).

or agonizingly pacing his dressing room. Georgina Hale, one of his leading ladies, vividly recalled his grueling struggle: "If he came on the set, he'd have his two hands stuffed into his pants pocket[s] with his shoulders folded together and with a scowl on his face. And he wouldn't do a thing. And he would let all the people wait. It wouldn't matter how many were being paid or how much it cost. And after he'd sit there in a daze for hours, he would leave and call it all off for the day. And then he wouldn't even call us back for a week."[14]

Lloyd would sneak off to soberly consider a sudden problem or plan for business in days ahead.

He said, "Comedy work doesn't end when the comedian finishes his scenes. He has to figure out new business for days to come. The dressing room, or some secluded spot, is where I head when not filming, and there I try to think. I must be quiet and alone. One of my best gags came to me the other day as I was sitting in a four-wheeled chariot that had been used by Theda Bara."[15]

As a way to relieve pressure, Lloyd regularly flew with the aviators of local military camps. He highly enjoyed the liberating sensation of air travel, although he admitted that he had shakily approached his maiden flight. While boarding the plane, he stuck a piece of hard candy into his mouth. He said that, upon returning to ground level, the candy was gone and he could not remember if he had swallowed it or if it had dropped out of his mouth. The ride, enthralling and dizzying, had addicted him to flying.

Lloyd found one other way to relieve pressure. During the hunting season, he would go in the blind and afield in order to shoot ducks. The more high-flying, the more fast-moving, the better. Fellow duck-hunters described him as an admirable wingshot.

Duck hunting allowed Lloyd an opportunity to escape into the wildest, simplest and most solitary places. These were otherworldly locales where a man could indulge in contemplation and revel in suspense.

The author of *The Duck Hunter's Bible*, Erwin Bauer, described the appeal of the duck hunter's world. He wrote, "As we waited, I wondered about something I had pondered over before. Why does a man go goose hunting? But in the next instant I knew. The honking was faint and far away at first, but it raised goose pimples just as it had when the phrase was coined a long time ago. As the honking came closer, it became a haunting Klaxon call which added a chill that played up and down my spine. No sound, it seems to me, unless it would be the hunting cry of a timber-wolf pack, is more primitive or more symbolic of the lonely places left in North America."[16] He later added, "Duck hunting gives a man [the]chance to see the loneliest places. Non-duck hunters, who wouldn't understand, might call these the unfriendliest places. I mean blinds washed by a rolling surf, blue and gold autumn marshes, a northern bay with ice forming on the perimeter, a rice field in the rain, flooded pine-oak forests on any remote river delta."[17] Bauer remembered one day in a valley when, after a rainstorm had turned into a sleet storm, "cold vapor enveloped the valley so thoroughly that I seemed suspended in a void."[18]

As an offshoot of hunting, Lloyd amassed a gun collection. He had an armory of modern pieces; several models of flintlock muskets and squirrel rifles; and a separate collection of early pistols and revolvers.

Apart from this activity, Lloyd was spending most of his spare hours at the Athletic Club. For him, this place had become so much of a home that he had his mail directed there.

In the spring of 1918, Lloyd and White presented *A Waiter's Wasted Life*. The film, a drastic departure, did not depend on the obvious assortment of animals. Some action was created by mice, but they were limited to brief appearances—"scuttle-ons." Overall, *A Waiter's Wasted Life* was breezy, crazy and witty.

The multitude of critters returned to Lloyd and White's next collaboration, *A Tight Squeeze*. Lloyd, cast as a farm boy, was surrounded by all of Old MacDonald's favorites. A still featuring the farm boy character shows a make-up and costume design similar to what Lloyd wore in his early Kalem comedies, including *Ham and the Villain Factory* and *Ham the Lineman*. The most obvious similarities are the soup-bowl bangs and the hiked-up pants. Lloyd, however, is not wearing a protruding putty nose as he had worn earlier. Also, he is wearing a vest, which would remain part of his costume for the next three years. Lloyd would soon take to wearing tight-fitting shirts to give himself an "overgrown boy" look.

Ethel Teare, whose Sennett contract had expired, joined Lloyd and the animals on this production. Lloyd made a point to work with old friends. It was at Lloyd's initiation, according to a press release, that two friends, Dave Morris and Hugh Fay, were also hired as cast members of Lloyd's Sunshine unit. Lloyd had previously given Morris a job while he was working at Kalem. Since then, Morris had been making the rounds at Keystone, L-KO and Christie. Fay, a former stage actor, had come from a well-known theatrical family. His father, Hugh Fay Sr., was part of the comedy team Barry and Fay, which achieved fame in vaudeville playing farcical Irish stereotypes in various sketches. Fay himself worked on vaudeville circuits with his wife, Elsie Mynn. The couple performed a number of musical comedy sketches, including "Love is Everything," "Chinese Honeymoon" and "The Girl and the Man." Fay's

Hamilton acts as catcher for the Sunshine baseball team. Pitching the ball is the comedian's notorious friend Hugh Fay. The other actors are unidentified (courtesy of the family of Lloyd Hamilton).

specialty, according to a review in *The Oregonian*, was "songs, dances and merriment." The actor might sing a song, tell the audience a funny story, and close with an eccentric dance.

An animal stunt concocted for *A Tight Squeeze* proved impossible to shoot. Lloyd said, "We figured out a splendid gag for a mule that was supposed to be led out onto a springboard, but it had to be abandoned because no mule was silly ass enough to do it. We tried this several times, but they all stopped dead when they saw the water below them, and turned it down."[19]

Lloyd was pushing himself harder with each Fox production. It took a case of the measles to force him to take a break. He was resting in bed, awaiting the tiny red spots to fade from his face, when he learned of a tragedy on the Sunshine set. During the production of *The Diver's Last Kiss*, it was proven that leading a mule onto a springboard was more difficult than leading a stunt man onto the wing of an airplane. It was Slim Summerville's stunt man, Earl Burgess, who had accepted the hazardous assignment. Burgess was to climb onto the wing and then drop a weighted dummy to make it look as if he fell. After the harrowing aerial business was shot, members of the film crew went to retrieve the dummy. Where the group expected to find a broken dummy, they found a man's crushed and bloody body. The body was entangled in a jumbled mass of wood and high-tension wires.

In the opinion of the *Moving Picture World* critic, *A Waiter's Wasted Life* was an extraordinary Sunshine release, a comedy "full of new ideas." The critic specifically noted that "a great deal of amusement comes from the nonchalance of the players." However, *A Waiter's Wasted Life* was not a large moneymaker. Financial success was achieved by *A Tight Squeeze*, which one critic ranked highly because "the animals were worked very cleverly into the action."

Months after the debut of the Sunshine series, Lehrman stopped meeting his release obligations, compelling Fox to fill their schedule with reissues. It was at this point that Lehrman's relationship with Fox began to deteriorate.

In the fall of 1918, Lloyd slipped into a darkened theatre showing his latest comedy and hid himself in the back row. He said he believed this film "was about the funniest thing ever."[20] So, as the film unfolded, he was amazed to find that most members of the audience were not laughing. He quickly recognized that he had blundered by making his character act too bright. He concluded that his audience wants to laugh "at" the comedian rather than "with" him. "If a comedy character displays too much intelligence," he said, "the audience would resent his brilliancy — unless his planning results in embarrassment to him."[21]

Buster Keaton would reach the same conclusion. Decades later, Keaton claimed that an audience does not like it when a comic is smarter than they are. He explained, "The audience wants their comic to be human, not clever."[22] While Lloyd remained clever on screen, he took care to reserve his wit. Joe Franklin, nostalgia king, said that Lloyd adopted a "crazy like a fox" technique.[23]

White encountered a problem while directing *Roaring Lions on the Midnight Express*:

> [If you worked with animals, you couldn't] anticipate what you're going to get. You'd just gamble. A man named Al Herman was one of my many assistant directors at Sunshine Comedies. Before coming to Hollywood, he had been a prizefighter, and his muscles bulged like two giant-sized salamis. We were shooting with Curley Stecker's lions.... Nero, a giant African with a black mane, weighed at least 325 pounds. The scene was a circus train; the lions had got loose. Nero was running down an aisle of a sleeper car....[24]

White explained that Billie Burke, an actress in the car, was menstruating and her blood attracted the lion.

> [Nero] grabbed Billie's arm in his mouth. Herman didn't hesitate; he grabbed Nero by the tail and pulled the beast backwards, sliding him and Billie.... Al huffed and puffed, then yanked Nero's rear right up off the floor. Nero roared with pain and dropped Billie's arm. He snarled at Al, then charged him. Fortunately, Curley fired a couple of blank pistol shots into Nero's face, and Nero retreated.[25]

In late 1918, the Hamilton-White company assembled on the massive mock-up of a country lodge. The occasion of the gathering was a production called *His Musical Sneeze*, a film designed to spoof Lloyd's duck-hunting activities. Determined to furnish his screen self with a permanent and readily identifiable outfit, Lloyd was meticulous about dressing his duck hunter. In the end, he garbed the character in a tie, a speckled vest, and a loose-fitting cutaway coat.

By the completion of *His Musical Squeeze*, Lehrman and Fox had terminated their relationship. Fox was committed to continuing the Sunshine company's operations without Lehrman, whose absence was evident in the February promotion. Contrary to the usual notes on their latest animal acquisitions, the comedy company reported the recruitment of two directors who were bipedal and utterly furless.

His Musical Sneeze achieved popularity due to Lloyd's performance. Most of Lehrman's leads remained indiscernible among the animals, bathing beauties, and comical cops. However, Lloyd was the one actor to rise above the chaotic amalgam.

Near the end of 1918, Lloyd's brother-in-law, Pierce Morehouse, died of influenza. Morehouse had been a prominent figure in the Oakland real estate business. He worked for years as the sales manager of the Realty Syndicate, which owned a large amount of property in the area. Their holdings included housing properties, a transit company, a sky railway, hotels, and an amusement park.

Lloyd took time off from work to travel back home and attend the funeral. He didn't get to visit his family much, but he was always in good spirits when he was around them. Virginia, his niece, said of Lloyd, "I did not see him often, but I remember him as jovial and friendly."

On December 1, 1918, a group of Sunshine comedians went to San Diego to entertain the soldiers at Camp Kearney.[26] Hugh Fay hosted the event. The highlight of the show, as reported in the *Oakland Tribune*, was a skit performed by Lloyd and Mack Swain.

Shortly after, it was reported in an exhibitor periodical, *The Sunshine Comedy Special*, that a big-budget Sunshine comedy was underway. Lloyd took the lead in a farcical sea adventure set aboard a sixty-foot sailing yacht. For the rousing climax, the yacht had been sunk in a studio tank, dumping several lions and an estimated fifty extras into the water.

On January 17, 1919, Fox published a full-page notice in trade magazines to let theatre owners know that a Sunshine comedy, *A Lady Bellhop's Secret*, had been stolen and they shouldn't accept it for exhibition in their theatres.

Details of the theft came out in New York papers.[27] An editor named Charles Hochberg was responsible for sending the negative to Fox's New York offices. Hochberg was expected to enclose the negative in a metal box and insure the box and its contents with Wells Fargo for $25,000. The box soon arrived in New York, but all that the New York officials discovered inside were sand and rocks. Fox fired Hochberg, charging the editor with embezzlement. Two days after a warrant was issued for his arrest, Hochberg surrendered to the authorities. He denied any knowledge of the theft. He claimed that he had not written or signed the shipping directions. Hochberg was eventually released under a $2,500 bond.

In 1919, a rash of film thefts marked the emergence of film pirate rings. Early in the year, a negative of *Treasure Island* was mysteriously removed from a van parked outside of a London transport company. During this period, Federal authorities were working especially hard to break up a ring based in Syracuse, New York. It was suspected that this ring was the leading distributor of illegal prints. Film producers moved quickly to oppose the pirates. Six major film companies, including Fox, organized the Film Theft Committee. By tightening security, the committee was at least able to end the daring daylight heists.

Still, the theft of *A Lady Bellhop's Secret* was strictly an inside job and Fox knew that Lehrman was behind it. Fox was losing patience with Lehrman over excessive spending and production delays and Lehrman knew his days were numbered. On January 19, two days after announcing the theft, Fox made it clear to the press that they had fired Lehrman.[28] Fifty members of Lehrman's staff, including Lloyd Hamilton, Fred Fishback, Hugh Fay, Gertrude Selby, Billie Ritchie and Ethel Teare, left the company with Lehrman. The departure occurred before Lloyd's sea adventure was completed. Eventually, Fox filed criminal charges against Hochberg and Lehrman. The case was brought into court following a grand jury indictment, but by then Lehrman had returned the film to Fox. It was reported in the *Los Angeles Times*, on May 7, 1919, that the presiding judge dismissed the charges and discharged the defendants.

White talked about helping Lehrman to steal a film from the L-KO company in 1917.

Either White's memory was faulty and he transposed events or Lehrman found this past strategy so effective that he decided to repeat it.

White recounted, "We had been waiting for Lehrman to come back from New York with financing.... While Lehrman was in New York, we thought the Stern Brothers were trying to put something over on him because they owed him money. They hadn't paid him for completing a picture he had made. A friend of mine and I boxed the negative and the positive and sent it to American Express, 'To Hold.' The Stern Brothers found this out and fired me."[29]

Hochberg, the editor who was arrested, was one of White's closest friends and could have been the friend mentioned in White's story.

In the spring of 1919, Fox hired Sennett veteran Hampton Del Ruth to produce the Sunshine series. Under Del Ruth's supervision, the Sunshine comedies continued to rely on the deranged and indelicate style established by Lehrman. Story and characterization were not what people got out of watching these films. They, instead, sat back to enjoy wild and elaborate effects that no other comedymaker had the money to produce. *A Schoolhouse Scandal*, one of the rare Sunshine comedies to survive, opens with Slim Summerville parachuting out of a plane, crashing through the roof of a boarding house, and landing in a dining room chair just as dinner is being served. Other people seated at the table don't react to this extravagant entrance and the filmmakers don't bother at all to explain it. Animation combines with live action when Fox's cartoon stars, Mutt and Jeff, make a brief appearance in the film. Animation is also utilized to show a Model T drinking out of a trough. A bottle of liquor has fallen into the trough by mistake, which causes the car to become inebriated and give its driver Jack Cooper a wild ride. By the end of the film, a cyclone travels directly into a home, causing the place to spin around wildly. A bed, with a person sleeping under the covers, lifts off the floor and floats in mid-air. Other furniture is blown around the place. At one point, a car comes flying through the air. This was just business as usual in the mad world of Sunshine.

More than assuring that comedians took calamitous spills and recklessly drove speedy autos, Del Ruth was able to ensure timely delivery of the Sunshine comedies. By the fall, these comedies were reportedly showing in more theaters than all two-reel comedies except those of Chaplin.

The success of the Sunshine comedies inevitably influenced other producers. At their zenith, the company's influence was clearly seen. Comedy brands that suddenly materialized were "SunKist," "Sun-Lite," and "Sunbeam." The Stern Brothers replaced their L-KO series with "The Rainbow Comedies." All comedy producers, including Sennett, now used numerous and varied animals in their productions. "Century Comedies," a Universal series, became a showcase for animals, including the Century Lions. Their releases included *African Lions and American Beauties*, *Weak Hearts and Wild Lions*, *Naughty Lions and Wild Men*, *Loose Lions and Fast Lovers*, and *Lion Paws and Lady Fingers*.

William Campbell parlayed his credit as co-director of the *Roaring Lions and Wedding Bells*. Campbell was granted a namesake series, "Campbell Comedies," which featured a large variety of animals. When the "Our Gang" series became popular, he threw some child actors into the mix.

The popularity of the Sunshine series did not only influence comedy producers. It was due in part to the animal performances in the series that trained animals, including Strongheart and Rin Tin Tin, were put front and center in feature films and attained celebrity status in Hollywood.

The "lion comedy" was a common form of entertainment in the twenties. Sennett produced the most astoundingly wild and silly lion comedies, including the 1926 comedy *Circus Today*. The jungle king managed, in the end, to occupy an important place in the annals of silent film comedy.

In February, 1919, Lehrman reported that he was erecting a new studio in Culver City, Los Angeles. It was disclosed that, when construction was complete, Lehrman would begin producing two-reel comedies of his "usual intense character." In full-page ads, Lehrman promised exhibitors a series of twelve *Lehrman Comedies*. He informed the press that, in addition to short subjects, he would create five-reel films in which comedy and drama were blended. It was not generally believed at the time that pure slapstick could support a feature.

Lehrman contracted First National as his distributor. First National, which had originally been known as National Films, was a unique organization. Exhibitors had formed the company to combat the motion picture conglomerates, which were demanding high rental fees. First National formed partnerships with directors and stars. The company advanced these artists production money in return for exclusive rights to exhibit their pictures. The joint venture was firmly established by the first Hollywood adaptation of "Tarzan."

First National largely expanded in early 1919. Their talent pool included D.W. Griffith, Mary Pickford, Jack Pickford, Constance Talmadge, and Marshall Neilan. Neilan had stopped acting in 1916. In the last three years, he had directed numerous features for Paramount and Goldwyn. Most of his Goldwyn features had been designed as vehicles for Blanche Sweet. Lately, he had been working mostly with Mary Pickford. Between 1917 and 1919, he directed several of Pickford's most popular vehicles, including *Daddy-Long-Legs*, *Amarilly of Clothes-Line Alley*, *Stella Maris*, *The Little Princess*, and *Rebecca of Sunnybrook Farm*.

First National's latest inductee was Chaplin. Under their contract, Chaplin was paid one million dollars. In return, the comic agreed to provide First National with eight comedies in a period of eighteen months.

Though this arrangement allowed him to become his own producer, Chaplin would become dissatisfied. Years later, he described his treatment by First National executives as inconsiderate, unsympathetic, shortsighted and ruthless.

During the construction of Lehrman's studio, regular press releases kept the trade abreast of his efforts. In April, the filmmaker reported that he would produce ten *Lehrman Comedies* within the next ten months. Ads featured a portrait of the producer, clearly designed to convey Lehrman as proud and prestigious. In one ad, it was noted that Lehrman had organized the successful Sunshine company and had "trained a great number of screen comedians who have since become famous."

Evidence exists that, in 1919, Lloyd had a short-lived association with Mack Sennett. First, the Sennett Company's papers reveal that the studio's scenario department wrote a vehicle for Lloyd in 1919. The script, titled "The Lesson Story," is available at the Academy of Motion Picture Arts and Sciences. "The Lesson Story" was later readapted for Ben Turpin and became the comedy *No Mother to Guide Him*.

Second, the New York Public Library for the Performing Arts had cataloged, as indicated by their card index, a still of Lloyd Hamilton from a 1919 Sennett comedy entitled *His Best Foot Forward*. The still, unfortunately, could not be found in their holdings. *His Best Foot Forward* could have been another comedy that Lloyd had been preparing to do before Sennett fired him.

The third and final clue in this mystery is a 1932 newspaper item which describes some trouble Lloyd had working with Sennett fifteen years earlier. As the story goes, Sennett agreed to let Lloyd direct his own comedies. Sennett wasn't expecting any problems until, one morning, he walked on his stages and found extras gathered around Lloyd. Lloyd, a big cigar jutting out of the side of his mouth, was parading back and forth, demonstrating a busy stride. The extras were laughing. Sennett soon realized that his new comedy star was performing a disparaging imitation of him. Sennett told Lloyd that it wasn't the job of the director to stand around making the extras laugh. He was so angry that he dismissed Lloyd on the spot. "[S]omehow news of my imitation had gone all over Hollywood," said Lloyd, "and nobody would give me a directing job."[30]

The story came out as a publicity item circulated to newspapers. It was written in a jokey style, meant to entertain a person reading their newspaper over breakfast. Publicity items in this jokey style, like the one about an aunt leaving "Ham" a Texas ranch with 200 head of hog, were at times fabricated just for a laugh.[31] But this item about Sennett firing Lloyd seems largely true. Without a doubt, the episode corresponds with other known incidents. Lloyd did, in fact, have a reputation for clowning with the crew. He liked to walk on the set and get people laughing. Also, this was a man who once, while back stage at a musical comedy show, broke up stage hands by doing a disparaging imitation of the stage manager. This incident was even more typical of Sennett, who was notorious for his rash firings. The only real question is whether the incident in fact happened fifteen years earlier, which would place it in 1917, or if it happened in 1919, which would fit in it with the other available evidence.

Lloyd's filmography shows a nine-month gap in 1919. Rob Farr, who has done much research on Lloyd, refers to this as Lloyd's "lost year." Lloyd's trouble with Sennett could explain the gap. The only other likely explanation is that Lloyd and White took time off while waiting for Lehrman to get financing for a new company. A similar situation occurred when Lehrman left L-KO in 1917. White said, "I waited a whole year for Lehrman to come back from New York.... He paid me for twelve months at fifty dollars a week. I didn't do a damn thing but have a good time."[32]

Lehrman was able to set up a deal with First National. He immediately signed Lloyd to work as his star comic and White to work as his director. With Lehrman as their vanguard, Lloyd and White were about to experience a bold advance in their careers.

9

Further Adventures on an Ostrich Farm

The Jans Corporation had recently had great success reissuing old Tom Mix one-reelers. Jans, encouraged that a package of Keystone reissues had recently completed a profitable run, planned to make their next investment in a comedy series. The company, in the end, bought the rights to ninety-two *Ham* comedies, which they intended to release on a weekly basis starting in the Spring of 1919.

Jans launched a large exploitation campaign to sell state rights. Ads noted that the marketplace had experienced great growth in the last few years and only about ten percent of the current theatergoers had ever seen a Ham and Bud comedy. Jans claimed, weeks later, that their promotion had attracted a strong turn-out of exhibitors. The fact that reissued comedies could compete successfully with first-run comedies supported Lloyd's belief that the demand for comedy was great.

During the summer of 1919, Lehrman inaugurated pre-production work on the first *Lehrman Comedy* titled *A Twilight Baby*. The film was to satirize the enforcement of the recent Volstead Act, a Federal law that forbade the manufacture, transportation, sale or possession of alcoholic beverages. The lead role, that of a hapless moonshiner, had been written for Lloyd. Lehrman employed Virginia Rappe, his live-in companion, as Lloyd's leading lady. Billie Ritchie, though not fully recovered from recent injuries, joined the cast in a supporting role.

By this time, Lehrman was ecstatic, savoring the sight of constructors inserting the last bricks into the picture plant bearing his name. But erroneous news stories regarding the studio's ownership soon spoiled his good mood. Roscoe Arbuckle had leased space from the comedy producer, who had been a friend since Keystone's early days. Misconstruing the facts, the press reported that Lehrman's grand studio was the product of a Lehrman-Arbuckle partnership. This so upset Lehrman that he rushed to release the following statement:

> The new studios are entirely my own property and I have no partners or associates whatsoever in the ownership. When I contracted with First National Exhibitor's Circuit.... I was determined to build a production home which would in every respect meet my ideas of what a modern studio should be, and the plant which I am now bringing to completion is the result.
>
> Mr. Arbuckle has leased space for the making of his pictures, but his position at the studio will be solely that of tenant. I am moved to make this point clear in justice to both Mr. Arbuckle and myself.[1]

Production of *A Twilight Baby* began in August. Lehrman estimated that the comedy would be shot within a dozen weeks. He planned to ship the negative print to New York on the first of November.

As production commenced, First National executives compelled Chaplin to visit Lehrman's facility in a show of fraternity. Chaplin had, to date, produced two three-reel films for First National. His latest production, currently in the planning stages, was shaping into a much longer film.

In a photo released to trade magazines, Chaplin is posed awkwardly beside Lehrman. It is hard to believe, considering the history of these two men, that Chaplin stayed around longer than it took the photographer to frame him and Lehrman in his view-finder and squeeze a finger down on the shutter-release.

Lloyd, aided by Lehrman and White, progressed in the look of his comic character. Lehrman advised Lloyd to wear a cap. He believed that, less associated with adult males than a derby, the cap would enhance Lloyd's boyish face. As the traditional headgear of a Lehrman comic was a crash helmet, Lehrman seemed determined to alter his style.

Lloyd could not immediately find a cap that was big enough to fit his size 7 7/8 head. On a whim, he squeezed on a smaller-sized cap and quickly checked himself in a mirror. Pleased with the sight of the overgrown boy that looked back at him, he settled on wearing the tight-fitting headpiece.[2]

During production of *A Twilight Baby*, White invited a tailor to the set and had him abbreviate Lloyd's cutaway coat.

Lloyd developed a more polished version of his odd walk, which he realized was important. Chaplin's walk made the comic readily recognizable over much of the world. Alice Howell, formerly one of Lehrman's L-KO players, had gotten much attention with a penguin-like walk. Larry Semon, by walking on tip toe, had gotten himself both laughs and notice. Lloyd would refine his own walk over the next two years.

Lloyd made it a strict point not to emphasize his size or fitness as, he feared, his character would become less empathetic. This was a concern Lloyd had when he first started making comedies. Neilan had convinced him that he could be funnier if he played up his larger size, but it doesn't appear that Lloyd ever believed being bigger gave him the vulnerability he needed for audiences to be concerned for his well-being. This was a concern that would remain with the comic in the coming years. Lloyd reported in a *Moving Picture World* article, dated April 23, 1927, that he preferred to work opposite a leading lady who was taller than him so that his character would appear more sympathetic.[3]

Lehrman was unwilling to let Lloyd totally command his inaugural comedy. The producer developed scenes around farm animals. Lehrman said that he carefully studied animals to fit gags to their individual characteristics.[4] He said, for example, that he observed a rooster strutting around with its tail feathers jutting proudly in the air. This inspired him to set up a gag in *A Twilight Baby* where a rooster got his tail feathers blown off. He was sure that the appalled reaction of the rooster, whose vanity had been horribly abused, was something that would make an audience roar with laughter.

Lehrman also arranged a scene pairing Ritchie with a bevy of ostriches. It has been reported that Ritchie's physical condition had deteriorated due to past injuries and the abuse of medication he had taken to control the pain. By what was later known about Ritchie, he may also have been suffering from the early effects of cancer. In any case, the comedian's reflexes were sluggish as he grappled with the ostriches, which were being less than cooperative. An ostrich, a skittish and territorial creature, cannot be expected to react well to being used as a stooge in a slapstick routine. And an ostrich is not an animal you want to get riled. The ostrich is an extremely large bird, as tall as nine feet and as heavy as 250 pounds, and it is able to kick forward with enough force to fracture a man's ribs. The keen edges of an ostrich's hooves have been known to create deep gashes and even puncture internal organs. Making the bird even more lethal is the fact that its deft maneuvers can make it difficult for an unprepared victim to get away. Actor Tommy Kirk had to perform with an ostrich for Disney's *Swiss Family Robinson*. Kirk said, "The animal guy would always tell me, 'Don't *ever* stand in front of the ostrich.' If they kick you, it's goodbye Charlie." Eventually, an ostrich did attack and injure Ritchie. Allegedly, other ostriches, roused by the attack, rushed forth and caused Ritchie further injuries. Ritchie was escorted off the set and remained sidelined for the rest of the production.

Another cast member also fell ill. While trying to ride a bicycle, Rappe stopped and clutched her side. She could not continue to pedal. With little discussion, White eliminated the action from the scene and moved to the next set-up. However, the episode would come to assume great significance.

Lehrman continued to say that much would come from his forthcoming release. To remain on schedule, the grand comedymaker ordered that the footage of *A Twilight Baby* be spliced together during production.

Lehrman apparently made a last-minute, unceremonious decision to increase his debut comedy to feature length. By all indications, audiences were ready for comedy features. Sennett had recently devoted much time and resources to a five-reel production. This was Sennett's first feature since *Tillie's Punctured Romance*, which had been produced five years earlier. In the end, Lehrman assembled three-reel and four-reel versions of *A Twilight Baby*.

"Mr. Lehrman is the proud father of a lusty infant prodigy, that will shake the roofs of the world with laughter." Neither Lloyd or White was ever mentioned in Lehrman's persistent press notices. Ads released in November were mainly concerned with Lehrman. In a typical ad, it was proclaimed: "Henry Lehrman is the Punch!"

The fact that two versions of *A Twilight Baby* were in release may contribute to the varying comments from exhibitors, some of whom said it was a pleasant and original film while others said it was too long. The "debate" began with the remarks of a theater owner in Jacksonville, Texas, who had done good business with an early preview of the film. The Texas man wrote to *The Exhibitor's Herald*: "This one is a knockout but a little too long." The critic of *The Exhibitor's Herald* promptly countered this statement, writing: "There is reason to believe his too long objection will not hold water. It probably impressed him that way because it was not shown properly."

Other comments followed. A Michigan exhibitor wrote that he had found *A Twilight Baby* to be an exceptional comedy ("Something different in this one"), but he followed his praise with this severe qualification: "First two reels continual laughter, when it begins to drag." An Arizona exhibitor also faulted the film's length. "Good comedy, but a little too long. Two reels is all they want for a slapstick comedy." A disgruntled Minnesota exhibitor commented on the film's weak second half. He added that, though he had thought the first half was good, "I did not think that *A Twilight Baby* was as good as they would have a person believe. It lost money for me and did not please those that came. Only a few laughs."

Twilight Baby allowed Lloyd moments of drama. At one point in the film, Lloyd's dog is shot trying to protect Lloyd from a wicked rival. Lloyd is sad at first, but he quickly summons his courage to defeat the rival. Richard M. Roberts, a film historian who has viewed the rare film, has noted that, in this critical scene, "Hamilton successfully manages pathos."[5]

Lloyd believed that, for him, *A Twilight Baby* marked a long-awaited turning point. He now felt ready to take the next step in his artistic development.

10

A Fresh Start

Lloyd and White went shopping for a studio facility. White said, "We inadvertently heard a rumor that a French director by the name of Louis Gasnier had a studio under long-term lease from Pathé, but wasn't shooting any pictures. We went out to see him."[1]

The studio, named Astra, had housed the *Ham* company in Kalem's twilight days. Lloyd and White informed Gasnier that they wanted to rent the studio but couldn't immediately pay him. White promised him "the first money we get." Gasnier accepted the arrangement.

The Hamilton-White company commenced shooting in the spring of 1920. Their pilot film had been given the double-edged title *A Fresh Start*. Reportedly, Lloyd and White invented this title because a brief title would receive more prominent newspaper and marquee display.

A Fresh Start relied on at least one stale feature: lions. White figured this trusty gimmick would assure the film's success. While poised atop a ladder, Jimmie Adams is inadvertently lowered into a lion's pit at the zoo. A series of mishaps cause the ladder to raise and lower repeatedly so that Adams has to ride the ladder like a seesaw. Soon, the lions escape. At this point, White repeated a scene from *Hungry Lions in a Hospital*. The tenants of a boarding house pile up chairs as a barrier against the lions, but one determined lion is able to leap into the air and crash through the chairs. This scene, which utilizes no apparent trick photography, can be jolting to a viewer accustomed to comedians facing wild beasts through rear screen or split screen effects. Lige Conley, Adams' diminutive co-star, got highly favorable notices for his spry performance. White liked Conley. "Lige was a good comic," he said. "He didn't have a dime's worth of his own creativity to sell, but he could do what I wanted him to do."[2]

The question becomes why Lloyd wasn't featured in the pilot film. White never explained that when interviewed in later years. He talked much about his efforts to sell the film, but not the reason he didn't rely on a more marketable star. White said:

> With *A Fresh Start*, I had another hit on my hands, but I didn't realize it. It was coming along day by day, the hard way. I made a deal with Curley Stecker ... so I wrote into the picture some terrific gags about lions that got away from a zoo next door. The audience screamed at this preview.... Sol Wurtzel, a manager for Fox who had been at the preview ... soon asked me to come back to Fox ... I told him, 'Okay. If you put up the $25,000 this negative has cost the studio and myself, you can have it and my services for $500 a week.' He wouldn't take the deal.
>
> Gasnier was going to New York, and we had creditors down our neck. We owed everybody in town but couldn't pay our bills. I gave the negative and print to Gasnier, who gave it to one of his stooges. They ran it in New York for several aspiring distributors. None of them thought it was good except E.W. Hammons, who gave Hamilton and me a deal right off the bat.[3]

Hammons was the president of Educational Films, a new comedy distributor. The company, as indicated by its name, had intended to produce scholastic films. However, the organization's silent instructionals had proven to be painfully boring. *The "Why" of a Volcano* and *Constantinople, the Gateway of the Orient* were among the company's failed titles. Hammons, whom White described as a "slick operator,"[4] moved to one of the film industry's more lucrative channels.

Hamilton on a hunting trip (1920) (courtesy of the family of Lloyd Hamilton).

Hamilton (right), between scenes on *Duck Inn* (1920), examines a prop with director Gilbert Pratt (courtesy of the family of Lloyd Hamilton).

Lloyd and White intended to establish individual production units to turn out a monthly two-reel series. Lloyd would function as star, story man and supervisor of his unit, but White would help him as necessary to oversee production.

Lloyd wanted to put forth his best and achieve a faultless product. He wanted to no longer be preoccupied with time and money where his ideas were concerned. Hammons' financing would help Lloyd to reach his objectives. Each comedy would have a budget of $20,000. White recalled, "Most of the time, we'd come within a hairbreadth of the $20,000. Sometimes we'd go to $22,000; then we had to do one for $18,000 to balance them out."[5] The production time on each film would be one to two months.

Lloyd and White wasted no time assembling their crew. They hired directors John Noble and Gilbert Pratt. They hired Lloyd Bacon and Archie Mayo to head Lloyd's scenario staff. They brought together an ensemble of actors, including Lige Conley, Marvel Rea, Hugh Fay, Frank Coleman and Jimmie Adams. Lloyd was familiar with most of the new crew. Bacon, one of Lloyd's oldest friends, had worked steadily since he had left the *Ham* company, appearing in several westerns and in nearly a dozen Chaplin comedies. Pratt had been a heavy at Kalem. Fay, Coleman and Adams had been members of Lloyd and White's Sunshine team. Mayo, a former New York stage actor, was struggling for six years to find steady employment in Hollywood. Then, one day, he was working as a sales clerk in a clothing store and Lloyd walked into the door to buy a shirt. The story, as reported in *Photoplay* magazine, was that Lloyd was so impressed with this well-spoken, energetic man selling him a shirt that he offered him a job on the spot.[6]

The program of Educational's forthcoming season, which represented their first year of general release, included four comedy series. Astra's series was named the *Mermaid Comedies*. White explained:

> I went to Balboa [Beach] and made a picture about bathing beauties. New York chose to call the entire series *Mermaids*. They didn't ask me; they just went ahead and made the main title *Mermaid Comedy*.[7]

A second series was produced by a pioneer comedymaker, Al Christie. The other series, less distinguished, were the *Chester Comedies* and *Torchy Comedies*. Lloyd's first *Mermaid* vehicle was *Duck Inn*, a fast-paced comedy principally set at a hunting lodge. Lloyd enjoyed pun titles. "Duck Inn" was the name of the lodge in the story; it also referred to the opening scene wherein the lead character repeatedly ducks indoors to avoid an erratic rainstorm. This established a precedent. Lloyd's comedy *Waiting* would mainly concern Lloyd waiting on tables at a restaurant, but would open with Lloyd anxiously awaiting the arrival of a date. *Framed* would be about Lloyd being falsely incriminated by a band of thieves, but would first focus on Lloyd patronizing a photography studio. *Hooked* would begin with Lloyd fishing, but would climax with a dockside lunch wagon inadvertently becoming fastened to the side of a steamship.

For the script to *Duck Inn*, Lloyd revamped proven material, including a popular Sunshine sequence in which he had battled a squirting duck. He was determined to combine slapstick, fast action and unusual escapades with a more natural humor. He wanted to create a hybrid that would not support a pie fight, a chorus of bathing beauties, or meaningless gags.

At this time, Lloyd admitted that he was not devoted to story lines. He professed that a plot, which did not corroborate with fast action, hindered the creation of an ideal comedy; "[There should be] just enough of a story to hold interest.... There must be a constant variety of events, for the development of a single line of story will become tiresome."[8]

The story of *Duck Inn*, which varied the plot of *Roaring and Wedding Bells*, echoed old stories like "Jason and the Argonauts." To win parental consent to wed his sweetheart, Lloyd must set forth on a quest for a rare and elusive bird.

Lloyd explained, "The story itself is simple enough, but there are so many variations that the audience is kept guessing—and laughing. I believe that the average person, after seeing *Duck Inn*, will say that every portion of it is part of the story, yet analyze it and you'll find it is not. But it brings laugh after laugh, and every event is the logical development of another. I would call *Duck Inn* a splendid example of possible nonsense."[9]

Pratt directed *Duck Inn* and Monte Banks and Marvel Rea acted as Lloyd's main support. Banks, a guest player, was a diminutive comic who would later gain some popularity. Rea, a twenty-year-old local girl, had been the female lead of *A Fresh Start*. During a prior period, she had worked at Sennett and Sunshine. In costuming himself for his new film, Lloyd buried his feet into a pair of scuffed, misshapen slapshoes and affixed to his head a plain gold cap.

Lloyd continued to develop the serious character evident in *A Waiter's Wasted Life*. He acted solemn in depicting a hapless but enduring hero. Ads referred to Lloyd as "that versatile comedian with a sad face" and "the plump comedian with the wan smile." Eddie Cantor would observe a similar style in Laurel and Hardy. Cantor remarked that Laurel and Hardy acted as if they were performing in *Macbeth* or *Hamlet*.[10] Tragedy held a particular attraction for Lloyd and succeeded in activating his creative germ. In part, he remained the serious actor of the Hackett troupe. Director Pratt enjoyed working with Lloyd. He said that Lloyd was "always willing to give to the limit of his resources."[11]

Overall, the *Mermaid* crew was surprised by their employers' stringent standards and practices. In particular, Pratt was impressed that Lloyd and White would willingly reshoot flawed scenes.[12] Lloyd, who was in search of perfection, routinely studied his company's footage and reshot or discarded the parts that failed to satisfy him. As they shot an extraordinary amount of footage, the young producers could easily jettison weaker scenes.

Lloyd developed a method of working. He said:

> Comedy situations are invented by the director, star and by a crew of "gag men" on the staff at the studio. These gags are submitted to star and director, and if they meet with their approval, they are passed on to the mechanical and technical staff of the studio.
>
> Although 2,000 feet of film is used in the finished comedy, many times that footage is used in making the picture. "Gags" which look funny — on paper — are found to be dull and lifeless on screen and must be rejected; the difficulty of photographing other funny bits prevents them from coming up to expectations and they are also rejected.
>
> When the picture is finished, it is gone over with careful scrutiny by a staff composed of director, star and others. After eliminations, substitutions and many changes, the picture is at least ready for the public, and then we know whether or not we have made a successful comedy.[13]

According to a pressbook item, Educational intended to make the name "Mermaid" as popular as Ivory Soap. Inaugurating a flash publicity campaign, they marketed the series with the line: "Mermaids for Merriment."

A Fresh Start was a rousing success. In late July, Educational released ads promising that *Duck Inn* would "renew the roars of *A Fresh Start*." Another ad featured Lloyd cautiously projecting his head and rifle through a clump of shrubbery. The headline read "Loaded with Laughs."

Lloyd had, with the debut of the *Mermaid* series, set forth on a real quest.

A Pause for Analysis II

Walter Kerr wrote, "[Hamilton] worked out a costume and a cast of mind that owed nothing to anyone else."[14] Kerr defined this character as "a plumpish man with dainty fingers, a waddle for a walk, and a pancake hat set horizontally on the prim, doughy moon of his face."[15]

Lloyd's screen character, though at times eccentric, was endearing. He was an everyman, providing areas of identification for a wide audience, but he still had his own individual nature and point of view.

An explanation for Lloyd's comedy can come with an exploration of Lloyd's life. The actor created comedy of depth and distinction because his comedy had real-life parallels. Ultimately, he produced an exaggerated version of himself. Lloyd stated, "The successful comedy character depends largely on psychology — I must say the psychology of the comedy star himself."[16] Lloyd explained, on another occasion, that his manner of taste, as much as it determined how he dressed and what he ate, had determined the aspects of his screen character. A person's taste, he said, was something that develops from a person's heredity, environment and associations.[17]

Who was this character so comparable with Lloyd's actual personality? Above all else, this comic alter ego was a faintly effeminate, overgrown boy. Early on, he resembled a timid child whose mother had sent him out to play. His cute and corpulent face was cherubic; his hair was neatly combed; and he behaved as if being obedient to the motherly instruction "Be a good boy." This man of uncommon size demonstrating boyish behavior created an amusing picture. Harold Lloyd and Roscoe Arbuckle had exhibited a natural boyishness, but neither comic had ever realized the "man-child" as purposefully and vividly as Lloyd Hamilton did.

Evidently, it had been faulty rearing that had prevented this character from maturing into a responsible adult. He looked to have been suppressed and intimidated in his upbringing. Even as an adult, he was not free of his mother's control. This is particularly evident in *A Homemade Man*. A small, gray-haired woman leads Lloyd into an establishment. While Lloyd tranquilly stands at her side, she implores the owner to give her "little boy" a job. This mother figure is a visible force in many of his films.

With his father being distant and hostile, the character lacked a masculine influence. He possessed a gentle and sensitive nature. His style inspired some critics to define Lloyd as "sissyish." In leaving home, the lad would enter a world filled with harm and adversity. This world was absurd and unpredictable. It was a pirate steamer with a vicious captain and mutineers. It was a power plant besieged by union agitators and terrorized by a murderous villain. It was a cannibal island, a Wild West town, a zany immigration center. It was big, mad cities modeled after New York, San Francisco and Los Angeles. In several films, including *Extra! Extra! Extra!*, *Uneasy Feet*, *Crushed* and *The Movies*, the young man became lost on a merciless urban sprawl. Lloyd conceived much of his comedy by forcing a timid, delicate and methodical lad into the middle of a chaotic, fast-paced and hostile environment. It was an engaging conflict model. Introverted individual vs. extroverted society. Lloyd was an oversized babe toddling through a wild forest.

Many vehicles revolved around Lloyd being propelled into adulthood. This step was represented by Lloyd finding a job, leaving home, seeking to marry or, as in *No Luck*, simply smoking his first cigar. Whether prepared for it or not, the young man advanced from one stage of life to another. It was as if he was being carried on an incessantly moving conveyor belt. In *April Fool*, Lloyd was abruptly snatched out of adolescence by a derrick, which dumped him into the hold of a global steamer. In *Dynamite*, Lloyd was called upon to leave behind a placid life and succeed his deceased father as a power plant chief. In *Moonshine*, he came of age to join his family's moonshine trade. In *The Simp* and *Going East*, Lloyd faced a more forceful impetus. His father, frustrated with his son's unmanliness, became furious and literally kicked his boy out of their home.

Lloyd, now an adult, commenced with his dreams, ambition and faithful dog to make something of himself in the world. These films were Lehrman's comedies of fear and disorder enhanced by Lloyd's performances, which embodied a width of emotion. Strong characterization brought the comedies more than the simple human features of dread, lust and confusion. Lloyd's subdued performances tended to reveal intimate feelings and observations. He provided a beating heart at the center of the comical chaos.

Beneath the baby face, checkered cap and other superficies, Lloyd became Protestantism's definitive mime. His strict religious instruction was reflected vividly in his cinematic alter ego, who was sober, modest, prudent, industrious, and solitary. His performances, in all their subtlety, showed a Puritan austerity and Protestant thrift.

Lloyd downplayed his acting while everything else around him was exaggerated. *Dynamite* had plenty of rapid action and huge explosions, but Lloyd was engaged in small-scale occupations. At his introduction, he was patiently dropping flies into a brook so as to coax fish to come within clubbing distance. This fishing technique evolved into a laughable pantomime routine. Not many comics could take such a simple idea and turn it, as Lloyd did, into classic comedy. Stan Laurel, in the role of a caveman, would recreate the routine a few years later. Director Sergio Leone, a Laurel and Hardy fan, resurrected the routine for a spaghetti western nearly a half-century later. This time, Terence Hill employs the fishing technique to demonstrate his lightning speed as a gunfighter.

Leonard Maltin has observed, "The gags and stories in a Hamilton short might be broad and slapsticky, but Hamilton himself was delicate and subtle. He communicated with his audiences through 'camera looks' and quiet gestures that made the incident on screen that much funnier." [18]

Lloyd could draw human comedy from improbable situations. Donning a coat, he fails to notice that he has not completely removed the coat from a stand. Consequently, the entire rack strolls with him as he walks down the street.

A. Edward Sutherland, a veteran comedy director, found Lloyd to be "terribly funny" and thought he was one of the great movie comedians.[19] He was particularly enchanted by the wacky bent of Lloyd's comedy: "He had a terribly strange approach to things. For example, he had a picture called *The Rainmaker*, where he would come out and it would start to rain and he'd go back and get his umbrella, and it would stop raining. There, he made God the heavy.... [He] would do completely off-balance things. He had a routine where there were three clams, and they were all open, until he started to eat one, and that one would close.... This wonderful, sad, never-growing-up, Peter Pan face he had. He was just wonderful."[20]

Another big fan of Lloyd's was Edward Dryhurst, who knew Lloyd while working as a gagwriter with Hal Roach in the 1920s. Dryhurst had a long career writing, producing, directing and composing music for British features, but Lloyd Hamilton was one person he remembered fondly after all his years in the business. Dryhurst realized that the off-center comedy in Lloyd's films came very much out of Lloyd's own personal sense of humor. He remembered, with particular amusement, being in Lloyd's bedroom and seeing a signed portrait of the comic displayed with the message "To myself for no reason at all." This is probably the reason that those people who knew him off-screen found him to be even more funny and charming than the fans of his movies. "I loved him," said Dryhurst.[21]

With the *Mermaid* series, Lloyd took a significant step in the development of a comical myth. He knew that, by familiarizing the public with a single character, he would strengthen his comedy. He explained, "We laugh at a person because we can understand his nature and what the predicament means to him."[22] He offered as proof, "Situations that are screamingly funny with a certain performer are without a single laugh when performed by another."[23]

Once fully developed, the character determined Lloyd's material. Woody Allen has said, "Jokes become a vehicle for a person to display a personality or attitude."[24] With Lloyd, much of his comedy was derived from his characterization. It was important to Lloyd that the audience recognize and understand his character. "Just as sympathy must be felt for a dramatic or emotional star," he said, "so must understanding be felt towards a comedy performer."[25]

On screen, Lloyd had great difficulty in resolving problems. It was not that he wasn't intelligent. He was incompetent because he was unable to deal well with anxiety. Lloyd said that his character was so sensitive that he became overwhelmed with embarrassment whenever he made a mistake. It was out of fear of failure that he was inclined to overdo. He would try so hard and act so persistently in performing a task that he would fail and, perhaps, exacerbate a problem. For example, he managed to open a grocer's cider barrel at the expense of the cider. Lloyd described his character, plainly, as "the big good-natured person who is always striving to be helpful — and who is always getting it wrong."[26] Appropriately, the working title for one of his comedies was *Distress*.

In the silent film era, the average, brash, cocky comedian had no shame and would dare any situation for a laugh. But this didn't at all describe Lloyd, who got laughs playing a timid, socially awkward character often forced into embarrassing situations. Today, the brash comedian remains dominant in movies due to comedians like Will Ferrell, Jack Black, Vince Vaughn, and Jim Carrey. The one modern comedian who remains a staunch advocate of Lloyd's comedy of embarrassment is Ben Stiller, who has perfected a socially awkward and easily embarrassed persona in *There's Something About Mary* and *Meet the Parents*.

Lloyd, in this way, also reminds me of three other comedians, Woody Allen, Jerry Lewis and Harold Lloyd. The following episodes help to establish the connection:

1. Woody Allen, trying so hard to act nonchalant with a date, accidentally spills a drink and breaks a glass.
2. Jerry Lewis, as a hospital orderly, maddens a head nurse with his excessive efforts. Overwhelmed, the nurse bellows: "*Don't Try So Hard!*" Lewis anxiously responds: "I'll try hard not to try so hard."
3. Harold Lloyd gets his hand caught in a vase as a pretty lady approaches him. Harold, smiling awkwardly, hides his hand behind his back. He tries to sustain a conversation while desperately trying to shake the vase loose.

These comics transformed anxieties into absurdities. A shallow, studio-packaged version of the pathetic, diffident blunderer would be common in the forties, a time when the leading comics included Danny Kaye, Lou Costello and Red Skelton.

Jacques Tati, a French comedian who made his feature film debut in 1949, was closer in nature to Lloyd's "poor boy" character. Tati's characters mean well but their clumsiness and social ineptitude invariably get them into trouble.

Tati, like Lloyd, did not like to put great emphasis on plot. Tati's *Jour de fête*, or *The Big Day*, is about a postman who repeatedly interrupts his duties to help out local residents. He helps a cross-eyed carnival worker pound a stake. He directs laborers setting up a flagpole. He joins a group of farmers raking hay. He goes to great lengths to help these people but he tends to bungle the job and create mayhem instead. Tati was able to successfully extend this simple plot, very similar to the plot Lloyd used in *Good Morning*, for a span of 79 minutes. Tati wasn't afraid to construct a feature-length comedy without plot restrictions, contrary to the conventions established in the early days of feature comedies. It was these same conventions which were to later prove a dire challenge for Lloyd.

Authority figures strongly affected a Lloyd character, simultaneously drawing and frightening him. Lloyd, seeking parental approval, was trusting and obedient to any authoritative person who treated him nicely. He would work extremely hard to please these people. He eagerly followed the instructions of a friendly man who, unbeknownst to him, was burglarizing his parents' home.

Lloyd's screen character was a genteel person. As a situation overwhelmed him, he tried his best to maintain the appearance of dignity. Lloyd explained that he was playing "a shabby gentleman who keeps the semblance of immaculate respectability through all poverty and the adversity of his experiences."[27]

Lloyd made much of small matters. During *Mermaid*'s first season, a critic for *Moving*

Picture World described Lloyd as "the clown who takes infinite pains to solve what is obviously simple."

Stemming from Lloyd's unsparing efforts was "building," a remarkable comedy invention introduced as early as *Duck Inn*. Building involved drawing a succession of gags, one funnier than the last, from a simple, everyday problem: removing a firmly set cork from a bottle; retrieving a windblown cap; catching a fish; donning a life preserver; tying a shoelace on a busy city street; parking a car; swatting a fly. Lloyd aimed for the loudest laugh with a big, climactic gag, what he called "the payoff." He explained, "[The audience] does not want to be simply led to a big laugh, they must be chuckling all the time."[28]

Lloyd, a sad and lonely clown, retained a moving essence in his subdued countenance. This was different from the blank look of Ben Turpin, which Walter Kerr called "the permanently stunned expression of a haddock on ice."[29] Lloyd's expression, which was dubbed "his lost hope look" and "baby stare," was more meaningful than the expression Turpin employed to comically off-set silly situations. Lloyd conveyed his deepest self through widened eyes, which radiated innocence, vulnerability, tenderness, melancholy and wistfulness. By humanly reacting to his dilemmas, he provided his comedy with a warmth beyond his character's never-ending calculations and blunders.

To a great extent, Lloyd was an exponent of reaction comedy, which operated under the premise that a comedy situation could be made much funnier by a character's particular reaction to it. This distinction established Lloyd as a precursor of Laurel and Hardy, who took reaction comedy to its highest levels. Norman Taurog, one of his directors, would say of Lloyd: "He was a funny man. He didn't have to do terrifically broad gags — just a look, and the way he would react."[30]

Once, in a supermarket, I observed a man trying to extract a wire basket from stack of wire baskets. He attempted to rattle the basket loose from the others. He pulled the handle to the right and to the left. Then he angrily brought his foot into play. Despite this exertion, the basket did not come free. As he deliberated over what to try next, the man became aware that the eyes of other shoppers were fixed upon him. The man became so embarrassed that he quickly surrendered the cause and walked away. For me, the scene was made engaging by the many emotions that the man had expressed during this simple plight. That was what Lloyd Hamilton was all about.

Lloyd had translated his silent character into purely physical terms. The "quiet gestures" to which Maltin has referred were a distinct reflection of Lloyd's nature. They mirrored the performer's exactness, delicateness and timidity. It was so as not to risk invading another's space that Lloyd would extend his fingers within limited confines. And then it was in fearing harm that he would promptly retract his fingers whenever a person revealed anger.

Calculating to impress, Lloyd had developed his ludicrous walk into a trademark feature. He realized that, in the silent comic's wholly visual world, such a distinct physical mannerism would be beneficial. The walk was given various labels. It was labeled the "ducklike waddle" and "sissy walk." Taurog called it "the walk of a man wearing tight underwear."[31] A publicist termed the walk the "hip-knee-ankle walk," a clinical name indicating the successive body parts that were employed. Most fans simply knew the gait as his funny walk.

With his funny walk and all, Lloyd Hamilton portrayed one of the most unique and imposing characters of screen comedy.

11

Lloyd on His Own

Duck Inn was a groundbreaker. The comedy intrigued critics, who praised Lloyd for his effective characterization and deftness of mimicry, and it drew a large audience. Due to *A Fresh Start* and *Duck Inn*, the *Mermaid* series secured a prominent place in theatre programs within its first two months.

All in all, *Duck Inn* introduced a fresh and strong force into the comedy field. *One Week*, a two-reel comedy released weeks later, introduced a serious rival: Buster Keaton. Competition between these two men would become evident and Keaton would still remember it many years later.

The contrast between Lloyd's *Mermaid* character and "Ham" was so great that it baffled theatergoers. Educational reported that, following the release of *Duck Inn*, people of nineteen countries inquired if this was the same Lloyd Hamilton who had starred in the Kalem one-reelers. After Educational informed the press that their comic had in fact been half of the "Ham and Bud" team, a *Motion Picture News* critic referred to *Mermaid*'s extraordinary principal as "Lloyd 'Bud' Hamilton."

Lloyd followed his auspicious *Mermaid* debut with *Dynamite*, a comedy on which he was billed as: LLOYD HAMILTON Your old friend "Ham."

Dynamite was an even bigger success than *Duck Inn*, entertaining audiences at such major theaters as New York's Strand and Detroit's Majestic.

An unexpected incident disrupted the production of Lloyd's third *Mermaid* vehicle, *The Simp*.[1] In the script, Lloyd enters his home at a late hour. He tries hard not to wake his parents but the family cat, who persistently meows, threatens to betray his arrival. During the filming, the cat became frightened. She jumped across Lloyd's shoulders, dug her claws into the comic's neck, and then froze in place. The terrified animal had to be carefully pried loose. The irony couldn't have been lost on Lloyd, who had survived Stecker's lions only to fall victim to a common house cat.

Jack White wasn't receptive when Bud Duncan approached him for work. White explained: "When Bud was looking for a job at my studio, Lloyd said, 'If you hire this guy, I won't work for you.' We never did hire Bud. He used to hang around my back door, day after day, trying to buttonhole me for a job. I walked past him all the time. I felt sorry for him, but I knew Lloyd wouldn't work with him."[2]

In the fall of 1920, Lloyd hired Charley Chase as his director. Chase, like Lloyd, was a hard worker. He was hailed by his peers as one of the brightest writers and reputed to produce work of incomparable polish and precision.

Hamilton woos the actress Beatrice Monson in *Moonshine* (1920) (courtesy of Cole Johnson — Slapstick Archive).

Lloyd and Chase became drinking buddies. This remained a way for Lloyd to unwind from a hard day's work. But it wasn't that he and Chase didn't have qualms about drinking. Chase's daughter said that, on a $100 bet, the two friends competed to see who could refrain from drinking for the longest period. After a week, Lloyd appeared at Chase's front porch. Casually relinquishing a $100 bill, he said, "Let's go have a drink."³

Lloyd and Chase combined forces on two films, *April Fool* and *Moonshine*. *April Fool*, a farcical sea-adventure, was reminiscent of Lloyd's unfinished Sunshine comedy. *Moonshine*, like *A Twilight Baby*, concerned the Volstead Act. In late 1919, when ratification of the Volstead Act initiated Prohibition, the Athletic Club transformed into a speakeasy under an altered name, the Hollywood Athletic Club.

Chase did no more films with Lloyd. Instead, he accepted a lucrative offer to join the Hal Roach studio, beginning an association that would last fifteen years. Chase, who would return to acting, would become one of Roach's most popular stars.

Chase admitted using Lloyd as his comic model. This was confirmed by comic Billy Gilbert, who was one of Chase's closest friends. Gilbert said:

> I remember one theory he had — he said all comedians should pick another comedian whom they admired, one who was as different physically as possible from themselves and play each scene as they thought he would play it. His model was "Ham" Hamilton. He said that when other people saw the end results they could see no resemblance, that he couldn't even see it

himself because it came out different. But when he played a scene he always thought, "How would Ham play this?"[4]

Chase, like Lloyd, created much of his comedy by placing his character at the center of an embarrassing situation. He also, on many occasions, wore a checkered cap.

Another one of Lloyd's drinking buddies was a gag man named Walter Morosco. Morosco became a source of friction between Lloyd and White. White said, "Lloyd and Walter were both heavy drinkers and it was starting to affect us. Lloyd was late for work and wasn't up to par, so I let Morosco go."[5]

At this time, Lloyd and Ethel were living in Venice, a seaside resort district in West Los Angeles. Its major attraction was an amusement pier, which included rides, game booths and an aquarium. A tourist could enjoy a scenic ride on a miniature railroad or see the town by riding a gondola through miles of canals. The resort's tax revenue was so strongly dependent on the income of bar owners that Venice became the one community to defy Prohibition laws. In 1920, Venice was the official party capital of Los Angeles. Chaplin frequently attended parties at the Waldorf Hotel, which was just off the beach, and Keaton and Arbuckle threw lavish parties every Saturday night at the Sunset Inn on Ocean Avenue. Actress Viola Dana, who was a guest at many of the Arbuckle-Keaton parties, said, "Venice was

Hamilton, as an immigrant, encounters hostile officials at Ellis Island in *The Greenhorn* (1921). The other actors are unidentified (courtesy of the family of Lloyd Hamilton).

Hamilton receives a medical examination from a pretty nurse played by Kathleen Myers in *The Greenhorn* (1921) (courtesy of the family of Lloyd Hamilton).

what we called a 'wet' town. You could drink there, and many of us got drunk there. A lot of cash flowed across the counter."[6] Lloyd was hunkered down in the middle of the action.

During his nightly outings, Lloyd became close friends with Lew Cody, a handsome and roguish leading man notorious in Hollywood for his womanizing and public exhibitions of drunkenness. Jeanine Basinger, a professor of film studies, described Cody as "a heavy-drinking disaster of a man."[7] Cody's bad reputation developed, at first, from the determined efforts of the actor's very own publicists. It was, in this regard, about marketing an image. The playboy characters that Cody portrayed in movies like *Don't Change Your Husband* and *The Butterfly Man* made their way through high society circles drinking and philandering. The studios saw it as a way to sell tickets to Cody movies to promote Cody as a real-life "he-vamp."[8] In public, Cody presented himself in every way to encourage this reputation. He played the part down to the smallest of details. In acting like an ostentatious playboy, he made a point to carry his cigarettes in a silver case and smoke them in an ivory holder. It was only a matter of time before the line blurred and the image and the man got jumbled up together. Legend grew about the actor's wild escapades. The most famous story of Cody had him getting drunk at a party and proposing marriage to Mabel Normand, to whom he had made advances only hours earlier. Normand, who was also drunk, accepted, the proposal and eloped with Cody the same night. Cody was reportedly so drunk while filling out the marriage license that, when it came to writing in his family history, he was unable to remember his mother's name.[9] Normand later indicated in her diaries that, on at least one occasion, Cody got "terribly drunk" and "raised hell."[10] Normand described Cody coming home in a drunken rage, smashing in a window and threatening to break a servant's neck.

Lloyd was a regular visitor at Cody's mansion, where guests were welcomed inside a special party room and instructed to memorialize their presence by writing their names on the door. Cody, more than getting Lloyd to put his name on his door, found a supporting role for his comedian friend in his latest feature, *Occasionally Yours*.

Lloyd was, in general, having fun and spending lots of money. It was while on location in San Pedro, filming waterfront scenes for *April Fool*, that Lloyd accepted delivery of a Dorris sports car. Lloyd, who had a passion for shiny new sports cars, got into the habit of buying a new sports car every couple of years.

Lloyd's final comedy of the season, *The Greenhorn*, was written and directed by Chuck Reisner, who was on loan from Chaplin (for whom he was employed as associate director). Reisner, who was reputed to be a human gag encyclopedia, was a vital member of Chaplin's team. He was available to direct *The Greenhorn* as, during this period, Chaplin was infrequently in production. *The Greenhorn*, like Chaplin's *The Immigrant*, presented the experiences of a foreigner entering the United States.

By now, the partnership of Hamilton and White was in jeopardy. Lloyd said that the two were so serious about their work that they often got into rows. He said that they were recently having lunch when a discussion about a scene got so heated that a waiter came over to break them up.[11]

White bitterly recalled:

> We weren't getting along too well, so I advised him [Lloyd] to hire outside directors.... He didn't mind. He had buddies like Chuck Reisner that were very anxious to direct him, now that he was a "comer." I came on the set and they were doing very well. Hamilton sat in the director's chair like he was directing.[12]

Lloyd's opening season of *Mermaid* releases had been a succession of hits. The series, which had impressed viewers with outlandish, elaborate and clever gags, had lifted Lloyd high above the rank and file. It had ensured him continued success and recognition as a unique and valuable personality.

Of late, Roscoe Arbuckle had become the first clown to cross alone into the domain of feature films. Arbuckle, who was contracted to Paramount, had starred in several five-reel comedies since the preceding fall. Also, Buster Keaton had starred in Metro's *The Saphead*, a seven-reel adaptation of a successful Broadway play. *The Saphead* did not mark Keaton's emergence as a feature star. The script was inappropriate, bridling the comic with a tame role ill-suited to his special talents. Keaton asked his producer, Joseph Schenck, to allow him to continue making features, "He wouldn't agree," said the actor. "Schenck insisted that I return to the two-reel field. I couldn't convince him that comedy features were the coming thing. If I'd won that argument, it could have made a big difference in my career. Neither Chaplin or [Harold] Lloyd were making features at that time, and I would have had a headstart on both of them."[13]

Yes, a race was on.

In February, 1921, Chaplin released a six-reel feature called *The Kid*, the First National film that he had been preparing while *A Twilight Baby* was in production. *The Kid* was Chap-

This still, dated 1921, shows Hamilton still developing his make-up and costume design. He has added to his existing outfit — striped shirt, gray vest, checkered Windsor tie — a checkered cap (courtesy of the family of Lloyd Hamilton).

lin's greatest triumph to date. In the film, he performed opposite a precocious child named Jackie Coogan. Decades later, Keaton would express envy and regret regarding this "kid." Coogan's father, who was a comic, had worked with Keaton in 1919. Little Jackie, who had routinely followed his father to the studio, would entertain Keaton and others in between scenes. Keaton lamented that he did not recognize the boy's potential.

In March, 1921, the formal presentation of a new contract brought Messrs. White and Hamilton to New York City. Lloyd and White, who had severed their ties with Astra, were in the midst of establishing Hamilton-White Comedies, Inc. According to the new arrangement, the second *Mermaid* series would number twenty entries: six comedies produced by Lloyd's crew and starring Lloyd; six comedies produced by White's crew and starring Lige Conley; and eight comedies produced by Astra and starring Jimmie Adams. Soon, the collapse of Astra would end plans for Adams' series.

In New York, Lloyd attended entertainment celebrations that E.W. Hammons held in the star's honor. Lloyd surprised fellow celebrants by sitting quietly during the entire evening.[14] As kudos were heaped upon him, he reacted modestly. Some guests said that they found it hard to believe he was a comedian. Lloyd, by all accounts, maintained this divided personality. He was a fun guy when he walked around the set in costume. He was a fun guy when he was out on the town drinking with close friends. But he was serious in the privacy of his home and shy and subdued at business events.

Lloyd may have been quiet at Hammons' party, but he was visibly stirred by White's tour of the city. The points of interest were largely situated within the confines of White's old boyhood turf, but White ended up taking him all over town. Lloyd found himself intrigued and charmed by the great metropolis. Lloyd and White seriously considered opening their new company in New York. This was a radical notion considering that, by then, the American film industry was almost entirely based on the West Coast. By their return to Los Angeles, the pair had dropped this plan as impractical.

Lehrman's series had fallen from the high mark set by *A Twilight Baby*. Directly after losing Lloyd and White, Lehrman hired Charles Conklin (a.k.a. Heinie Conklin) and Al Ray as his featured comics. Conklin and Ray had very different styles. Conklin, a farcical comic who had performed many supporting roles at Sennett, wore heavy eyebrow lining and an upside-down Kaiser Wilheim moustache. Ray, who had acted in both comedies and dramas at Fox, looked and acted relatively normal. Lehrman might have thought that he could use Ray to transition to a more reserved style and move into the feature film market. Ray and Conklin, however, were anything but reserved in their first Lehrman Comedy, *A Kick in the High Life*. As rival suitors, the comedians erupt in a jealous rage and attack each other with clubs, plates, chairs and dynamite. The outcome of their battle is the complete and utter demolition of their sweetheart's bungalow.

Lehrman's next comedy, *Wet and Warmer*, was even more violent. A hotel and bathing establishment was filled with lively and eccentric characters, whose lives are threatened when the building catches fire. People who have seen the film at the festivals tend to remark on the realism of the fire. Did Mr. Suicide really burn down the set? Billie Ritchie makes a brief appearance as a hotel guest who remains sound asleep while his bed goes up in flames. This proved to be Ritchie's last appearance on screen. The Lehrman perennial died as the result of stomach cancer on July 6, 1921.

After his latest comedies failed at the box office, Lehrman persuaded Lloyd to lend his drawing power to a new comedy, *A Game Lady*. The shooting was arranged to coincide with the Hamilton-White company's hiatus. *A Game Lady*, concerning yet another comic duck hunt, contained several proven laugh-getters, including Lloyd's all-out effort to shoot a duck that can squirt a powerful and prolonged stream of water. On the completion of this production, Lehrman's grand picture plant was permanently closed.

Before the start of the new season, the Hamilton-White company moved. White explained, "Hammons came out to visit. When he saw the facilities we were working in, he didn't like them. We left Astra studio and rented D.W. Griffith's Fine Arts studio at Sunset and Hillhurst."[15]

Lloyd sought a permanent leading lady for the new season, settling on lovely 21-year-

Hamilton performs with future wife Irene Dalton in *The Vagrant* (1921) (courtesy of Cole Johnson — Slapstick Archive.)

old Irene Dalton. Irene was the younger sister of Dorothy Dalton, a popular screen actress who had been briefly married to Lloyd's friend Lew Cody. Dalton left a job as a stenographer in Chicago and was almost immediately hired by comedy producer Al Christie for a starring role in his *Vanity* series. She had made a number of comedies for Christie when she accepted the role of Lloyd's leading lady.

Mermaid opened the second season with *Robinson Crusoe, Ltd.* This spoof, directed by White required the Hamilton-White company to build a cannibal village in Malibu. *Robinson Crusoe, Ltd.* was the sum of Lloyd's comedymaking know-how. The comedian produced polished versions of his best routines, blending them together in one grand confection. At the same time, his character had become solid enough to pull together the various parts. The result was Lloyd's biggest box office success to date. Cross-breeding broad comedy with laughable observations of human nature, the film allowed critics to easily draw comparisons between Lloyd and Chaplin.

White's comments on his partner's triumph are utterly sour and somewhat improbable:

> After we moved to the Fine Arts studio, the home office asked me to direct Hamilton. They weren't satisfied with what they were getting. Hamilton and I worked out a story called *Robinson Crusoe, Ltd.*, which saved Hamilton's ass. We happened to be lucky; we had a goody, but that was it. We split right after the picture was made.... [Hamilton] got cocky

again and didn't want to work with me. I said to myself, "He can jump in the lake," and I never made any more pictures with him.[16]

Early in his second *Mermaid* season, Lloyd added a few embellishments to his screen uniform: An undersized checkered cap and a matching necktie were adopted as prominent elements. Magazine writers called Lloyd's neckwear a Windsor-knot necktie, but that did not fully describe this flamboyant tie with the floppy wings, the streaming tails, the checkered design pattern, and the big fat knot in the middle. It was the type of necktie to be worn by a clown with Victorian tastes. Lloyd's checkered cap quickly became, as one writer called it, the dominant "Hamiltonian symbol."[17]

Lloyd's following film *The Vagrant*, filled with non-stop, off-the-wall gags, used material from the "Ham" comedy *A Flyer in Flapjacks*, but also included many new ideas inspired by Lloyd's recent visit to New York City. The Hamilton-White company erected for the film an elaborate set resembling Manhattan's East Side tenement district. The mock-up covered more than an acre of ground. Tom Wilson played a vigilant and omnipresent cop, much as he had in *The Kid*. Thirty-two-sheet ads posted outside of major theatres launched a successful run for *The Vagrant*.

Hamilton and Keaton, as the leaders of the two-reel comedy pack, had become head-to-head competitors. Both men controlled their creative destiny, a privilege that loosed those eternal students inhabiting their psyches. Keaton, as described by Walter Kerr, was "compulsively analytical."[18] Lloyd was reputedly one of the film industry's most serious and hardworking craftsmen. His intense regard for his work inspired admiration and dedication in many of his colleagues. His third comedy of the season, *The Advisor*, allowed the comic to poke fun at an old family livelihood: the legal profession. The *Motion Picture News* critic submitted a favorable review in which he good-naturedly stated, "It hasn't any trick ducks in it, for which we are thankful."

Lloyd's next comedy *Rolling Stones* in which Lloyd was paired with child actor Bobby DeVilbiss, bore somewhat of a resemblance to Chaplin's *The Kid*. Lloyd, who revealed a tenderness and sympathetic nature, was often compared by critics to Chaplin. These comparisons led Lloyd and Mayo to believe the comedian would have similar appeal being matched up with a child. *Rolling Stones* again cast Lloyd as a tramp, only now the tramp is the loving guardian of a seven-year-old brother. The film focused on Lloyd working with DeVilbiss to perpetuate audaciously absurd scams to get a meal at a cafeteria and help a pretty young lady sell hats. This was much like Chaplin's use of Jackie Coogan in a scam to sell windows. *The Kid* promised "a smile, and perhaps a tear," but *Rolling Stones* remained sob-free in its pursuit of laughs.

DeVilbiss was Lloyd's first knee-high co-star since Bud Duncan, but he was certainly not the last. *Rolling Stones* in fact started a trend for Lloyd. In the coming years, the comedian shared scenes with a number of child actors — Coy Watson in *No Luck*, Ben Alexander in *A Self-Made Failure*, Josephine Adair in *The Educator*, and Douglas Scott Lloyd in *Peaceful Alley*. He interacted with groups of children in *The Vagrant, Going East, Here Comes Charlie*, and *Listen Children*. Publicity items emphasized that the comedy star got along ideally with children. He was described patiently talking with children in between scenes, breaking open a watermelon for a young group of extras, and having candy purchased for schoolchildren who had gathered to watch him film exterior scenes. Exhibitors reported that their preadolescent patrons responded well to the comedian's childishly awkward antics and this certainly gave Lloyd a reason to foster relations with the younger crowd.

As his peers' screen activities influenced him, Lloyd was also influenced by his brothers' off-screen activities.

In its passion to be entertained, the American public had violently showered the film industry with coins. Within a few years, this influx of cash transformed Hollywood into a lavish community. In most cases, the recipients of this wealth became overjoyed and celebrated their success with extravagant parties. Roscoe Arbuckle, a prominent figure on the party scene, experienced a harsh reversal of fortune while hosting a holiday party in San Francisco. It was September, 1921, and Arbuckle had been charged with murder. The alleged murder victim, a 30-year-old actress, was Lloyd's onetime leading lady Virginia Rappe.

According to Arbuckle, Rappe had approached him in a hotel suite to obtain money for an abortion. Rappe startled Arbuckle when, unexpectedly, she burst out in screams and tore at her clothing. Several people attended to her, but nothing they did helped. Rappe, as it was later determined, died when her bladder burst. Prosecutors claimed that Rappe's bladder was damaged when Arbuckle lay on top of her during a sexual assault. The defense set out to establish that Rappe's bladder had been inflamed for years and, due to this chronic cystitis, the bladder had spontaneously ruptured. Musty medical records were brought forth. In court, White produced the outtake from *A Twilight Baby*. The footage showed Rappe, in the process of riding a bicycle, grasping her side and looking to be in obvious pain.

News of Rappe's death plunged the motion picture colony into a widespread and destructive scandal.

Hamilton tries to escape from Ellis Island in an expert disguise. *The Greenhorn* (1921) (courtesy of Cole Johnson — Slapstick Archive).

In retrospect, Jackie Coogan said, "The whole motion picture industry was in that dock with Roscoe. Hollywood front offices decided to go moral. Guys were told to cut down to two or three mistresses."[19]

The motion picture industry was fearful that outside forces would release fierce, uncontrollable watchdogs into their community. Hoping to dissuade such action and maintain control, Hollywood's twelve most powerful producers sought an honorable person to lead a clean-up campaign of the film colony. Their search ended with the selection of Will Hays, a former postmaster general. Hays' appointment was announced in January, 1922. Upon the occasion, Hays proclaimed that he would make Hollywood a wholesome place. The Motion Picture Association of America, which was informally known as the Hays Office, went into operation two months later.

The murder of William Desmond Taylor, a leading director, incited further scandals. Among the discoveries made in the murder investigation was that Taylor had been involved in adultery, sexual perversion, drug trafficking and witchcraft.

Lloyd was spending little time at home. He was more often at the studio or carousing. Whenever he was home, he was buried in the preparation of a new comedy. Ethel demanded a vacation, but Lloyd was avoiding any letup. He feared that, by being absent from the studio, he would severely fall behind in his work.

Hamilton with Irene Dalton in *The Rainmaker* (1922) (courtesy of Robert Arkus).

Lloyd had long alienated himself from his wife. Ethel, resentful of being pushed out, grew irritable and, in early 1922, sued Lloyd for separation. Soon after, the couple abruptly reconciled their differences and Ethel dropped her divorce action.

Lloyd ended his second *Mermaid* series with *The Rainmaker* and *Poor Boy*, films reflecting Lloyd's perpetual pursuit of change and growth. In *The Rainmaker*, Lloyd employed a curious device: To indicate that a gag was forthcoming, he included a close-up wherein he would wink at the camera. These asides, which forestalled the gags, could have conceivably proved a burden.

Critic James W. Dean found it daring for Lloyd to have set much of *Poor Boy* in a church, a setting that other comedymakers saw as sensitive and were careful to avoid. *Poor Boy* exhibited a great lessening of slapstick and more concentration on what Lloyd called "human and serious comedy."[20] In describing this effort, Lloyd said, "There isn't any resort to mechanical tricks to get a laugh."[21] He was seeking to rely on "real humor and real situations to get laughs."[22] This ambition required many alterations in his style and character, but Lloyd was not distressed. He simply stated, "In the course of the various types of comedy I have played, my character has undergone several changes."[23]

Poor Boy clearly exhibited artistic growth to Dean and other critics. Lloyd claimed that he was feeling cramped in the confines of two-reel comedies. He believed that he had progressed to a point where he could endure the responsibilities and challenges of a feature film.

At the outcome of the 1921–22 season, Lloyd established Lloyd Hamilton Corporation. He announced that his company would produce a series of two-reel comedies for Educational and possibly produce longer comedies for First National.

Lloyd's break from White was the source of great resentment. White alleged that Lloyd "didn't keep his word." According to White, Lloyd had agreed that they would negotiate their contracts as a bloc. "Instead of that," White exclaimed, "he talked to Mr. Hammons, got himself what he wanted, and practically ran out on me.... [He] didn't tell me a damn thing about it. When I found out what he had done, I was furious. I said, 'We've been together four years, getting a great deal accomplished, and you sign up without me when you agreed not to.' He was so dumb, or maybe scared...."[24]

When questioned if there was a particular occurrence that effected their split, White responded: "Hardly. There were a lot of things that I've dismissed from my mind because I didn't want to dwell on them at the time, so I've forgotten them; it's like burying something. The main thing I remember is that Hamilton crossed me."[25]

White and Lloyd remained on the same lot. White said that, whenever he saw Lloyd, he would say no more than "Hello, how are you?" The one exception was the time that White rode through the lot in a new customized car and Lloyd stopped him to get a ride.

Lloyd's new arrangement was not easily apparent. Lloyd would continue to use the Fine Arts facilities. His new company would consist of virtually all the members of his *Mermaid* crew. Lloyd, having established a solid team in the last two years, was unwilling to make too many changes. The one person who didn't move to Lloyd Hamilton Corporation was Irene Dalton, who returned to Christie. Irene was a promising ingenue by the estimation of the critics, but she soon found her career winding down. After appearing as support in two light-comedy features, she completely retired from acting.

Lloyd, though, was certainly on a rise. At this time, critic James W. Dean wrote, "... Hamilton is hereby nominated for a place in the hall of comic immortals. Chaplin, Lloyd and Keaton must crowd up a bit to give him room."

In March, 1922, D.W. Griffith offered Lloyd a lead role in a feature-length comedy entitled *One Exciting Night*. The role, that of black servant Romeo Washington, would require Lloyd to perform in blackface. Lloyd, who had scenes in both *Dynamite* and *The Greenhorn* where he appeared in blackface, had said only nine months earlier that he wanted to play a blackface role entirely through one of his new comedies.[26] Still, Lloyd refused the offer. Instead, he and Ethel set forth on a month-long vacation that marked their first time abroad.

The couple began their vacation in Oakland. Lloyd enthusiastically informed an Oakland reporter:

> I'll be gone ten weeks or three months, and I am going to see London and Paris and Germany and all those places over there. I shall stop in New York for about a week and take in the new shows. It will give me new ideas. When a man travels and sees something it broadens him, I think.
>
> I am going to take along my cap and my shoes and my stage pants — I know I can find a cameraman over there — so if I see something I think would be good in a picture, I'll just have it shot and put it away for future use.[27]

The inner taskmaster was along for the voyage.

12

The Man in Blackface

Roscoe Arbuckle had gone to trial three times before he was acquitted of murder charges on April 12, 1922. The jurors, who felt that Arbuckle had been treated unfairly in the proceedings, accompanied their verdict with an apology.

By now, though, the adverse publicity had permanently tainted Arbuckle, and forces had amassed to make him a scapegoat for the excesses of Hollywood. Hays, feeling the need to demonstrate the power and commitment of the MPAA, barred the controversial comedian from working in motion pictures. On April 20, two days after the ban against Arbuckle, another scandal shook Hollywood. It came to light that Wallace Reid, an enormously popular action star, was struggling to overcome a morphine addiction. Blame was placed on Reid's employer, Paramount Pictures, which had subjected the leading man to a nonstop production schedule. Reid, bowed by exhaustion, had botched a stunt and suffered injuries that made it too painful for him to work. Paramount executives, determined to complete the film, had a doctor provide Reid with addictive pain-killers.

Reid was in a weakened condition when he contracted a virulent strain of influenza. He spent months in agonizing pain, struggling to regain his strength. His health continued to deteriorate and he eventually fell into a coma. He died in an asylum on January 18, 1923.

Reid's addiction had a profound effect on his wife, Dorothy. Following her husband's death, Dorothy initiated a crusade against drug addiction. Author Michael H. Price wrote: "With a missionary zeal, [she] embarked upon a campaign to expose the drug evil through motion pictures."[1] She produced a film depicting the dangers of drug abuse. Dressed in black, she engaged in a cross-country tour to lecture on narcotics.

Hugh Fay, one of Lloyd's closest friends and most valued associates, was later implicated in the Reid scandal by director Eddie Sutherland, who identified Fay as the dealer who kept Reid supplied with heroin.[2] The story goes that, while starting out as a bit player with Keystone, Fay found he could earn extra money acting as a courier for a dealer supplying heroin to Keystone employees. Under the alias "The Count," he managed to become the busiest dealer in town. The actor is said to have also supplied heroin to Mabel Normand, Alma Rubens and Barbara LaMarr, all of whom died as a result of drug abuse.

It is an accusation worth exploring as Fay was closely connected to Lloyd. Fay worked with Lloyd, on and off, for more than seven years, directing some of Lloyd's most profitable and best reviewed comedies, including *The Vagrant*, *Poor Boy* and *The Rainmaker*. He lived near Lloyd in Venice, which kept the two men within the same immediate social circle. These friends, who had taken up flying during their days at Fox, had a special connection in the fact

Hamilton, as usual, runs afoul of the law. The police officer is unidentified (courtesy of Steve Rydzewski).

they flew together in their spare time. Lloyd would have known if Fay was selling drugs and it would not have reflected well on him to have had this man in his employ or to have had this man at his side when he was out on the town.

It certainly does not reflect well on Lloyd, or dispel the accusations about Fay, that Jess Weldon, another longtime member of his stock company, was convicted during this time for drug trafficking. Weldon died in a prison hospital in 1925.

In Fay's defense, Sutherland was the only person who ever alleged that the actor was a dealer. William M. Drew, author of *Speaking of Silents: First Ladies of the Screen*, has pointed out that even Rubens, who was supposed to be one of Fay's regular clients, did not bother to mention Fay when she detailed her drug problems in a lurid confessional titled *This Bright World Again*. Also, drug dealers have to be serious about their business, which entails a great deal of risk. At the time, local and federal law enforcement officials were cracking down on the drug trade in Hollywood. Assistant District Attorney Tom Green focused his resources on getting drug dealers off the studio lots. Fay, a friendly and charming man, had a fulltime career in movies, alternating between acting, writing and directing. He was devoted, as his show business father had been, to making people laugh. Nothing in his background suggests that he was the type of person to bother with an activity as shady, illicit and hazardous as the drug trade.

Sutherland, though, remains a reliable source. He was prominent in Hollywood, putting him in a position to know what was going on behind the scenes, and he had no known motive to slander Fay. Sutherland acknowledged that it was hard to believe that Fay was the notorious Count. "He was," said Sutherland, "one of the quietest, nicest actors I've ever known."

On May 10, 1922, Lloyd was one of more than 100 stars who attended a charity ball at the Hotel Astor in New York. The highlight of the ball came when the guests voted to elect

Hamilton is the new teacher at school. *The Educator* (1922) (courtesy of the Everett Collection).

a King and Queen. Lloyd, who competed with at least 35 celebrities, received 1,427 votes. He ended up in twelfth place, beating out such prominent leading men as Buster Keaton, Harold Lloyd, Douglas Fairbanks, and John Barrymore.

After a month, Lloyd relinquished his role as tourist and party guest and devoted himself to mobilizing his new corporation. He was able to occupy one of the company's key positions with a trusted person. Lloyd Bacon, besides continuing as a writer and supporting actor, would be his assistant director.

Lloyd experienced the most difficulty in his search for a leading lady. To fill the position, a number of interviews and screen tests were conducted over a two-month period. At one point, Bacon asked Lloyd to meet his friend Ruth Hiatt, a teenager who had just arrived from San Diego. Ruth had minor screen experience, having acted for film companies in her hometown. Lloyd was skeptical, but he was willing to please his friend. He set up an interview with Ruth. Not only did he find her photogenic, but she proved to him she could act as well.

Lloyd's efforts were disrupted by a death in the family. After suffering a stroke, his father, William Hamilton, died on May 18, 1922. Lloyd brought his mother to Los Angeles to spend a few months at his home.

The premiere *Hamilton* comedy, *The Speeder*, was in an early stage of production when

Hamilton was often paired with child actors. The girl is Josephine Adair. *The Educator* (1922) (courtesy of the Everett Collection).

its director fell ill. His ready substitute was Lloyd Bacon. Bacon's more than competent work convinced Lloyd to keep his friend in the director's chair.

Bacon, as devoted as he was to his new duties, remained an actor at heart. He became known as a loud and colorful director. He regularly called attention to himself with outlandish behavior and funny outfits. Joe E. Brown said that, if a character wore a uniform in a scene, then so would Bacon.

Orral Humphrey, another associate from Lloyd's early stage days, also contributed to the latest series. Humphrey, the former stage star who had once mentored Lloyd, had retired to a quiet thousand-acre ranch. Lloyd convinced him to visit Los Angeles to appear in *The Educator*.

Lloyd's niece Virginia, who was six years old at the time, had vivid memories of *The Educator*, which she found to be "very enjoyable." She was particularly amused by Lloyd's outfit, which included a long frock coat and a pair of slapshoes. She explained that this attire was in sharp contrast to her uncle's usual fine dress.

Robinson Crusoe, Ltd., Lloyd's previous season opener, proved memorable. Maybe too memorable. Many automatically scaled the beloved film against *The Speeder*. A *Moving Picture World* critic explained that, though Lloyd must be tired of the comparisons, everyone was looking for another *Robinson Crusoe, Ltd.* That film, this critic believed, was "one of the greatest comedies ever made." Nevertheless, *The Speeder* was a success, doing well enough for Broadway's Rivoli and Rialto to book the five remaining entries of Lloyd's new series.

The first season of *Hamilton Comedies* won praise and profits. According to notices in trade journals, their drawing power proved to be greater than that of the features that they had been contracted to support.

By early 1923, Lloyd was a worldwide box office attraction. He had never attained a higher level of riches, respect or fame. It confirmed Lloyd's celebrity status when he was cast as himself in a big-budget Paramount release, *Hollywood*. A more tangible sign of Lloyd's status was a palatial residence in Laurel Canyon, one of Hollywood's most exclusive communities. Lloyd, whose family was in the real estate business, understood the value of land and made a point to buy up a large portion of undeveloped land in Laurel Canyon.

Many people would admit that Lloyd was deserving of success. He was not only an extremely funny man. As Leonard Maltin described him, Lloyd was "in every sense a comedian's comedian."[3] He was hardworking and innovative. He extended himself beyond performing, participating in every stage of production. He knew to gravitate to strong creative partners.

Lloyd had proven sturdier than most of his colleagues. During the most fertile period for film comedy, he had more than endured. Of the countless comics to appear, he had remained one of the most outstanding.

Lloyd, as a character comedian, was different from most of his contemporaries. Under the mass production of two-reel comedies, the industry had withstood a proliferation of wind-up comedians. These were spiritless and indistinct performers carried along, without personal control, by a wild and rapid succession of fantastic mechanical gags. These were comics who wore hooks on the back of their necks so they could glide from one gag to another across wire-rigged stages. The most popular of these comics were Billy Bevan, Ben Turpin, Snub Pollard, and Larry Semon. The mechanical gags had caused, to use a phrase of existentialist Karl Jaspers, "a wearing down into uniformity all that is individual." This was certainly not Lloyd's type of comedy. Lloyd said, "A screen comedian must have a distinct individuality. Without it, he is a mere automaton — a puppet who moves through the scenes

... getting laughs only through the situations in which he is placed by the mechanics of the picture."[4]

Lloyd had a number of admirers in Hollywood. Other comics were his most enthusiastic admirers. In the 1960s, Keaton praised Lloyd in an interview for *The Massachusetts Review*. Keaton, as quoted by Herbert Feinstein, called Lloyd "one of the funniest men in silent pictures."[5] Several writers allege that Chaplin revered Lloyd, although no one has been able to produce an exact quote to that effect. Oscar Levant wrote in his memoir *The Unimportance of Being Oscar*, that he once asked Chaplin if there was any other comic he had ever envied. Chaplin, according to Levant, instantly named Lloyd Hamilton. Adolph Green, another of Chaplin's friends, told film historian Kevin Brownlow that Lloyd was "Chaplin's favorite."[6]

Lloyd was lavish in spending his money. He bought many gifts for himself and he was extremely generous to others. One of the first things he did with his new riches was to buy his mother her first car. Lloyd had the admiration of peers, the approval of the public, and the favorable acknowledgement of critics. Yet, he remained unrelieved by his success. He needed to aim for more. He visualized at least one final hurdle he had to clear. He wanted to star in features. The press, which saw Lloyd on the verge of such an ascension, was clamoring impatiently for him to make his move.

Hamilton tries, with the assistance of actress Ethel Teare, to teach unwelcoming townsfolk that education is power in *The Educator* (1922) (courtesy of the Everett Collection).

A select fold had begun forming with the rise of feature-length comedies. Chaplin and Harold Lloyd clearly dominated the market. In the past year, Harold Lloyd had starred in four successful features. That gave him more presence than Chaplin, who was deeply immersed in the preparation of his second feature. It is likely that, if it had not been for the San Francisco scandal, Arbuckle would have turned this duo into a triumvirate.

Max Linder, France's great pioneer of screen comedy, had recently reappeared in three feature vehicles. This venture was unsuccessful and Linder did not react well. The comic, intensely depressed, arranged a suicide pact with his wife. The couple died after taking poison and slitting their wrists. In his defense, friends insisted that Linder had been exposed to poison gas during the war and this had afflicted his mind.

For comics, features were a fresh and fertile realm. Fox strove to install a comic in this new place and looked to Englishman Lupino Lane. Lane's feature, the five-reel comedy *A Friendly Husband* (released in January, 1923), received a tepid response and immediately concluded the studio's relationship with Lane.

In 1923, Sennett deviated from his ensemble slapstick features with *The Shriek of Araby*, a five-reel vehicle for Ben Turpin. No other Turpin features followed.

It was only a rare comic who could successfully carry a feature and this success could only occur under the appropriate circumstances. Keaton had recently managed to surpass Lloyd Hamilton with an awesome series of short subjects, including *The Playhouse*, *The Boat*, *The Paleface* and *Cops*. Seemingly, Lloyd Hamilton and Buster Keaton were the only screen comics who possessed the talent to contest Charlie Chaplin and Harold Lloyd. It was time for them to move out of the two-reel class and into the screen dimensions of Chaplin and Lloyd. Reporters pushed this notion as far as it would go.

During the spring of 1923, Keaton's company conceived a six-reel comedy titled *The Three Ages*. To lessen the risk of the venture, Keaton had interwoven three period pieces into one film. If audiences could not accept him in a feature, he could simply cut the film into three short comedies.

Lloyd remained ambitious. He tensely eyed this hurdle, on the other side of which lied full acceptance and the greatest of fame. Fame is greater to some men than the fleeting property of life.

At Fine Arts, recently the subject of extensive renovation, Lloyd devised a grand season-opener entitled *The Optimist*. With this comedy, he intended to test new ideas and demonstrate what a *Moving Picture World* critic would later recognize as "a decided change of motive."

Lloyd believed that, while dramatic actors could rely on tried and true situations to get an audience to cry, a comedian was required to create new situations to get an audience to laugh. He described, as a prime example, the premise of the old woman about to be ejected from her home by a skinflint mortgage holder. Her long-lost son makes an emotional return just in time to save the old homestead. Lloyd said that this situation, though "older than Nero's pet bulldog," could get an audience "crying so hard that the theatre is left damp for three days." But, he maintained, that an audience expects to be surprised watching a comedy and they would be unlikely to laugh seeing the same situation twice.

Lloyd Bacon and Hank Mann collaborated with him on the script. Gil Pratt was assigned to direct.

Hank Mann, a tough and spirited man from the East Side of New York City, was another "comedian's comedian." A subtly expressive and sympathetic comic, he was similar to Lloyd. His screen character, a popular principal of Keystone and Fox comedies, reminded one film historian of a "soulful basset hound." Stories of Mann's pranks and dares have surely enlivened

Hamilton confers with Uncle Eph (Tom O'Malley) in *His Darker Self* (1924) (author's collection).

the Keystone legend. Mann, unable to revive his career after a stint in the military, proved how important it was for an actor to maintain momentum in Hollywood.

During the production of *The Optimist*, Lloyd became the focus in an ongoing, well-publicized squabble between a foremost Hollywood director and a celebrated singer. Those squabblers were, respectively, D.W. Griffith and Al Jolson. Jolson agreed to make his screen debut as the star of a Griffith feature. Griffith had a "blackface comedy" story developed specifically for Jolson.

Jolson was filled with doubt about the film. Up to that point, most motion pictures starring reputable stage performers had been remarkable failures. The celebrity of stage stars did not extend into rural areas, where most film fans lived. Also, movies were a different element than the stage. Not accustomed to playing to a camera, many stage stars had given awkward performances. Jolson feared that he would embarrass and possibly even ruin himself in a silent film. It terrified him that he would have little appeal without his singing voice. Could the great Jolson woo an audience by simply embracing a song in his heart?

Production began at Mamaroneck, Griffith's New York studio. Screening of early rushes intensified Jolson's fears. In a state of panic, the singer fled to Europe, placing an ocean between himself and the picture plant. Griffith, angered by Jolson's flight, reciprocated with legal action.

Industry insiders expected Griffith to simply drop the enterprise and eat his losses. However, the man was blinded by rage and egotism. He deliberated over replacing Jolson with

Eddie Cantor, another stage entertainer who frequently wore blackface. Then, in August, he announced that his new film would star Lloyd Hamilton. By this time, the film was entitled *Black and White*. The director's casting selection was widely applauded.

Before beginning work on *Black and White*, Lloyd pushed hard to get ahead on his series. He made elaborate precautions, as documented by memos, to ensure his company's efforts would proceed in his absence. He arranged for Jack White to oversee the company's continuing operation. White would supervise the pre-production work on the season's remaining *Hamilton Comedies*, enabling filming to resume upon the comic's return.

The event of Lloyd's first feature attracted considerable press attention. One reporter wrote that, with this undertaking, Lloyd had become one of the "Big Four" screen comedians.

Keaton felt the heat. Forty years later, he remembered: "In our day, there was tremendous competition in our field.... Jerry [Lewis] doesn't have Chaplin, Lloyd, Hamilton and a half dozen others on his heels."[7]

Publicity men met the press' demand for material. According to one of their releases, *Black and White* was fulfilling Lloyd's ardent and enduring desire to be a blackface comedian. It was claimed that, as a child, Lloyd had staged a juvenile minstrel show in his father's barn.

Soon after Lloyd signed onto *Black and White*, Griffith's direct involvement in the undertaking quietly ended. Producer chores were shifted to Albert Grey, Griffith's brother-in-law. Griffith asked Lloyd to find himself a suitable director.

Meanwhile, Griffith set his attention on a new project. Will Hays had inspired him to make a patriotic film. He settled on a historical epic called *America*.

13

The Manageable Chaplin

Griffith's abrupt abandonment of *Black and White* had soured Lloyd's grand opportunity. Three years later, Lloyd remembered, "I felt like a soldier in the ancient battalion whose general was called on to surrender. As an answer to the emissary of the enemy, the general marched a whole company to the edge of a cliff and commanded them to jump."[1] Lloyd was legally blocked from his own retreat. In the end, he resolved to assume the job and put it behind him as soon as possible.

Delight Evans, a writer for *Screenland* magazine, described Lloyd being impressed when he arrived at Griffith's romantic and picturesque estate at Mamaroneck.[2] Griffith, to show he was a big fan of Lloyd's comedies, reportedly did an imitation of Lloyd's walk when the two men first met.

Lloyd spent six weeks filming on the East Coast. On his return home in October, he was greeted by a bitter wife. On October 29, Ethel filed a separate maintenance suit in Los Angeles Superior Court, she charging Lloyd with cruelty and nonsupport. The legal action, despite Ethel's charges, would soon be dropped.

The Optimist had been greeted with many favorable notices, but its success had been overshadowed by the even more enthusiastic response to Keaton's *Three Ages*.

Throughout November, Lloyd concentrated on creating a personal film called *Lonesome*. *Lonesome* was the work of a man contemplating failure and ruin, maybe a man transforming fear into creative material. In the film, he played an ambitious lad who becomes poor and lonely following a series of setbacks. Prevented by his pride, he cannot return home to his mother and sister. *Lonesome*, dominated by biting humor and grim reality, was not the usual two reels of nonsense and fun. *My Friend*, possibly recognized as a more commercial offering than the oddly downbeat *Lonesome*, was used instead to open the new season.

Around this time, Lloyd immersed himself in Hollywood's social nightlife. In 1929, this subject would be addressed in a *Motion Picture Classic* article.[3] According to the author, business managers urged Lloyd to abandon his aloof tendencies and attend industry parties. They told him that, to persuade producers to usher him into features, he needed to increase his visibility and socialize among Hollywood's prime movers. Acting on this advice, Lloyd courted studio executives at merry, booze-sodden gatherings. He frequented speakeasies and occasionally threw open his doors to all sorts of partygoers, no matter if they were souses, sycophants, players, chatterers, swankies, phonies or troublemakers.

Lloyd, an accomplished entertainer, acted well in the role of host. He was jolly and generous to his guests. He was a good fellow. He gained a reputation as a soft touch, letting more and more of his money be siphoned to hangers-on. Marvel Rea, Lloyd's leading lady in *The Simp*, told a story about a man who showed up on the set every day saying he was an out-of-work actor and needed money. It bothered Rea that Lloyd kept giving the man money.

Lloyd used his grand parties as occasions to drink heavily. Alcohol has been known to allow a tense, driven man to drop below his conscience, where self-esteem and achievement don't matter. Lloyd may have pursued in drinking the feeling of weightlessness, much as he did whenever he flew or swam. With alcohol, he could have let his body glide the stress-free bliss.

First National had distributed several successful slapstick comedies over the last three years. They had released *The Kid*, *A Twilight Baby*, several Sennett features, and eleven Keaton short subjects. Most recently, they had contracted to release Larry Semon's first feature-length comedy. In the market for a new and more manageable Chaplin, First National had been negotiating with Lloyd to star in a feature film since 1922. Finally, the two parties came to an agreement and a contract was signed on February 29, 1924. The project required Lloyd's services for at least six weeks starting on March 8. The comedian's base salary, for the minimum production period, was $1,200 per week. If the production went over schedule or the comedian had to come back for retakes, he would be paid an additional $1,500 per week. This was a relatively inexpensive production as indicated by the star's salary and the six-week production schedule. By comparison, Buster Keaton was paid at a weekly rate of $2,500 and was given as long as six months to produce a feature.

The First National contract allowed Lloyd no creative control in the project. According to the agreement, the nature of the production was to be designated by First National and Lloyd, as "said artist," would work "faithfully and conscientiously ... under the instructions and directions of [First National]." Still, the fact that the contract was signed just eight days prior to shooting meant that the script had to be ready by the time of signing and Lloyd was in effect approving the script by going forth with the agreement. In light of the *Black and White* fiasco, it is conceivable that Lloyd was eager to bear down and prove himself and willing, in the process, to accept less than ideal conditions.

Based on the recent controversies, a standard morality clause was also included in the contract. The provision simply read: "Said artist agrees that during the life of this contract, he will do nothing that will injure his standing as a motion picture actor."

Educational prepared to lose their top clown, whose contract concluded at the end of the season. To fill the anticipated void, Hammons contracted three established favorites, Bobby Vernon, Al St. John and Walter Hiers. Ruth Hiatt, Lloyd's find, became the new star of the *Mermaid* series.

Early on, it was producer J.K. McDonald who assumed creative control of Lloyd's First National feature. McDonald, determined for the film to contain a good amount of Chaplin-style pathos, went as far as borrowing the very poignant and very familiar premise of Chaplin's *The Kid*. Lloyd was to play a kind-hearted tramp responsible for taking care of an orphan boy. The script was prepared under the title "Sulphur Springs," but the title was changed during production—first to "Misunderstood" and later to "The Goof."

Ben Alexander was cast as the orphan. Although only thirteen years old, he had nine years of experience in films. Alexander had worked with top directors, including King Vidor and D. W. Griffith. He recently starred in comedy shorts for Jack White. Within the last few months, he was directed by William Beaudine in the J.K. McDonald productions *Penrod and Sam* and *Boy of Mine*. McDonald looked to be grooming Alexander as a rival to child star Jackie Coogan. It was no surprise for the producer to be heading in that direction. In the brief time that McDonald had been making movies, children had become a specialty of his. He, in fact, got his start producing "Johnny Jones," a short comedy series depicting a boy's lively adventures with his neighborhood buddies. The series, produced in 1922, has the distinction of debuting more than a month before Hal Roach's similarly themed "Our Gang" series.

William Beaudine, a former "Ham and Bud" director, was engaged to direct the feature. Beaudine was accomplished at directing short comedies and had recently graduated to directing feature films, but he may not been the ideal person for this assignment He had directed eleven features, in quick succession, in the last year and a half, but not one of these features had been an outright comedy. To date, his features included a domestic melodrama, a crime melodrama, a family melodrama, a society melodrama, and a newspaper melodrama. He was only slightly less serious with a "Taming of the Shrew" adaptation, a Tom Mix western, and a light comedy starring Viola Dana. He had also directed *Penrod and Sam* for McDonald. Cole Johnson, a film historian who got to see a rare print of the film, describes *Penrod and Sam* as a good light-hearted comedy about children getting into mischief, fighting bullies and experiencing puppy love. Victor Potel briefly shows up as the town drunk and provides broader, less light-hearted comedy. Then, the film turns dramatic, presenting scenes not found in the original Booth Tarkington novel. In the novel, the worst thing to happen to Penrod's little dog Duke is for him to have to endure his winter bath, but Duke ends his film appearance getting hit by a car. Many tears flow from actor Alexander, after which the cast gathers for a somber funeral service. These scenes, more than the children's antics, drew the attention of the critics. It is questionable if this, or any other film on his résumé, prepared Beaudine to direct a wild and wacky Lloyd Hamilton feature.

The feature-length comedy had, for Lloyd's peers, required a decidedly different style, form and content than the short comedy. It had proven, for sure, to be a challenging and unwieldy creature. It was in appreciating this fact that Chaplin was progressing slowly on his current feature.

The feature comedy, in the end, tested the substantiality of its star. As a meteor entering the Earth's atmosphere, the comedian diving into this realm would be dissipated if he was not sufficiently brilliant. To endure for the extended length, Lloyd would have to modify his established laws and draw more from his screen character. He would need to pace himself differently and design a new structure and new mechanics.

Lloyd admitted to problems. He said that, having to devote "so much footage to story development," he was forced to abandon humor that was continuous and fast.[4] Years earlier, he spoke out against comedymakers relying on a single storyline. He believed that stories grow tiresome and intrude on the essential action. The fact was that the comedian didn't even work with a script. During an interview in 1922, he told a *Salt Lake Telegram* reporter that his team planned out a general situation and then invented gags on the set. Lloyd was focused on being funny and spontaneous and he did not express his strongest skills when it came to continuity. For now, though, Lloyd had no choice but to uphold a strong narrative.

It had been necessary for those who preceded Lloyd, including Harold Lloyd, Charlie Chaplin and Buster Keaton, to accomplish the same radical passage. None of these comedians had found a need to develop storylines for their short comedies. Harold Lloyd explained that his writers would develop ideas "more or less piecemeal" and work out no more than a "little basic plot." Keaton said that he and his staff simply figured out enough of a story to know what sets they had to build. Now, in making a feature, Harold Lloyd had to provide his character with a serious basic intent and supply his storyline with a strong central idea. Keaton, in much the same way, had to enclose his comedy within a plausible dramatic context. Chaplin had, in making *The Kid*, provided his lead character with an extremely serious situation: the discovery of an abandoned baby. Chaplin, who acted mockingly towards the silly and repetitious plots of his early films, had learned to carefully nurture a strong and original story.

This is not to say that these men had completely shifted their allegiance from gags to plots. The fact was that, once established in features, Chaplin, Keaton and Harold Lloyd tended to vary their dependence on stories. Harold Lloyd wrote in 1928: "I like the story pictures as well as anyone, yet I am a little afraid of overdoing them and forgetting one of these days that we are makers of comedies."[5] Chaplin, although usually allowing a story line to take precedence over gags, still believed a story should never interfere with the "fun and games."[6]

In March 1924, ads proclaimed:

LLOYD HAMILTON
in
His Darker Self
His first 5-reel comedy

A somber mood: Featured from left to right are Mary Corr, Patsy Ruth Miller, Ben Alexander, and Hamilton. *A Self-Made Failure* (1924) (courtesy of George Eastman House Motion Picture Department Collection).

During its run, Lloyd's blackface comedy competed with Keaton's *Sherlock Jr.* and Harold Lloyd's *Girl Shy*, both outstanding successes for their respective stars. *His Darker Self*, which drew minimal profits, was a disappointment. It did not prove to a snooty *New York Times* critic that Lloyd Hamilton was in the same class as Chaplin "or even Harold Lloyd." However, for all the reviewer's faultfinding, he did acknowledge that Lloyd's performance caused "many persons to laugh very loudly."

A twenty-minute version of *His Darker Self* would eventually be released to theatres as a short subject. Evidently, the distributor believed that Lloyd's proper place was in short subjects. *His Darker Self* was, in Lloyd's estimation, an irrefutable failure.

In June, 1924, Lloyd's First National feature was released as *A Self-Made Failure*. Again, it was no more than a moderate moneymaker. The film did not join Lloyd with Chaplin, Harold Lloyd and Keaton. It did not inspire the immediate investment in a third Hamilton feature. The Earth's position shifted, with Lloyd brought out of line with his ultimate target.

Lloyd was devastated by the inadequate performance of his features and his loss of prestige in the industry. The principles instilled in him as a child controlled his perceptions of work, prosperity and respectability. A Protestant is taught to hold his life as an absolute whole. They are to demand from oneself not single good works, but a life of good works combined into a unified system. The displacement of a single pin will destroy all the merit that they might have been accumulated by good works. Lloyd, like his screen character, was a shy and sensitive individual who worked hard to do the right thing. He wanted to create work of substance and quality and to be acknowledged for his success. The failure of his features was an overwhelming embarrassment for him. Lloyd's work soon went into decline and his drinking got out of hand. His image changed abruptly from serious artist to party guy. Irene May Selznick, daughter of MGM mogul Louis B. Mayer, said, "Every studio had problems with drinking. If people weren't drinkers before they got to the studios, the tension helped make them drinkers."[7]

Lloyd tried to assure himself that, as long as he continued to do his best, he would eventually be rewarded. At least this is what he suggested years later when he discussed the situation with writer Frank Capron. So, for now, he signed with Educational for three more seasons. To inaugurate a series of "Bigger and Better Hamilton Comedies," Hammons agreed to invest more money in them.

Lloyd left his wife in late June and voluntarily moved out of their home. He was discontented. He wanted a change of scene. So, he packed some belongings and traveled alone to New York.

A Pause for Analysis III

What went wrong with *A Self-Made Failure*? The film itself is not available for evaluation, but we at least have the finished script, which provides exceptional detail of the scenes. It was in fact these details which became a source of irritation to producer J. K. McDonald, who apologized to the First National executives for what he termed "minutia." He wrote, "The continuity writer, who 'sat in' with us, has made extraordinary, and possibly unnecessary, endeavor to outline and detail all 'shots' as to atmosphere, etc., with the result that there may appear to be a superfluous amount of reading matter in delineating inconsequential scenes which are not in any manner a Master Scene."[8]

The script provides Lloyd with the role of a kindly, easygoing tramp named Breezy. Under the mistaken impression that Breezy has become a successful businessman, a dying friend leaves his young boy Sonny in the tramp's care. The story unfolds in a little country village known as Sulphur Springs. Grandma Neal, a gentle old woman, has made her living operating her humble, old-fashioned cottage as a boarding house, but now visitors are being drawn to a new sanitarium near the town's hot springs, and the scarcity of lodgers has reduced the old woman to poverty.

Prosperity is very much in evidence at the sanitarium. A small path leads from the sanitarium to a steamy pool surrounded by shade trees and benches. The springs, which are believed to cure lumbago, gout and rheumatism, attract an abundance of senior citizens.

Cyrus Cruikshank, the proprietor of the springs and hotel, is presented as a miserly, crotchety old man. Cruikshank prepares for the grand opening of a swimming pool and rubbing parlors. It is announced in posters that visitors to the event will be treated by a famous German masseur and entertained by bathing beauties. On this day, the masseur is expected to arrive at the train station.

A train pulls into the Sulphur Springs station. Breezy, Sonny and their canine friend, Cameo, crawl down from the rods. They are covered in coal dust. The trio strolls by the engine. As they pass beneath the cab, Lloyd notices the engineer slouching out of the window. He glances at an old wrist watch, then indignantly asks, "Can you imagine him bringing us in twenty minutes late?" The engineer, angered by the remark, yanks a rope to discharges a blast of steam in Breezy's path. Breezy jumps aside in alarm.

Breezy and Sonny wash up at a water hole. Sonny sternly inspects Breezy's ears. When he discovers dirt behind one ear, he scolds his friend. Breezy drops his eyes in shame and holds still while Sonny scrubs off the dirt.

Underneath a tree, Sonny guides Breezy through a lesson in penmanship. Sonny takes out a book with the letters "A-B-C" printed on the cover. Breezy is distracted from study. He reaches into his pocket and pulls out a well-worn letter. The illiterate tramp looks at the letter fondly before holding it out to Sonny and asking him to read it. Sonny objects. "None of that," he exclaims, "we've got to study!" Breezy persists. "Please read it *again* for me," he implores. Sonny reads aloud, "My old friend Breezy, there is no one to whom I can trust my son as I can to you. I am sending him to you, hoping that you will make him the same success in life that you have been...." Breezy beams with pride to hear those words. Sonny continues reading as his proud guardian takes a moment to adjust his battered shoe, covering a toe that sticks through a split seam.

Sonny soon begins the penmanship lesson. He writes: "I hope we won't be tramps all our lives." Sonny hands Breezy the paper and asks him to copy it. Breezy grips a pencil in his hand and forces the point against the page. He frowns from deep concentration and guides his hand awkwardly to form the words.

In the meantime, Cameo steals a lunch pail from a truck driver. Breezy is suspected of the theft, and a chase ensues. To elude a constable, Breezy hides behind a stack of trunks. He is revealed when one of the trunks is removed. Breezy is inadvertently rescued by a hotel runner, who mistakenly assumes that this new visitor is the masseur. Breezy accompanies the runner though he has no idea who this man thinks he is or where he is taking him.

At the hotel, Cruikshank welcomes Breezy. In this greeting, it becomes clear to the tramp that the hotel proprietor believes he is this masseur celebrated for his great strength and therapeutic skills. Breezy accepts the role with poise. Cruikshank introduces Breezy to a crowd of guests, at which time he presents Breezy with a large dumbbell made of flowers. Breezy avoids an unattractive waitress who wants to feel his muscles. When the assembly disperses for dinner, Cruikshank receives a wire explaining that the actual masseur had to cancel his

13. The Manageable Chaplin

visit. Cruikshank, though infuriated, decides that it would be better to keep Breezy around than to admit his mistake.

Spike Malone, an arrogant and aggressive road show manager, arrives with an alluring collection of bathing beauties. Cameo helps carry the ladies' cases. Peering into a keyhole, Cameo spies Spike's shapely wife getting undressed. The provocative sight causes Cameo's ears to point straight into the air. Breezy shoos the dog away from the door, but he cannot resist peeking into the keyhole himself. Spike arrives in time to see Breezy bent over in front of the door and pressing his eye to the keyhole. Breezy, finding Spike standing behind him, fearfully leaves the scene.

Cruikshank, unmoved by Sonny's sorrowful pleas, ejects Cameo from the hotel. Sonny and Cameo wanders off down a dirt road. The boy and his dog eventually reach Grandma Neal's home, where they are welcomed as guests.

At the grand opening, the bathing beauties are in prominence. Breezy appears in white trousers and a fancy sweater. Confident in his impersonation, he struts importantly over to a megaphone and introduces the bathing beauties. After parading before the crowd, the bathing beauties engage in a diving exhibition and play aquatic basketball. Breezy obviously remains attracted to Spike's wife. To get a better look at the lady, he uses his megaphone as a telescope. Spike does not approve of this continued attention. In the rubbing rooms, Breezy persists in irritating Spike, who ends up chasing Breezy throughout the resort.

Breezy visits Sonny at his new residence. Instantly, he becomes infatuated with Alice, Grandma Neal's orphan granddaughter.

John Steele, a tenant at Cruikshank's hotel, is a quiet, unassuming man who has deserted his law practice to become a novelist. Unable to pay his board bill, he is evicted from the hotel. Breezy assumes that Steele is leaving because he was dissatisfied with the hotel's accommodations. He eagerly grabs Steele's baggage and leads him to Grandma's boarding house. On returning to the hotel, Breezy learns the real reason that Steele vacated his room. He races back to Grandma's cottage. By now, there is obvious affection between Steele and Alice. Breezy sadly realizes that, besides burdening his friends with a destitute boarder, he has introduced a superior rival to his beloved Alice. The group gathers to chat in the parlor. Grandma informs her guests that her deceased son, James Neal, had once owned the springs. She explains that, shortly before his death, her boy had relinquished the springs to Cruikshank in payment of a debt.

On returning to the hotel, Breezy seeks a sheet of paper to practice his penmanship. He finds a receipt. The receipt indicates that James Neal had made a payment which settled his debt with Cruikshank and nullified the agreement to transfer ownership of the springs. Failing to understand the significance of the paper, Breezy simply turns it over and writes on the back. Afterwards, he visits Grandma's cottage to show his writing to Sonny. As he steps on the front porch, he finds Steele and Alice cozied up together in a hammock. Alice asks Breezy if he knows that Steele is a writer. Breezy smiles and says, "So am *I*." At this point, he proudly exhibits his writing. Steele smiles while Alice struggles to conceal her amusement.

In the parlor, Grandma is busy sewing a garment. Distracted when Breezy enters the room, she drops her thimble underneath a table. Breezy looks under the table, but he cannot see anything. He figures to light the receipt at a gas lamp so he can hold the flame underneath the table and see the thimble, but Sonny finds the thimble before the receipt catches fire. Sonny then notices the receipt and shows it to Steele. Steele explains that, though the receipt raises question about the ownership of the springs, Cruikshank's rights cannot be challenged without the corroboration of the deed.

Hamilton looks over the shoulder of young Ben Alexander who plays the brains of this outfit. The shady onlooker is played by Sam De Grosse. *A Self-Made Failure* (1924) (courtesy of George Eastman House Motion Picture Department Collection).

    Breezy gets the idea to practice his penmanship in the middle of the night. He is dressed in a long striped nightgown and shoes as he sneaks inside Cruikshank's office in search of paper. His arrival interrupts a burglar cracking the hotel safe. The thief silently vanishes into the darkness. Breezy finds the deed to the springs, which the burglar threw out of the safe. He stuffs the document down the front of his nightgown, but it slips through and drops to the floor. Breezy steps in glue that has spilled from an overturned bottle. The glue causes the contract to become fastened to the sole of his shoe. Breezy strikes a match to see what this paper is that's sticking to his shoe. When the match burns down to his fingers, he flings it away. The match drops on the safecracker's kit of explosives. An explosion occurs. Flames from the explosion burn away the tail of Breezy's nightgown. Breezy tightens the gown around himself as several other people appear. Assuming that Breezy was trying to rob him, Cruikshank demands that the constable arrest the tramp. The constable orders Breezy to raise his hands. Breezy lifts his hands, but he has to squat down in his gown to stop from exposing his posterior. Breezy follows the constable's lead. When the door is opened, he is suddenly assailed by the cold night air. He grabs a fur boa from a rack and wraps it around his shivering shoulders. In departing, the constable assumes a tight grip around Breezy's arm. A passerby is startled to see Breezy and the constable walking down the street. Observing Breezy's fur boa and loose, flowing garment, he presumes that the lawman is keeping company with a homely mistress.

Lugging a basket of food, Sonny visits Breezy in prison. At first, the tone of the scene is intensely sad. However, Sonny becomes enthusiastic when he learns that the deed fell out of Breezy's nightgown and may be somewhere in the hotel lobby. Sonny races out of the building before handing the basket over to Breezy. Breezy wriggles his way between the bars and strains his arm to reach the basket outside the cell. Meanwhile, another hand extends from an adjoining cell and steals food from the basket. When Breezy finally reaches the basket with his foot, he looks inside and only finds a small piece of white cake. He sits remorsefully and raises the cake to his mouth. Before he can take a bite, a fly settles on the cake. Breezy swats at the fly with a stick, but only manages to crumble the cake. He sees the fly settle on a wall. He is removing his shoe to crush the pest when he notices the deed stuck to the sole. He promptly tosses the deed to Cameo, who has been loitering outside of the cell.

Cameo promptly delivers the deed to Steele, who is in the middle of a conversation with Cruikshank. At first glance, it appears that James Neal did sign the springs over to Cruikshank, but then Steele sees that the signature is dated two weeks after the date of Neal's death. Steele shows the signature to Grandma, who confirms that it is a forgery. Cruikshank tries to kick Cameo but the dog moves out of the way, causing the old man to lose his balance and fall.

Several weeks later, Grandma Neal hosts a grand opening of a new Sulphur Springs Resort. Amid the festivities, Breezy is sad to see Steele and Alice sharing an embrace and a kiss. Breezy leaves to be alone. He notices a slip of paper in his primer. It bears the hopeful sentence that Sonny scrawled as a sample of penmanship: "I hope we won't be tramps all our lives." By now, Breezy understands the significance of these words. He glumly retrieves his carpetbag and walks to the train station.

Meanwhile, Sonny desperately searches for his missing dog, who he suspects has been killed by Cruikshank. While searching the train yard, Sonny notices Breezy crawling underneath a freight car. Bewildered, he rushes to Breezy and pulls him off of the drawbars. Breezy cannot conceal his embarrassment. Sonny reaches out and touches the carpetbag. "Where are you going?" he asks. Breezy responds bravely, "You stay here and help Grandma make a success of the baths—I have to leave." Sonny becomes frantic. He clutches at the carpetbag and looks up wildly. His lips quiver. He cries. "If *you're* goin'—*I'm* goin' too!"

Breezy shows Sonny his note. "Don't you remember this?" he asks. Sonny ignores the note. "You got to take me," he insists, "Now that Cameo's gone—you're all I've got." Breezy weakens. "Alright," he announces, "we'll go together."

As they climb onto the rods of the freight car, Breezy and Sonny hear Cameo's familiar bark. Cameo, trotting across the tracks, is led by a procession of puppies. Breezy and Sonny laugh. Breezy agrees to stay so that he can help raise the puppies.

THE END.

Lloyd had gone with a dramatic premise "older than Nero's bulldog"—the old woman about to be ejected from her home by the skinflint mortgage holder. The sad scenes derived from this situation play a far greater role in the script than the funny scenes. Lloyd is often guided in stage directions to act sad. Breezy is sad in prison. Breezy is sad when he sees the girl he loves with another man. Breezy is sad when he sets out to leave the boy at the end of the film. At one point, the script describes a close-up where "Breezy looks off, wide-eyed ... a little expression of sadness steals over his face ... a feeling of pathos." It is clear, throughout the script, that the writers' priority was pathos. The script comes off, in the end, as cloy-

Breezy the tramp gives his orphan charge, actor Ben Alexander an impromptu math lesson in *A Self-Made Failure* (1924) (courtesy of George Eastman House Motion Picture Department Collection).

ing. Frank Capra, who could make an audience cry better than anyone, said that pathos has to come naturally out of the situations being created. He said that it didn't work to "deliberately *try* for pathos" and any contrived effort to the play a scene for pathos was bound to turn out "silly."[9]

Buster Keaton said that, when he started to make features, he recognized that he couldn't sustain the audience's interest unless he got them to care about his character. "You had to get sympathy to get any story to stand up," said Keaton. But the stoic comedian, not one to wallow in self-pity, refused to make any direct pleas for sympathy or act in any way that compelled the audience to care. "If the audience wanted to feel sorry for me," he said, "that was up to them."[10]

The screenwriting team which worked on *A Self-Made Failure* made an effort to create scenes with pathos, but they did not put forth the same clear effort to make scenes that kept the audience laughing. On paper, *A Self-Made Failure* offers no comedy incidents, gags or stunts that were original or exciting. It needs to be considered that, this same year, Keaton amazed audiences with groundbreaking technical effects in *Sherlock, Jr.*, which featured the surreal adventures of a projectionist who leaves his booth to step up to the screen and join the movie in progress. This was also the year that Harold Lloyd climaxed his romantic comedy *Girl Shy* with the chase scene to end all chase scenes. Harold, determined to stop his sweetheart from marrying a cad, races through the streets using whatever means of transport is available to him. At first, he steals a ride on the floorboard of a car without realizing that the car is being used to train a student driver. The student driver, who doesn't know how to operate the steering, pulls out into the street and drives the car in circles. Harold then hijacks a car without knowing that bootleg liquor is in the backseat; soon a police car is in hot pursuit and detectives are shooting at him. He eventually gives up on automobiles and, in quick succession, uses a variety of vehicles, including a racehorse, police motorcycle, streetcar, fire engine and wagon, to get to the wedding before the couple is pronounced man and wife. This sequence is still regarded as must-see for the aspiring filmmaker who wants to stage and edit action scenes. *A Self-Made Failure* didn't, by comparison, give Lloyd Hamilton anything special to do. Breezy gets involved in a case of mistaken identity. Breezy gets chased around by a big jealous husband. Breezy accidentally sets off explosives and gets blown up. This was overused comedy material that Lloyd would have had to execute well if he wanted to make it fresh and funny.

Pathos showed up in these other comedy features of the year, but it was an element used effectively in collaboration with other elements. *Sherlock, Jr.*, has a moment of pathos, but just a moment. Keaton is ejected from his girlfriend's home after his rival frames him for stealing a watch. He briefly stands out on the front porch hanging his head, but then he sees his rival leaving the house and takes off to follow him. The master of slapstick is immediately back in action. A minute later, he is hanging off the spout of a water tower and getting blasted with a torrent of water. This was how Keaton framed his films dramatically, but then let the comedy be their true and overriding substance.

Harold Lloyd had made a point to create a sympathetic character in *Girl Shy*, but he remained restrained in his use of sentimentality. Harold and his leading lady, Jobyna Ralston, share scenes that are sweet, tender and romantic, but the sentiment in these scenes never becomes excessive and never gets in the way of the laughs. Harold sits down by a lake for a romantic moment with Jobyna. The scene is soon interrupted when Harold realizes that he sat on a big turtle, which has decided to walk off into the lake with him. Later, Harold is led to believe that a publisher is interested in buying his book "The Secret of Lovemaking," but his dream of becoming an author is shattered when he finds out his manuscript has become the joke of the publishing house. The publisher tells him his book is "ridiculous" and demands that he get out of his office. Harold now feels that he'll never be successful enough to marry Jobyna and acts callously towards her to get her to break up with him. This is definitely pathos, but it's not drawn out and the actors are skillful enough to make the scenes feel genuine. The scenes where his manuscript is rejected and Harold breaks up with Jobyna run for no more than five minutes, just long enough to generate emotion for the big climactic chase.

Harold Lloyd shared Keaton's belief that a comedy character shouldn't wallow in self-pity. This comedian, at his best, relied on a contagious optimism that made an audience root for him to win. This was a character that, no matter what adversity he had to face, remained hopeful about his ambitions and was determined to succeed in the end.

Another major weakness in *A Self-Made Failure*'s script, perhaps even greater than the overuse of pathos, is that Lloyd's character is depicted as a hopeless imbecile. Breezy sorely lacks the abilities that a lead character needs to drive a plot forward. He doesn't overcome adversity through an act of strength. He doesn't thwart the villain and save the day. He doesn't take definite measures to make a better life for the child Sonny. His main objective in the early scenes is to scope out the bathing beauties at the sanitarium. His main objective in the later scenes is to practice his penmanship. He is the irrelevant comic relief in his own film.

The script, in fact, fails to focus on its lead character. Breezy, the kind-hearted tramp, is out of view for large portions of the story, including an elaborate scene that had been devised to showcase the standard bevy of bathing beauties. The script also introduces a wholesome couple to furnish the film with a romantic interest. Conrad Nagel and Mae McAvoy were originally cast as the couple, but they were later replaced by Matt Moore and Patsy Ruth Miller. Sonny and Cameo, the orphan boy and his clever dog, are mostly in charge during Breezy's absences. Early on, Cameo playfully disrupts Sonny's efforts to wash dishes. In a more extended sequence, Sonny and Cameo befriend Grandma Neal and set forth to acquire tenants for her boarding house. Their mission places the pair at the local train depot, where they are forced into vigorous competition with a hotel runner. Later, Sonny chops wood for the old woman. Cameo carries the kindling to a woodpile, where he arranges the pieces into amazingly neat rows.

McDonald and Beaudine had very much wanted to use Cameo in the film. Cameo, also known as "Cameo the Wonder Dog," had made some memorably funny appearances in Sennett comedies. In one film, he is playing poker with Billy Bevan and he keeps sneaking a peek at Bevan's cards. Beaudine realized that audiences like dogs and they especially like funny dogs. It was evident, during the nine years that Cameo worked in films, that he had no bigger fan or greater employer than Beaudine, who cast the dog in seven feature films. But the fact that the director found him talented was not the only reason he was used extensively in *A Self-Made Failure*. Cameo, who had played Duke in *Penrod and Sam*, had proven he could work well with Alexander. McDonald recognized that the relationship between the boy and dog had been a major reason for *Penrod and Sam*'s success and this relationship was something that was worth recreating. Still, the scenes between Alexander and Cameo took away from Lloyd's screen time and managed to dilute the strength of the comedian's well-meaning tramp character.

Lloyd himself mostly blamed the eight-reel running time of the film. "[It] was three reels too many," he said.[11] He surely must have recognized, in line with this thinking, that the elimination of subplots and the diminishment of supporting characters could have significantly improved the film.

The faults in this script cannot be blamed squarely on writers Violet Clark, John Grey and Lex Neal. Grey would become an important writer for Harold Lloyd, managing to effectively suffuse comedy and drama in *The Freshman* and *The Kid Brother*. Neal would, in the next few years, contribute considerable material to successful features for Buster Keaton and Harold Lloyd. He later reunited with Grey, with good results, on the Harold Lloyd feature *Speedy*. The problem was that the direction of the film was clearly set by McDonald, who provided the storyline that screenwriters had to follow. McDonald explained that the scenes were fervently developed in several meetings, with gag men and situation men debating to achieve a fair balance. He assured First National executives that every gag was an integral part of the story. He promised that the film would include an ample amount of fast-moving, farcical comedy but the absurd action would be contrasted by "sufficient pathos and quiet, subtle humor."[12] But, in the end, it remained McDonald's chief objective to have the script provide numerous occasions for pathos. It was to that end that Clark was put in charge of developing the story. Clark had sixteen feature films to her credit, which gave her considerably more experience than Grey or Neal, but her experience had been in woman's dramas, including *Slander the Woman*, *The Woman Conquers* and *A Woman's Business*. She could not have been

The tall comedian had to cast even taller actors as heavies to make himself look vulnerable, as shown here in *Lonesome* (1924). The identity of this particular heavy is unknown (courtesy of Cole Johnson — Slapstick Archive).

expected, based on her lack of comedy experience, to have developed a storyline with ample comedy opportunities.

More than 100 production stills are available for *A Self-Made Failure* and the action on display in the stills consistently matches the action described in the script. This is sufficient proof that Beaudine did not deviate in any major way from the script. Still, the quality of a film is often in the details.

Lloyd had a couple of opportunities in the script to do what he did best and he may have used these opportunities to bring more comedy to the film than what the writers had put on the page. Breezy, alone in the prison cell, struggles to swat a fly. This was one of those simple, common predicaments from which Lloyd was able to get a good deal of comedy. Described a few pages earlier in the script is a scene where the back of Breezy's nightgown has been torn off and he has to be careful to keep people from seeing his bare behind. Lloyd, who was at his funniest in embarrassing situations, likely made this scene a highlight of the film.

What is truly sad more than anything that happens to Breezy, is the fact that the film is no longer around for anyone to see exactly how Lloyd executed this material. Lloyd, who was at the top of his game at this time, was able to get big laughs with his subtle reactions and bring real warmth and emotion to the simplest moments of a story. Maybe it was true that Lloyd Hamilton swatting at a fly was dull compared to Harold Lloyd's epic chase sequence, but not every film has to be daring and breathtaking to be good. It can be enough for a film to be sweet, charming and, most of all, human.

14

Tumbling Back to Shorts

For the 1924–25 season, Fred Hibbard was contracted to write and direct the *Hamilton Comedies*. During the previous season, Hibbard had directed *My Friend* and other successful Educational releases.

"Hibbard" was, in fact, an alias; the director's real name was Fred Fishback. He was 28 years old when he started his film career working for Thomas H. Ince in 1912. He directed two-reel comedies for Sennett from 1915 to 1919. Then, in April, 1919, he went to work at Universal, where he got to direct and produce his own series, *The Fishback Comedies*.

Fishback ran into trouble in September, 1921, when production broke for the Labor Day weekend and he drove out of town to attend a party in San Francisco. He was accompanied by a close friend, Roscoe Arbucle, who had made arrangements for the party. Fishback didn't expect anything eventful to happen that weekend. The only plan he had made other than the party was to visit the San Francisco Zoo, where he intended to look over some seals he might be able to use in an upcoming film.

As it turned out, though, Fishback was present when Virginia Rappe died. He wanted to do something to help when Rappe started to scream hysterically and he thought it would be a good idea to lift the woman and dump her into a cold bath. Unfortunately, it could be that Fishback's actions are what caused Rappe's bladder to rupture. He became a central character in the press' running drama. While Arbuckle's name became synonymous with "murderous beast" and "mad rapist," the references "Arbuckle pal" and "wild party guest" also transformed Fishback into a notorious figure. Universal executives, wishing to avoid bad publicity, terminated the director's namesake series.

It was soon after the San Francisco scandal that Fishback discovered he had lung cancer. Though his illness lingered, Fishback resumed his career in 1923. Under the alias "Hibbard," the comedymaker directed Century and Educational comedies. As the cancer had damaged his larynx, he principally addressed his crew through a megaphone.

Fishback organized Lloyd's supporting cast. He added Dick Sutherland, a popular comic heavy, to the stock company. He hired Dorothy Seastrom, a hardworking 19-year-old dancer from Dallas, to succeed Ruth Hiatt, who had embarked on her own climb to stardom. In a highly publicized annual election, the Western Association of Motion Picture Advertisers had ranked Ruth as one of the year's most promising young actresses. This placed her in a collection known as the "WAMPAs Babies." Another member of the group was Clara Bow, who would become the sex symbol of the decade. Lloyd was apprehensive over having lost Ruth, an actress with whom he shared great trust and admiration.

Hamilton loses his clothing in *King Cotton* (1925) (courtesy of the family of Lloyd Hamilton).

Lloyd, preferring to brood in his dressing room, participated less in the creation of his films. Before the cameras, he demonstrated a slackening of effort.

According to the *Jonah Jones* exhibitor book, Lloyd said, "It is an established fact that the most successful motion picture comedies are the two-reel ones. The fast-moving action demanded by the shorter picture gives the comedian the best opportunity to display his ability. It is also known that laughter cannot be sustained beyond a certain length of time, after which there is a sobering reaction."[1]

Lloyd wrote a script called *Crushed*, which described a traveler's introduction to the New York City subway system. Set builders constructed a facsimile of a Manhattan subway station. Mock cars could run back and forth within a short span. A platform was crafted to withstand the weight of the numerous extras needed to depict a ruthless stampede of rush-hour commuters.

By the time *Crushed* was released the following fall, its central gag sequence was no longer novel or inventive: Theatergoers had recently seen virtually the same sequence played out by Harold Lloyd in the feature *Hot Water*. *Hot Water*, released four weeks earlier, was still in theatres when *Crushed* debuted, which made it conceivable for the audience at the Strand to be watching Harold Lloyd on a crowded trolley car struggling awkwardly with a live turkey and groceries while the audience down the street at the Capitol was watching Lloyd Hamilton on a crowded subway car struggling awkwardly with a live goose and groceries. John Grey had worked as a writer on *A Self-Made Failure* shortly before going to work on *Hot Water*. It is open for conjecture if Grey had come up with the idea for this sequence and had ended up suggesting it to both comedians.

One evening in September, Hollywood police received complaints from neighbors that an unruly, three-day-old bash was in progress at the Hamilton home. Patrol officers interrupted a festive gathering that included Lloyd, seven male guests, and a young lady dressed in men's pajamas. The police would only tell the press that Lloyd's lone female guest was a "former film actress." On suspicion of drunkenness, the police took Lloyd into custody. Lloyd was able to bail himself out of jail in the morning.

Due to his illness, Fishback was forced to forestall his efforts on the *Hamilton* series. While the director rested, Lloyd played himself in *Hello, Hollywood*, a *Mermaid* comedy starring Lige Conley. For the film, Lloyd and Conley performed a popular stage routine where two comics get on opposite sides of a bare mirror frame and one mimics the actions of the other. Chaplin used this routine as early as 1916, Max Linder used it in the 1921 feature *Seven Year's Bad Luck*, and the Marx Brothers took final ownership of the routine in a wild and wacky variation performed in *Duck Soup*. In the *Hello, Hollywood* version, which was arranged by a young director named Norman Taurog, Conley has snuck onto a studio lot and is trying to avoid detection. When Lloyd steps in front of the mirror, he finds Conley standing where his reflection is supposed to be. Conley tries pretending he is Lloyd's reflection by mimicking the comic's every movement and expression. Lloyd knows his own face, but Conley is so accurate in his mimicry that Lloyd can't be sure whether this is his reflection or not.

During his absence, Fishback received bad news: Thomas Ince, the renowned filmmaker who had ushered him into the industry, had died of a heart attack. Despite great pain, Fishback was determined to concentrate on his work. For the latest *Hamilton* comedy, he wrote a script entitled *Waiting*.

Waiting was dogged by a dark cloud. The premise of the comedy required a strong antagonist, but Sutherland had been persuaded to leave Lloyd's company and lend his frightening visage to dramatic features. Soon after, Dorothy Seastrom fell ill. Lloyd promptly turned to Ruth Hiatt for help. At Lloyd's request, Ruth stepped into Seastrom's role. On January 6, 1925, just prior to the production, cancer ended Fishback's life.

Fishback had reinforced Lloyd's top rank in the short subject field and carried the performer beyond the failure of his feature films. In the months ahead, his loss would severely impact the Hamilton Company.

In spite of Fishback's death, the Hamilton Company proceeded with the production of *Waiting*. Based on inferior results, the comedy's release was postponed.

Seeking to capitalize on the recent publicity of *His Darker Self*, Educational

Hamilton in a wary mood (1924) (courtesy of Cole Johnson — Slapstick Archive).

Hamilton gives a friendly wink in this publicity photo distributed in 1927 (author's collection).

asked the Hamilton team to conclude their current season with a blackface comedy. Lloyd's writers responded with *King Cotton*, the plot of which revolved around an irrigation system. California's Imperial Valley, which possessed an appropriate irrigation system, was selected as the film's principal production site. Imperial Valley was also part of Brawley, a duck-hunter's paradise. For his visit to Brawley, Lloyd packed a shotgun alongside his comic outfit.

On August 7, 1925, Ethel Hamilton revealed to the Los Angeles press that she was divorcing Lloyd on the grounds of desertion. Lloyd had never returned home. He was refusing to live with Ethel any longer. Ethel reported that her attorneys had negotiated a property settlement. In the agreement, Ethel surrendered rights to the Laurel Canyon home. Lloyd committed to relinquish possession of all furniture and furnishings in the home. He waived interest in a player piano and a 1924 Buick Coupe. He also promised to buy a home for Ethel. Under this arrangement, Ethel would select a residence to cost not less than $15,000, the extent of Lloyd's required contribution. Lloyd would provide a down payment of $3,000 and, in the diminishment of the mortgage, he would impart $12,000 in monthly increments of $150. Lloyd further agreed that, on a weekly basis, he would contribute $100 for Ethel's support and maintenance. Additionally, he stated that he would pay $750 to satisfy all attorney and court fees.

On August 10, Lloyd was served a summons on the divorce matter. The notice was never answered. On October 9, Ethel pleaded for the court to hasten her suit to trial. She claimed that, due to Lloyd's prominence as a motion picture actor, the divorce proceedings were drawing extraordinary notice. Her allegation was broadly defined in an affidavit, which partly read:

> This action has come to the attention of large numbers of people and has been freely commented upon and publicly discussed throughout the United States and particularly by friends and acquaintances of the plaintiff and defendant in Los Angeles, California, and has created great notoriety, publicity and scandal.

Ethel alleged that the situation was causing her "great mental anguish." It was observed in the affidavit that Ethel behaved "extremely nervous and temperamental." Recorded at the closing of the document were the following remarks:

> The affiant has become nervous, hysterical and ill in body and in mind, and at times is near a nervous collapse.... An early trial and disposition of this action ... will enable affiant to take a complete physical and mental rest and recover her health. Plaintiff therefore prays that said action be set down for trial at an early date convenient to the Court.

Lloyd was called to appear in court.

White said, "Hamilton was having wife trouble all the time — Ethel, his dear wife, whom he hated. He was trying to get rid of her and she was trying to take all the money she could get from him. Everybody cheated the poor guy. That's why I felt sorry for him."

Lloyd's personal problems hindered the progress of his latest season-opener, *The Movies*. A past experience had inspired the premise. Lloyd, who portrays himself, becomes incapacitated when he breaks his leg. Following the mishap, his director encounters a smalltown boy who bears a striking resemblance to the comic. Desperate, the director uses the boy to replace his star.

Roscoe Arbuckle directed the comedy. The infamous man concealed his identity by assuming the alias "William Goodrich." Actress Louise Brooks said that Lloyd liked Arbuckle adding, "[Arbuckle] knew what Lloyd Hamilton could do. He just gave him blocking, and let Hamilton do the rest."[2]

One critic highly recommended *The Movies,* predicting that this funny two-reeler would lead to a third Hamilton feature. As the short comedy was now an inconsequential part of an exhibitor's program, this was something that Lloyd would have liked to believe.

It was apparent, by now, that another comic was in line to ascend into the feature film constellation. A dynamic comedy character had deftly emerged from Harry Langdon, who was starring in a series of short comedies for Mack Sennett. This screen persona, which was sympathetic and childlike, showed a kinship to Lloyd. The similarity went farther. Like Lloyd, Langdon performed in a delicate style and patiently pursued laughs. By the end of the year, critics would hail Langdon as the freshest comer in screen comedy.

Ending his association with Sennett, Langdon signed with First National on September 15, 1925. The contract provided for Langdon to produce and star in four features within sixteen months. (Langdon's demand for creative autonomy had stalled negotiations, but First National had finally bowed to the actor's wishes.) According to the contract, First National accepted "Harry Langdon's judgment, management, supervision and control, solely and exclusively and uninterruptedly exercised by him at any and all times and places and in the manner determined by him alone." First National was contractually powerless to interfere with Langdon's decisions unless a film went over budget. This astounding contract was dozens of pages. In comparison, Lloyd's contract with First National had been three pages. It pleased First National executives that Langdon intended to model his features after Chaplin's films.

Keaton, ever the maverick, had defied Chaplin's influence and thumbed his nose at all the Little Tramp's drippy sentiment with his recent feature *Go West*. The comedy star spoofed Chaplin's appeals for pity by playing an unlucky drifter, named Friendless, who develops a touching relationship not with a woman, not with a child—but with a cow!

In 1925, Hollywood was producing more comedies than ever before, but had still not caught up to the exhibitors' demand. Lloyd, who had been a forecaster of the current trend, elaborated on earlier statements. He explained:

> The plays long ago were nearly all tragedies. Comedies were very few. Tragedies were gradually succeeded by melodramas, and these have largely been replaced by the comedy-drama, the farce comedy, and the musical comedy on stage.
>
> The motion picture scene is passing through the same stages. More and more comedies are being made each year and it will only be a little while before comedy predominates the screen. People like to laugh. They get enough tragedy and drama from everyday life.[3]

Ignoring Ethel's complaint, Lloyd did not appear at a scheduled hearing. On October 21, 1925, the default was noted in court papers. On the same day, Ethel testified that Lloyd thought more of his film career than married life. She told the judge that that she had recently followed Lloyd to New York to plead for a reconciliation. "Judge," said Ethel, "he told me that he had to be *free*. He said there was something in him that clamored for freedom and that could not tolerate restraint."⁴ A *Los Angeles Times* reporter who attended the hearing stated the next day, "Even comedians yearn for the great open spaces."⁵

On October 28, the court issued an interlocutory decree of divorce. This temporary judgment was scheduled to elapse in a year. Unless a reconciliation occurred before the decree expired, the marriage would be terminated automatically.

Framed, Lloyd's second offering of the season, was a lackluster comedy. Following its production, Hammons moved to provide the Hamilton company with a strong director. The company obviously needed a man who could place the current series onto a sure and steady course. Elected for the job was Norman Taurog, who had directed a successful series of *Mermaid Comedies*. It was Taurog who had recently guided Lloyd through the old mirror routine.

Taurog had originally aspired to be a comic but, discouraged by the sight of himself on screen, he promptly quit acting and resolved to become a director instead. His big break came when he was working as an errand boy at Fox and got to meet Jack White, who was directing Lloyd in one of the Sunshine comedies. White was staging a scene where a speeding car zooms past Lloyd and sucks off his pants. Lloyd was looking silly standing in his underwear, but not as silly as the chubby errand boy running across the street and dodging traffic. White broke into laughter. He called over Taurog, whom he ended up hiring as his assistant.

Between 1920 and 1922, Taurog co-directed thirteen of Semon's Vitagraph productions. It is generally believed that this batch of films includes Semon's best work. Taurog attributed his success as a comedy director to his ability to understand the psychology of comedians. He said that he learned he had to act patient and firm with his comic charges, who were in essence big kids.

Taurog, whose comedy centered on fantastic mechanical gags, seemed ill-suited to direct Lloyd. His second *Hamilton* comedy featured a powerful wind driving Lloyd, his hot dog wagon and customers along roller coaster tracks and, finally, dumping the entire load into the Pacific Ocean. After a momentary pause, Lloyd, his wagon and the customers reappear resting atop a U. S. fighter submarine. This type of approach, though effective with Larry Semon and *Mermaid*'s interchangeable principals, failed when applied to Lloyd. Lloyd, who was at his funniest strolling down a street and mixing it up with people, had no need for miniatures or stop-motion animation.

Taurog soon moved to change his ways. He

This illustration, which was used in Educational's annual exhibitor's program, was found among Hamilton's personal effects. Hamilton noted on the back that the artist was named Randall (courtesy of the family of Lloyd Hamilton).

listened carefully to Lloyd, whom he saw as a precious story man, and adapted himself to the comic's distinctive style. The accomplishment of this shift was marked by *Move Along*, a subtle and clever comedy that was the company's final release of the season. The plot of *Move Along* was so simple that it can be adequately described in a single sentence: After being tossed out of his boardinghouse room, Lloyd draws upon his resourcefulness to establish an immediate home on the street. The gags were continuous. At one point, Lloyd neatly lays his trousers in the street in time for a steamroller to come along and press them.

Though *Move Along* was an improvement over *Framed* and Taurog's earlier *Hamilton Comedies*, the film prompted an Illinois exhibitor to write: "It seems to me the Llyod [sic] Hamilton Comedies are getting poorer and poorer. When my present contract is run out I am through with Llyod [sic] Hamilton Comedies."

In June, 1926, Lloyd revealed to the press that he had recently injured his foot while making a comedy.[6] He said, now that his foot had become infected, he was going to take time off to stay with his mother and make sure to rest his foot.

15

Erratic Behavior

Much activity was going on at Lloyd's Laurel Canyon mansion. Lloyd was continuing to host parties. The Hays Office had received unconfirmed reports that orgies were common at the gatherings.[1] They had also been informed that Lloyd was drinking excessively. The MPAA advised Lloyd that, before word of his intemperance spread beyond the confines of Hollywood, he totally refrain from alcohol consumption.

Educational's profits were plummeting. Several problems were responsible for the decline. A determined effort by major film companies was smothering independent producers. In addition, a glut of short comedies had created a backlash. William K. Everson wrote in *American Silent Film*, "Because of the ready market for comedy in the twenties, supply far exceeded realistic demand. Many potentially major comics were just lost in the shuffle."[2] Everson used Lloyd as an ideal example. Lloyd, he contended, had deserved a lot more attention. He wrote, "The laconic duck-waddle and off-hand brashness of Lloyd Hamilton were unique. He was a major and extremely successful star of two-reelers in the twenties, elevated by some to a near–Chaplin status."

Educational's 1925–26 season had been a severe financial failure. The company had, in particular, fared poorly with their last *Hamilton* series. As a consequence, Hammons drastically cut the Hamilton company's annual budget. Under the new arrangement, Lloyd's crew was committed to producing eight comedies for the upcoming season. Hammons maintained the less restrictive production schedule for Jack White's *Juvenile* series, which starred a popular young performer nicknamed "Big Boy," and a promising new series starring Lupino Lane.

The Hamilton company opened their new season with *Jolly Tars*, a mindless but amusing comedy featuring Lloyd as an inept sailor. Comedymakers have frequently turned to the reliable "service" premise, but *Jolly Tars* was more immediately inspired by the success of a recent Beery & Hatton vehicle, *We're in the Navy Now*. For *Jolly Tars*, Taurog had assembled a good supporting cast that included three familiar Hamilton cronies: Henry Murdock, Dick Sutherland and Phil Dunham. The director climaxed *Jolly Tars* with Lloyd riding atop a missile. A less effective version of this exact gag had been part of *Great Guns*, a Bobby Vernon vehicle of the preceding year. *Jolly Tars*, a straight "gag" comedy, reportedly did well with audiences.

Unfortunately, Lloyd's latest series did not live up to its promising start. The season's remaining comedies were mechanical and uninventive. They were used as a dump for hackneyed and impersonal gags. The balance of the action was padded with pointless slapstick. Lloyd was not stopping his gag writers from indiscriminately borrowing gags. Worse, his performances were lethargic.

Hamilton (right) visits Petaluma (man at left is unidentified) (courtesy of the family of Lloyd Hamilton).

In the early seventies, Kerr wrote, that it was "disheartening to see Lloyd Hamilton, in a two-reeler made relatively late in the 1920's, making use of business with a vacuum cleaner — sucking drapes from the walls, clothes from men's backs, hair from a dog — that the undistinguished Billy Bevan had exhausted, to no particular effect, some three or four years earlier."[3]

It may have shown a decline in the state of comedy that, at the time Kerr made this statement, a movie enjoying a lucrative theatrical run featured a very similar scene. In *The Return of the Pink Panther*, Peter Sellers wielded an equally forceful vacuum cleaner that ended up devouring a noisy parrot.

Lloyd's uninspired battle with the vacuum cleaner was a key scene in *Breezing Along*. The scene is not as surreal or funny as it could have been. The drapes, rather than magically slipping into the bowels of the vacuum cleaner, become awkwardly affixed to the nozzle. Lloyd, trying to pull the hose loose, rips the drapes from the wall. The drapes envelope Lloyd, covering up the expressive comedian and leaving him as no more than a jumpy bulge for much of the scene. *Breezing Along* is, overall, a lackluster film. The first reel, in which Lloyd demonstrates incompetence as a chauffeur, offers nothing remarkable except for a well-staged car crash, which results in part of a home collapsing.

The second reel opens with the film's one funny gag. Lloyd, a butler, greets guests at the front door. The first guest retracts the crown of his top hat and hands over the flattened headpiece. Then, the man bends a folding cane and slips this into the servant's hands. A second guest approaches and hands Lloyd a top hat. Lloyd, trying to compress the hat, manages to crush it. The guest, who has been inattentive to the butler's actions, also offers his cane. Attempting to fold the cane, Lloyd snaps it in half. The film goes downhill from there. Trite humor is derived from a box of exploding cigars. Further gags surround Lloyd serving up a crab dinner. The prop crab, with its string-operated claws twitching every few seconds, shows more energy and personality than Lloyd.

Somebody's Fault, released two months before *Breezing Along*, is equally poor. Here, the gagwriters indulged in sadistic humor. Lloyd has trouble helping out in an electrician's shop. Bulbs slide off shelves and burst on his head. He gets his hand caught in a steaming hot waffle iron. Even worse agony befalls him on a service call. He's working atop a utility pole when a woodpecker lands on his shoulder. He swings a hatchet at the bird, but the bird suddenly flies off and he drives the hatchet blade into his own Adam's apple. Lloyd, in his boundless ineptitude, eventually causes a high-voltage current of electricity to overrun his body. The electrical shock, although predictable, is humorously conveyed. When Lloyd clutches a live wire, his cap rises and expands like a cake. Much of the humor seems aimed at the comedian's younger fans.

In *The Toy Bulldog and His Times* boxing legend Mickey Walker wrote of an encounter he and manager Doc Kearns had with Lloyd during this period. He said, "We went to a party one night in 1926 and got high, which was par for the course. Lloyd Hamilton, the deadpan comedian of silent pictures, was there.... Hamilton was near the end of his career. He had lived high, had blown millions and needed money. He owned a large track of land in Laurel Canyon, in the hills above Hollywood. Ham wanted to leave Hollywood. He was sick of the place and was washed up in pictures, too. Anyway, he wanted some quick dough, hoping to go to New York and make a fresh start. Doc and I were feeling no pain and it didn't take much salemanship on Ham's part to sell us his real estate. We bought it for $55,000, sight unseen. It was a rather unbusinesslike transaction. Lloyd was as looped as we were." Walker said that the land was later developed and sold for millions of dollars.

Tension developed between Lloyd and Hammons. Because Lloyd's dissipations were adversely affecting his work, Hammons was concerned even more than the Hays Office. Lloyd often appeared on the set looking tired and not feeling up to working. He publicly questioned having been sidetracked on his way to becoming a dramatic actor. Lloyd was wearing his checkered cap, tie and cutaway coat increasingly less. Briefly, in 1926, he had replaced his cap with a straw hat for the comedies *Nobody's Business* and *Here Comes Charlie*. He had recently worn a derby in *Goose Flesh*. The trend continued in his latest comedies. He was dressed as a marine for most of *At Ease* and dressed as a woman for much of *His Better Half*. An item in pressbook for *At Ease* indicated that Lloyd had no qualms about discarding his familiar habit for other outfits.[4] He no longer seemed to care about developing this funny individual in the checkered cap.

Estelle Bradley, Lloyd's leading lady at the time, remembered Lloyd being the nicest guy in the morning, but then he would have a few drinks at lunch and come back to the set unfit to get through his scenes. One particularly bad experience occurred while she and Lloyd were filming a scene on a dirt road. Lloyd, said Bradley, "stank like a skunk from boozing." He stumbled against her suddenly, knocking her into a ditch and falling on top of her. "He was a big fellow," said the 5' 2" actress, "and all I thought was, 'Oh, no, I'm going to be squashed like a bug!'" Bradley also saw Lloyd at clubs and parties. She said that Lloyd generally came across as preoccupied and distant.

Taurog clearly recognized the situation. In 1922, the director had become mixed up in a similar clash between Larry Semon and Vitagraph. Semon had aggravated Vitagraph executives with his unreasonable spending and generally eccentric behavior. Taurog surrendered nearly two years on a lucrative contract so he wouldn't have to be in the middle of this situation. In the face of his current dispute, he left Educational and took charge of Universal's *Andy Gump* series.

Roscoe Arbuckle filled in for Taurog on the next pair of Hamilton productions. Both films were domestic comedies occasionally enlivened by a dose of slapstick. When Arbuckle was engaged to direct a Marion Davies feature, Taurog was persuaded to rejoin the Hamilton team.

In the latter half of 1926, Harry Langdon scored big with two features, *Tramp, Tramp, Tramp* and *Short Pants*. On the release of the first film, a *Photoplay* author wrote, "Langdon has graduated and this film is his diploma." The press and First National indefatigably referred to Langdon as "the new Chaplin."

In January, 1927, a magazine writer named Frank Capron set out to discover how Langdon's success had affected Lloyd. Capron acknowledged that Lloyd, a previous heir to the Chaplin crown, was one of his personal favorites. Capron had arranged for Lloyd to meet him on the set, but he didn't find Lloyd around when he arrived. The writer was eventually directed to Lloyd's dressing room. Lloyd wasn't anywhere to be seen when the writer got there. Resting on a table was a starched batwing collar and a plain gold cap. From what Capron could hear, his arrival had roused someone in an adjoining room. Lloyd, misty-eyed and haggard, appeared in the doorway. Capron introduced himself and apologized for having disturbed Lloyd. Lloyd explained that he had been napping because a toothache had kept him awake all night. He appeared to have forgotten about the interview, but Capron remained enthusiastic. He wrote that the comedy star came across as a modest person, "not a bit upstage."[5]

Capron had barely begun his interview when a bearded, professional-looking man came into the room. The man set a small black bag on the table, brusquely pushing aside the cap and collar. "All right, Mr. Hamilton," he impatiently announced, "I'm ready for you."

Lloyd looked bewildered. The man, realizing he hadn't been expected, dully explained his visit. He was a doctor summoned by Educational to give Lloyd a complete physical examination. As a matter of business precaution, the company was taking out a quarter-million dollar life insurance policy on the comic. Grasping the situation, Lloyd excused himself and led the medical man into the other room. Capron had been waiting for a half-hour when Lloyd finally reemerged. Lloyd was breathing heavily, but seemed encouraged. He told Capron that, according to the doctor, he was in satisfactory shape. It is possible that Capron was being coy in describing this highly suspicious scene.

Capron resumed his interview, establishing feature films as the topic. He mentioned Langdon's swift rise in features. Lloyd told Capron that he was not disturbed by Langdon's success. He said that he was holding to his aspirations, without envy and malice, and patiently continuing his work. He claimed that he was looking forward with hope to a third attempt. In relating their discussion, Capron spoke of "the favor of the gods" and Lloyd's "eventual ascension to the select fold."[6] Capron started out talking about a comedian taking pratfalls and ducking custard pies, but he ended up talking about grace, destiny and rapture. Lloyd, according to Capron, could only pray that "the gods" were not opposed to his rise.

The interview had become, in effect, a religious discussion. Lloyd might have done well to remember a sermon his old pastor had given about confronting disappointment with a fullness of spirit. Pastor Brown warned against a person giving up to disappointment, which would most likely end their usefulness. He maintained that, even when everything goes against you, you should "rejoice in the goodness of God ... and keep the face bright."

"I hope some day to get a chance under better conditions," said Lloyd. "Not to satisfy any personal vanity, but I believe it is possible to do better work in the longer comedies. There is more leisure, more range for story and situation, and more freedom to concentrate on artistic efforts."[7]

Capron believed that, considering how it was difficult for a comedian to establish themselves and remain popular, Lloyd was to be admired for his achievements. He said that it was important for the young ambitious comedian to see what others before them have done to be successful. He warned that comedy was a dangerous business, with many having had to suffer dire consequences for failing to make the right choices. "[I]nstead of attaining enduring stardom," he wrote, "[they] have flickered a moment or two and burned out."[8]

16

Ain't It a Crime?

In February, 1927, John V. Martin rented the Crescent Night Club, a fashionable cafe located on one of Hollywood's major routes. Martin officially recorded that he would operate the club as a tea room. In truth, he planned to use the palatial establishment as a speakeasy.

During the early hours of Saturday, March 26, Charles and Irene Meehan arrived at the Crescent. The club contained a peppy crowd which had not yet called an end to Friday evening. These patrons included, among several show business people, a number of prominent actors and directors. The Meehans paused at the entrance. Louis Menney, the doorman, allowed them to proceed into the building.

Mrs. Meehan had been a film actress prior to her marriage. Under her maiden name, Irene Dalton, she had been one of Lloyd's leading ladies.

Irene wasn't wise when it came to picking men. This was evident two years earlier, when she became a central figure in the highly publicized divorce of John Raymond Owens, a millionaire oil man, and his wife Florence.[1] Irene met Owens in April, 1921, and the two soon became involved in an affair. Owens, who had homes in Toledo, Detroit and Los Angeles, traveled around the country with Irene. At one time, the couple traveled by train from Los Angeles to Chicago, where they visited Irene's mother. They later drove from Chicago to Detroit to attend a party at the Cadillac Hotel. They next went to Toledo to attend an all-night party at the Secor Hotel. Based on a complaint filed by Florence, Irene and Owens were arrested for violating the Mann Act, which prohibited the interstate transport of a female for immoral purposes. The law was originally designed to combat white slavery, but the United States Supreme Court decided in 1917 that the law could be applied in cases of consensual extramarital sex.

Irene went on to marry Charles Meehan, a 24-year-old professional criminal. To hear Meehan tell it, he was an actor turned real estate man. The fact was that Meehan had utterly failed in an effort to become an actor and was currently drawing a minor income from selling real estate. For the past few years, he had earned most of his income by bootlegging liquor under the alias "Charles E. Mayo." Since 1924, he had been convicted five times for violating the Volstead Act. Meehan, like his wife, had been acquainted with Lloyd. Being a perennial party guest, he had been part of several gatherings at Lloyd's home. This evening, as he walked into the Crescent, he was in a drunken stupor.

In the dining room, the Meehans noticed Lloyd sitting at a table. At the same table were film director Jimmie Sinclair; a full-time stunt man, Billy Jones; and a part-time stunt man, a cheerful and likable guy named Eddie Diggins. Of Lloyd's companions, Diggins demands a more explicit description.

Diggins, a lightweight boxer, was, at 23 years old, already regarded as a has-been. He had been trying lately to use stunt work as a bridge between his dwindling boxing career and an acting career and he had been encouraged by his acquisition of minor roles in the features *Goat Getter* and *One-Punch O'Day*.

Much material existed for a conversation between Lloyd and Diggins. First, each man was a fan of the other's profession. Second, both the comic and the boxer had risen from the same area of the country. Third, eerie similarities were evident in their respective careers.

Diggins was born and raised in Antioch, a small neighbor of Oakland. As a teenager, Diggins won numerous American titles wearing the winged "O" of San Francisco's Olympic Club, an amateur athletic organization that had once been represented by "Gentleman Jim" Corbett. In 1921, Diggins turned glove pro under the management of Johnny Herger, a world welterweight champion who had retired undefeated. Diggins subsequently fought one four-round main bout every week for a full year. In these fights, which were presented at San Franciso's Dreamland Rink, Diggins phenomenally defeated many admirable lightweights. At that time, observers predicted that Diggins would become a world champion. In 1923, Diggins was unexpectedly knocked out two rounds into a bout. Several of the boxer's following showings were equally poor. As a result, acclaim of Diggins quickly diminished. By 1925, observers were reporting that the fighter's glory days were over.

Irene walked to Lloyd's table. After saying hello to everyone, she casually joined the gathering. Meehan, who was too drunk to participate in the table talk, alternated between frustration and boredom.

Eventually, Meehan rose angrily from the table. Trying to pick a fight with anyone, he began to stagger through the club. He went from one man to another. He firmly stopped when he came before Diggins. He stared menacingly into the eyes of the noted boxer. He paused on him longer than he had with any of the other men.

"I'll fight you, too," Meehan finally challenged.

Diggins, who had little interest in Meehan's drunken threat, pushed the man aside and started to walk away. Meehan responded, immediately, by charging Diggins. The attack triggered a scuffle between the pair.

Due to the liberating effect of alcohol, a building packed with heavy drinkers is a volatile place. This may explain the reason that, immediately after Diggins and Meehan began trading blows, a furious free-for-all erupted. Billy Jones said that he gave "everything I had to get to [Diggins]." In running for the nearest exit, thirty to forty people, including Irene, Sinclair and numerous screaming women, reportedly created a stampede. Seeking a less troubled environment, Lloyd cautiously hurried to the barroom.

A chair appeared suddenly above Jones' head. As the cracking of wood exploded in his ears, his head felt as if it had caught fire. He fell to the floor, whereupon he was repeatedly kicked.

Above Jones, the activity grew more frenzied. Another chair supposedly knocked Meehan unconscious. Bottles were sailing across the room. Patrons smashed chairs, broke a large chandelier, and collapsed tables. In order to have something with which to batter each other, some tore legs from the overturned tables. The departing throng was choking doors and windows. Once they escaped the club, Irene and Sinclair got into Meehan's car and rode around the block.

It was around the time that someone hurled a chair into his stomach that Menney moved to leave. He instructed the club's bartender, Walter Erickson, to gather the night's proceeds and follow him out of the building.

Then, abruptly, the lights went out. The sudden darkness settled the commotion. Witnesses would claim that, within the next few moments, they heard thumps that they understood to be an exchange of rough blows and a crash that suggested that a body had hit the floor. One female witness would later state that, right after these sounds, she heard "a scream of pain."

The lights came back on. Jones lifted himself to his hands and knees. Almost immediately, he noticed Diggins lying still amidst broken chandelier glass. Jones could see a copious stream of blood escaping from his friend's chest. Upon becoming aware of this deathly form, patrons even more anxiously struggled to leave the scene. Outside the Crescent, the night became misty from exhaust fumes and dotted with taillights. Within a remarkably short time, the club was quiet and virtually empty.

By this time, Lloyd had returned to the dining room. With Jones' help, he promptly checked Diggins' life signs. Since Diggins still exhibited traces of life, the pair worked desperately to revive him with artificial respiration. Minutes later, a chef named Joe S. Santinelli and a young Japanese dishwasher emerged from the kitchen. They found Lloyd and Jones administering first aid to a jagged wound situated directly over Diggins's heart. The two men assisted Lloyd and Jones.

Irene and Sinclair were around the corner, deliberating over what they should do. Irene finally decided that they should retrieve her inebriated spouse. "Charlie will get killed," she reportedly told Sinclair.

Nearly everyone had cleared out by the time the couple returned to the Crescent. Irene found Meehan unconscious in a room adjacent to the dining area. After reviving him with hot and cold towels, Irene walked into the dining room. It was there that she found the large, sweet-faced comedian supporting the bloodied body of the boxer. Lloyd, she later told police, was struggling vainly to revive the man.

The police arrived at this point. Witnesses remember them making a loud entrance. They rammed open the doors and marched through the club. A couple of uniformed men unceremoniously ushered Lloyd aside. The police promptly concluded that a knife had caused Diggins' wound.

Diggins died before the arrival of an ambulance. Detectives on the scene quickly began an investigation. In an effort to locate witnesses, they instructed their men to collect the club's lingering employees and patrons. From this group, they gathered the names of some of those who had departed the club since the row. They also ordered their officers to search for liquor.

Meehan was found collapsed in an alley located behind the club. His clothing was severely disarranged. His head carried a puffy lump and cuts. After officers revived him and lifted him to his feet, Meehan drunkenly boasted of having connections. He arrogantly informed his escorts that his brother was a special agent of the Justice Department. As the officers guided him into the club, Meehan remarked, inexplicably, "I slugged him through the window." He reiterated this statement several times before an ambulance finally removed him from the scene.

Police filled the club. They dragged six gallons of wine, five gallons of alcohol, and twenty-six bottles of gin from the barroom. They managed to assemble several potential witnesses. The witnesses included a pair of waiters, Tim Tooline and Columbo Kelley, and two checkroom girls, Rosie and Josie St. George. Other officers combed through debris in search of a knife.

Ultimate command of the investigation was assumed by Herman Cline, captain of the Los Angeles Detectives, and Ed Slaughter, chief of the Hollywood Detective Division.

Captain Cline initiated a search for the Crescent's proprietor, who was listed as "John Martin." Slaughter ordered that those who had been singled out as material witnesses be immediately arrested. To determine if any of these principals had ever been arrested, Slaughter dispatched an officer to the police record bureau.

Eight people were questioned while under detainment at Hollywood's central police station. The group included Jones, Lloyd and Santinelli. Lloyd told the police: "When the fight started, I beat it out of the room because I didn't want to get mixed up in it. After the commotion had died down, I came back in and saw Diggins on the floor. I was trying to revive him when the police came in." Jack Waggoner, a film director, also explained that he had fled from the fight before the stabbing and had not returned until afterwards. The accounts of the remaining witnesses conflicted, only succeeding in frustrating the investigation. For undisclosed reasons, the police soon eliminated Meehan as a suspect. This left the detectives without a clue as to who had stabbed Diggins.

Later in the morning, Lloyd and six other vital witnesses were released. From Lloyd's appearance at the time of his arrest, it was obvious that he had not participated in the fight. Also, Lloyd's remarks had been supported by other testimony. The police had no doubt that Lloyd had told them the truth. Only Santinelli was held for further questioning. Meehan remained under guard at a receiving hospital.

Shortly before noon, Slaughter faced the press. He reported that investigators had formed

Hamilton clowns around as a trapper in an ill-fated production of *Rose Marie*. The actress is unidentified (courtesy of Cole Johnson — Slapstick Archive).

"four definite theories." When you hear the police say something like this, it essentially means that they're completely baffled. The press corps publicized the most sensational of the authorities' hypotheses, according to which members of an underworld organization had provoked the Crescent fracas as a diversion. It was surmised that, under the cover of the battle, the gangsters had murdered Diggins. In line with this premise, police officials were seeking six unidentified men who had swiftly driven away from the crime scene.

The news reporters fashioned the jumble of facts into a suspenseful crime-drama. In order to elicit sympathy for the murder victim, the reporters overstated Diggins' recent screen work. They wrote that the boxer had been on the threshold of a promising new career. Sports editors, whose comments were usually confined to the back of their papers, were given front page space to reminisce about the boxer's career. In the *L.A. Record*, the main headline read:

JAIL 6 IN MOVIE MURDER
BOXER SLAIN WITH KNIFE

The photo that accompanied the bold type did not display Diggins — it featured Lloyd Hamilton. The picture, a characteristic promotional portrait, exhibited the diffident comic with a bleached, fearful expression. By surrounding that face with such dramatic words as "speakeasy," "tragedy," "murder" and "underworld," the editor had created a striking image that would sell papers.

Sometime on Saturday, Erickson surrendered to the authorities. He admitted that he had purchased the liquor uncovered in the barroom. Asked what he remembered about the fight, Erickson said simply, "I didn't see anything." When his interrogators pursued these remarks, Erickson qualified that he did recollect that there had been a "fracas of some sort." The bartender was released on $500 bail.

Before the end of the day, Menney surrendered to the authorities. He admitted that he was the sought-after "John Martin."

Deputy District Attorney E.J. Dennison advanced a new hypothesis, less exciting than the earlier one: Dennison insisted that Diggins' death was not a conspiratory murder. He concluded that, perhaps struck down in the dark, Diggins had fallen on a piece of the broken chandelier. The police probe, in his mind, showed no direct evidence of murder. It is possible that, in his drunken haze, Meehan mistook the sound of the shattering chandelier as a window breaking, hence the remark "I slugged him through the window." Dennison ordered that Diggins' body be examined again. He asked that, this time, examiners meticulously search for glass particles.

At Monday's coroner's inquest only one of an eight-member jury submitted a verdict in Dennison's favor. The remaining jurors decided that Diggins had been stabbed with a pocketknife. On Tuesday, investigators announced that they had inaugurated a manhunt. They explained that their suspect was a "notorious thug of the local underworld."

Today, the death of Eddie Diggins remains a mystery.

17

"Drank Himself Out"

Lloyd's career remained intact despite the scandal. In April, 1927, Educational signed him to a new three-year contract. Then, within the next month, Lloyd accepted a leading character role in a prestigious, big-budget feature. *Rose Marie* was based on Rudolf Friml's operetta, a version of which had recent success on the London stage. Metro-Goldwyn-Meyer, the premier film company, was behind the project.

Since this silent-film adaptation couldn't accommodate songs, the studio looked to focus on the romantic melodrama inherent in the story, which outlined the obstacles in a passionate and illicit love affair. Rose Marie, a married woman who operates a Canadian trading post, falls in love with Jim Kenyon, a fugitive who has the Mounties in hot pursuit. Kenyon claims to have been wrongly accused of murder and Rose Marie has no doubt about his innocence. Despite the couple's wretched situation, the audience was to be treated to a tidy, happy ending. The trapper would be cleared of the murder charge and Rose Marie's husband would break his back and die. Well, perhaps that ending is more tidy than happy. Lloyd was cast as Kenyon's sidekick, a rugged trapper named Fuzzy. The role was added to lend comic relief to the grim proceedings.

As two-reel comedies no longer sustained a lucrative business, many screen comics were now playing supporting characters in leading features. The most prolific of the character comedians were Slim Summerville, Chester Conklin, Mack Swain, Ford Sterling, and Hank Mann. Lloyd had the chance to join their ranks.

Lloyd was dating Irene Dalton, who had recently divorced Charles Meehan. On a Saturday evening in June, they drove to Santa Ana, where they were married by a justice of the peace. The couple had originally planned to follow their wedding with an extensive automobile trip, but Lloyd's commitment to *Rose Marie* made the romantic excursion impossible. The newlyweds curtailed their honeymoon, spending the first few days of their marriage in quiet seclusion.

As *Rose Marie* was scheduled to begin production in August, Lloyd made sure to get an early start on his latest series. He shot as much as he could and then took time off to grow a full beard for the trapper role.

Two more comics, unable to remain effective in features, had suffered severe and abrupt professional reversals.

Larry Semon, a former cartoonist, was inclined toward exaggerated and improbable comedy. He failed to develop a screen personality with which an audience could identify. Walter Kerr described Semon as "a face and a walk without an idea to see him home."[1] Semon relied mostly on extravagant gags and long, frantic chases. As Taurog explained, "[Larry's failing was that] a person couldn't take those wild gags and that fast stuff for five reels."[2] Semon made five features and every one of them lost money. His last feature, *Spuds*, was released in April, 1927. According to Leonard Maltin, Semon's experience in features left the comic "bankrupt, financially and emotionally."[3] Semon became increasingly depressed and his health deteriorated. He died in 1928 at the age of 39.

Harry Langdon was also having problems. His *Long Pants*, released in March, 1927, featured a peculiar and surreal shift in story and characterization that alienated many of the comedian's fans. *Variety* reviewer Alfred Rushford Grearson said of the film, "[T]he sympathetic element is overdeveloped at the expense of the gags and stunts that made *The Strong Man* a riot."[4] A month later, *His First Flame*, a feature that Langdon had made while still at Sennett, found its way into theatres after a two-year delay. Theatregoers, unaware of the film's history, were disappointed by the lesser production values and the relative crudeness of the writing and acting. This pair of box office failures put Langdon under pressure to reassert himself with his next feature, *Three's a Crowd*, but the creative team responsible for his success had recently broken up and Langdon made a bold decision to turn the situation around on his own. Behind the cameras, he took control of writing, directing and producing, which was perhaps more responsibility than he was equipped to handle. Poor planning and extensive re-takes caused budget overages, which angered the executives at First National. *Three's a Crowd*, an uncomfortably strange and depressingly dark film, was poorly received on its release in August, 1927. Langdon was accused of manufacturing too much Chaplin-style pathos and losing sight of being funny. The film managed to chase away more of Langdon's fans and put the comedian on an unstoppable downward slide.

Lloyd was possibly responding to Semon and Langdon's failures when, in July, 1927, he renewed his pronouncements against the feature-length comedy. He said, "Two-reel comedies are the logical place for a comedian," he said. "The longer pictures are too burdened with story which slow the action too much for successful comedy business."[5]

In 1927, Warner Brothers purchased the screen rights to a Broadway hit called *The Jazz Singer*. The prime candidate to lead the film version was Al Jolson, who had been evading film producers since his bad experience with Griffith. Warner Brothers managed to land the performer only after committing themselves to furnish the film with a soundtrack. The soundtrack technology had been available for several years, but previous trials did not encourage studios that the technology had a commercial use. Warners arranged for *The Jazz Singer* to be silent except for its song segments.

Problems arose soon after production started on *Rose Marie*. The studio became displeased with the leading lady, Renee Adoree. Despite the investment of $242,000, the production was scrapped. Director Lucien Hubbard reshot the film with an entirely new cast. The title role was assumed by Joan Crawford. In the new production, Lloyd was replaced by George Cooper. Lloyd returned to his series. Using the extra production time, his company was able to produce an additional comedy for its new season.

From 1921 to 1926, Educational had opened their annual exhibitor book with a page devoted to Lloyd. However, the first page of the 1927–28 annual featured an ad for the Lupino Lane series. For those exhibitors of Lloyd's earlier series, the text of this announcement had a familiar ring: "The Lane comedies have been one unbroken succession of hits. A big attraction and growing bigger with every release." The next page of the exhibitor book was wholly given to Jack White's *Big Boy* series. The *Hamilton Comedies* had been pushed to page three.

Conspicuous by their absence from the program were the properties of the prolific Christie

Company. Al Christie had ended his seven-year association with Hammons and contracted with Paramount, who agreed to give Christie the money to produce short comedies and feature-length comedies.

In the last year, Educational had seen its largest percentage of profits come from *Felix the Cat*, a bi-weekly series of one-reel cartoons. Not only did the ink-based feline entertain children and adults, he was also a relatively inexpensive star. He posed a serious threat to his live-action rivals. From a historical perspective, the paw prints were on the wall.

The *Hamilton Comedies* of the new season exhibited a marked improvement over the releases of the previous year. These comedies were tolerable, ranging in quality from fair to good. One exhibitor commented of Lloyd's latest series: "Not the best that Lloyd has made, but will pass."

The most successful of the latest *Hamilton Comedies* was *At Ease*. Comedy writer John Grant would later lift key segments of the film for Abbott and Costello's service vehicles. Even further down the road, a matching of Taurog and Grant would lead Martin and Lewis to rework the same material.

Two other highlights of the new *Hamilton* series were *A Homemade Man* and *Between Jobs*. The Athletic Club, still Lloyd's principal purlieu, provided the inspiration for *A Homemade Man*. *Between Jobs* was a partial remake of *The Vagrant*. Educational's publicity department reported that the film gave Lloyd "his best opportunity in many days." It was scenes from this comedy that had been so delightfully described to me in the halls of the New York Public Library. Richard L. Fox had recalled Lloyd plastering himself inside a room and trying to drill an exit. When the pointed end of the drill bore through the wall, it attached to a co-worker and twirled the man around.

Lloyd's latest leading ladies were interchangeable. They were physically appealing but their performances were bland. Two of these actresses were nearly half Lloyd's age, a disparity which strained their credibility as Lloyd's love interest.

As early as November, 1927, Irene moved to take legal action against Lloyd. According to the *Los Angeles Times*, Lloyd and Irene permanently separated on February 1, 1928, only seven months after their marriage. Irene went to stay with friends from Chicago. On April 7, Irene sued Lloyd for divorce, the action petitioned on the grounds of cruelty. The following was reported in the *Los Angeles Examiner*:

> Mrs. Hamilton in her complaint stated that her husband often used language unbecoming a gentleman, that he prevaricated and she had lost confidence in him. Mrs. Hamilton said that on January 7 last Hamilton induced her to pledge her jewelry to his manager, Mrs. Adelle Daniels, and obtain a loan of $1,000.00. Hamilton, she said, received the money and never returned money for jewels, although, she asserts, he is financially able to redeem them. While in San Francisco, she said, Hamilton struck her, causing her severe physical injuries.

Irene also charged that her husband regularly staged "wild drinking parties."

Over the years, Irene's accusations have attained undue prominence in the comedian's story, contributing to persistent rumors that the man went out of control when he drank. Rumors told to the author during research for this book allege that when Lloyd had too many drinks, he had a tendency of getting into fistfights. One story depicts Lloyd tearing off his shirt in a drunken rage and running up the street screaming. But these stories, which are not supported by newspaper coverage, public records or eyewitness accounts, are not likely to be true and should be written off as the type of dark lore that grows up around tragic, mysterious figures.

The inevitable problem is that, when random facts get loose in the air, they will be picked up, shared, misconfigured and exaggerated. It is true that Irene accused Lloyd of getting drunk and hitting her. It is true that the comedian was arrested a number of times for public drunkenness. These facts could lead to the reasonable assumption that Lloyd became disorderly and even violent when he drank. But it would be wrong to accept the story of the combative, bare-chested, screaming man as fact. The type of disorderly behavior that attracted police to Lloyd was never, by any means, violent. And one needs to be wary about accusations that arise during divorce proceedings. Even assuming that this accusation was true, Irene never indicated that this was anything more than an isolated incident that occurred during a heated argument.

In her suit, Irene requested that Lloyd return a car that she had lent him. She asked to regain possession of her jewels. She sought an award of permanent alimony, which would provide her with monthly payments of $1,500. Finally, she applied for $5,500 to pay counsel fees and court costs.

The loan from his business manager was not the only indication that Lloyd was living above his means. Within the last few months, Lloyd had defaulted on his mortgage and lost his home. It was in describing this incident that Jack White expressed sympathy towards his former partner: "He mortgaged a house he had in Laurel Canyon, forgot to make his payments, and they took the house away from him after he had paid almost two-thirds of its value."[6]

The new divorce action didn't improve Lloyd's reputation. Without a tantara, Hammons broke Lloyd's contract in April. This meant that *Hamilton Comedies* would not return in the next season. In the May issue of *The Exhibitor Herald*, a letter made it obvious that at least one exhibitor was not distressed by the event. In evaluating Lloyd's latest release, *Blazing Away*, a Kansas City theater owner observed, "Pretty weak. Hamilton is about done, I guess, and evidently Educational knows it. I see he's missing from their 1928–29 schedule."

In an interview with Sam Gill, archivist at the Academy of Motion Picture Arts and Sciences, Taurog would readily acknowledge that Hamilton had been defeated by his alcoholism. Jack White declared, "Here was a man who had been good for seven years. He was a big star, yet all of a sudden exhibitors didn't want his pictures anymore."[7]

Charles Lamont, the director of the Lane and *Big Boy* series, had known Lloyd for a long time. Lamont was married to Estelle Bradley, a former beauty queen who was the leading lady in six Hamilton comedies during 1926 and 1927. Lamont told film historian Kevin Brownlow that he and his wife would go out with Lloyd and he would get so drunk that they had to prop him up.[8] In an interview for this book, Lamont summarized the situation as follows: "Lloyd was a friendly and amiable fellow; unfortunately, he overindulged in his drinking. Eventually he became an alcoholic, so the studio dropped him."[9]

In between the production of his final scenes, Lloyd was said to have been quietly entertaining the children in his cast.[10] Lloyd had, in the last few months, become unassuming on the set. His crew rarely heard him raise his voice and he spoke with very few people.

Educational's complete abandonment of Lloyd roused the Hays Office, who barred Lloyd from working in the local film industry. Lloyd offered no public statement in response. He showed no resistance at all.[11]

Jules White, Jack's younger brother, was a *Cameo* director at the time. Years later, White spared words and delicacy in describing the event. He stated, simply, "Lloyd drank himself *out*."[12]

18

The Vagrant

The Jazz Singer and its follow-up, *The Singing Fool*, were phenomenal hits, their success triggering a "sound craze" throughout Hollywood. *The Jazz Singer*'s most influential scene simply involved "Jolie" playing a piano and singing to his screen mother. Upon completing the song, he suddenly adlibs a speech that film historian Walter Kerr identified as "a lengthy piece of nonsense."[1] He promises his mom, "I'll take you up to the Bronx where you'll meet your friends, the Goldbergs, the Friebergs, and all the other bergs."

By the middle of 1928, sound was the predominant issue in Hollywood. Trade publications were neck-deep in the subject. The major film companies were investing much of their capital into the purchase of sound-recording equipment.

Educational commenced their latest season, their first without Lloyd, as if there was nothing extraordinary about it. There was not the slightest trace of Lloyd Hamilton in fan or trade magazines. The performer's name had suddenly vanished from their pages.

The *L.A. Examiner* printed Lloyd's name in one story. Rugby Ross, who had rented a home to Lloyd and Irene, named Lloyd as the defendant in a damage suit. Ross alleged that, by staging "wild parties," the comedian had caused much injury to the rental property. The hearing occurred on July 3, 1928. As Lloyd did not appear to contest the suit, the judge automatically ruled in favor of the plaintiff. He ordered that, as equity, the absent defendant pay $1,023 to his former landlord.

In an interview with Edward Watz, actor Eddie Quillan remembered seeing Lloyd on July 10, 1928, when celebrities gathered to see singer-comedian Bert Wheeler perform at the Los Angeles' Orpheum Theatre.[2]

It was sometime during this period that the 36-year-old comic seemed to vanish into thin air. What had suddenly become of him?

Acting was a trade Lloyd had plied passionately for two decades. A person cannot suddenly quit a job they have been doing for that long. Now, barred from the studios, he had lost more than his livelihood; he had lost his identity, too. In his idleness, it was unlikely he could find coherence, balance, or self-worth.

Lloyd was not disposed to reuniting the scattered pieces of his life. He shunned his pressing problems. He simply quit. Indulging his addiction, he consumed two quarts of alcohol per day. As the liquor clouded his mind, he sealed himself from his difficulties, slipping into a black and silent void. The massive and continuous doses of alcohol devastated his body. His athletic build melted away. His sweet childlike face dissipated as its features became emaciated. But the large amount of alcohol failed to dematerialize him entirely.

Depleted, as well, were his savings. Incapable of paying his mortgage, Lloyd was cast out of his home. Charleson Gray, who later explained the situation in an article for *Motion Picture Herald*, decried the incompetence of business managers and described the comic's excessive generosity in lending money.³

Lloyd initially sought the kindness of friends, who provided him with food, money and temporary lodgings. One of his hosts was Edmund Lowe who, with Lloyd and Bacon, had once formed an inseparable trio at the Alcazar Theatre.

Lowe, who had entered motion pictures in 1917, had recently enjoyed a major comeback. The actor had been typecast for years as a drawing-room Romeo, which made his screen appearances dull and repetitive. In 1926, he accepted an unconventional role in the war drama *What Price Glory?* This blood and mud adventure, which featured the actor as a comically scrappy sergeant, transformed his career, bringing him a variety of new roles.

Lloyd assumed the role of freeloader, although he hated to be an object of charity or impose on his friends. Worried he would wear out his welcome, he wouldn't stay at one place for long. He was too embarrassed to ask for help from his family. He was soon a dislocated man adrift on the streets.

Whenever he stepped onto a busy boulevard, his heart would sink and his stomach would tighten. Gray wrote about him "[constantly] ducking down alleys and side-streets in order to avoid the tightlipped disapproving stares or the curious grins of passersby."⁴ She wrote about his "shamed avoidance of everyone connected with the picture business." It hurt him more than anything to be recognized. He dreaded coming upon the old acquaintance who might suddenly call out his name. Gray described him "slinking down a back alley" to make sure that a friend or a co-worker didn't see "the wreck he had made of his flesh."

Lloyd's existence was bleak, harsh, and unreal. Contrary to the adventures of Lloyd's cinematic tramps, nothing was charming or fascinating about life on the street. This alcoholic man, who was without a home or job, did not demonstrate the buoyant enterprise of Oofty Goofty. He wandered along, instead, in a disoriented and catatonic state.

Lloyd told Gray that, during this period, one of his more painful moments occurred in a drug store, where he had gone to purchase wine tonic. A boy who recognized the former comic came up to him and asked him for his picture. Lloyd was crushed by the encounter.

Lloyd said that, whenever he was especially desperate for money, he was able to depend on Henry Lehrman. Lloyd, who was getting around in any way that he could, could remember riding to Lehrman's home in a tailor's delivery truck. Lloyd was also given money by several actor friends, including Charley Chase, Lew Cody, Richard Dix and Joe E. Brown.

For a respite, Lloyd would wander along a deserted stretch of beach. When the metal pin in his foot was causing him pain, he would stop to rest on the sand. The seaside setting was placid, conducive to meditation, but Lloyd had managed to erase most thoughts. He wasn't inclined to sift and weigh his notions in order to identify his mistakes. Instead, he descended into a sturdy sleep.

The sight of the sleeping derelict attracted curiosity. Observers contemplated the origin of this person. As the helpless, rangy vagrant roamed the shore, some onlookers worried that he would stray into the ocean and drown.

But, one evening, one man demonstrated more than passive concern. Charles Ray Ouelette, struggling with heavy cargo, came lurching into the Athletic Club. Locked under his arm, hanging limply, was a gangly white goblin. This creature was a longtime club member, yet no one in the place recognized him. No one knew this was Lloyd Hamilton. Ouelette

Hamilton (right) provided comic relief as a stuttering valet in Great Britain's first "all-talkie," *Black Waters* (1929). His costars are Hallom Coaley (left) and Noble Johnson (courtesy of Cole Johnson — Slapstick Archive).

dragged Lloyd downstairs to the Turkish baths, where he instructed a masseur to clean up his companion and give him a thorough working over.

The sight contrasted a scene out of a popular old Chaplin comedy, *The Cure*. The setting of *The Cure* didn't just happen to look similar to the Athletic Club — it had been designed, under Chaplin's instructions, as an elaborate reproduction of the club. Chaplin, as an inebriated man who subjects himself to a rubdown, made a point to parody the Athletic Club's aggressive masseurs. Rebelling against the rough treatment, he transforms the massage into a wrestling match. Now, though, there was no silly action. Lloyd, settled on the masseur's table, was as inert and somber as a corpse on a morgue slab.

For the rest of the night, Lloyd slept soundly in one of the club's bedrooms. In the morning, Ouelette sat with Lloyd and explained that he was an associate of Dorothy Davenport, the widow of Wallace Reid. He informed Lloyd that he and his colleagues had "something for a gland in the chest" that could quickly break his alcoholism. He asked Lloyd if he would consent to their treatment. Dubious "quick cures" were prevalent in the late twenties and thirties. Alcoholics were treated with potent drug cocktails typically fortified with morphine and phenobarbital. Quick cure sanitariums would flourish for a time. But evidence mounted that, worse than being unproductive, these treatments were often damaging. Stories spread about the physical and mental abuse of patients. Under a cloud of disrepute, the sanitariums would draw fire from legal and medical authorities and would be forced out of business.

For now, though, the friendly man's proposal was a summons from darkness into light. Lloyd was being asked, perhaps for the last time, if he was going to renew his commitment to life. Lloyd's thoughts were divided. It was bound to cross his mind, in these familiar surroundings, that this same good fellow could easily get him a drink.

In minutes, Lloyd resolved to essay a resurgence, but he didn't tell Ouelette his decision right away. He knew that, before he began this critical undertaking, he needed some strength.

"It sounds good," he said, "but I'd like to have a drink first."

It wasn't until he consumed three quarts of whiskey that he allowed a physician to insert Ouelette's elixir into his veins.

Lloyd did withstand the horrors of withdrawal and, in a few weeks, he experienced a clear improvement in his fitness. Throughout his recovery, he devoted most of his time to exercising in the club gym. It was reported in *The Los Angeles Examiner* that Lloyd was "on the water wagon."

Still, the alcohol had done its job well. Lloyd recalled very little of the last year. His memories were vague and disconnected. He started to record his impressions in a notepad.

Lloyd eventually assembled a few of his homilies into a composition entitled *Maxims of an Ex-Mutt*. The full text, as published in Motion Picture Classic, appeared as follows:

> *Maxims of an Ex-Mutt*
> *by Lloyd Hamilton*
>
> *The best way to end up a bum is to start out as a good fellow.*
> *Living life is a whole lot different than reading about it.*
> *Liquor is all right. It was the way I handled it that was bad. I never came up for air.*
> *My mother is happy for the first time in years. I would be a fool ever again to endanger that.*
> *I'm going to bear down and finish the routine.*
> *There must have been a reason for all that I went through.*
> *I'd hate to think it all had no purpose, all was futile.*

Buster Keaton, who would also suffer through a period of alcoholism, could have learned from these maxims. Five years later, Keaton's mother and brother would track their errant kin to a vagrant camp. Rudi Blesh, Keaton's biographer, described the scene as follows:

> Around the fire, which had been built on the right-of-way on the lee of a gully, was a seated circle of tramps. At the center Buster Keaton was performing a slapstick pantomime, executing neck rolls and pratfalls ... over the open fire. The tramps were laughing and applauding, and after each fall, one or another would hand a wine bottle to their entertainer.[6]

Keaton, acting more sociable than Lloyd, plunged into the middle of the tramp community and performed a scaled-down version of his former act.

Hays was encouraged enough by Lloyd's recovery to lift the MPAA ban against the comedian. Acting on the reinstatement of his old friend, Marshall Neilan engaged Lloyd to appear in his latest film, *Black Waters*. *Black Waters*, a murder-mystery about a serial killer stalking victims aboard a fogbound schooner, was a low-budget independent feature put together by British producer Herbert Wilcox. Wilcox, who normally made films in London, had transported his production crew to Hollywood to have access to sound equipment. The film's script was written by John Willard, author of the stage play *The Cat and the Canary*. *Black Waters* had the same basic plot as *The Cat and Canary* except that the "old dark house" had become an old dark houseboat. The writer still offered a murderous lunatic lurking in disguise among a group of guests. Lloyd, as a stuttering valet, tried his best to provide comic relief between the multiple murders. Audiences weren't likely to have laughed much when the nervous valet ends up getting beaten to death with a blowpipe.

Black Waters, as a "poverty row" feature, was an indication of Neilan's own sharp decline. This was the result of Neilan's contentious nature and sensitive artistic impulses, especially unsuitable traits amid the industry's growing corporate culture.

During the twenties, Neilan became known as Hollywood's foremost ladies' director. He created the best vehicles of the decade's most popular actresses, including Mary Pickford, Blanche Sweet, Colleen Moore and Constance Talmadge. Still, his reputation did not give him the authority he needed to make films as he thought they should be made.

Neilan was willing to battle studio executives when their interference imperiled his creative ideas. Joe E. Brown stated: "Neilan only got mad when he should." Whether justified or not, the numerous battles were costly. Struggling under the constant conflict, the director extended his drinking habits. Pickford complained that Neilan's drinking had become a problem as early as 1924, when the two worked together on *Dorothy Vernon of Haddon Hall*.[7]

Drink, worry and strife had caused Neilan to age prematurely. The director was in his thirties, but he had already lost the color in his hair, developed deep creases in his face, and suffered a loss in vision. Nonetheless, his features were still sharp and handsome. He looked, with his silver hair and wire-rimmed spectacles, like a stately elder.

During the 1920s, somber and inartistic businessmen had taken control of Hollywood. With word having gotten around that Neilan was a difficult employee, the film industry's new rulers quietly banned him. Joining the new order would be only the filmmakers who displayed no extravagancies. *Black Waters* followed Neilan's brief employment with two minor studios, FBO and Pathé.

To at least one critic, Lloyd's performance in *Black Waters* demonstrated that the actor "knew how to use his voice." Whenever Lloyd's stuttering valet got stuck on a word, he would detonate the verbal jam by whistling. This would instantly clear the air and enable him to begin his statement anew. For Lloyd, his stage accomplishments accounted for his effectiveness in the speaking role. As the "sound" film was quickly replacing the silent film, vocal skills were a valuable asset.

A young producer, Harry Donald Edwards, approached Lloyd in early 1929 proposing a series of *Lloyd Hamilton Talking Comedies*. Some discussion followed, at the end of which Lloyd agreed to star in twelve two-reel comedies. The series would be produced by a new independent organization called Lloyd Hamilton Productions Inc. and would be distributed by the Educational Film Corporation. Lloyd Hamilton Productions Inc. would be a subsidiary of the Metropolitan Sound Studio Inc., a property of Al and Charlie Christie. Printers prepared a two-page magazine spread to announce "HAMILTON BACK WITH EDUCATIONAL IN NEW SERIES OF TALKIES."

By this time, cartoons, double features and live prologue presentations were greatly lessening the exhibitor's need for the short comedy. The only survivors were the foremost independent producers, Roach, Sennett, Hammons and Christie, and the short subject divisions of the major studios. Chiefly, these companies had managed to endure by drastically lowering their budgets. With his latest series, Lloyd would not receive the time and money to be artistic.

On March 30, 1929, Ethel Hamilton notified the court that Lloyd was in contempt of their divorce decree, having failed to pay alimony since November, 1927. He had made his last payment on Ethel's home in May, 1927. Ethel reported that, to meet the terms of her mortgage, she had been compelled to borrow $2,763.16. Ethel solicited a prompt execution of the judgment. Based on her complaint, Lloyd was served a summons on April 5.

On April 10, Lloyd was drawn into another legal matter. Attorney Leslie Ross examined Lloyd as a judgment debtor. Ross' client claimed that Lloyd owed him $1,250, the outstanding rent on a Hollywood home. To determine if Lloyd was concealing assets, the lawyer subjected Lloyd to a rigid examination. The inquiry proved fruitless — Lloyd had no money.

On April 24, the Court appointed Ouelette as a receiver. It was his duty to collect and distribute Lloyd's earnings. The Court ordered that, in the capacity of receiver, Ouelette pay Ethel one-third of the money that came into his possession. Ouelette resumed alimony payments on April 27.

Meanwhile, a Los Angeles Superior Court judge issued a decree legally ending Lloyd's second marriage. Irene told Judge Walter Guerin that she hadn't had a good laugh since she married Lloyd. Receiving a cash property settlement of $1,000.00, Irene used the money to abandon Hollywood and relocate to Chicago.

It was pointless now for Lloyd to look back to his marriages. Instead, he chose to look forward to a happy screen match. He expressed his desire to work again with Ruth Roland, a figure of sunnier days. This pairing, though, was unlikely. Ruth, who had garnered wealth from fortunate real estate investments, had comfortably retired from motion pictures in 1926. Her retirement came at just the right time considering her movies weren't selling as many tickets as they once had. Ruth volunteered her talents to humanitarian causes. Via radio, she sang to disabled vets living at government hospitals. Her singing was so well-received that it eventually led to a radio program called *The Ruth Roland Hour*. By early 1929, Ruth was working on her radio show and touring on vaudeville's renowned Orpheum Circuit.

Lloyd more seriously considered working again with another Ruth: Ruth Hiatt. Since 1926, Ruth played Mrs. Smith in Sennett's *Smith Family* series. Edwards, though, could not get Ruth to leave the series. The principal female role of *His Big Minute*, the first comedy of Lloyd's new series, was given to Gladys McConnel. McConnel had been the leading lady in two comedy features starring Harry Langdon and three shoot-'em-up westerns starring Ken Maynard.

With his new income, Lloyd departed the Hollywood Athletic Club and moved into the Bradford Apartments.

19

The Comeback

Lloyd had been given no authority in the creation of his new series. He had not demanded any. His creative spirit had faded long ago. At this point, his life was dedicated more to survival than artistic achievement. Studs Terkel referred to financial need as mankind's lot, writing, "No matter how demeaning the task, no matter how it dulls the senses and breaks the spirit, one must work. Or else."[1]

The production team of *His Big Minute* included at least two of Lloyd's old colleagues. Gil Pratt had scripted *His Big Minute*; William Watson, a Sunshine associate, had been hired to direct. Upon reporting to work, Lloyd donned a checkered cap and a matching bow-tie. The bow-tie had replaced the quaint Windsor tie he had once been known to wear.

He had laid up a great deal of energy for the assignment, but he was far from rejuvenated. Despite a spark of vigor, he did not look well. The corrosive effects of drink had caused extensive and irrevocable damage to his body. His shrunken form was startling, but the ravages of alcohol were most evident in his face.

He walked onto soundproofed stages, a peculiar place crammed full of bulky new equipment developed for sound productions, included a menacing-looking camera larger than the typical dressing room, countless electrical wires tangled together, and microphones hovering overhead. He had to make his way through this obstacle course to get to the set.

The cameras, which were encased in massive soundproof boxes, could not be easily maneuvered, and they restricted directors to static shots. Consequently, the general pace and visual flair of movies had diminished from what had been done in silent movies.

While Lloyd was at work, a publicity team wrestled with a difficult albeit unavoidable question: How were they going to fit an explanation of Lloyd's recent absence among their fluffy press releases and exhibitor suggestions? The answer arrived in the form of a common three-letter word: lie. Educational would employ, at alternate times, the three following explanations:

1. Finding his career at a standstill, Lloyd Hamilton had elected to retire. His comeback had been prompted by the new opportunities that talking pictures offered him.
2. The screen comic had deserted the short subject field in favor of feature work. (*Black Waters* was mentioned in a weak attempt to substantiate this claim.)
3. Lloyd's year of unemployment represented a brief and temporary career slump brought on by the public's fickleness.

To justify Lloyd's sickly appearance, it was reported that he had recently engaged in a vigorous gym program to drop excess pounds. The publicity team, who probably felt that

Rita La Roy, as a comely moll, mistakes a shy coin collector for mob boss Nick the Shiek. *Don't Be Nervous* (1929) (courtesy of the family of Lloyd Hamilton).

this was the best they could do, devoted more space in press and exhibitor materials to outlining a contest for "kiddie" Lloyd Hamilton impersonators.

The *Lloyd Hamilton Talking Comedies* were lightweight. The principal character of the new series was a shallow and distorted shadow of Lloyd's "poor boy" character. The material only allowed Lloyd to employ the character's basic mannerisms. The emphasis was, instead, on verbal play.

Lloyd had to lend his voice to this new talking series. He spoke in a childish, sissyish voice. When frightened, he emitted a whiny moan. It was taking a big risk to have this character speak for the first time in eleven years. The imposition of speech caused severe damage to many silent clowns, who were the delicate and graceful spirits of an awesome dream world. With Langdon, his voice strongly entered into his character turning from a lovable innocent into an irritating idiot. A greater controversy exists regarding Keaton's voice. Walter Kerr believed that Keaton, by his speech, profoundly hurt his "sound" work. In describing to Keaton's voice, Kerr wrote: "Unexpectedly deep, and with a peculiar drag to it, it directly contradicted the instantaneous flexibility of his physical outlines."[2] This opinion is opposed by Rudi Blesh, who believed that Keaton's flat voice was appropriate as it was as uncommunicative as the comic's face.

Still, the *Hamilton Talking Comedies* satisfied their audience. Two early stand-outs of the series were *Don't Be Nervous* and *Peaceful Alley*. The former, a spoof of underworld crime dramas, won highly favorable notices from all the top trade publications. Lloyd drew special praise for his laughable and convincing characterization of an underworld chieftain, one of dual roles.

The latter, a quaint comedy, combined elements of three films: Chaplin's *The Kid*, Lloyd's *Poor Boy*, and a 1921 Monte Banks comedy called *Peaceful Alley*. Gil Pratt, the director of the original *Peaceful Alley*, collaborated with Lloyd on the film. Lloyd was featured as a pathetic lad who lives on the bleak and somber streets of an urban slum.

Following the production of *Peaceful Alley*, Edwards allowed Lloyd the time to handle outside assignments. Louis Lewyn, a producer who had been among Lloyd's longtime fans, hired the comic to host a *Voice of Hollywood* reel. A former newspaperman, Lewyn had originated the *Screen Snapshots* series for Columbia in 1920. *Screen Snapshots*, which presented light-hearted newsreels about stars at work and play, was the earliest forerunner to *Entertainment Tonight*. *The Voice of Hollywood*, his latest series, presented a combination of newsreel footage and variety acts. As host, Lloyd is disrupted by a salesman from a hat company. The salesman tries convincing him to abandon his cap for a straw hat. Defending the cap, Lloyd insists, "That's my livelihood." Then he glumly concedes that, due to back alimony, he doesn't have the money to buy a new hat.

Other work came. Courtesy of Marshall Neilan and RKO, Lloyd received a supporting role, as an inept detective, in the light "society" comedy *Tanned Legs*. Also, Lloyd was one of the many guest stars in *The Show of Shows*, Warner Brothers' all-talking and all–Technicolor variety extravaganza. Lloyd enjoyed a significant role in this highly publicized production. His co-stars, representing a large number of Hollywood notables, warmly welcomed back their errant brother.

Frank Fay, the master of ceremonies, overtly adlibs throughout the show. Fay was the father of the comedy monologue. Bob Hope and Jack Paar, who would later bring the comedy monologue to television, would never be shy about acknowledging their debt to Fay. At one point, Fay steps up to a piano to sing. He lifts a corner of the piano's ostentatious drapery and remarks to the audience, "I spent all night crocheting this."

Lloyd acts relaxed while confined in one of the film's sketches, but he seems less comfortable playing in more loosely scripted scenes. One such scene opens with Fay preparing a poetry recital. At the outset, Fay warmly introduces "the celebrated and world-known Lloyd Hamilton." On this cue, Lloyd employs his popular gait to join Fay at center stage. Fay tries to engage Lloyd in small talk, but Lloyd is withdrawn and avoids eye contact. Fay says, "We haven't seen you around for awhile." Lloyd seems at a loss for a reply. He hangs his head. The conversation seems torturous for him. Fay figures to put him out of his misery. He brightly states, "You're looking good!" Then, he moves to introduce Louise Fazenda and Bea Lillie. In the meantime, Lloyd appears distant and preoccupied. Before beginning, Fay again acknowledges the participants of the recital: "myself, Miss Fazenda, Miss Lillie and ... *Mr. Hamilton*." The sudden mention of his name startles Lloyd, causing Fay to wisecrack: "He's the one napping on the end."

The Show of Shows attracted many theatergoers anxious to see the musical variety show. An alarming mob assembled at the film's New York City premiere. To check the rush of overeager film fans, a mounted unit of the NYPD was forced to ride their horses onto the sidewalk.

Ruth Hiatt, who had recently fulfilled her Sennett contract, rejoined Lloyd soon after his company resumed production.

20

The Final Fade

On July 20, 1929, Romaine L. Hogan replaced Clyde Triplett as Ethel Hamilton's attorney. Hogan was more aggressive than the two attorneys who preceded him. On October 22, Hogan demanded that Lloyd pay roughly $12,500. Lloyd owed $7,500 in alimony from the period of December, 1927, to April, 1929. He was also obliged to pay an accrual of $4,050 towards Ethel's mortgage. Hogan inflated the debt by seven percent, the maximum interest rate allowed by law.

Lloyd was aggravating the situation with showy acquisitions. He remained an impeccable dresser, spending much of his income on clothing. His records show many receipts from the cleaners, where he brought his finery to be professionally laundered and pressed. On November 1, he spent $1,517 on a new Packard car. Lloyd had shown, over the years, that he could never resist a shiny new automobile. Consider the time he saw former partner Jack White driving a new car onto the studio lot. The two men had avoided speaking to one another since a bitter break-up, but Lloyd was willing to forget all the disagreement and ill feelings for a spin around the block.

By sending garnishment notices to Ouelette and Metropolitan Sound Studio, Hogan challenged the receiver's disposition of funds. On November 10, Ouelette responded to his notice, asserting that he was not financially indebted to Lloyd Hamilton and "possessed no personal property belonging to said defendant." A similar response was received from W. S. Holman, secretary of the Metropolitan Sound Studio.

On November 14, Ouelette obtained an attorney for his defense. In a court motion, the attorney directed Ethel to justify her demands. He also required Ethel to "show cause why she should not be held in contempt of court in levying upon moneys in hands of the Receiver."[1]

In September, Lloyd was approached by an old colleague to work in a feature film. The colleague, Archie Mayo, had written some of Lloyd's most popular comedies, including *Robinson Crusoe Ltd.* and *Poor Boy*. In the last three years, Mayo was able to rise to a key position at Warner Brothers. The studio executives had started him out directing women's dramas, but they had recently assigned him to develop a series of comedy vehicles for Edward Everett Horton. The latest, *Wide Open*, was to feature Horton as a clever bookkeeper who is hindered in his career by his meek and clumsy manner. It wasn't far off from the type of storylines that Mayo had tailored for Lloyd's "poor boy" character. Horton, at this time, acknowledged a debt to Lloyd. The actor, who tended to play his characters in a dithery and prissy fashion, commented that he had been inspired by Lloyd's "goofy" characteristics.

Warner Brothers offered no explanation when Lloyd was suddenly dropped from the project.

On December 19, Ouelette submitted a report to the court. As the basis of the report, he requested the cancellation of the divorce decree. He provided a complete statement of the moneys that he had collected and disbursed as receiver. These papers showed that Ouelette had properly directed the money and none of the funds remained in his possession. Between April 27 and December 14, Ouelette had supplied Ethel with slightly more than $100 per week, payments totaling $3,516.62. A lengthy list of the cash receipts and cash disbursements ended with the following notation: "Balance on hand — nil."

A curious cash disbursement is $11.25 that Lloyd paid to the Hollywood Florist. That amount, based on inflation rates, comes to $135 in current dollars. Lloyd, for that amount of money, had to have bought a bountiful bouquet. A bouquet like that was most likely purchased either for a date or a funeral. This is intriguing as no other evidence exists that Lloyd was dating during this period.

In late December, the Court was notified that not all of Lloyd's income had passed through Ouelette's hands. Within the two months preceding Ouelette's appointment, Lloyd had procured salary advances totaling $7,600. Metropolitan, who was loaning out Lloyd's services, had arranged for Warner Brothers and RKO to divert the comic's wages to them. They had retained this money as reimbursement of the salary advances. An earnings statement yielded the following information:

Picture # 1 March 2	$ 900.00
Picture # 2 April 6	$ 1,125.00
Warner Brothers check	$ 2,750.00
RKO check	$ 3,000.00
Picture # 3 May 18	$ 1,250.00
Picture # 4 July 6	$ 1,250.00
Picture # 5 August 7	$ 1,250.00
Picture # 6 September 14	$ 1,875.00
Picture # 7 October 7	$ 1,875.00
Picture # 8 November 20	$ 1,250.00
Total	$17,525.00

On January 9, 1930, Judge Guerin complied with Ouelette's request to be discharged as receiver. Guerin instructed Lloyd to pay Ouelette's attorney the sum of $150. He also ordered Lloyd to immediately begin rendering weekly alimony payments of $150. Al S. Keller, Lloyd's business manager, was appointed receiver. Guerin announced that, at a later date, he would designate a "dispassionate party" as a joint receiver.

On January 20, Lloyd changed attorneys, replacing N.J. Kendall with Griffith Jones. On February 19, Hogan filed a motion alleging that Ouelette "failed to collect and pay plaintiff in accordance with court order the sum of $1,650.66, which sum the defendant received to his own use and benefit."

As of February 21, Lloyd was no longer employed. In ongoing negotiations with Educational, he was offering his services for the ensuing year. On March 1, he signed an affidavit that simply read:

> The affiant has no work and when he does work his salary is smaller than the amount he was earning at the time of the making of the order. Affiant requires more for his personal needs at the present time than when the order was made and the plaintiff does not need more than $50.00 per week to live upon.

Medical bills were the reason that Lloyd was requiring more for his personal needs.

Clarence W. Horn, an accountant, was assigned to share the duties of receiver. Horn meticulously maintained Lloyd's financial records and, in preparing reports, cut through the dry legalspeak. The documentation he left behind is a valuable source of information.

Horn recommended that, on a monthly basis, Lloyd pay $175 in alimony and apply $75 to Ethel's home loan. Apart from the back alimony that he owed to Ethel, Lloyd's debt totaled $20,019.93. The debt included delinquent income tax of $13,851.42, an amount which had accumulated over three filing periods. The government had originally demanded payment of back taxes in December, 1928. Horn asserted that the demands for alimony were unreasonable unless they were in keeping with Lloyd's other obligations.

Horn provided the following itemization of Lloyd's debt:

As of March 1, 1930

1924 Income Tax	$2,753.91
1926 Income Tax	$2,312.14
1927 Income Tax	$8,785.37
Walter Lundren	$50.00
Joe E. Brown	$200.00
Charley Chase	$200.00
Lew Cody	$5.00
Henry Lehrman	$350.00
Charlie Christie	$200.00
Mary Hamilton	$25.00
Dr. Ed Ruth	$1,800.00
Dr. Leo Schulman	$950.00
Dr. G.J. Crandall	$65.00
Al Frates	$250.00
Auto Club of Southern California	$13.00
Renew It Cleaners	$5.00
Elite Garage	$115.00
Hollywood Athletic Club	$245.56
Wheat Gill	$343.50
The Masque	$102.00
Scott & Roth	$153.45
Dr. MacKenzie	$6.00
William Jiller	$110.00
Nan Israel	$95.00
Dr. Charles Pflueger	$750.00
Exhibitors Herald World	$135.00

As this list indicates, several film folk were among Lloyd's sympathetic contributors.

To determine the status of Lloyd's employment, Horn visited the Metropolitan Sound Studio in late February. Following the visit, he reported:

> I was informed that there is nothing assured as to his future employment other than they are mapping out a program for the balance of 1930, and perhaps can use the defendant's services, but it is evident that if they can use his services it would not be at a higher figure than they have been paying.... At the present time the defendant has no ready funds that I could find through his representative or the studio, and is now receiving sufficient amount to take care of his actual expenses by advances made through his representative, Mr. Keller.
>
> That the defendant has certain living conditions to maintain that are probably necessary to a man in his position and the people he is associated with, and while his personal expenses may seem a little excessive they do not appear to me to be higher than would be required under the circumstances.

This report was accompanied by the following earnings statement:

1929 Income

Metropolitan Sound Studio	$14,400.00
Warner Brothers	$2,750.00
RKO Studios	$3,000.00

Expenses

Publicity	$51.50
Wardrobe	$458.03
Managers	
C. R. Ouelette	$2,149.20
Al S. Keller	$375.00
Car Expense	$450.68
Car Depreciation	$359.38

January and February 1930 Income

Metropolitan Sound Studio	$4,070.00

Expenses

Advertising	$56.90
Photos	$32.50
Managers	$556.25
Car Expense	$355.37
Wardrobe	$20.00
Attorneys	$550.00

Hamilton gets roughed up by smugglers in *Are You There?* (1930). The other actors, from left to right, are Richard Alexander, Gustav Von Seyffertiz, Henry Victor and Nicholas Soussanin (courtesy of Cole Johnson — Slapstick Archive).

Hamilton takes a break from his groundskeeping duties in *Are You There?* (1930) (courtesy of Cole Johnson — Slapstick Archive).

In an application, Ouelette alleged, "Your petitioner has acted without compensation." However, Horn's statement clearly shows that Lloyd had provided Ouelette with a living wage.

On March 31, Judge Crawford ruled that Lloyd's alimony obligations would end if the comedian immediately paid $10,000 in overdue alimony. Because he lacked the money, Lloyd was forced to disregard the proposal.

During the next several weeks, Lloyd worked on two projects. He acted as a hostler in *Are You There?*, a musical-comedy starring *Show of Shows* co-star Beatrice Lillie. Also, the Richfield Oil Company featured Lloyd in *Service Wins Again*, a film shot at the Metropolitan Sound Studio and advertised as the "first industrial talking picture comedy."

Lloyd was working on *Are You There?* when he was approached by an association of menswear dealers to promote straw hats. The premise of the promotion was that the comedian had become so enamored of straw hats that he was willing to discard his checkered cap to wear one. On May 1, 1930, Lloyd had a straw hat secured on his head as he sat in the back of a new V16 Cadillac and led a parade of automobiles down Hollywood Boulevard.

In July, Metro-Goldwyn-Mayer announced that Lloyd would be the comedy lead in a feature, *The New Moon*. Lloyd's role, however, was not specifically described. *The New Moon*, which was to showcase the love affair of a princess and army lieutenant, was another operetta. Sigmund Romberg had long ago fashioned *The New Moon* as a traditional opera, but his score had been recently updated for Broadway audiences by Oscar Hammerstein, Frank Mandel and Lawrence Schwab.

At MGM, *The New Moon* was to be afforded lavish treatment. Cast as the musical and romantic leads were Grace Moore and Lawrence Tibbett. Tibbett, a Metropolitan Opera baritone, had recently made his screen debut in another MGM operetta, *The Rogue Song*. This previous effort, seeking to provide a balance of melody and mirth, had relied on extensive comic relief from two popular funnymen, Laurel and Hardy. Tibbett's performance in *The Rogue Song* had earned the singer an Academy Award nomination. Moore, who had also come from the Metropolitan Opera, was new to Hollywood.

Production was postponed when Tibbett and Moore, who carried animosity from a past collaboration, refused to work together. Moore's escalating weight caused further delay. During the pre-production lags, major cast changes occurred. George Fawcett, who had been cast as a villainous governor, was replaced by Adolphe Menjou. Lloyd was also dropped from the cast, but it is not clear which role he was supposed to play or which actor succeeded him. The obvious assumption would be that Lloyd was replaced by Gus Shy, who contributed some low comedy as a faithful member of the lieutenant's garrison. Shy gets a dramatic moment, though, when his character, Potkin, is killed by a marauding tribe of hillmen.

Up until the last few months, Shy had been a comic dancer on Broadway. His perform-

Hamilton performs with musical revue star Beatrice Lillie in *Are You There?* (1930) (courtesy of Cole Johnson — Slapstick Archive).

ance in a popular Broadway musical, *Good News*, had garnered him many good reviews. Irving Thalberg, who was producing MGM's version of *Good News*, had engaged the dancer solely for the purpose of recreating his stage role. Shy, this attractive newcomer who was available on the MGM lot while Thalberg was initiating production on *The New Moon*, could have inspired a last-minute casting change.

However, it is more likely that Lloyd was meant to assume another role. Early promotion for *The New Moon* simultaneously named Lloyd and Shy as members of the supporting cast. Roland Young, who played a larger comic role in the film, was not mentioned in the same publicity releases. Young, a busy actor for forty-five years, is best remembered for originating the movie role of Topper, a sleepy milquetoast who is befriended by fun-loving ghosts. In *The New Moon*, Young played Count Stroghoff, the princess' rascally uncle. The role, though mostly subdued, lapses at times into broad comedy. In a wilderness fort, the count warily sleeps with a machine gun strapped around his chest. When suddenly awakened, he springs to his feet and fires several rounds. To conceal his panicked response, he calmly replies that this is the way a military man starts his day. It wouldn't be hard to imagine Lloyd handling this scene.

On September 12, Lloyd hauled an injured man into the Hollywood Hospital. The man's

The bad guys are no match for Hamilton (center) in *Won by a Neck* (1930). The bad guys are played by Dan Welheim (left) and Glen Cavendor. The arresting officer (right) is played by William McCall; the actor at left is unidentified (courtesy of Cole Johnson — Slapstick Archive).

leg was covered in blood. When the medical staff learned that a bullet was embedded in the man's thigh, they called police to investigate.

The wounded man, Douglas Kendall, told police that he had been hurt while hosting a party. Guests, he admitted, got a little out of control and decided it would be fun to take turns firing a small-caliber pistol at a kitchen door. He was allegedly examining a bullethole in the door when a would-be marksman shot prematurely, hitting him instead of the target. The detectives, who had counted more than thirty bullet holes in the door, accepted the story as fact. The *L.A. Enquirer* reported that the guests of Kendall's merry party included several screen players. When Kendall was shot, most of these guests had fled in panic. Lloyd claimed that he reached the scene just as the members of the gathering were dispersing. He said that he immediately placed Kendall in his car and rushed him to the hospital.

Ray Hanford, a character actor, came forth to confess responsibility for the shooting. Hanford explained to police that guests were betting who could make an accurate hit firing at bric-a-brac. The bets came down to ten dollars per shot. Hanford said that he accidentally shot Kendall as the host handed him the gun. Kendall, whose injuries weren't serious, refused to file charges. The case was closed.

Hamilton (right) teams with fellow comedy star Al St. John for the domestic comedy *Marriage Rows* (1931). St. John inappropriately cozies up to his host's wife, played by Addie McPhail (courtesy of Cole Johnson — Slapstick Archive).

In October, Lloyd drove his car into a pedestrian, Thoroddur Oddson. Oddson, at the time of the collision, had been standing to the rear of the car. Four months later, the man sued Lloyd for damages, claiming that he had received serious and painful injuries. The suit called for Lloyd to pay, in damages, $50,837.

On November 19, Horn reviewed Lloyd's finances. In the process, his opinion of Lloyd soured. Horn discovered that Lloyd had been employed from April 8 to October 1. During that period, he had earned $27,328.33, which he disbursed through his agent, Al Keller. Towards Lloyd's debt, Keller had paid nothing except $250 to the government, $850 to Dr. Schulman, $65 to Dr. Crandall, and $25 to Lloyd's mother. He had paid no more than the monthly sum of $250 in alimony. Horn noted, "The Plaintiff informs your Receiver she cannot live on the reduced allowance and pay the interest and other expenses on this house."

Horn learned that Lloyd's contract had expired on October 1. Under the terms of the contract, Metropolitan had briefly held an option to retain Lloyd for another six months. The option had been allowed to elapse on November 17. Mr. Cahane, general manager of the studio, told Horn that the reason for this action was his company's inadequate funds. Horn wrote: "Mr. Cahane also informed me that he thought after the first of the year conditions would change with all producing companies to warrant them starting the making of pictures on a regular schedule."

Horn concluded that, based on Lloyd's earnings, he would expect a substantial amount of the actor's debt to have been paid. "However," he noted, "only a small amount was used for this purpose and now that his revenue has temporarily stopped he is faced with the past bills payable and no balance on hand to even meet current expenses. I would call the attention of the Court to the fact that in little over 6 months of 1930 the total income exceeds by over $7,000.00 the total for the entire year of 1929."

Horn further stated:

> The conditions have reversed themselves during the period elapsed since my last report. At that time the Defendant had the accumulated debts and no funds with which to meet them or pay his alimony demands. Shortly thereafter, he obtained the new contract and for present conditions had a very fair income, but this has not altered his position one bit and he still has all the debts plus the previous account owing the Plaintiff.
>
> The Defendant is not employed at present, but prospects are good for a contract in the near future.

As part of his report, Horn furnished the following list of disbursements:

Loan to Alf Goulding	$582.65
Pacific Finance Company (on car)	$1,475.26
Furniture	$1,357.67
Miscellaneous Item	$300.00
Rent, groceries, laundry, telephone gas, light	$2,642.74
Meals, care for dog, hunting supplies, flowers, taxi, theatre tickets, diamond ring	$7,704.95
Publicity	$398.93
Wardrobe	$1,353.90
Al Keller, service	$1,631.25
Auto Expense	$1,229.11
On old accounts	$915.00
Doctors expense	$603.60
Legal expense	$1,275.55

C. W. Horn, report and expense	$150.00
On old income tax $250.00	
1929 income tax $265.98	
Old accounts (see list)	$1,057.00
Clubs	$345.00
Edward Small Co., agents	$1,062.49
Chauffeurs	$892.00
Misc.	$12.25
Interest	$289.81
Paid Ethel Hamilton, 7 months	$1,750.00

Most conspicuous is the sixth listing (meals, care for dog, etc., and diamond ring). The amount, adjusted for inflation, is equivalent to roughly $88,000 in present-day terms. How much of this money went to the diamond ring, as listed, and who was the recipient?

By this time, Lloyd owed Ethel $21,000. On November 26, Lloyd agreed to pay $1,500 "in full settlement, satisfaction and release of any and all judgments." He accepted the following payment schedule:

$1,000.00 payable on or before November 28
$250.00 payable on or before January 1
$250.00 payable on or before February 1

The balance was "payable at the rate of not less than $500.00 per month, with interest on deferred payments at the rate of 6 percent per annum, interest payable monthly; the said $500.00 payments to commence on or before the 1st day of March, 1931, and to be made on or before the 1st day of each and every succeeding month thereafter until the said balance of $13,500.00 with said interest has been paid." At the signing of the agreement, Ethel received the opening payment.

This portrait was used to promote Hamilton's Universal series (1931) (courtesy of the family of Lloyd Hamilton).

Hammons, gratified with the latest returns on the *Lloyd Hamilton Talking Comedies*, signed Lloyd for a third season. For Roscoe Arbuckle, contracted to write and direct the new series, this assignment represented a return to Hollywood. For the last three years, he had been working on stage exclusively. Easing the impact of his comeback, Arbuckle surrounded himself with several longtime associates, including Al St. John, Glen Cavender, Del Henderson, Doris Deane, Addie McPhail and Harry McCoy.

Arbuckle's *Hamilton Talking Comedies* were domestic situation comedies. The response to these films was generally favorable. A *Hollywood Reporter* critic called the series' *Marriage Rows* "a swell comedy ... [with] practically one laugh after another.... Twenty minutes of good entertainment, whether you're a Hamilton fan or not." The critic of *Motion Picture News* was an ungracious dissenter. He expressed harsh disapproval of Lloyd's "pansy pantomime."

Due to Educational's financial problems, the series ended prematurely.

During this period, Lloyd starred in a comedy short called *Wedding Belles*, produced by Cavalcade Film Corporation. There is not much known about its origins. It presumably represents the comic's only affiliation with Cavalcade, an obscure company that wasn't around long. The release, not mentioned in trade journals, came to light when a print was discovered at the Museum of Modern Art.

In the spring of 1931, Universal announced that they would greatly enlarge their output of two-reel comedies. In the last year, Universal's short subjects had been limited to the production of weekly newsreels, *Oswald the Rabbit* cartoons, a Slim Summerville series, and *Cohen & Kelly* comedies. Seeking to improve their position in this area, the studio had drawn up an ambitious expansion program that called for the immediate establishment of four production units. Each unit would spotlight a single comic.

Universal hired Lloyd to star in one of their new series. The film company contracted to pay Lloyd $2,700 per picture for a total of eight pictures. Similar agreements were made with Daphne Pollard, Eddie Gribbon and Bert Roach. Universal launched a publicity blitz for these series.

Harry Edwards, a longtime comedy director and a former *Ham* director, was assigned to lead the production company of the new *Hamilton* series. The associated scripts were notable in that they extracted a large amount of material from Lloyd's silent vehicles.

Unable to meet his bills, Lloyd drew more court summonses. He had induced Adelle Daniels, one of his former business managers, to accept checks totaling $4,126. When the bank refused to make payment, Daniels took legal action against him. Her suit was filed in April, 1931.

On June 23, Hogan submitted an affidavit to address Lloyd's excessive spending. In part, it read:

> The defendant is now making and will in future make certain money which, unless a receiver be appointed in this matter to collect, hold and disburse according to the order of Court, will be dissipated and spent and diverted by defendant.... That the defendant by reason of his personal disadvantages is totally unable to handle his own business affairs, to collect, hold and pay out any money received by him for his services and by reason thereof has employed and is now employing Al S. Keller, as his business manager. That the said Al S. Keller is unable and will continue to be unable without order of Court to control the defendant in his expenditures of money collected for his services and said Al S. Keller has permitted the defendant to borrow sums of money from various persons with the result that the defendant has been, now is, and will continue to live beyond his means and income ... and that the defendant will continue to exhaust the money that he is to receive from his services before the same becomes due.

Based on this affidavit, Keller was served with a summons, which read:

> You are hereby ordered to appear in the above entitled court ... on 30th day of June, 1931, at the hour of 2 P.M. then and there to show cause, if any you have, why you should not be adjudged guilty of contempt of court and punished accordingly for willfully conspiring with defendant Lloyd Hamilton and advising him and causing him to willfully disobey the Court's order heretofore made on the 21st day of November, 1930, ordering that said Lloyd Hamilton to pay to Clarence Horn the sum of two hundred fifty dollars, fees as temporary receiver.

Lloyd visited court on June 30. He testified that Keller was fully in charge of his earnings. Keller explained that, because Lloyd wasn't working, he had no money to pay his client's alimony. Hogan argued that Lloyd's other creditors had received payments. "There's got to be more cooperation in meeting this court alimony order," Judge Guerin stated. "I'll continue the matter in a week. I'm warning you, Mr. Hamilton, that unless satisfactory arrangements are made with Mrs. Hamilton, you'll go to jail."

It was agreed that Lloyd would be temporarily pardoned if he paid the nominal sum of fifty dollars. This money needed to be in the hands of Lloyd's attorney, G. V. Weikert, by noon of July 10. On the morning of the 10th, Weikert waited two hours for his client to arrive. Three minutes before noon, there was a commotion in the hall. The door burst open. Lloyd entered, breathing heavily and waving a paper. "Saved," he shouted. Upon reaching Weikert, he thrust forward a cashier's check for $50. On the same day, Horn became the exclusive receiver. Mayer & Lancaster replaced Al Keller as Lloyd's representation.

In the meantime, Jack White entered into a divorce action. The suit had been filed by White's movie star wife, Pauline Starke. White was worried about the California Community Law, which would allow Starke to demand half his worldly possessions. Lloyd never said a bad word about his ex-wives no matter what they said about him. White, in contrast, attacked his wife in the press before she had a chance to comment about the divorce. He said that, if she insisted on enforcement of the Community Law, he would "start saying things himself."

Lloyd's Universal comedies were bad, but critics panned the series without laying blame on the star. While Edwards and his writing staff were sharply attacked, Lloyd was commended for making the best of slight material and resources.

The *Lloyd Hamilton Comedies* was the only new series that Universal renewed for a second season. For their 1931–32 season, Universal executives signed Vince Barnett, Louise Fazenda and James Gleason to each star in a two-reel comedy series. Lloyd began work on a talkie version of his best comedy, *Robinson Crusoe, Ltd*. The *Crusoe* remake would never be completed.

On the evening of September 26, Lloyd came strolling down Fifty-fourth Street, approaching Crenshaw Boulevard. It's not certain what happened next. None of the news stories would probe into Lloyd's purpose or condition. All that's known is that he ambled into traffic, bounding before an onrushing car, and the impact knocked him to the ground.

Lloyd lay motionless, reduced to a crumbled heap, his scalp leaking blood. An ambulance corps rushed him to Benedict Hospital. The police did not find any reason to hold the driver, C.W. Shaffer. Lloyd was all patched up when he awoke in the hospital. His scalp, which had sustained gashes, had been shaved, cleaned, stitched, and bandaged. His left leg, which had been fractured in several places, was buried in a gauze and plaster cast and suspended in a sling. A cotton dressing was wound around his waist. Various aches likely plagued his body, but it was better than being celebrity road kill. Days later, Lloyd was joking with his nurse, Dorothy Kiefer. His behavior belied the grimness of the situation. From his hospital bed, Lloyd contacted an attorney, who immediately sued Shaffer for $52,350. The suit, not considered to have merit, didn't get very far. Lloyd remained in the hospital for the next two months. He had been in this predicament once before but, unlike that earlier experience, he was resigned to his confinement. No studio chief or legion of film fans awaited his recovery. A grand banquet would not honor his comeback.

Based on his injury, Lloyd received an insurance check in the amount of $2,350. Between October 3, 1931, and February 29, 1932, he would satisfy $1,377.72 in medical expenses. Lloyd was released from the hospital in November. With the aid of crutches, he uneasily departed the medical building. It was expected that Lloyd would quietly complete his recuperation.

A few nights later, Lloyd suffered another accident while visiting Rex Lease, a romantic leading man and one of Lloyd's many show business friends. Various explanations for the accident reached newspapers. A reporter for *The L.A. Examiner* wrote: "As he [Hamilton] was leaving, he slipped on a rug, his crutches went out from under him and sat down heavily on the floor." It was alleged in *The L.A. Times* that Lloyd's crutch slipped on a polished oak floor. The most believable account, though, was described in *The Oakland Tribune*. The cause of the mishap, as stated here, was that Lloyd attempted to demonstrate his maneuverability and perform a wild dance on his crutches. This was just the sort of silly stunt Lloyd might have performed after a night of drinking at a buddy's home. He was said to have been briskly hobbling towards his car when he suddenly spun around as if to accomplish a balletic step. He lost his balance, with his crutches collapsing beneath him, before he was able to complete the playful pirouette. The misadventure, whatever version was true, caused Lloyd to break his other leg and sent him back to the hospital.

During the two months he spent in the hospital, he received much bedside companionship. His visitors, which included Charley Chase, inscribed their names on his leg casts. When Lloyd was released from the hospital, his mother came to care for him.

Universal edited the footage of Lloyd's partly finished comedy into a barely coherent release. *Robinson Crusoe and Son*, as it was called, inspired much brighter notices than Lloyd's previous Universal comedies. However, these notices failed to benefit their subject. By the time Lloyd's bones knitted, Universal was no longer interested in resuming the *Hamilton* series. It was not specifically this series that had dissatisfied the studio's management. The executives were generally disappointed with the box office performance of their two-reel comedies and were moving to dismantle their short subject department.

Mary Hamilton approached Horn. She informed the receiver that she was returning home and, since she did not reside close to Los Angeles, she could not regularly call on Lloyd. She asked Horn if he could assist her in watching over her disabled son. Horn agreed that, "although a personal matter," he would assume this responsibility. Months later, Lloyd ended his convalescence at his mother's home in Porterville.

Early in 1932, Mack Sennett announced that he was assembling an all-star cast for his first feature film in four years.[2] Among the stars included on Sennett's ambitious cast list was Lloyd Hamilton, who was still recovering in the hospital when the announcement was made. Other stars included Clara Bow, Lupe Velez, Andy Clyde, W. C. Fields, Jean Harlow, Dorothy Burgess, Edmund Lowe, Roscoe Ates, Mack Swain, Ben Turpin, and the blackface comedy team Moran & Mack. When asked about the plot, Sennett would simply say that it would be big and it would involve lots of animals. He said that one scene he was working out would feature whales and sharks. Soon after, fourteen writers worked out a story about a circus worker who travels on a ocean liner to retrieve a sweepstakes prize. Complications arise when a nefarious hypnotist uses his skills to steal the sweepstakes ticket. The film was in production from July 21 to August 13. Ben Turpin and Moran & Mack were only performers on Sennett's wish-list to appear in the film, which was released under the title *Hypnotized*. It is unknown if Lloyd was unavailable to work on the film due to his recent medical problems.

Still, Sennett remained interested in employing Lloyd, who had long been one of his favorite comedians. On a 1955 episode of the Arthur Friedman–hosted radio program *Turning Point*, Sennett spoke admiringly of Lloyd, saying that Lloyd ranked with Chaplin and Langdon for his skills of "comic motion" He said, "[Hamilton] would walk just across the room and apparently do nothing but just make you laugh." In the fall of 1932, he signed Lloyd to star in a series of two-reel comedies. He paired the veteran star with rowdy 22-year-old comedienne Marjorie Beebe, who was dating the comedy producer at the time.

By this time, the Sennett studio had passed into its winter. In bridging the silent and sound eras, Sennett had employed Andy Clyde, Harry Gribbon and Thelma Hill as his principal players. Clyde, Gribbon and Hill were eventually succeeded by a large assortment of supporting players, an ensemble including Beebe, Patsy O'Leary, Daphne Pollard, Nick Stuart, Arthur Stone, Frank Eastman and Dorothy Granger. Now, Sennett was retreating from the ensemble comedies and looking for solid principals. Besides Lloyd, his new stars included Charlie Murray, W.C. Fields, Walter Catlett, and a young man named Ben Alexander. Alexander had reached adulthood since playing the orphan boy in *A Self-Made Failure*.

Nowadays, Lloyd was feeling extremely weak and looking much older than his forty-one years. He had continued to drop weight, which made him look horribly gaunt.

In *False Impressions*, his first Sennett comedy, Lloyd finds himself in a predicament where he has to don an elaborate disguise to crash a high society ball. His disguise, which included a bushy moustache and a baggy tuxedo, recalled the grotesque makeup and costuming that Lloyd had adopted in his early Frontier and Kalem films. Dorothy Granger, who had a leading role in the film, said that Lloyd impressed her as a "very quiet and extremely sad man."[3]

Lloyd's second Sennett comedy was *Doubling in the Quickies*. Dressed in his trademark outfit, he is endearing and amusing as a smalltown grocer who pursues his girlfriend to Hollywood.

The film teams Lloyd with a couple of comedy icons from his past. First, he rides in a car with Charlie Chaplin. It isn't actually Charlie, it's a mannequin that Lloyd dresses as Charlie so that he can gain access to a movie lot. Lloyd explains to the guard that he and "Charlie" are having lunch with "Freddie March." Once he gets onto the lot, Lloyd encounters an old animal friend, a roaring lion, inside a dressing room. Trying to rationalize away his fear, he tells himself, "Don't be afraid, Joe. Lions can't hurt you. They didn't hurt Daniel so they won't hurt you." Another lion harassed Lloyd in his third Sennett comedy, *The Lion and the House*.

On November 7, Ethel Hamilton presented an affidavit to justify the continuation of alimony. She asserted that her ex-husband continued to earn money, pointing to a thousand-dollar payment he received in November. She noted that Lloyd, having lately filed for bankruptcy, would soon be rid of all of his bills except her award and his income tax debt. She interjected that the back taxes, which Lloyd had arranged to pay in small increments, were not a pressing obligation. The balance of the affidavit read as follows:

> That affiant has no other source of support and maintenance except from payments made by said Lloyd Hamilton on the said judgment and has bills demanding immediate payment as follows, to-wit:

1932 taxes on real property	$175.68
Electrolux payment due 10/29	$8.18
Gardner at Beverly	$18.00
Interest due 10/25/32	$129.06
Telephone bill	$5.15
Moving to Beverly	$10.00
Alley assessment now due	$18.89
Battery for Buick	$7.85
Due on Jewelry	$300.00
Interest to date	$30.00
Total	$703.01

> That it will be equitable and just and well within the means of said Lloyd Hamilton to pay affiant through the said Receiver one-third of all of the income and earnings by him received until affiant's said judgment is paid and satisfied.

In response, the Court ordered Horn "to show cause why certain monies should not be paid to plaintiff in above entitled action."

Horn replied on November 16. In an affidavit, he deposed:

> That he was, in July, 1931, appointed Receiver for the above entitled defendant, and that at that time the defendant was out of employment and had no funds on hand; that during July and August, 1931, the defendant was living in an apartment at the beach in Los Angeles County, California, with funds advanced by his mother, and in September, 1931, affiant took him to affiant's home because of his destitution.
>
> That on September 29, 1931, the defendant was injured in an automobile accident, and broke his leg, and was confined in the hospital until the latter part of November, when he, upon his release, slipped and broke his other leg, thereby confining him in the hospital until April, 1932. At this time, when he released from the hospital, he went to Porterville where he was supported by his mother, and by reason of his unfortunate accident, sixty more days elapsed before he was able to apply for engagements, and at last he received employment on October 1, 1932 for two short pictures with the Mack Sennett Studios; that on October 13th, 1932, he finished the first picture, and your affiant received in behalf of his employment the sum of Seven Hundred and Fifty Dollars. His second picture was finished November 11, 1932, and affiant will receive in his behalf, the sum of One Thousand Dollars.
>
> That the question of whether or not defendant will have further work depends upon the favorable reception by the public of his pictures, and the discretion of the producers as to further productions. Therefore, since July, 1931, your affiant has received Seven Hundred and Fifty Dollars, with the prospects of One Thousand Dollars within the near future.
>
> That at the time affiant was appointed receiver for the defendant in the above entitled action, the defendant's debts were in the sum of over Sixteen Thousand Dollars. The Federal Government has a claim of over Ten Thousand Dollars due for income taxes and penalties, and there are outstanding promissory notes held by attorneys which must be settled, or further litigation will ensue.
>
> Your receiver, affiant, when he received the check for Seven Hundred and Fifty Dollars paid past rent and upkeep for defendant, thereby releasing his clothes which were under attachment for past due rent, and at the present time has no money on hand.
>
> That defendant's mother has advanced over Fifteen Hundred Dollars in caring for her son during his disability, and monies owed to Dr. Taylor for necessary dental work.
>
> That by reason of the uncertainty as to defendant's future earnings capacity, as well as his outstanding obligations, your affiant is unable to compute what, if anything, could be given to the plaintiff herein. Therefore, it is submitted that it would be unequitable and unjust for the court at this time to arbitrarily order your Receiver to pay one-third of the defendant's income to the plaintiff by reason of the aforesaid conditions and situation.
>
> That plaintiff is an able-bodied, healthy woman and cannot dispute the unfortunate circumstances surrounding the defendant. That if she is unable to recognize the conditions and situation, this Honorable Court should protect the defendant until he is sufficiently secure in his employment.

A financial report was attached to the affidavit. This statement delineated Lloyd's expenses down to charges for a haircut and cigarettes. It also showed that, on January 4, Lloyd spent $6.65 to purchase a sweater; in October, he had his radio repaired; on November 7, he spent $61.15 to acquire shirts, a hat and a robe. Reoccurring entries of the report suggest that Lloyd was employing a personal attendant named Edward Howard.

Lloyd's next Sennett two-reeler had started out as a vehicle for W.C. Fields. Fields was no longer available as he had argued with Sennett and refused to work with him again.

The argument had been brewing for months. Fields agreed to write and star in a series for Sennett on the condition that he was allowed complete control until he "went wrong." Fields, who considered Sennett a good friend, expected Sennett to honor the agreement and trust him to know what he was doing. Fields took the extra precaution of submitting script outlines to Sennett, never intending to move forward on a script unless he had Sennett's approval. Sennett, however, would get second thoughts once he got the finished script and he would take it upon himself to change scenes. In the case of the script "His Perfect Day," Sennett wanted to include what Fields described as an "indelicate castor oil sequence."[4] Fields objected to this material, which he found to be inappropriate. A series of letters went back and forth between Fields and Sennett. Sennett's final answer was curt. He said that either Fields approve the script in its new form or it would be given to Lloyd Hamilton. Lloyd wasn't expected to defy Sennett. He wasn't expected to be so discriminating as to question the appropriateness of an indelicate castor oil sequence.

The film went into production with Lloyd under the title *Too Many Highballs*. The direction was handled by Clyde Bruckman, who had collaborated with Fields on the script. It was to Lloyd's benefit that much of Fields and Bruckman's material was left intact. Lloyd, in one funny scene, has trouble parking his car and is arrested by an ill-tempered cop for drunk driving. In a case of movies reflecting real life, Lloyd is then forced to undergo a "quick cure" for alcoholism. One critic said that he could not entirely enjoy the film because the comic's "disturbing appearance ... spoiled the fun." Lloyd was certainly not looking his best and not looking very funny due to his ill health. *Too Many Highballs* was Lloyd's last Sennett film. Lloyd said in court papers that he decided at this point to unceremoniously retire.

Four months later, Sennett had to permanently shut down his studio.

In the spring of 1933, Hal Roach considered hiring Lloyd for a new series.[5] Roach, at the time, was the preeminent producer of short comedies, responsible for popular series starring Laurel & Hardy, Our Gang, and Charley Chase. Lloyd could have had a good home at Roach. However, it was Lloyd's relationship with Chase that caused Roach to pass on hiring him. The producer feared that, if he had these two good drinking buddies working on the same lot, they were bound to have a bad influence on one another.

Lloyd started off his retirement with some travel. On December 2, he went on a hunting trip. Later, on Christmas Eve, he went to stay at his sister's home.

Horn tendered a report in April, 1933. The report read:

> Owing to personal business that at present requires most of my time and makes it necessary that I make trips out of the City, and I feel I cannot devote the time the above case requires, the parties to the action and myself have mutually agreed upon my retiring from the case. I hereby resign and will assist the party appointed by the court in my place, in anyway that I can, and will give any information I have knowledge of whenever same is desired.

J. B. Mandell, Lloyd's latest attorney, responded with a petition, which read as follows:

> That within the past few months the said receiver Clarence W. Horn has been engaged in sundry business matters that require all his time and attention and it has not been possible for the said receiver to adequately carry on his manifold duties as receiver of said defendant, Lloyd Hamilton. That it will be impossible in the future for this receiver to give any of his time to the affairs of this defendant which now require almost daily attention upon the part of the receiver.
>
> "That in view of the foregoing this petitioner asks that an order be made directing the discharge of Clarence W. Horn as receiver....

At this time, Lloyd's liabilities totaled $49,716. This included alimony amounting to

$12,500 plus $18,000 due to the Federal Government. On June 3, 1933, Lloyd's bankruptcy petition was approved.

In 1933, producer Louis Lewyn reunited Lloyd with Bud Duncan for a *Hollywood on Parade* reel. Lloyd initially appears in the film persuing the finalists of Paramount's highly publicized international beauty contest "Search for Beauty." He has brought along a Brownie box camera to take pictures, but he has trouble operating the camera and ends up unraveling a roll of film. He has even more trouble with a fellow photographer played by Bud. Bud is holding a flash pan close to Lloyd's face as he ignites the powder and sets off a blinding flash. Later, Bud gets in the way as Lloyd tries to photograph Mae West at a movie premiere. Lloyd, just like old times, contends with this persistent little nuisance by giving him a hard kick in the rump.

Lloyd's old pastor, Charles Reynolds Brown, had recently embarked on a campaign against motion pictures, which he blamed for reducing attendance at Sunday church service. He said that movies had, in effect, made people deviate from spiritual development and had diminished the public's "readiness to share in Christian activities."[6] As he saw it, the moviegoing experience — people staring at pictures on a screen — added no real value to society. Movies, he said, were "a cheap, easy kind of diversion which cannot by any stretch of the imagination be called a form of art." Real actors, he believed, were theatre actors, who worked on stage to be "engaged with real people" and get a "sense of response from an audience." He believed that their efforts to make personal contact with their audience made them interesting and admirable. The theatre actor, in this way, respected Christian fellowship and adhered to the example of God, who "was made flesh [to] dwell among us in the fullness of grace." Movie actors, in contrast, worked in a "social vacuum." Their efforts for the camera — "rolling their eyes up and down, pulling their features this way and that ... [and] vainly trying to express something which they do not feel"— was, in his estimation, "pathetic."

By now, a schism existed between Lloyd and his family, one that went beyond mere geography. The family members interviewed for this book were reluctant to say much on the subject. Richard Bishop was asked, directly, if his uncle's lifestyle as a movie star had created conflict within the family. He replied, "Some." That one word, delivered grimly and emphatically, seemed to imply a great deal, but that was all Richard was willing to say.

Mary Hamilton was, at this time, living with her daughter's family. Mabel had married Otis M. Judson, a real estate developer. The Judsons were well-established fixtures of Piedmont's upper class. Otis was a major shareholder in a local oil refinery.

Lloyd, who now only traveled for short distances, did not attend the elaborate wedding ceremony of his niece, Virginia Joy Morehouse. Virginia had waited until she graduated from the University of California to marry her fiancé, Charles James Hawksley.

A rare mid–1920's portrait of Hamilton without costume or makeup (courtesy of Billy Rose Theatre Division, New York Public Library for the Performing Arts, Astor, Lenox and Tilden Foundations).

The wedding took place in the fall of 1933. Officiating was Dr. Reverend Clarence Reidenbach, the new pastor at the First Congregational Church of Oakland. Pastors at this church had faithfully presided over all the family's religious functions. The bride was given away by her stepfather. Also present was Virginia's one other uncle, a prominent artist named Charles Chapel Judson. Although he worked with various mediums, Mr. Judson was best known for his paintings. He had once been a Professor of Graphic Arts at the University of California; now, he was a trustee of Oakland's California College of Arts & Crafts. His name was listed in *Who's Who in American Art*.

Virginia's older sister, Claudia, attended the wedding with her husband, John Bishop, and her daughter, Claudia Jean, who was one of the maids of honor. The Bishops had driven up from Hollywood, where John worked as a cameraman. John and Claudia also had a five-year-old son, Richard, who had stayed at home. Richard was aware of his uncle at the time — he was, in fact, told that he looked like his Uncle Lloyd — but he rarely had contact with this celebrated member of his family. "I think I saw him two times," said Richard.

Virginia Hawksley, in discussions for this book, was reticent. When asked if her grandparents disapproved of her uncle being an actor, she answered curtly, "Not at all." She was later asked to describe, in general, her grandparents' relationship with her uncle. "They were very fond of him," she replied. She made the point that her grandmother was devoted to her uncle and took care of him when he became ill.

Richard and Virginia, cryptic and evasive as they were on most subjects, were clear and decisive when it came to Mary Hamilton. Virginia made it clear that she was a devoted mother. Richard went out of his way to say that she was "a wonderful, wonderful woman." They were, in speaking of their grandmother, affectionate, loyal and, perhaps, protective. They stressed, as if attempting to head off criticism, that this was a good woman. Her son may have come to a bad end but this was not something for which she should be blamed. Lloyd was left, in this scenario, as the bad son who had given his mother grief and disrepute.

On October 4, 1933, police officers in a patrol car observed Lloyd erratically wandering along Windsor Boulevard. On further examination, the officers confirmed their suspicion that Lloyd was in an intoxicated state. Before a night court judge, Lloyd pleaded guilty and was fined ten dollars. He was detained in jail until the next day.

Two weeks later, the scene was virtually replayed. While patrolling Sunset Boulevard, police officer George T. George saw Lloyd walking around and bumping into people. He stopped Lloyd and asked him what he was doing. Lloyd explained that a man had come by slandering the police and he had felt compelled to chase down the man to defend the police. The officer arrested Lloyd on a charge of drunkenness and escorted him to the Lincoln Heights Police Station. Lloyd was held in jail for a day. The *Los Angeles Examiner* headline read "Lloyd Hamilton Defends Police."

Jack White may have been recalling these incidents when he described Lloyd drunkenly falling down "somewhere around Santa Monica Boulevard." "He was so full of booze," said White, "he didn't know where he was."[7]

Towards the end of 1933, Harry Edwards coaxed Lloyd back before the cameras. Under Edwards' direction, Lloyd acted in two Educational comedies. The veteran comic was prominently billed in the credits as "Guest Star."

The first film, produced by Jack White, was *Pop's Pal*. Lloyd doesn't show up until the climactic scene, at which time he gets into the middle of an argument between Billy Bevan and George Bickel. As the scene opens, Bevan's son is getting ready for a visit from an important businessman. His warring father and father-in-law, Bevan and Bickel, are down in the living room when someone knocks on the door. Bevan opens the door to find Lloyd in a characteristic pose. His old costume hangs loosely from a skeletal frame. His eyes are not clear. Wan and frail, he offers a ghostly figure. When he finally delivers a line, he speaks with a slur. Bevan and Bickel, who resume their bickering, physically attack one another and mistakenly strike the visitor. Lloyd desperately flees the scene, but the two men want to apologize and

Hamilton makes his final screen appearance in *Star Night at the Cocoanut Grove* (1934) (courtesy of Cole Johnson — Slapstick Archive).

chase after him. He tries to outdistance the pair on a bicycle. Since Lloyd could not handle the slight physical demands of the role, it is an unconvincing double who runs a couple of yards, hops onto the bicycle seat, and promptly pedals away. Bevan and Bickel pursue Lloyd on a motorcycle.

The second film, an Andy Clyde comedy, briefly featured Lloyd as a sheriff. Lloyd is a bit more mobile here, but only one of his legs is fluent. This is particularly obvious when, while pursuing a criminal, he drags the stiff leg across the length of the screen. Lloyd also appears infirm in an encounter with Andy, reciting his lines in a flat and weary voice.

On December 5, Lloyd entered into a partnership to open a small cafe. His partners included Edward Howard and Ethel Fenner. Ethel Fenner had, until a recent marriage, been Ethel Hamilton, Lloyd's first wife. Ethel, who furnished the venture with capital, became upset when she failed to receive any return on her investment. It disturbed her even more when Lloyd and Howard failed to comply with her demand for an accounting. On February 6, 1934, she was granted a decree to dissolve the partnership. Shortly after, the cafe was closed.

Lloyd's name wasn't in the newspapers again until August 15, 1934, when his second wife died suddenly at her home in Chicago. That wasn't the only death Lloyd had experienced this year. One of his closest friends, Lew Cody, died May 31, 1934. Cody, a heavy drinker to the end, was a frequent passenger on Buster Keaton's notorious "land yacht." This was a mobile home that Keaton bought following his divorce from Natalie Talmadge in 1932. The vehicle became, according to writer Sam Marx, "the greatest party place I've ever known."[8] Marx said, "It rocked back and forth day and night with the drinking that was going on. It was like New Year's Eve every day."

In the fall of 1934, Lloyd was overcome by intense pain, the cause of which was cancer of the liver. He tried to conceal his condition from his friends, but the secret could not remain hidden. Jack White claimed that Chaplin came forward to pay Lloyd's medical bills.[9]

Louis Lewyn, who had produced the *Voice of Hollywood* series, gave Lloyd a non-strenuous role in *Star Night at the Cocoanut Grove*. This MGM short subject presented a variety show in Colortone, an early color process that offered a garish palette. In a musical number, Lloyd depicts a rich man who has purchased a Hawaiian island. The setting is a serene beach surrounded by blue water. Wafting through the air is a lively tune, dominated by the sweet strain of a piano, the wailing of horns and the ringing of guitar strings. Lloyd, sitting on the white sand, looks drawn. He is outfitted in a top hat, black leotards, a red lei, and a long grass skirt. A string of shells adorn his hat and dress cuffs hang loosely from his wrists. A long, smoky cigar juts out of his mouth. The costume is reminiscent of the one Lloyd wore in his classic *Robinson Crusoe Ltd.* Two native girls are devoutly fanning the island king with large, leafy swatches from a palm tree. Lloyd, while enjoying the breeze, is dangling a monkey doll at the end of an elastic cord. He yanks the cord repeatedly to make the doll dance. A line of hula girls dance and sing while they encircle the chieftain. Lloyd sleepily smiles as he stares at his bouncing doll. His gestures are ungraceful. It seems genuine when, in trying to puff his cigar, he falters and slightly misses his mouth.

In the end, Lloyd strikes an erect pose and sways feebly to the music. He has one hand set on his hip while his other hand proudly draws the bloated cigar from his mouth. With a contented grin, he blows a cloud of white smoke into the air. As the melody dwindles, the camera moves behind Lloyd and slowly withdraws from the scene. Lloyd, with both his hands on his hips, continues to rock in place as the scene fades.

At the outset of 1935, Lloyd's home was a single room in a small Hollywood hotel. On

January 17, a Thursday evening, he was visited by two close friends. On entering the cramped room, the friends immediately noticed Lloyd lying beside his bed. They pulled him onto the bed and asked him if he was feeling all right. It was obvious that he was weak. As he tried to speak, he coughed up blood.

One friend stayed close to Lloyd as the other got on the phone to call Dr. J. J. Tobinski, who made a quick assessment of the situation. He realized that, if Lloyd was coughing up blood, he was hemorrhaging and needed emergency care. He summoned an ambulance to move Lloyd to Hollywood Community Hospital.

Determined that an ulcer in Lloyd's stomach had ruptured, Dr. Tobinski promptly made arrangements for surgery. The procedure was completed by morning, at which time Lloyd was being given blood transfusions. The newspapers didn't go into detail about Lloyd's operation, but it can be expected that surgeons performed a gastrectomy to remove the ulcer-bearing part of his stomach. Today, treatment would likely be less intrusive. A surgeon would reach the ulcer using a small tube called an endoscope and possibly insert a heating probe to cauterize the ulcer. A gastrectomy was, at the time, a much more traumatic operation.

Lloyd rallied in mid-afternoon. He was conscious, smiling and exchanging quips with the nurses. Minutes before five o'clock, he dropped into unconsciousness. Twenty minutes later, he died.

John Bishop, who had spent the night at the hospital, phoned Mary Hamilton to notify her of her son's death. That evening, the 76-year-old woman and her daughter boarded a southbound train in Berkeley. They reached Hollywood in the morning, by which time photos of Lloyd were appearing in newspapers across the world. Most of the photos were promotional stills of Lloyd in his prime days. He had on his funny hat and funny coat, and he looked out with a funny look that expressed fear or sadness or confusion. The front page of the day's *San Francisco Chronicle* featured a headline that told the tale:

COMEDY ENDED
MIRTH MASTER HAMILTON
DIED AT HOLLYWOOD

The premature posing of the beloved screen comedian, who had turned 43 in August, caused great sadness in the Hollywood community. Friends said that Lloyd had dropped out of sight and they didn't know that he was ill. Some reporters focused on this, referring to Lloyd as a loner. The headline in the *Fresno Bee* read "Lloyd Hamilton, Comedy Veteran, Dies as a Recluse."[10]

Mary Hamilton, who must have thought that Lloyd had gotten enough attention in his life, told the press, simply, that she wanted a private, quiet service for her son. Reporters assumed that the service would be held in the Oakland area, but Lloyd's body was laid out for viewing in Los Angeles at Edwards Brothers Funeral Home. Final respects were paid by seventy-five close friends and ex-associates, who attended a chapel service on January 21. In newspaper accounts, it was emphasized that none of Lloyd's "playday pals" were present. Some of the playday pals, including Lew Cody and Hugh Fay, had died years earlier. Others were struggling with dire health problems related to their drinking.

Charley Chase attended the chapel service. By this time, heavy drinking had severely damaged Chase's stomach. In the last ten years, he had to be hospitalized twice to remove parts of his stomach.[11] He had barely any stomach left, but he couldn't stop drinking. He would die of alcohol poisoning less than five years later.

Joe E. Brown had sought help to dry out when his drinking got out of control.[12] In the end, he became such an avid teetotaler that he could no longer tolerate drinkers. At one point, he fired longtime agent Ivan Kahn for what he regarded as excessive drinking.[13] The clean and sober comedian outlived all of his old drinking buddies, dying in 1973 at the age of 81.

Lloyd Bacon was on hand to console Mary Hamilton. Virginia held onto a letter of condolence that the family received from the director.

Reverend James H. Lash of Hollywood Congregational Church officiated at the service. In his eulogy, the reverend said of the deceased entertainer, "He accomplished his purpose — to bring happiness to millions around the world through clean comedy." Wesley Tourtellotte, an organist, played a group of Lloyd's favorite selections. Ivan Edwards sang "Abide With Me" and "Oh, Sweet Mystery of Life." For the interment of the body, Lloyd's brother-in-law had provided a public cemetery lot located in Plano, California. Following cremation, Lloyd's remains were to be buried alongside William Hamilton's grave. The Judsons, who owned the lot, were descendants of one of Plano's early ranching families.

Plano was situated in Northern California, 246 miles from Oakland and near Lake Success and the Great Sequoia Forest. The town, a small one, lied in what had always been a low-yield farming region. Reflecting what the district's average taxpayer could afford, the cemetery plot and maintenance charges in Plano were meager. Plano had recently been absorbed by Porterville, a larger neighbor with an estimated population of 2,000.

Lloyd's body reached Porterville in late January. Porterville was not exactly Avalon, but it was pleasant. It formed a picturesque setting at the foot of the Sierras. The weather was mild although it was in the middle of winter.

Lloyd's body were finally brought to Plano's Vandalia Cemetery, the oldest of the district's eight. Up until then, Vandalia's most notable occupant had been a nineteenth-century woman who had been killed by Indians. Lloyd's remains were buried without grand ritual.

On January 29, 1935, the file on Ethel Hamilton's divorce action was closed. This litigation had endured for a decade. During this period, Lloyd had changed attorneys four times. The last document in the file was a brief affidavit from R. E. Allen, the latest receiver in the case. Allen swore: "I am informed and believe and I allege upon such information and belief that the defendant, Lloyd Hamilton, has died."

Except for her Uncle Lloyd, Claudia Bishop was the only member of the Hamilton family to make her home in Hollywood. Her husband, John, became the head of Paramount's camera and film processing departments and, in 1955, he won an Oscar for developing VistaVision.

Claudia's son, Richard, said that he grew up around movie stars and he did not come to think well of the Hollywood lifestyle. He said that he saw, up close, the anxieties that result from working in the movie industry. His parents told him that they were willing to support him in any endeavor as long as he steered clear of the film business. He made sure to follow their advice.

Claudia's daughter, Claudia Jean, attended Van Nuys High School, then continued her education on the University of California's Berkeley campus. To be within commuting distance of the university, she left behind Hollywood and moved into her grandparents' home in Piedmont. Claudia Jean joined Chi Omega, an exclusive sorority which had once welcomed her aunt as a member.

During her college education, Claudia Jean became engaged to her high school sweetheart, John Marvin Owen. After attending the California Institute of Technology, John completed specialized training at a school sponsored by the U.S. Army. It was as a fullfledged engineer that John married Claudia Jean in 1945. Mary Hamilton, who attended the ceremony, finally got to welcome an engineer into the family.

Mary Hamilton died in 1949. Her body was cremated, her ashes buried along with her son's remains. In 1961, the ashes of Mabel Judson were also buried at this site.

By 1935, Educational had come full circle in more ways than one. To start, the company had secured the rights to an Oscar-winning documentary about the Krakatoa volcano disaster, which probably covered a lot of the same ground as their early documentary *The Why of a Volcano*. Hammons had revived one of the company's original series, *Torchy*. Al Christie, one of Educational's early comedy producers, had come limping back to the fold after suffering some financial reversals.

Educational no longer possessed any major attractions. Their best-known stars, Buster Keaton and Harry Langdon, had seen better days. Most of their other comedians, like Tom Patricola and Buster West, were forgettable. An exception was Ernest Truex, who did well playing milquetoast husbands in domestic comedies, but Truex would do better as a character actor in feature films. Any money still to be made in the short subject market was being made by Columbia and RKO. The Three Stooges, Columbia's newest comedy stars, were creating the biggest ripples in this Hollywood side-pond. The Stooges' series was produced by Jules White, a younger brother of Lloyd's former partner. Jules had once worked as Lloyd's errand boy.

In the late thirties, Educational went on to what has been termed "a quiet death."[14] Soon after, a fire ignited at Educational's warehouse. Lost in the blaze were the master negatives of all Lloyd's Educational releases.

As a result, it was not assured that future generations would know of Lloyd Hamilton. Despite an expansive body of work (over 250 films), the current remains of the comic's output is slight.

The Final Years of Hamilton's Partners

Marshall Neilan

During the twenties, Neilan had achieved prominence directing features for Famous Players-Lasky, Mary Pickford Films and Marshall Neilan Productions. Now, as he entered a new decade, he found himself struggling to find work. His first production of the decade, *Forever Yours*, had been shut down after one month of shooting despite production costs estimated at $300,000.00. Mary Pickford, the star and producer of the film, was so unhappy with the production that she had the negatives destroyed. As a follow up, Neilan completed an undistinguished romantic comedy, *Sweethearts on Parade*, for Columbia Pictures.

Based on Neilan's growing reputation for arguing with his bosses and drinking heavily, the major studios were unwilling to trust him to direct a feature film. Left little choice, Neilan returned to short subjects. During 1931, he directed one Sennett comedy and two entries of Roach's Thelma Todd-Zasu Pitts series. *Catch as Catch Can*, one of Neilan's Todd-Pitts comedies, was an exceptional effort. According to Leonard Maltin, the film possessed a "pure wistful charm"[15] and a distinctive technical style. Bud Duncan, diminutive half of the Ham and Bud team that Neilan created twenty-seven years earlier, appeared in a climactic boxing scene as a referee.

In 1934, following three years of inactivity, Neilan traveled to Florida to direct Buster Keaton in an independent feature, *The Fisherman*. Misfortune plagued the production. Keaton, his morale soured, went to the financial backers and convinced them to withdraw from the project.

Neilan stayed in Florida to direct *Chloe, Love Is Calling*, a low-budget horror film about a voodoo priestess and her zombie slaves. Afterwards, he returned to Hollywood and directed three studio features in quick succession. The first, *The Social Register*, was a Columbia production starring Colleen Moore. Moore had worked with Neilan on the 1920 feature *Dinty* and remained close friends with the director for the remainder of her life. Neilan also directed *The Lemon Drop Kid*, a Paramount adaptation of a Damon Runyon short story, and a vehicle for child star Jane Withers called *This Is the Life*.

In 1937, Ambassador Pictures hired Neilan to direct a series of B-musicals starring a popular Arkansas singer-songwriter named Pinky Tomlin. Tomlin's biggest hit, "The Object of My Affection," is best remembered for a comical rendition essayed by Carl "Alfalfa" Switzer in *Our Gang Follies of 1936*. Neilan directed three Tomlin vehicles before Ambassador abandoned the series.

Neilan lived in obscurity over the next two decades. He didn't return to films until 1957, when he played Senator Worthington Fuller in Elia Kazan's *A Face in the Crowd*. This was the entertainer's final bow; he died of throat cancer on October 27, 1958.

Bud Duncan

Bud had worked steadily in films since 1911, performing in short comedies for Biograph, Apollo and Kalem. But the failure of his *Clover* series in 1919 prompted him to temporarily desert his motion picture career to headline theatre prologue bills and perform in vaudeville shows.

Later in the year, Bud worked to launch *Bud and His Buddies*, a one-reel series designed to team the comedian with a variety of ingénues. Bud started his own production company, Shiller, and established distribution through Reelcraft Films. Bud's father, who was employed as Shiller's General Manager, assembled a technical crew while Bud, avoiding competition with Hollywood's major producers, auditioned recent beauty contestants in New York. Although Bud worked hard to produce the series and managed to sell it rapidly through independent exchanges, *Bud and His Buddies* ended after a mere fourteen releases.

In 1927, Bud ended a seven-year absence from films. He was a transient figure in a Tiffany-Stahl feature entitled *The Haunted Ship*. He starred in the Jack White comedy *Dear Season*, which involved a party of motorists who unwittingly invade an all-girls camp. The following year, he was prominently featured in two-reel comedies for Weiss Brothers Artclass Pictures.

During the following year, Bud attracted the attention of FBO producer Larry Darmour and director Elmo Boyce, who were adapting Jimmy Murphy's newspaper strip *Toots and Casper* into a series of two-reel comedies. Thelma Hill was cast as the pretty, vivacious blonde Toots and Bud was transformed into her harried spouse, Casper. The couple was, in many respects, a forerunner of Blondie and Dagwood. Surviving series entries, including *Fooling Casper* and *Smile, Buttercup, Smile*, have proven to be delightful farces about married life.

The series, though well received, ended after only a dozen productions. It was hurricane winds stirred by the sound craze that had crushed *Toots and Casper*. FBO, in an effort to survive the talkie revolution, merged with Radio and Pathé to form RKO. The RKO executives wanted their short subject department to produce fresh vehicles that emphasized the vocal talents of their actors. Born from this change was *Nick and Tony*, a series that showcased the misadventures of two heavily accented Italian immigrants, and a series starring Clark & McCullough, Broadway comedians who specialized in snappy wisecracks.

Bud had trouble getting work in movies at this point. In 1931, Marshall Neilan cast him as a referee in a Roach comedy, *Catch as Catch Can*. Otherwise, the actor found more opportunities in radio and publishing. He was heard on numerous radio shows in the next few years.

Most notably, he hosted the CBS series called *The Whopper Club* and played the title role in *The Cinnamon Bear*, a fantasy program produced in 1937. *The Cinnamon Bear* became an annual Christmas special and stands today as a cherished classic of oldtime radio. A fan club, The Cinnamon Bear Brigade, distributed a monthly newsletter in the 1980s. In 2007, the seventieth anniversary of the show was marked by an illustrated coffee table book. Duncan also wrote two cookbooks during this period.

Bud returned to movies in 1941 when Monogram Pictures, a producer of low-budget films, cast the runty comedian as another popular comic strip character, shiftless hillbilly Snuffy Smith. The film, *Private Snuffy Smith*, was modeled after Abbott & Costello's *Buck Privates*, a highly profitable "service" comedy that had capitalized on wartime sentiments. It was not out of the ordinary for Monogram to have Snuffy to lift arms against the Nazi hordes. Hollywood had, in fact, already enlisted many renowned fictitious characters, including Tarzan, Sherlock Holmes and the Invisible Man, to fight against the Nazis. Bud, fitted with an oversized putty nose and baggy uniform, announced with rigor, "Bodacious! Bring on those Natzy varmits!"

Bud worked on the film with two fellow comedy veterans: director Edward Cline and slow-burn comedian Edgar Kennedy. Kennedy, then the star of a popular series at RKO, was featured as Snuffy's commanding officer, Sgt. Gatling. It was his familiar likeness that dominated ads.

John Grey, a former writer for Lloyd Hamilton and Harold Lloyd, worked on the script with two newcomers, Jack Henley and Doncho Hall. Hall ordinarily worked as a puppeteer and showed no interest in pursuing a career in screenwriting. Henley, though, was more committed to the project. He, in fact, became adept at scripting cheaply-produced, low-brow comedies. Prominent in his later credits are four "Ma and Pa Kettle" films, a half dozen installments of "Blondie," two "Bowery Boys" vehicles, and the infamous *Bonzo Goes to College*.

Despite its low production values, *Private Snuffy Smith* performed satisfactorily as half of a dual bill. A sequel, *Hillbilly Blitzkrieg*, reached the market a few months later. This time, radio double-talker Cliff Nazarro joined the cast as Smith's friend Barney Google. *Hillbilly Blitzkrieg* climaxed with Snuffy being launched on an experimental missile. With scuffling forces bumping into control levers, the missile achieved a wide variety of wild aerial maneuvers. Unfortunately, Bud's skills riding this rocket did not leave any producer with the urge to hire the comic.

Bud found work where he could. Alfred Santell, a former Ham and Bud director, remembered Bud working as a waiter "in a cheap restaurant."[16] Eventually, Bud found a steady job as a shipping clerk for a company called Radio Recorders.

In 1954, Bud received a bit part in *Princess on the Nile*, a costume nonepic starring Debra Paget, Jeffrey Hunter and Michael Rennie. Dee Monroe, a friend close to Bud at the time, said that Bud reacted enthusiastically when he secured the role. In his one scene in the film, he can be glimpsed as a thief sitting atop a bulky partner's shoulders. It was an image reminiscent of his long ago partnership with Lloyd.

The remainder of Bud's days was difficult. Bud, who had never married, lived by himself. He was, by all indication, destitute. Monroe described Bud as sad, disillusioned and bewildered. Bud often complained to Dee about times in his life when he wasn't treated fairly. Bud retired in 1955. He lived simply in a trailer home and made frequent outings to fish, hike and camp. Whenever he met someone, he would speak to them ardently about his film career. In 1960, he developed heart disease and lost possession of his trailer. In an act of kindness, Dee took the 77-year-old retiree into her home and cared for him. Bud's condition rapidly deteriorated. Due to thickening and hardening of his artery walls, Bud found the pain unbearable and had to be registered into the L.A. County Osteopathic Hospital. A doctor told Dee that Bud's heart was struggling to maintain circulation and the old man did not have long to live.

On November 26, 1960, Bud quietly succumbed. The Monroes provided information to the officials preparing the death certificate. They also paid for the funeral. Bud's body was attired in a suit that Dee had purchased for the occasion. On the first of December, the service was held in Woodlawn Cemetery; when it ended the remains of the diminutive comic were buried in a pauper's grave.

Jack White

Jack White, after more than thirteen years of turning out comedies for Educational Pictures, closed his production company in 1933. By this time, Jack had become overwhelmed by personal and professional problems and had lost his confidence and drive. He explained, "I got tied up in divorce problems with Pauline [Starke] and I had no appetite for filmmaking."[17] At the same time, the demands of his job caused him physical exhaustion. In regards to his Educational comedies, he said, "I lived them, wrote them, directed them, produced them. We eventually made as many as forty-two a year. That's a hell of a lot of pictures."[18] When he developed thyroid disease, he was sure that this was caused by the stress and fatigue. He felt, under the circumstances, that he was at the brink of a breakdown and it was time for him to get out. He was certain that filmmaking could kill a person after seeing his two hardest working protégés, Stephen Roberts and Mark Sandrich, suffer premature deaths.

After resting for a few months, Jack journeyed to New York to produce a stage show. "It wasn't any good," he admitted.[19] During the run of the show, he commuted to Long Island to produce the three-reel musical comedy *Poppin' the Cork* at the Eastern Service Studio. Al Christie opened this studio facility with the specific intention to feature Broadway entertainers and nightclub performers in motion pictures. Jack's project, a tuneful tribute to the repeal of Prohibition, is best known today for having up-and-coming stand-up comedian Milton Berle in the lead role.

By 1935, Jack was feeling washed up and no longer wanted to work in movies, but his brother Jules used some tough talk to get him to join his production unit at Columbia. Jack operated at the studio under the alias "Preston Black." "I was having divorce trouble and the lawyers were hounding me everywhere I went to work," he explained. "So I changed my screen name so they couldn't tell who the hell I was. I worked under the name Preston Black for, on and off, ten years."[20] Jack would retain vivid memories of lawyers "molesting" him. "Everytime I wanted to talk about a job, her lawyers were already there before me. It was murder."[21] Jack directed several of his brother's stars, including the Three Stooges, Andy Clyde, Harry Langdon, El Brendel and Walter Catlett.

With the coming of World War II, Jack volunteered for military service. He worked in the Photo Battalion of the Signal Corps until he got sick and came home. Once back on the West Coast, Jack obtained employment at 20th Century Fox. He recounted:

> I worked there as an assistant director ... and I learned a lot that I hadn't come into contact before. I had a deal with the studio; I was to stay there until the war ended, at which time the regular guy whose job I had would be able to reclaim his position. When he returned, I went back to Columbia.[22]

Jack focused his attention on writing for the next thirteen years. He wrote a number of Columbia's two-reel comedies and, in the early fifties, he wrote an autobiography. It proved a disappointment to him when he failed to interest a publisher in his autobiography. Health troubles prevented Jack from working steadily. He was unable to even sell the occasional script when Columbia closed its short comedy department in 1958.

In 1977, I tried to locate Jack through the Directors Guild of America. Jack was not listed with the union, but the membership roster did include an address for Jules White. I wrote a brief letter to Jules, asking him to forward a message to his brother.

I should have expected that Jules' response would be less than friendly. During his career, Jules had been known to be overbearing and pugnacious. He was proud to say that he had achieved success by being a "bastard" and he insisted that it was his gall and combativeness that earned him the admiration of Columbia president Harry Cohn. The hard-boiled Cohn, nicknamed "King Cohn," did in fact expect his managers to hold their own against him. Samuel Marx, a Columbia story editor, said of the studio chief: "The people he respected the most were the people who fought him the most."[23]

In answering my letter, Jules demonstrated that his old hard-edged manner remained intact. He complained bitterly that he was plagued by writers' queries.[24] He told me that Three Stooges fan clubs "write all the time from all over the U.S." He alleged that he was always being asked about Buster Keaton, Harry Langdon, "and countless other comics." He grumbled that, due to the large volume of inquiries, he refuses to cooperate. "At first I did," he said, "but it got out of hand."

In a second letter, I demonstrated my own combativeness. I reminded Jules that my inquiry had been intended not for him but for his brother. Jules responded promptly and, this time, he assumed a more congenial tone. He assured me that he was not a "heel" and he offered a few brief comments for the book. He cheerfully reported, "Jack is living and quite well, thank God." However, he brought the correspondence to an unpromising conclusion. He wrote: "I'll show Jack your letter. IF (?) he cares to answer it, you'll hear from him (which I doubt)." Jack never replied.

A few years later, the Directors Guild of America engaged David Bruskin to conduct an oral history of the White Brothers, which included Jack, Jules and a younger brother named Sam. Bruskin spoke to Jack while conducting interviews in the spring of 1983, but these conversations weren't productive and most of Jack's history came from Jack's unpublished autobiography. Jack died the following year. Jules, who had suffered from Alzheimer's Disease, died in 1985.

21

In Reference to Relics

The known remains of Lloyd Hamilton's 250 films are scant. Work from his peak years, 1920 to 1924, is largely missing. Some of his silent Educational comedies came to light in the late eighties. Arising from the private collection of David Wyatt were *Dynamite*, *The Simp*, *April Fool*, *Moonshine* and *His Baby Daze*. Discovered in Czechoslovakia were *The Vagrant*, *Crushed*, *Waiting*, *His Better Half* and *Always a Gentleman*. Long available to private collectors were *Dynamite*, *Somebody's Fault*, *Breezing Along*, *Papa's Boy* and the two-reel version of *His Darker Self*. In 1976, Blackhawk Films had converted *Breezing Along* from pre-print material. In general, the prints are of poor quality. In faded footage, the features of Lloyd's powder white face are often invisible.

Ironically, Kalem's *Ham* comedies have fared slightly better. Of these reels, at least 37 of 118 remain in existence. Since the sixties, the home movie market has offered *Ham in the Harem*, *Raskey's Road Show*, *The Blundering Blacksmith* and *The Bathtub Bandit*. In the late seventies, the Library of Congress transferred thirteen *Ham Comedies* from nitrate film stock to the much safer acetate film stock. Many of these films came from Marlu Telefilms, which, in the early 1950s, distributed a package of *Ham* comedies to television stations.

Lloyd's work is missing mostly as the result of callousness and shortsightedness on the part of studio executives. In the 30s, 40s and 50s, a particular apathy existed in regards to preservation. The rare exception in the area of silent comedy was Chaplin's films, which were consistently valuable to distribution companies. Due to their continuing popularity, these comedies were never in danger of being lost or destroyed. For this reason, we now have nearly all of the Tramp's adventures. However, no other silent film comic was prized in this critical period. The bulk of Buster Keaton and Harold Lloyd's work survived only because both men had preserved personal prints.

The existent vehicles of other prominent silent clowns, including Lloyd Hamilton, Roscoe Arbuckle, Larry Semon, Raymond Griffith and Max Linder, have remained severely limited. The best-known of Griffith's surviving films, *Hands Up*, shows that Lloyd had some influence on Griffith. The film begins with a sober presidential conference, much like the scene that opens *The Advisor*. It was indicated in reviews of *The Advisor* that the conference scene, which depicted Woodrow Wilson with his cabinet, carefully avoided caricature. Griffith also reworked scenes from *Robinson Crusoe, Ltd.*, simply replacing Hamilton's island cannibals with savage Indians. Griffith distracts the Indians by teaching them to dance the Charleston. He is later able to get the upper hand when he offers to teach the chief how to play craps. In the next scene, when Griffith and the chief emerge from behind a rock, Griffith is wearing the chief's headdress and other garb, which he has managed to win in the game. Without more examples of their work, no decisive evaluation can be made on the full merit of Hamilton, Griffith and these various other comedians.

Much of Mack Sennett's output is missing; but it is a loss that, based on existing Sennett productions, may favor the comedymaker. In his autobiography, Sennett wrote indifferently of his lost films. The situation did not seem to excite or depress him. Perhaps this was because Sennett realized that his legend far exceeded the quality of his output.

For years, not enough of Hamilton's work was available to form a definite opinion of the checkered-capped comic. But what does exist is promising and suggests that the recovery of Hamilton's missing comedies would likely benefit the comic's historical standing.

The life cycle of a film has never been made to automatically include preservation. Studio heads have long avoided this costly and bothersome process. In the movie industry's early days, studios would simply destroy the prints of a "played-out" release. Great Hollywood artists were building wonderful sandcastles on a turbulent beach.

This attitude is not limited to that remote period. In the 1970s, an NBC executive managed to gain storehouse space by destroying a large number of irreplaceable *Tonight Show* videos. That is not the only instance of television videos being destroyed. It is, in fact, rare to find videos of many favorite series, including *The Hollywood Squares* or *The Soupy Sales Show*. Like me, many fans of silent film comedy discovered Hamilton from Herb Graff's PBS series. Graff told film collector Cole Johnson that he was asked all the time how a person could get a copy of the series and he felt bad to have to tell them that PBS destroyed all the tapes. So, the program that made an issue of Hamilton's lost films has, itself, become lost.

Elsewhere, the archivists of museums, libraries, national institutes and municipal universities have lacked financial support to save films.

In 1975, Walter Kerr wrote, "Having gathered good evidence that a print of Raymond Griffith's *Wedding Bills* had been in the vaults of a distinguished museum five or six years ago, though it was no longer listed in the files, I made something of a nuisance of myself pressing inquiry. I was at last reluctantly told that the print had indeed been there but had, alas, been allowed to disintegrate before it could be copied.... The museum authorities were by no means indifferent to the fate of the film; they simply hadn't the money to recopy rapidly enough everything currently in their possession."[15]

Kerr continued, "One recent Christmas week a friend who was then an archivist for a national institution called me in despair: Did I know any way to raise a great deal of money *fast*? It seems that Fox Film, or its present ownership, had agreed to give the institution's library everything stored in its New Jersey vaults. My friend had made a trip out to the vaults, sequestered — because of the hazard of fire — in unsettled woodland. There were masses of aged films for the taking. But the walls of the building had long since cracked, portions of the roof had caved in, snakes were slithering about in the interior undergrowth, foxes were eating the Fox Film. He didn't get the money fast enough to save everything."[16]

It was not until recent years that this deplorable situation has started to improve. On May, 1, 1990, leading directors championed film preservation with the creation of The Film Foundation. It has been their objective to deliver multi-million dollar contributions from the major studios to America's five principal archival institutions: the Library of Congress, the Museum of Modern Art, the UCLA Film & Television Library, the George Eastman House, and the American Film Institute. Scorsese, who envisions twentieth century films affecting distant generations, has declared, "Rescuing the first century of film is our unique cultural responsibility."[17]

* * *

A Brooklyn boy, Herbert "Jackie" Gleason, had been one of Lloyd Hamilton's many fans. Lloyd had a great influence on Gleason's later work.

Joe Franklin, talk show host, told me, "There was no question that Gleason was motivated either subliminally or deliberately by Lloyd Hamilton. On my program, many times, Gleason has told me that he was inspired by Lloyd Hamilton. He was motivated by the country bumpkin style ... or the 'crazy like a fox' technique."[18]

The "Poor Soul," a popular Gleason character, had no doubt been patterned after Lloyd's screen character. In *The Great Clowns of American Television*, Karin Adir described the Poor Soul as "a baby-faced bumbler" who has to "deal with a cruel, uncaring world."[19] She adds, "[A]lthough he means well, [the Poor Soul] usually manages to exasperate those with whom he comes into contact.... Infantlike, he clenches and unclenches his fingers as if trying to grasp onto the air for support. His bug-eyes stare with exaggerated awe at the world around him; his awkward gait propels him from one pathetic situation to the next." Everything that Adir writes about the Pour Soul could easily be applied to the character that Lloyd portrayed on screen.

Gleason's most famous character, Ralph Kramden, shared a more subtle resemblance to Lloyd. Kramden, like Lloyd's "Poor Boy," was a romantic dreamer and perpetual loser who struggled to retain his basic dignity. The author of this book corresponded with Gleason, who described Lloyd as "a fine comic."[20]

A more superficial imitation of Lloyd's celluloid alter ego came along in the early forties. In the costuming of the Three Stooges, an attempt was made to fashion Curly Howard into a new Lloyd Hamilton. The boyish Stooge, attired in a checkered cap and matching Windsor tie, re-created several of Lloyd's gags. At one point, he wound up in an elaborate entanglement with a squirting duck. But Curly didn't resemble Lloyd as much in these gag sequences as he did when he simply performed timorous hand gestures.

It was a testament to Lloyd's special genius that the comic left a lasting impression on many of his writers and directors. The White brothers and Archie Mayo weren't the only former collaborators to recast another comic as Hamilton. Three decades after he directed *A Self-Made Failure*, William Beaudine had Huntz Hall imitate Lloyd's dress and mannerisms in the Bowery Boys comedy *Blues Busters*.

No man can physically survive in this world forever. Not even a man who is healthy, clever, courageous, and incredibly fortunate. This means that, to secure immortality, a man must accomplish that which is eternal or at least memorable. Motion pictures offer a man immortality.

In the 50s and 60s, a great interest arose in Hollywood's early comedy stars. From this interest came a number of books, articles and film retrospectives. The Cannes Film Festival welcomed Harold Lloyd to an elaborate retrospective of his films. After one of the films was presented, a standing ovation brought Harold to his feet. Swept up in the applause, the elderly guest leapt to the railing of the balcony, grabbed an upright support with one hand, and grandly leaned out over the audience. He hadn't felt this much affection since his heyday in the 1920s.

Buster Keaton, Charles Chaplin and Stan Laurel were also on hand to participate in this great revival. A Keaton autobiography was published in 1960; an autobiography of Chaplin was published in 1964; released in the same general period was John McCabe's *Mr. Laurel and Mr. Hardy*, a biography for which Stan Laurel had provided a vast amount of information and inspiration. From viewing available films and interviewing surviving comedymakers, several writers penned many other books focusing on film comedy's bygone days.

Books, which can be read, discussed and debated many years hence, also offer a man immortality. Behaviorist B. F. Skinner shocked many people by stating: "I would bury my children rather than my books." In qualifying this statement, Skinner later declared that he would also bury himself rather than his books. He wrote: "If some Mephistopheles offered me a wholly new life on the condition that all records and effects of my present life be destroyed, I should refuse." Some eternal achievement is worth more than life itself.

Having perished, Lloyd Hamilton and his work did not constitute even a small part of the resurgence. In the loss of his films, the comic had lost his claim upon the future. During the 60s, he remained a forgotten figure.

In 1958, during an interview with *Film Quarterly* magazine, Keaton was asked what comics he liked. He spoke of some comics who were popular at the time. Then, he added briefly, "I liked an old one called Lloyd Hamilton."[21]

In October, 1991, Lloyd Hamilton was honored at the Ninth Annual Pordenone Silent Film Festival. The festival marked the centennial of Lloyd's birth. Film collectors and official film archives have perfectly integrated in Pordenone, a small town in Northern Italy. Their association has been successful in discovering many lost films. The group has been devoted to the preservation and public presentation of the unearthed treasures. The festival boasts careful screenings. Whenever exhibiting a film, the festival staff assures the correctness of aspect ratio, projection speed, shutter operation and musical accompaniment. Through their efforts, the Pordenone festival has become a laboratory for the reevaluation of early cinema. It has become a place where the "black hole" of early cinema is systematically explored.

Following a $2,000,000 renovation, the Hollywood Athletic Club had reopened in October, 1990. The club was now an ornate billiard hall complete with coral-colored ceilings and background music featuring INXS. It possessed forty-five pool tables, three antique snooker tables, a chic bar-and-grill and a library with a roaring fireplace. This upscale billiard parlor attracted a new generation of entertainers, including Sean Penn, Charlie Sheen, Keanu Reeves, Kiefer Sutherland, Sinead O'Connor and Jason Priestley.

Oakland had strayed far from its pristine origins. In August, 1992, CBS News declared Oakland "one of the deadliest cities." It was reported that, in the first seven months of the year, 125 murders had occurred there. Because of the high murder rate and heavy drug trade, the city had been nicknamed "Croakland" and "Cokeland."

In neighboring San Francisco, the theatres on O'Farrell Street were now presenting nude dancers. In many ways, though, San Francisco had become the Oakland of Lloyd's youth. In 1994, Joe Queenan wrote in *Spy* magazine: "San Francisco is Arcadian and relatively safe. But that's because, years ago, it shipped all its problems across the bay to Oakland. Determined to turn itself into a city that exists for no reason than to be pretty, San Francisco has banished everyone who isn't presentable — the poor, the homeless, anyone who can't spell *caffe latte*— to the smoldering junk heap across the water.... The ugly truth is, the charm of San Francisco is inversely proportional to the squalor and gloom of Oakland."

In 1991, several hundred people attended the festival. These guests were treated to twenty-nine of Lloyd's films.

Porterville's population had increased tenfold since 1935. The area, which calls itself "The Sierra Wonderland," is devoted to family fun. It accommodates vacationing households with water sports and campgrounds.

According to cemetery records, Lloyd Hamilton simply had been an "actor." Even less is told by Lloyd's marker, one in a line of three thin and flat squares of bronze. Simply, it provides the deceased man's name, year of birth, and year of death.

The grounds of the Vandalia Cemetery are nicely maintained. The lawns contain manicured rows of white marble headstones bearing florid and sentimental elegies. Inconspicuous in this marble orchard is the modest marker of Lloyd Hamilton, the Oakland boy who had so relentlessly struggled to shine.

Providing a better statement of Lloyd Hamilton's existence are the rare strips of film that survive from comedy shorts like *Move Along*.

Appendix I: Profiles of Select Sunshine Personnel

Billy Armstrong (1891–1924) Armstrong was a mainstay of Chaplin's Essanay series in 1915 and 1916. He also worked as one of Sennett's supporting players. In 1920, he appeared in a popular Sennett feature entitled *Down on the Farm*.

Billy Bevan (1887–1957) Bevan, a diminutive Australian comic, was enlisted into Sennett's supporting ranks in 1920. Within the next two years, he became one of the studio's top attractions. For the balance of the decade, his only equal on the Sennett lot was Ben Turpin. In the sound era, he played character roles in numerous feature films, including *Cluny Brown*, *The Picture of Dorian Gray* and *The Lost Patrol*. At times, he provided no more than brief comic relief. This was certainly the case when he appeared as a passenger car attendant in the moody mystery film *Terror by Night*. In one scene, the camera moves slowly down a shadowy corridor until it comes upon Bevan sleeping in a chair. The comedian is leaning backwards, the backrest of the chair propped against the wall, when his nap is put to an abrupt end by a scream. It is then, with arms flailing, that he looses his balance and topples backwards, managing an effortless pratfall in the true Sennett tradition.

Jack G. Blystone (1892–1937) Blystone received his filmmaking training as a writer-director of *Joker Comedies*. After the series' demise in 1915, he found work at L-KO, directing Hank Mann and Alice Howell. Within a year, he succeeded Henry Lehrman as the general director of L-KO. In 1917, Blystone created an independent company, Century Films, to produce a new series with Howell. While Blystone was putting together financing, the Stern Brothers bought a controlling interest in the company and incorporated its output into Universal's program. By 1919, Blystone and Howell were no longer associated with Century Films, and the Stern Brothers had reorganized the company to produce animal comedies. Blystone worked for Fox (later 20th Century–Fox) from 1920 to 1936. He directed short comedies for three years, after which he graduated to directing Tom Mix features. The studio later assigned him to direct other stars, including Spencer Tracy and Will Rogers. Blystone also directed *Mr. Lemon of Orange*, which Fox hoped would make Swedish dialect comedian El Brendel into a star. The film, though a failure at the time, has aroused interest among film historians in recent years. Blystone took a break from Fox in 1923 to work with Buster Keaton on *Our Hospitality*. At the end of his career, he directed two Laurel and Hardy features, *Blockheads* and *Swiss Miss*.

Eddie Cline (1892–1961) Cline spent six years with Sennett before Roy Del Ruth convinced him to move to Sunshine in 1919. From 1920 to 1923, Cline was credited with co-writing and co-directing many classic Keaton vehicles, including *Cops* and *The Paleface*. In later years, he would concede that the Keaton comedies were chiefly directed by their star. He rejoined Sennett in 1924. By the thirties, he was directing feature-length comedies. From this period, his most notable films are *Million Dollar Legs*, *The Villain Still Pursued Her*, and several Wheeler and Woosley vehicles. In the early forties, he worked for Universal, where he principally directed Olsen & Johnson and W.C. Fields. His best known collaboration with Fields was *The Bank Dick*. Finally, the director worked at Monogram, where his chief responsibility was a series alternately known as *Bringing Up Father* and *Jiggs and Maggie*. In 1948, illness forced Cline to retire while in the midst of making *Jiggs and Maggie in Court*.

Jack Cooper (1890–1970) Cooper was born and educated in Manchester, England. Prior to working as a Sunshine principal, he spent three years in Fred Karno's legendary music hall troupe and appeared in Sennett comedies. In 1923, Cooper and pint-sized Billy Engel supported child stars Buddy Messinger and Baby Peggy in a series of Universal comedies. Cooper then returned to Sennett, where he assumed supporting roles.

Harry Depp (1883–1957) Depp was highly active during the twenties. In short comedies, he specialized in playing "drag" roles. He also worked as skirtless support in various feature films.

Roy Del Ruth (1895–1961) Roy Del Ruth was given his first big break by his brother Hampton, who hired him to take charge of a Sunshine unit. Del Ruth enjoyed a golden period working for Warner Brothers from 1925 to 1934; along with fellow director William Wellman, he turned out Warners' earliest classics. The best of these features included *Taxi!*, *Blessed Event*, *Lady Killer*, and the original *The Maltese Falcon*. Unlike Wellman, who went on to become a major director, Del Ruth failed to fulfill this early promise. His later films included *DuBarry Was a Lady*, *The Babe Ruth Story*, *Topper Returns*, *Kid Millions* and *The West Point Story*. The director's pace of one or two features a year slowed after 1954. His last two films were *The Alligator People* (1959) and *Why Must I Die?* (1960).

Charles Dorety (1898–1957) Coupled with Monte Banks, Dorety starred in *Bulls-Eye* comedies in 1919. From 1927 to 1928, he starred in a two-reel series based on Rube Goldberg's *Ike and Mike* comic strip. For the remainder of his acting career, he exclusively played in supporting roles. During the early thirties, he worked as a foil to Laurel and Hardy, Andy Clyde and the Three Stooges. He played dozens of small uncredited roles for the remainder of his career. His last film appearance was as a watermelon peddler in *Abbott and Costello Meet the Keystone Kops* (1955).

Dot Farley (1890–1971) Farley, a Chicago girl who was distinguished by an oversized pair of front teeth, followed a screen debut at Essanay with work at a long string of companies, including American, Universal and Keystone. During 1915, Farley paired with Sammy Burns for a series of Vogue's *KuKu Comedies*. Upon leaving Fox, Farley appeared in Clover and L-KO releases, and starred in six Universal *Century Comedies*. By 1919, Farley had collected credits for nearly 200 scenarios. The comedienne was featured in *Vin Moore Comedies* in 1921, after which she took supporting parts in Sennett comedies. Farley and Daphne Pollard provided the broader moments in Sennett's *Girl Comedies*, a series which was designed to showcase the Bathing Beauties. In 1931, Dot moved to RKO, where she played Edgar Kennedy's mother-in-law. Farley's character was removed from the Kennedy series in the late thirties, but was reinstated five years later. Kennedy's death in 1948 marked the end of the long-running series and prompted Farley's retirement.

Bryan Foy (1895–1977) Bryan Foy was the eldest of Eddie Foy's famed offspring, the Seven Little Foys. As a songwriter, Foy composed Gallagher & Shean's popular theme song. As a director, he made the first of Warner Brothers' "sound" shorts. However, it would be as the king of quickie film producers that Foy would gain major renown. In the mid–thirties, Foy became the chief of Warner Brothers' "B" picture unit. In this capacity, he briskly produced cheap films that were generally topical and unsophisticated. In 1941, 20th Century–Fox provided Foy with the opportunity to make films of higher quality. The results of this alliance include *Guadalcanal Diary, The Lodger* and *Hangover Square*. Foy next joined Eagle-Lion, where he worked as production chief until the company was absorbed by United Artists. After independently producing an early "skin flick," Foy returned to Warner Brothers. In his second reign at Warners, he turned out *I Was a Communist for the FBI*, the 3-D *House of Wax* and *PT-109*.

Billy Franey (1889–1940) Franey started in show business as a circus parachutist. In 1913, he made his film debut as a supporting player in Universal's *Joker Comedies*, a knockabout series starring Max Asher. Franey and the rest of *Joker*'s supporting cast, which included Louise Fazenda, Harry McCoy, Gale Henry and Bobby Vernon, proved more popular than Asher, so the series was reworked to feature the entire ensemble. In 1915, the group disbanded to pursue individual careers. Franey teamed with Henry, an Olive Oyl lookalike, for a series that lasted from 1915 to 1918. From 1920 to 1921, he starred in a relatively successful independent series, which was distributed by Reelcraft. He later appeared in silent and talkie features, including several westerns, and worked as support in the two-reel comedies of Clark & McCullough and Charley Chase. In 1937, Franey played a wily house painter in an installment of *Mr. Average Man*, a popular RKO series starring Edgar Kennedy. The series producer, Bert Gilroy, was so impressed with Franey that he gave him a regular role in the series as Kennedy's father-in-law. Franey remained in the role until his death.

Victor Heerman (1893–1977) After gaining experience at Sennett and Sunshine, Heerman worked as a writer-producer-director for Lewis Selznick. In his multiple functions, he turned out *Love is an Awful Thing* and *Rupert of Hentzau*. He later joined Paramount, where he directed *Rubber Heels, Paramount on Parade*, and the Marx Brothers' *Animal Crackers*. Heerman had to assume a disciplinary role with the unruly Marx Brothers, at one point chaining the brothers inside locked cells to keep them from wandering off the set.

F. Richard Jones (1894–1930) Jones gradually extended his professional name from "Dick Jones" to "Richard Jones" to "F. Richard Jones." He worked mostly at Sennett from 1915 to 1925. Sennett started Jones writing and directing short comedies. Later, Jones directed features and acted as production chief. Jones' Sennett features include three slapstick spoofs, *Yankee Doodle in Berlin, The Shriek of Araby* and *Down on the Farm*, and a failed dramatic venture, *The Crossroads of New York*. His most acclaimed work at Sennett was four features he did with Mabel Normand, *Mickey, Molly O,' Suzanna* and *The Extra Girl*. During this period, Jones worked outside of Sennett on three Dorothy Gish features and directed two Sunshine comedies for Henry Lehrman. In 1925, Jones became Roach's creative producer. Jones had much to do with Roach attaining dominance in the short subject field. At the end of 1927, Jones left Roach to direct features. These features include Douglas Fairbanks' *The Gaucho*, Beery

& Hatton's *The Big Killing*, and the 1929 version of *Bulldog Drummond*. Colleagues believed that Jones' intense drive ran him down and led to his early demise.

Erle C. Kenton (1896–1980) Kenton's Sunshine credits are sandwiched in between numerous Sennett credits. Later, while under contract to Paramount, the director guided Bebe Daniels and Raymond Griffin through silent vehicles and made the 1933 horror classic *Island of Lost Souls*. In the early forties, Kenton was employed at Universal, his work including three of Abbott & Costello's best comedies: *Pardon My Sarong*, *Who Done It?* and *It Ain't Hay*.

Charles Lamont (1898–1993) Lamont, who had sprung from five generations of theatrical folk, became acquainted with stage, circus, vaudeville and carnival work as a child. During his succeeding years of performing, he toured Africa and Europe as the top mounter of an acrobatic troupe. In 1919, Universal contracted Lamont as a comic. Soon after joining the studio, Lamont began to supplement his performances by serving as assistant director and gagman. In 1923, he directed his first film, a Grand-Asher comedy starring Sid Smith. During the next year, he accomplished a term as a Century director and began a long, prolific association with Educational. Working as an Educational contractee, he directed Al St. John, Lige Conley, Johnny Arthur, Dorothy Devore, Jerry Drew and Lupino Lane. He directed Lane's first Educational comedy and numerous other entries of the succeeding series, including the classic *Monty of the Mounted*. He also developed and directed Educational's popular *Big Boy* series. From 1931 to 1932, he experienced a short break from Educational: At this time, he worked for Universal, directing the *Daphne Pollard Comedies* and *Charles Lamont Comedies*. For the balance of the decade, he alternated between directing Columbia and Educational short comedies (including most of Keaton's Educational series) and making feature films for several Poverty Row independents (namely, Chesterfield, Monogram, Republic, Progressive and Grand National). He spent the remainder of his career at Universal. His earlier features for the studio include *That's the Spirit*, *Her Primitive Man* and Abbott & Costello's *Hit the Ice*; among his later Universal films are *Ma and Pa Kettle* and *I Was a Shoplifter*. *I Was a Shoplifter* was significant as it was one of the rare times the director ventured into drama. In 1950, Lamont became Abbott and Costello's permanent director. This position ultimately entailed introducing Bud and Lou to the Foreign Legion, Captain Kidd, Dr. Jekyll and Mr. Hyde, the Invisible Man, the Keystone Kops and the Mummy. Lamont's last films were *The Kettles in the Ozarks* and *Francis in the Haunted House*. He retired in 1956.

Del Lord (1895–1970) Lord worked through the 1920s as a Sennett director. Subsequently, he directed Roach's unsuccessful *Taxi Boys* series and Paramount's short-lived *Del Lord Comedies*. Lord was prosperous again once he joined Columbia's short subject department in 1935. For the next fifteen years, he created Columbia's best short subjects, including over three dozen Three Stooges comedies. Between 1944 and 1946, he also directed formula "B" features for Columbia. Lord's final feature was a Judy Canova musical comedy called *Singin' in the Corn*.

Polly Moran (1883–1952) Moran achieved great success playing Sheriff "Cactus" Nell in Keystone and Sunshine comedies. One of her popular vehicles was called *Roping Her Romeo*. As implied by this title, little Nell was a bold cowgirl whose chief occupation was husband-hunting. From 1927 to 1932, MGM teamed Moran and Marie Dressler for a series of comedy features. The MGM features allowed Moran to perform in the boisterous style that she had perfected over the years. After Dressler died in 1934, Moran teamed up with other actresses, including Mary Boland and Alison Skipworth, but failed to achieve the same success. Moran last appeared in *Adam's Rib* (1949) and *The Yellow Cab Man* (1950).

Paul "Poll" Parrott (1898–1939) After his work on the Sunshine series, Parrott starred in a series of Roach-Pathé comedies. He decided during this period to abandon acting and become a director. Under the name James Parrott, he became a leading director at Roach. His credits include several classic Laurel and Hardy comedies, including *Hog Wild*, *Brats* and the Oscar-winning *The Music Box*, although this shy and quiet director was known to let Laurel handle much of the direction. He also developed several shorts starring his brother, Charley Chase. Parrott remains a prominent figure in the Roach studio's history although, early on, Hal Roach came close to firing him. The problem was Parrott's wife. Parrott would wake up in the morning and find that his wife had vanished with their car. He would have to walk to work, which would make him late. His wife would eventually turn up at the Roach lot and hang around the stages. She would distract her husband by becoming overly friendly with other men. She would track down Roach and pester him. Roach warned Parrott that he would be canned if his wife did not stay away and stop telling him her problems. Parrott solved the problem by filing for divorce. Paul later developed alcohol and drug problems, which made him unreliable as a director, and he was demoted to gagwriter in 1935. He died from an overdose of pills.

Victor "Slim" Potel (1889–1947) After a few years as an Essanay star, Potel did extensive work at Universal and Keystone. Potel later played roles in numerous features and, at one point, scripted short comedies. His features include *A Self-Made Failure*, *Make Me a Star*, *Special Delivery*, *Doughboys*, and *The Big Store*. Potel was a stalwart of director Preston Sturges. He is also well known for playing Ma and Pa Kettle's daffy Indian pal, Crowbar, in *The Egg and I*. Potel is credited with appearing in 431 films between 1910 and 1947.

Albert Ray (1897–1944) Ray starred in feature films before 1920, when he joined Henry Lehrman as a principal comic and director. During the twenties, he took charge of Educational's *Cameo* series. In the early thirties, he worked in Paramount's short subject division, where he directed Al St. John and Dane & Arthur. For the remainder of his career, he directed low-budget features, including five Johnny Mack Brown westerns.

Joe Roberts (1871–1923) "Big Joe," as he was commonly known, was one of Buster Keaton's oldest and closest friends. The two men developed a friendship during their early years together in vaudeville. Later, Roberts became Keaton's principal heavy, appearing in every Keaton production from the 1920 short *One Week* to the 1923 feature *Our Hospitality*. The Sunshine series provided Roberts with his one starring role.

Jimmy Savo (1895–1960) In a review of the Sunshine series' *Say it with Flowers*, a critic dismissed Savo as a "Keaton imitator." The critic claimed that Savo utilized "the great comic's sad face and loose trousers" and borrowed a number of Keaton's stunts, including an elevator sequence from Keaton's *The Goat*. However, Savo was a reputable performer. Influenced by W.C. Fields, he went on stage with a juggling act at the age of ten. He later added comedy, singing, magic and rope walking into his act, which was featured in Broadway revues and musical comedies. Charlie Chaplin called him the "best pantomimist in the world." His career was at its peak in the 1930s. In 1931, he released a best-selling song, "River Stay 'Way from My Door," which he originated in the Broadway show "Mum's the Word." (The song was later re-recorded by many popular singers, including Frank Sinatra, Kate Smith, Barbra Streisand, Paul Robeson and Fiona Apple.) Savo soon followed up with another hit song, "(You Get No Bread with) One Meat Ball." Between 1935 and 1938, he starred in three feature films, including *The Merry-Go-Round of 1938*, *Once in a Blue Moon* and *Reckless Living*. In a review of *Once in a Blue Moon*, a *New York Times* critic described the performance of "that exquisite and adorable clown Jimmy Savo" as "lovely, fragile and infinitely touching." In 1938, Savo played Dromio in the original Broadway production of "The Boys from Syracuse." In 1944, Savo underwent a leg amputation for a malignant tumor and had to stop working. He made a comeback with a nightclub act two years later. In 1952, he appeared as Sancho Panza in a CBS production of "Don Quixote."

Lewis Seiler (1890–1964) Seiler continued to direct Fox comedies after the Sunshine series ended. He later made features for Warner Brothers, First National, Columbia and 20th Century–Fox. Seiler was more prolific than artful. His best features include *You're in the Army Now*, a comedy starring Jimmy Durante and Phil Silvers, and the back-to-back musical comedies, *Doll Face* and *If I'm Lucky*.

Gertrude Selby (1896–1975) Selby, a petite and pretty Philadelphia lady, worked at several comedy units throughout the teens. The actress appeared in short films for Universal, Fox, L-KO, Pathé, Sunshine, Metro and Sennett. She was a favorite of Henry Lehrman, who used her as a leading lady in many of the comedies he made between 1914 and 1918. In early 1919, the newly formed Macdon Pictures Corporation signed Selby to star in an elaborately produced series. Unfortunately, Macdon Pictures was unable to find a distributor and the series was never produced.

Noel Smith (1895–1955) Smith was footloose from the late teens to early twenties. During this time, he helmed Billy Bevan vehicles as well as installments of the following series: *L-KO Comedies*, *The Hallrooms Boys*, *Jimmy Aubrey Comedies* and Century's *Pal the Dog*. He worked as Larry Semon's co-director in 1924. Smith's work on the *Pal the Dog* series may have convinced Warner Brothers that Smith would be able to handle their dog star, Rin Tin Tin. In 1925, Smith directed the Rin Tin Tin vehicle *The Clash of the Wolves* as his first feature. He went on to direct features starring Rin Tin Tin imitators, including Klondike and Silver Streak. Between 1926 and 1935, he directed nine features starring action hero Richard Talmadge. In the late thirties, he directed six features starring singing cowboy Dick Foran. In 1939, near the end of his career, he directed Bert Wheeler in Warner Brothers' *The Cowboy Quarterback*.

Vera Steadman (1900–1966) When she joined Sunshine in December, 1918, Steadman possessed credentials as a classic dancer, champion high diver and expert swimmer. In light of the wild stunts that the Sunshine comics performed, these skills may have been vital to Steadman surviving her four-month stay at Fox. Afterwards, she worked as a member of Universal's comedy unit and also became one of Sennett's Bathing Beauties. In the latter capacity, the comedienne mostly posed for publicity stills. Dressed in a bathing suit, she would stand between a camera and cardboard waves and strain her lips to present her perkiest smile. In 1918, after three years of being part of the scenery, Steadman was promoted to an ingénue role in the Sennett comedy *The Summer Girls*. Steadman performed as leading lady in two Larry Semon comedies durng the following year. From 1919 to 1931, she worked at Christie, starring opposite Neal Burns, Bobby Vernon, Jimmie Adams and Billy Dooley. She also made a number of appearances in features. The height of her career came when she performed as leading lady role in Charles Ray's *Scrap Iron*.

Ben Stoloff (1895–1960) At Fox, Stoloff eventually graduated from two-reelers to features, becoming responsible for making rugged action pictures as well as feature-length comedies. This meant that Stoloff had to remain flexible enough to direct Clark & McCullough for one film and manage Victor McLaglen as part of his next assignment. His most notable Fox feature was 1933s *Soup to Nuts*, the first film to showcase the Three Stooges.

Harry Sweet (1901–1933) Prior to his work with the Sunshine series, Sweet was paired with Lee Moran for a Universal series. After Sunshine and a brief stint with Sennett, Sweet made a transition from performer to director. At first, he directed short films for Selznick's Standard Cinema Corporation. Then, in 1929, Fox hired him to develop a series of films for stage comics Clark & McCullough. Sweet later moved to RKO, where he established a permanent short subject department. In heading the division, he supervised, directed and occasionally acted in numerous two-reel comedies. His greatest creation was the series *Mr. Average Man*, which many regard as the original situation comedy. The series would regularly feature three other Sunshine alumni: Edgar Kennedy, Dot Farley and Billy Franey. Sweet directed *Mr. Average Man* until his sudden death in 1933. He was piloting a plane over California's Big Bear Lake when he got caught in a storm and crashed into a mountainside.

Appendix II: Profiles of Select Hamilton Associates

The Leading Ladies

Ruth Hiatt (1906–1994) In the '30s, Hiatt appeared in two-reel vehicles of Harry Langdon, Our Gang and the Three Stooges. As a minor player, she worked in several "B" features throughout the decade. Her last film appearance was in a 1941 release entitled *Double Trouble*. For several decades, Hiatt ran a successful makeup business in Los Angeles. She died of congestive heart failure.

Babe London (1901–1980) Many comedy makers relied on Babe when a sequence required a funny fat girl. Babe was a Christie comedienne in the twenties and, at various points of her career, worked with Chaplin, Keaton, Sennett, and Laurel & Hardy. She made her last film appearance in *Sex Kittens Go to College*, a 1960 stripper-goes-collegiate comedy starring Mamie Van Doren and Tuesday Weld.

Kathleen Myers Myers was born in San Francisco but raised in New York. Her career in film comedy began during a visit to the West Coast. In quick succession, the young woman was engaged as leading lady for Chester Conklin, Neely Edwards, Jimmy Aubrey, Larry Semon and Lloyd Hamilton. Her screen career reached its peak in 1925, when the actress appeared in Keaton's *Go West*. Though Myers was billed as a star of *Go West*, many regard an engaging cow named Brown Eyes as the film's principal female.

Ruth Roland (1892–1937) From 1915 to 1923, Roland starred in eleven Pathé serials, the popularity of which ranked the serial star second only to thrill queen Pearl White. By daringly taking on a variety of hazardous situations, Ruth and "Fearless Peerless" Pearl truly rescued the faltering Pathé organization. The pair's adventures were so profitable that, by 1917, a long line of screen actresses were prepared to brave rapids, rock slides, savage Indians, and runaway trains. Mollie King, Doris Kenyon, Marie Walcamp, Juanita Hansen and "Pretty Kitty" Clifford were the more successful of the subsequent thrill princesses, but none of them were able to surpass the success that Roland had. In 1930, upon the completion of a fourth Orpheum Circuit tour, Ruth starred in a drama entitled *Reno*. This Sono Arts–Worldwide release, which marked the actress' screen comeback, received relatively heavy promotion. Nonetheless, the film was a critical and financial failure. Ruth's next and final film was an obscure Canadian feature called *From Nine to Nine* (1936).

The Heavies

Stanley Blystone (1895–1956) During the '30s, Blystone played villains in several serials and appeared in feature-length vehicles of Laurel & Hardy, Eddie Cantor and Wheeler & Woolsey. He occasionally provided support in a short comedy, usually tormenting the Three Stooges, (he was the Stooges' malicious sergeant in *Half-Shot Shooters*). His career ended with appearances in three Martin & Lewis films.

Louise Carver (1869–1956) Carver played tough characters in several silent and sound features. She also appeared in many silent two-reel comedies and, in the '30s, supported two-reel comics Charley Chase and Andy Clyde.

Glen Cavender (1884–1962) Cavender earned France's medal of honor for his brave participation in the Boxer rebellion. However, the man exhibited his true mettle by working as a Keystone Cop. Courageously racing to the rescue, he would ride a police car that recklessly rolled forth on roads covered with soap and grease. By 1915, he was playing supporting roles in many Keystone releases. Most notably, he appeared as the real estate salesman in *Fatty and Mabel Adrift* and as one of Sydney Chaplin's opponents in *Submarine Pirate*. In 1918, he joined Arbuckle's Comique company as co-director and supporting player. The following year, he became one of Sunshine's principals. During the next decade, he occasionally starred in a short comedy. Most notably, the funnyman was teamed with Bobby Ray for a group of *Arrow Comedies*. More often, though, he worked as a supporting player. He most often played Lupino Lane's chief heavy and appeared in features, including *Main Street* and Keaton's *The General*.

Otto Fries (1887–1938) Fries traveled for two years in a medicine show. When the medicine show wagon rolled onto Los Angeles terrain, he quickly departed and joined the Keystone company. Credited with having been one of the original Keystone Cops, this husky performer was later typecast as other comical cops. He was part of Roach's stock company from the late '20s to the early '30s. In 1931, he appeared in the Marx Brothers film *Monkey Business*.

Kewpie Morgan Following his work in Bud Duncan's *Clover* series, Morgan played principal roles at Sunshine and Sennett. Morgan later had a role in Keaton's high-profile feature debut, *Three Ages*. But this role is not something for which Morgan is well remembered, (The fact is that, for decades, film historians misidentified Morgan as Oliver Hardy). It was in another debut, the first short in Clark & McCullough's RKO series, that Morgan had a more significant role. Morgan shows up in this 1931 comedy, *False Roomers*, as one of the team's more formidable nemeses. He is front-and-center in the film's memorable wind-up, when he becomes so determined to chase down Clark & McCullough that he races his car through Jimmy Finlayson's boarding house. Even more people know the portly comic for playing Old King Cole in Laurel & Hardy's *Babes in Toyland*.

Blanche Payson (1881–1964) Comedy makers enlisted Payson whenever they required an ugly, overbearing Amazonian. Payson started her film career at Sennett. During the '20s, she appeared in silent features and worked as leading lady to Al St. John and Stan Laurel. During the early '30s, she acted in three Laurel & Hardy comedies (most notably as Mrs. Hardy in *Helpmates*) and appeared as a cruel stepmother in Our Gang's *Dogs is Dogs*. She also co-starred with Charles "Heinie" Conklin in the Paramount short *Meet the Senator*. She last supplied support in *Hoi Polloi*, one of the Three Stooges' best films, and Olsen & Johnson's *All Over Town*.

Dick Sutherland (1882–1934) Sutherland, an apelike man, was a frightening heavy in several features. But it wasn't always that way for Sutherland, who initially drew attention for turning in laughable performances in Harold Lloyd features, including *A Sailor-Made Man* (1921) and *Grandma's Boy* (1922). Sutherland ultimately returned to comedy. In the memorable pie-throwing climax of Laurel & Hardy's *Battle of the Century*, he appears as the dental patient who is abruptly hit in his wide-open mouth by a wild pie. His final film was another Laurel & Hardy comedy, *The Hoose Gow*. In this 1929 comedy, set on a prison farm, the actor portrays a menacing, axe-wielding mess cook.

Tom Wilson (1880–1965) As a member of D.W. Griffin's stock company, Wilson appeared in two epochal films, *Birth of a Nation* and *Intolerance*. However, he is best known for having played the cop in Chaplin's *The Kid*. A popular still features Wilson standing ominously behind Chaplin and his "Kid" (Jackie Coogan). Walter Kerr eloquently captioned the still "the eternal trio." In the late '20s, Wilson played a fight trainer in Keaton's *The Battling Butler* and starred with Charles Conklin in *Ham and Eggs at the Front*. The *Ham and Eggs* film had been designed as Warner Brothers' answer to the period's popular "service comedy" teams. In a turnabout role, Wilson vigorously avoided Noah Young, who played his tough sergeant. Wilson last appeared in *Edge of Hell*, a 1956 film written, directed, starred and produced by offbeat filmmaker Hugo Haas. Haas was acknowledging Chaplin's influence by casting Wilson in this project, which concerned a pauper who cares for a homeless boy.

Other Support

Ben Alexander (1911–1969) As a child, Alexander appeared in *A Self-Made Failure*, *Penrod and Son* and *Hearts of the World*. *Hearts of the World*, which starred Lillian Gish, was a major success. As a young adult, he played one of the leads in *All Quiet on the Western Front*. He eventually grew into character parts, the most notable of which was the role of *Dragnet* officer Frank Smith. As Joe Friday's paunchy partner, he worked in a television series for seven years and appeared in a 1954 movie.

Phil Dunham (1885–1972) Dunham was born in London, England, and educated at the University of Cambridge. During his film career, he worked in comedy companies attached to Kalem, Century, Fox and Lehrman. Between 1921 and 1922, he appeared in five Charles Ray features. Later, he varied between being part of Hamilton's supporting cast and a star of the *Cameo* series. In the '30s, he appeared in Paramount features and RKO short subjects, including Clark & McCullough's *Jitters the Butler*.

Del Henderson (1883–1956) Henderson had been a Canadian stage actor before 1909, the year he joined D.W. Griffith's Biograph unit. He abandoned the acting profession when Mack Sennett, a fellow Canadian and former co-worker, appointed him a director of the Keystone company. He revived his acting career with the coming of sound films. From 1930 to 1933, he had several funny roles at Roach: a lunatic in Charley Chase's *In Walked Charley*; a prissy traveler's aid attendant in Our Gang's *Choo Choo*; and a murderous heir in *The Laurel and Hardy Murder Case*. The Laurel and Hardy film is remarkable in that its climax anticipates the climax of Hitchcock's *Psycho*. Henderson, disguised as an old woman, seeks to knife co-heirs to Uncle Laurel's fortune. During a frenetic struggle with Stan and Ollie, Henderson loses his gray wig and reveals his true identity. Henderson subsequently appeared in several Paramount feature comedies, including *The Old-Fashioned Way*, *It's a Gift*, *Poppy*, *Ruggles of Red Gap*, and *Artists and Models*.

Charles Inslee Inslee was originally part of D.W. Griffith's Biograph unit. Following his departure from the *Ham* company, he briefly worked in Chaplin's Essanay crew. In Chaplin's *The Bank*, he depicted the bank president. He later became an *L-KO* player.

Little Billy (1895–1967) Little Billy was a midget who entertained circus fans during the '20s and '30s. On screen, he was one of the principals in *The Terror of Tiny Town*, producer Sol Lesser's all-midget western. He also appeared in a feature called *The Side Show*. He worked in a few comedy shorts, including a couple of Three Stooges vehicles.

Gus Leonard (1856–1939) Following the end of Kalem's *Ethel Teare* series, Leonard joined Harold Lloyd's *Lonesome Luke* corps. He continued to support Harold in the comic's succeeding short series and made uncredited appearances in nearly every one of Harold's feature films. During the '20s, he worked at Educational; appeared in two Charles Ray features; played a hard-hearted shopkeeper in Keaton's *Go West*; and had a major role in the classic drama *Coney Island*. In the early thirties, he was memorable as "Cap" in Our Gang's *Mush and Milk*. The last film in which he appeared was MGM's *Maytime*, a 1937 MacDonald-Eddy operetta.

Henry Murdoch (1891–19??) Murdoch was born in Virginia, and was educated at the University of Southern Virginia. After spending five years in stock and two years in vaudeville, Murdoch joined the Kalem company. He later worked at Universal, where he eventually was featured in the *Century* series. The comic's work in *Hamilton Comedies* led to starring roles in *Cameo* productions.

John Steppling (1869–1932) Steppling was the stocky star of Essanay's numerous *Billy Comedies*. Besides his *Billy* series, he appeared as support in several 1920s features.

The Directors

Lloyd Bacon (1890–1955) Bacon began enjoying major success as a director in 1928, when he joined Warner Brothers. He managed to enliven all types of Warners standard programmers. He worked equally well with the lot's tough bunch (Jimmy Cagney, Edward G. Robinson, and George Raft) and its nicer heroes (Pat O'Brien, George Brent and Joel McCrea). While at Warners, he also directed seven Joe E. Brown vehicles and made two classic musicals, *42nd Street* and *Footlight Parade*. In 1938, he directed *A Slight Case of Murder*, a comedy starring Robinson as a former bootlegger. In response to its success, Bacon and Robinson followed a similar course with *Brother Orchard* and *Larceny, Inc.*. Bacon's other popular Warner Brothers releases include *San Quentin*, *Marked Woman*, *The Oklahoma Kid*, *Knute Rockne—All American* and *Action in the North Atlantic*. Bacon joined Fox in 1943. In the late '40s and early '50s, he directed for Columbia, 20th Century–Fox and RKO. He made several musicals and comedies during this period. These films were relatively mild ventures with the following exception: an enjoyable fantasy-comedy entitled *It Happens Every Spring*.

William Beaudine (1890–1970) After his work on Hamilton's *A Self-Made Failure*, Beaudine directed Mary Pickford's *Little Annie Rooney* (1925) and a variety of features for Warner Brothers, including the crime melodramas *Cornered* (1924) and the Dorothy Devore comedies *How Baxter Butted In*, *The Narrow Street* and *A Broadway Butterfly* (all 1925). He subsequently returned to the Christie company, where he remained for the balance of the decade. In 1930, he returned to feature films. Among his early "sound" features were two notable Paramount releases, *Make Me A Star* and W.C. Fields' *The Old Fashioned Way*. By the late thirties, he was a prolific director of low-grade features. For his ability to avoid retakes, he eventually acquired the notorious nickname "One Shot." He was responsible for a few of Warner Brothers' *Torchy Blane* films. William K. Everson professed that Beaudine's *Torchy Blane in Chinatown* was the best segments of the "Blane" cycle. Other Beaudine mystery films are *Detective Kitty O'Day*, *Philo Vance Returns* and five of Monogram's "Charlie Chan" series. Beaudine directed approximately thirty "Bowery Boys" comedies from 1943 to their series' close in the late fifties. The director was also responsible for "Z"-rank horror features of the mid–forties, including *The Ape Man* and *Voodoo Man*. These were trite films, with Bela Lugosi and John Carradine alternating as mad doctors. Beaudine's horror-oriented work of the next decade — *Jesse James Meets Frankenstein's Daughter*, *Billy the Kid Meets Dracula*, and *Bela Lugosi Meets a Brooklyn Gorilla* — at least produced some curious results.

Harry Edwards (1889–1952) Between 1917 and 1924, Edwards directed entries of various comedy series (*Foxfilm*, *Mermaid* and *Century*). He settled at the Sennett studio, where he directed Billy Bevan, Ben Turpin and Harry Langdon. He worked with Langdon for two years. The collaboration ended with Langdon's premier feature, *Tramp, Tramp, Tramp*. In 1926, Edwards made a few installments of Universal's *The Collegians*, a series of comedy-drama short subjects. Thereafter, he returned to Sennett for four years. From 1930 to 1931, he was in charge of Universal's *Slim Summerville* and *Lloyd Hamilton* series. Over the next three years, he directed most of Andy Clyde's Educational series. Between 1942 and 1946, he worked for Columbia's short subject department, where he was reunited with both Clyde and Langdon. It was during this period that Edwards became severely hampered by alcoholism. The Three Stooges were so unhappy with his sloppy direction that they refused to work with him again. Other actors, including Vera Vague, also complained about Edwards' drunkenness and the unit chief, Jules White, had to fire him.

Alf Goulding (1896–1972) Born in Melbourne, Australia, Goulding came to the United States as part of a vaudeville troupe which disbanded soon after its arrival. Over the next four and a half years, Goulding appeared on stages across the country. He worked three years on the Orpheum Circuit and a year with the Morasco organization. He also performed as a member of Marie Dressler's touring company. Upon settling in Hollywood, Goulding worked briefly on an early Fox comedy series and then alternated with Gil Pratt as Harold Lloyd's director. He got the job with Lloyd based on a referral from Snub Pollard, Lloyd's main support and a fellow graduate of Goulding's old Australian troupe. In 1920, Goulding moved from Universal's *Century* company to the Sennett studios. He erratically worked at Sennett for the remainder of the decade. In 1933, he was one of two directors assigned to Vitagraph, Warner Brothers' short subject division. In this position, he directed the first three installments of the *Big V Comedies*, a series which marked Roscoe Arbuckle's screen comeback. From 1934 to 1935, Goulding worked for the short subject departments at Columbia and RKO. In 1940, he directed Laurel & Hardy in the Roach feature *A Chump at Oxford*.

Gilbert W. Pratt (1892–1954) Pratt began in films as a Kalem heavy. He went on to work for the New York Motion Picture company. Then, in the spring of 1918, he joined Harold Lloyd's Rolin series. Lloyd allowed Pratt the opportunity to direct. Pratt, based on his initial success as director, abandoned acting. Early on, he directed Jimmy Aubrey's Vitagraph series and Monte Banks' *Welcome Comedies*. He became particularly busy over the next two years. He directed Hamilton's first two *Mermaid* comedies, *Hallroom Boys* shorts, Banks' Federated releases, and Al St. John's early Fox vehicles. He also made *Mud and Sand*, a classic Valentino spoof starring Stan Laurel, and directed Universal's *Star* one-reelers, a series featuring Neely Edwards. Between 1923 and 1926, he moved to Jack White, to Christie, to Sennett. At the end of this period, he accepted a scriptwriting post at Paramount. *The Hamilton Talking Comedies* brought about a short-lived revival of his directorial career. He helmed two Hamilton vehicles and two Roach comedies before returning to scriptwriting. Over the next few years, he wrote scripts for Roach as well as for Columbia's short subject department.

Stephen Roberts (1895–1936) Roberts was one of Jack White's directors from 1924 to 1930. Later, he was responsible for Slim Summerville's Universal series. In 1932, he was engaged to direct Paramount features. His most notable Paramount credits include *The Story of Temple Drake*, *Lady and Gent* and a segment of *If I Had a Million*. He joined RKO in 1934. His fifth RKO feature was *The Ex-Mrs. Bradford*, an effective "Thin Man"–inspired comedy-mystery starring William Powell and Jean Arthur. This was his last film. Jack White attributed Roberts' premature death to overwork.

Alfred Santell (1895–1981) From 1917 to 1918, Santell directed Goldwyn productions and a few of National's "Smiling Billy" Parson comedies. Santell was in the army from July, 1918, to April, 1919. When he returned from the service, he took charge of a series of Universal one-reelers starring Neal Burns. Later in the year, Universal assigned Santell to direct their *Joe Martin Comedies*, which featured the jungle escapades of a trained ape named Joe Martin. The *Martin* series was eventually re-titled the *Alfred Santell Comedies*. At the same time, Universal promoted Santell to supervising manager. In 1920, the studio loaned Santell to direct the *Hallroom Boys Comedies*. Santell left Universal two years later. In 1923, he made his first feature, an FBO release entitled *Lights Out*. He continued to direct features and had a big success in 1925 with *Classified*, a First National production starring Corinne Griffith. Santell signed a long-term contract with First National. With films like *The Patent Leather Kid* and *Orchids and Ermine*, he earned a reputation for being one of the industry's best "light comedy" directors. He worked under a Fox contract from 1930 to 1933 and spent the remainder of the decade directing features for MGM, Paramount, and RKO. His films of this period include *Polly of the Circus*, *The Life of Vergie Winters*, *Winterset* and *People Will Talk*. His output diminished by the end of the thirties. The only films that he directed between 1939 and 1942 were three Paramount "B" features, including two Dorothy Lamour sarong pictures and one Bob Burns hillbilly comedy. Next, he directed two prestigious dramas for United Artists, *Jack London* and *The Hairy Ape*. Santell followed his UA productions with a pair of poverty row releases: *Mexicana* (1945) and *That Brennan Girl* (1946). These were his final films. I contacted Santell in the late seventies. He had recently suffered a third stroke, which left him in a poor physical state. He was semiambulate, could not speak, had trouble seeing, and possessed a less than reliable memory.

Norman Taurog (1899–1981) Taurog was a prestigious director at Paramount in the early thirties. His most notable Paramount films of the period are *Skippy* (for which he won an Oscar), *A Bedtime Story*, *We're Not Dressing*, *The Big Broadcast of 1936*, *Strike Me Pink*, and *Rhythm on the Range*. Between 1936 and 1938, he directed two 20th Century–Fox productions; Selznick's *The Adventures of Tom Sawyer*; and Universal's *Mad About Music*, a popular Deana Durbin feature that would be remade in 1956. In 1938, MGM signed him to a long-term contract. One of his early MGM productions was *Boys Town*, which immediately brought the director prominence at the studio. His other MGM films include the *Boys Town* sequel *Men of Boys Town*, *Young Tom Edison*, and *Presenting Lily Mars*. After his career was interrupted by a two-year hitch in the armed forces, he rejoined MGM and remained with the company until 1951. Between 1952 and 1956, he shot six Paramount features starring Martin & Lewis. After a year of freelancing, he returned to Paramount. This time, he directed Lewis *sans* Martin. His efforts produced two of Lewis' best films, *Don't Give Up the Ship* and *Visit to a Small Planet*. When Lewis elected to write and direct his own films, Paramount put Taurog in charge of their Elvis Presley series. In 1963, Taurog again left Paramount to freelance. During 1965, he directed an Allied Artists production starring Presley and two AIP comedies featuring Frankie Avalon. His AIP work exhibited more skill and finesse than the company's typical fare. Taurog closed his career with four MGM Presley features: *Spinout, Double Trouble, Speedway*, and *Live a Little, Love a Little*.

William Watson (1896–1967) Watson joined the Sunshine company in 1918. Previously, he had rose from editor to assistant director at the Sennett studio. In 1922, following a brief stint at Roach, he came aboard Universal's short subject division. For the next two years, he directed Universal's *Neely Edwards* series. He later worked as a Christie director.

Appendix III: Filmography

The entries of this compilation hold to the following pattern: film title (release date) behind-the-camera credits. cast. (special information.) plot.

The abbreviations noted in the credits translate as follows:

> Dial   dialogue
> D   director
> Ph   photography
> P   producer
> St   story
> Sc   scriptwriter

Rob Farr's "Lloyd Hamilton Filmography," published in *Griffithiana*, was a helpful resource in the completion of this filmography. Mr. Farr's detailed listing provided plot information on three of Hamilton's later comedies, *The Lion and the House*, *An Apple a Day*, and *Wedding Belles*, and, in many instances, identified the locations of existing prints. Foremost, Mr. Farr's filmography provided most of the titles, credits and plots for Hamilton's Frontier films.

The Lubin Comedies (1913)

Hamilton worked for Lubin during the first half of 1913. Because of the absence of cast lists, it cannot be determined in which Lubin films Hamilton appeared.

A Hasty Jilting (July 31, 1913) Frontier Motion Picture Company. Dot Farley, Lloyd V. Hamilton, Victoria Forde and Joseph J. Franz. 1 reel. (The announcements of the Frontier releases did not include cast lists until December 20, 1913, but Bo Berglund, working in collaboration with Rob Farr, was able to identify the casts of earlier films by examining published stills.) A young man is preparing to attend a country ball when he sprains his ankle.

Masquerading in Bear Canyon (August 7, 1913) Frontier Motion Picture Company. Lloyd V. Hamilton, Dot Farley. 1 reel.

Sailing Under False Colors (August 21, 1913) Frontier Motion Picture Company. Lloyd V. Hamilton, Dot Farley. 1 reel.

Flirty Florence (September 4, 1913) Frontier Motion Picture Company. Lloyd V. Hamilton, Dot Farley. 1 reel.

Dorothea and Chief Razamataz (September 11, 1913) Frontier Motion Picture Company. Lloyd V. Hamilton (Chief Razamataz), Dot Farley. 1 reel.

The Juvenile Kidnappers (September 18, 1913) Frontier Motion Picture Company. Lloyd V. Hamilton, Dot Farley. 1 reel.

A Village Pest (September 25, 1913) Frontier Motion Picture Company. Dot Farley, Lloyd V. Hamilton (Walle). 1 reel. Walle drives everyone crazy with his magic tricks.

Curing the Doctor (October 16, 1913) Frontier Motion Picture Company. Lloyd V. Hamilton

(Count Von Gasbag), Dot Farley (Dorothy Vernon). 1 reel.

The Spirits Walk (October 30, 1913) Frontier Motion Picture Company. Lloyd V. Hamilton, Eva Thatcher, Joseph J. Franz, Buck Connors. 1 reel. To get rid of an unwanted suitor, Eloise dares him to sleep in a haunted house.

The Secret of Balanced Rock (November 29, 1913) Frontier Motion Picture Company. Lloyd V. Hamilton. 1 reel. *Drama.* The plot centers on a lost mine.

The Circuit Rider of the Hills (December 12, 1913) Frontier Motion Picture Company. Lloyd V. Hamilton, Joseph J. Franz. 1 reel. An old moonshiner (Hamilton) tries to ruin his daughter's romance with the son of a revenue agent.

Out of His Class (December 13, 1913) Frontier Motion Picture Company. Lloyd V. Hamilton. 1 reel. *Drama.* A gambler sacrifices his life for his beloved.

His Better Self (December 20, 1913) Frontier Motion Picture Company. Lloyd V. Hamilton (Harry), Eva Thatcher. 1 reel. *Drama.* Harry, a degenerate alcoholic, saves a girl from the evils of drink.

His Father (December 27, 1913) Frontier Motion Picture Company. Lloyd V. Hamilton, Edythe Sterling, Hampton Del Ruth, Betty Burbridge, Joseph J. Franz. 1 reel. *Drama.* A man who has shown no worth in the past helps his son to capture a bandit.

The Winning Stroke (January 3, 1914) Frontier Motion Picture Company. Lloyd V. Hamilton, Hampton Del Ruth, Edythe Sterling, Joseph J. Franz, Betty Burbridge. 1 reel. *Drama.* A Chicago detective works hard to apprehend counterfeiters.

Cross Roads (January 10, 1914) Frontier Motion Picture Company. Lloyd V. Hamilton, Edythe Sterling, Hampton Del Ruth, Joseph J. Franz. 1 reel. *Drama.* A battle breaks out over a gold mine claim.

Abide with Me (January 24, 1914) Frontier Motion Picture Company. Lloyd V. Hamilton, Mae Welles, Edythe Sterling, Arthur Allardt, Joseph J. Franz. 1 reel. *Drama.* A Quaker family adjusts to western life.

The Turning Point (January 31, 1914) Frontier Motion Picture Company. Lloyd V. Hamilton, Edythe Sterling, Arthur Allardt, Joseph J. Franz. 1 reel. *Drama.* Two men vie for the affections of Nell.

Put Yourself in His Place (February 7, 1914) Frontier Motion Picture Company. Lloyd V. Hamilton, Arthur Allardt, Edythe Sterling, Joseph J. Franz. 1 reel. *Drama.* A man desperate to buy medicine for his sick daughter resorts to theft.

The Fatal Card (February 21) Frontier Motion Picture Company. Edythe Sterling, Arthur Allardt, Joseph J. Franz, Lloyd V. Hamilton, Charles Huber. 1 reel. *Drama.* Disguised in Ralph's outfit, Bill assaults and robs the ranch foreman. Escaping with a wad of bills, Bill hides in a leafy bough of a tree. Ralph is hastily captured and condemned to death. A member of the hanging party climbs a tree and throws a rope over a sturdy branch. The rope is being tightened around Ralph's neck when Bill is discovered in the tree. A roll of money is found in his possession. A card wrapped inside the cash confirms that this was the money taken in the robbery.

So Shall Ye Reap (February 28, 1914) Frontier Motion Picture Company. Arthur Allardt, Willis L. Robards, Lloyd V. Hamilton, Edythe Sterling, Joseph J. Franz. 1 reel.

Pretzel Captures the Smugglers (March 5, 1914) Frontier Motion Picture Company. Lloyd V. Hamilton (Pretzel), Walter Rodgers, Harry Russell, Mae Wells, Betty Burbridge. 1 reel. [At the Pordenone Silent Film Festival, *Pretzel Captures the Smugglers* was presented as "the earliest Hamilton film in existence." A print is available at the UCLA Film and Television Archives in Los Angeles.] Pretzel leads a trio of inept custom agents in pursuit of smugglers. At one point, he rolls out a cannon to blow up them. The situation intensifies when the lawman accidentally kills the smugglers' mother. In revenge, the smugglers use a rope to suspend Pretzel and his patrolmen over a cliff and light the rope on fire to get it to break.

The Colonel of the Nutts (March 12, 1914) Frontier Motion Picture Company. Lloyd V. Hamilton (Colonel Pretzel), Harry Russell, Betty Burbridge, James S. Douglass. 1 reel. Colonel Pretzel is the proprietor of the Cuckooville County Nutt Factory.

The Mystery of Buffalo Gap (March 7, 1914) Frontier Motion Picture Company. Arthur Allardt, Joseph Franz, Lloyd V. Hamilton, Walter L. Rogers, Edythe Sterling. 1 reel.

Colonel Custard's Last Stand (March 19, 1914) Frontier Motion Picture Company. Lloyd V. Hamilton (Colonel Custard), Mae Wells, Betty Burbridge, James S. Douglass, Harry Russell. 1 reel. While trying to break up his daughter's romance, Colonel Custard inadvertently puts an Indian tribe on the warpath.

Black Hands and Dirty Money (March 26, 1914) Frontier Motion Picture Company. Lloyd V. Hamilton (Pretzel), Mae Wells, Betty Burbridge, James S. Douglass, Walter Rodgers. 1 reel. Captain Pretzel tries to break up a blackhand gang.

Why Kentucky Went Dry (April 2, 1914) Frontier Motion Picture Company. Lloyd V. Hamilton (Colonel Bourbon), Betty Burbridge, Walter Rodgers, Mae Wells, James S. Douglass. 1 reel. Colonel Bourbon and Colonel Sourmash battle revenuers and each other.

Pretzel's Baby (April 9, 1914) Frontier Motion Picture Company. Lloyd V. Hamilton (Pretzel), Mae Wells, Betty Burbridge, Walter Rodgers. 1 reel. Chief of Police Pretzel must contend with a gang of counterfeiters while also dealing with marital troubles.

That Cuckooville Horse Race (April 16, 1914) Frontier Motion Picture Company. Lloyd V. Hamilton (Pretzel). 1 reel. Pretzel and Schnitzel, competitors in a horse race, dope each other's nag.

A Neighborly Quarrel (April 23, 1914) Frontier Motion Picture Company. Lloyd V. Hamilton (Pretzel), Walter Rodgers, Mae Wells, Betty Burbridge,

Roy Weddle. 1 reel. Pretzel and Mike battle over a girl.

Cuckooville Goes Skating (April 30, 1914) Frontier Motion Picture Company. Lloyd V. Hamilton (Pretzel), Walter Rodgers, Mae Wells, Charles Hagenios. 1 reel. Pretzel opens a skating rink.

Whistling Hiram (May 7, 1914) Frontier Motion Picture Company. Lloyd V. Hamilton (Hiram), May Cruze, Mae Wells, James S. Douglass, Walter Rodgers, Roy Weddle. 1 reel. Flirtatious Hiram falls for a married woman.

McBride's Bride (May 8, 1914) Kalem Company. Written, directed and produced by Marshall Neilan. Ruth Roland, Laura Oakley, Marshall Neilan, John E. Brennan. 1 reel.

Dad's Allowance (May 14, 1914) Frontier Motion Picture Company. Lloyd V. Hamilton (Papa Huckleberry), May Cruze, James Douglass, Walter Rodgers. 1 reel. Papa Huckleberry, the patriarch of a wealthy family, is appalled by the extravagant spending of his two sons and decides to take away their allowance to teach them a lesson. May, who is dating one of the sons, decides that, by flirting with Papa and putting him into a compromising situation, she can get the brothers' allowance restored.

Johnnie from Jonesboro (May 21, 1914) Frontier Motion Picture Company. Lloyd V. Hamilton (Johnnie Jones), Walter Rodgers, Mae Wells, May Cruze, Roy Weddle. 1 reel. Two grocers, Johnnie Jones and his father, fall in love with a widow and her daughter.

Hiram and Zeke Masquerade (May 28, 1914) Frontier Motion Picture Company. Sc: James Douglass. D: James Douglass. Lloyd V. Hamilton (Hiram), James Douglass, Mae Wells, May Cruze, Roy Weddle. 1 reel. At the Cuckooville Skating Rink, Hiram and Zeke pose as the world's greatest man and woman skating team.

The Deadly Battle at Hicksville (July 31, 1914) Kalem Company. Written, directed and produced by Marshall Neilan. Ruth Roland, John E. Brennan (Jim), Lloyd V. Hamilton (Dick). 1 reel. Jim and Dick are the rival suitors of a Southern belle. With the outbreak of the Civil War, the men take opposing sides and pursue their competition on the battlefield. General Jim has lemons gathered from a nearby grove to replace his battery's depleted cannon balls. However, the officer's resourcefulness is wasted. Jim's army, which consists of union men, fails to complete a charge when distracted by a five o'clock whistle. Abandoned by his men, Jim is easily captured by General Dick. Jim, an artful dodger, avoids being shot by a firing squad. Two men are assigned to hold the general in place, but they are the only ones slain in the next volley. When a cannon is fired at him, Jim effortlessly catches the cannonball. Dick finally ties Jim to the muzzle of his gun. News that the war has ended stops Dick from pulling the trigger.

Don't Monkey With the Buzzsaw (August 7, 1914) Kalem Company. Written, directed and produced by Marshall Neilan. Ruth Roland, John E. Brennan, Laura Oakley, Victor Rottman. 1 reel. 1 reel. [A print is available at the UCLA Film and Television Archives in Los Angeles.] Lloyd may briefly appear in this comedy as a police officer.

A Substitute for Pants (August 14, 1914) Kalem Company. Written, directed and produced by Marshall Neilan. Sc: William Courtney. John E. Brennan, Ruth Roland, Marshall Neilan (Billy), Lloyd Hamilton (Sammy). 1 reel. Sammy and Billy are rivals in love and politics. Ruth, the ranch owner's daughter, is the object of their affections. Sammy interferes when he discovers Billy sitting close to Ruth. This angers Billy enough for him to kick Sammy to the ground. Sammy becomes worried that Billy's appeal with the fairer sex will allow him to gain the women's votes in town and handily win the election. He ambushes Billy on the morning they are scheduled to debate. He takes off Billy's pants and locks Billy inside a barn miles outside of town. Billy is plucky enough to escape the barn, but he still has to find a way to get dressed and make it to town. He sees Ruth riding up on a horse and scrambles to find a way to cover his lower extremities before she can see him. Later, Billy races into town atop Ruth's horse. When he dismounts, the crowd sees that he is wearing Ruth's riding skirt. Sammy realizes as the suffragettes cheer this apparent show of solidarity that he has lost the election.

Sherlock Bonehead (August 21, 1914) Kalem Company. Written, directed and produced by Marshall Neilan. Ruth Roland, Dick Rosson, Lloyd Hamilton (Sherlock Bonehead), John Brennan (Ivorytop), Chance E. Ward (Captain Kidd). 1 reel. Rottenport's Chief of Police, Ivorytop, and Chief of Detectives, Sherlock Bonehead, compete to collect a thousand dollar reward for the capture of notorious smuggler Captain Kidd. After their disorganized efforts result in the trampling of a Secret Service agent, the pair decides they would do better if they combined forces. Ivorytop and Bonehead run into trouble launching their boats to pursue the escaping smuggler. Meanwhile, a female undercover agent takes pursuit in a rowboat. When she catches up to Captain Kidd, she strikes him with an oar and knocks him unconscious. Back on shore, the smuggler is taken into custody by a Secret Service Agent.

When Men Wear Skirts (August 28, 1914) Kalem Company. Written, directed and produced by Marshall Neilan. Ruth Roland (Billy), Marshall Neilan (Freddie), Fanny Yantis (Fanny), Lloyd Hamilton (Percival), John Brennan. 1 reel. Billy operates a beauty salon. Upset seeing Fanny's mistreatment of Freddie, Billy kicks the adventuress into a lake and hires Freddie to work as a manicurist. Percival, Freddie's middle-aged and overweight brother, arrives at the shop when Freddie falls ill. A gang of hired gunwomen arrives to capture Freddie and force him to marry Fanny. Percival, mistaken for Freddie, has a bag thrown over his head and is carried off to Fanny. Forced to act as a groom while still tied up in the bag,

Percival marches down the aisle like a contestant in a potato sack race.

Ham the Lineman (September 11, 1914) Kalem Company. Written, directed and produced by Marshall Neilan. Lloyd V. Hamilton, Chance Ward, Ruth Roland, George Drumgold, Victor Rottman. 1 reel. Ham is an amorous lineman. After being caught flirting with Detective Johnson's wife, he finds himself outdistancing bullets. In the meantime, vengeful gangsters are plotting against the detective. The next day, Ham is sent to repair a phone at Johnson's home. When Johnson finds the lineman in his living room, he is quick to draw his revolver on him. Ham, spurred by this hostile greeting, leads Johnson on a frantic chase. When the gangsters arrive and join the chase, Johnson and Ham take refuge inside a bedroom closet. Soon, several policemen arrive and apprehend the gangsters. Johnson, who is relieved, happily emerges from between a pair of coats. Before the detective's mood changes, Ham is able to explain his presence at the house.

The Slavery of Foxicus (October 2, 1914) Kalem Company. Written, directed and produced by Marshall Neilan. Sc: Edwin Ray Coffin. Marshall Neilan, Ruth Roland, H.L. Forbes, Lloyd V. Hamilton (Villainus), Victor Rottman. 1 reel. Foxicus, a citizen of ancient Rome, is eager to win the love of the fair Ruthinus. He comes up with a scheme that requires him to darken his skin and have himself sold as a slave to Ruthinus' stockbroker father. While in disguise, Foxicus overhears investment information, which he is able to use to buck the stock market and subvert the evil Villianus.

The Tattered Duke (October 9, 1914) Kalem Company. Written, directed and produced by Marshall Neilan. Marshall Neilan (Duke of Tattenham Corners), Lloyd V. Hamilton (Greasy Bill), Alice West, Ruth Roland. 1 reel. Greasy Bill, a waiter, discovers a duke's wallet. With the enclosed cash and identification, he impersonates the nobleman at a fashionable summer resort. Soon after, the real duke arrives and saves a girl from being drowned. A romance between the duke and the girl ensues. In the end, the couple is able to prevent the girl's mother from marrying the fraudulent duke.

Si's Wonderful Mineral Spring (October 16, 1914) Kalem Company. Written, directed and produced by Marshall Neilan. F. Fralick, Lloyd V. Hamilton (Hiram), Ruth Roland, H.L. Forbes. 1 reel. Hiram spitefully unloads rotten eggs into Silas' spring. The new odor and taste of the spring's water lead people to believe that the water contains medicinal properties. By selling drinks of this new remedy, Silas soon amasses a fortune.

Ham and the Villain Factory (October 30, 1914) Kalem Company. Written, directed and produced by Marshall Neilan. Ruth Roland, Marshall Neilan, Lloyd V. Hamilton, Victor Rottman. 1 reel. Tad observes Ham and his girlfriend driving together. The sight inspires a frightening dream.

Lizzie the Lifesaver (November 3, 1914) Kalem Company. Written, directed and produced by Marshall Neilan. Ruth Roland, Marshall Neilan, Frank Lanning, Lloyd V. Hamilton, Bud Duncan. 1 reel. Ham and Bud are fired as janitors when, amidst their fighting, they unintentionally smack Mr. Wise with a mop. Ham, bent on revenge, chases Bud. Wise, still smarting from the swat, fires his secretary Ruth for flirting with his nephew. That same day, Ruth becomes a popular lifeguard at a beach resort. After saving Wise from drowning, the grateful businessman presents her with a $5000 check. In the meantime, Ham and Bud's chase has yet to be resolved. Too large to follow Bud into a sewer outlet, Ham secures a three-pronged gaff and patiently waits for his acquaintance to re-emerge.

Ham, the Piano Mover (November 13, 1914) Kalem Company. Written, directed and produced by Marshall Neilan. Ruth Roland, Marshall Neilan, Dick Rosson (Bert Chassem, a flirt), Seena Owen, Lloyd V. Hamilton, Bud Duncan. 1 reel. Ham and Bud arrive to the Newlyweds home to deliver a piano. While Ham flirts with the maid, Bud carries the piano on his back. Ruth Newlywed pays Ham to get rid of a flirt who has followed her home. The plan fails when Ham, who has mistaken Mr. Newlywed for the flirt, throws him down the front steps. Once Mr. Newlywed returns with a policeman, everything is set right and the flirt is captured. [Lloyd recalled *Ham, the Piano Mover* in a 1922 interview published in the *Salt Lake Telegram*. The comedian found it funny that a number of talented people who were now very successful in motion pictures (Marshall Neilan, Ruth Roland and Seena Owen) had worked for paltry sums to make this silly little slapstick farce. He also noted that Victor Fleming, who had since gone on to direct Douglas Fairbanks, Constance Talmadge and other major stars, had worked on the film as an assistant cameraman — a "$12 camera cranker." That's right, Victor Fleming, the future director of *The Wizard of Oz* and *Gone with the Wind*, was one of the people responsible for filming the fantastic and epic adventures of Ham and Bud.]

The Peach at the Beach (November 17, 1914) Kalem Company. Written, directed and produced by Marshall Neilan. Lloyd V. Hamilton, Lucille Kellar, Bud Duncan, Chance Ward, Ruth Roland, Dick Rosson. 1 reel. Ham makes plans to dally with Ruth, Hothead's flirtatious wife. After telling his wife that he must leave town on business, he steals his wife's purse and meets up with Ruth at the beach. While Ham and Ruth bathe, a cameraman records the couple in beach scenes and pickpocket "Billy the Dip" robs Ham's purse. Ruth has to lend Ham money for him to return home. All seems well until weeks later, when the beach footage is exhibited at the local theatre. The film incites Hothead and Mrs. Ham. A riot ensues and the participants are ejected from the theatre. After dragging Ham home, Mrs. Ham finds a package containing her purse along with a note from "Billy the Dip." In the note, Billy expresses his sincere regret for having stolen Mrs. Ham's handbag at the beach. Mrs. Ham, even angrier than before, pummels her cheating husband. [A similar plot was used as the basis of the 1933 Laurel and Hardy comedy *Sons of the Desert*.]

Ham the Iceman (November 27, 1914) Kalem Company. Written, directed and produced by Marshall Neilan. Lloyd V. Hamilton, Laura Woods, Bud Duncan, Porter Strong, Ruth Roland, Juanita Sponsler, Marshall Neilan. 1 reel. Ham, a brash and philandering iceman, pursues his more attractive female customers. He is oblivious to any aversion to his looks and manner, and he doesn't even care if his object of desire has a husband or boyfriend. This day, the iceman mistakenly invites two women to meet him at the same time and same place. The women, unaware of each other, each arrange for Ham to be greeted by their boyfriend. At the rendezvous, the two men mistake each other for Ham and get into a furious fight with one another. As the situation is untangled, Ham arrives and discovers the rankled men, who are quick run after him. Ham makes his way to the top of a sloping street and slides cakes of ice toward his pursuers. He appears victorious until his wife arrives. This frightening development compels the iceman to leap into a swiftly running stream.

Bud, Bill and the Waiter (December 1, 1914) Kalem Company. Written, directed and produced by Marshall Neilan. Ruth Roland, Bud Duncan, Marshall Neilan, Lloyd V. Hamilton. 1 reel. At an ice cream parlor, Bill complains that he has found a fly in his dish. The manager allows him to leave without paying. The incident prompts the manager to fire Bill's waiter, Ham. Later in the day, Bill woos Mildred away from his younger brother, Bud. Bill makes sure that he is carrying a pair of dead flies in his vest when he takes Mildred to dinner that night. He manages, with some stealth, to reenact the ice cream parlor incident. This causes the restaurant manager to comp his meal and also dismiss his new waiter, Ham. Bud learns that, for their next date, Bill and Mildred will patronize the fashionable Wrector's restaurant. Bud forges letters to six of Bill's girlfriends, inviting them to dinner at Wrector's. Ham is now employed at Wrector's. On seeing Bill enter the restaurant, Ham warns the manager of the customer's ruse. The manager intercepts Bill as he plants a fly on his plate. As Bill squirms, his difficult situation is made worse by the appearance of his other girlfriends.

The Bold Banditti and the Rah Rah Boys (December 11, 1914) Kalem Company. Written, directed and produced by Marshall Neilan. Lloyd V. Hamilton, Marshall Neilan, Porter Strong, Alfred Von Harder, Jack Dillon, Frank Lanning. 1 reel. Ralph, the pampered son of a wealthy businessman, becomes a freshman at Yarvard College. The new student meets Bill Stout, a senior who has been asked by Ralph's older brother to knock some of the conceit out of the cocky freshman. Bill and his friends are adept at playing pranks on freshmen. To frighten Ralph, the group disguises as a band of blackhanders. Ralph overhears Bill explaining the plot and decides to play a prank of his own. Meanwhile, Ralph becomes a target of real blackhanders: a nefarious couple named Spagettio and Macaronio, who have decided that, to inflict vengeance on Ralph's capitalist father, they will blow up the freshman's room. When confronted by the duo, Ralph assumes that they are members of Bill's gang. He acts boldly toward the anarchists and carelessly tosses their lit bomb out a window. The bomb lands in the path of Bill's gang and the explosion knocks the gang to the ground. Bill and his friends battle the blackhanders while police and faculty rush to the scene. Mistakenly, it is Bill's bruised bunch who the police end up arresting.

Cupid Back the Winners (December 15, 1914) Kalem Company. Written, directed and produced by Marshall Neilan. Ruth Roland, Fay Brierly, Marshall Neilan, Tom Hayes, The Kalem Baby (Cupid), Lloyd V. Hamilton (primitive man), Juanita Sponsler (primitive woman). 1 reel. Cupid fails with his arrows to join a young physician and his kid brother with a pair of sisters. Determined, the cherub conveniently plants a book recounting the courting habits of primitive man.

The Winning Whiskers (December 22, 1914) Kalem Company. Written, directed and produced by Marshall Neilan. Marin Sais, Lloyd V. Hamilton, Marshall Neilan, Bud Duncan. 1 reel. [A print of this film is available at the Museum of Modern Art.] Lizzie, a cook, is transfixed by the melodramatic plot of a dime novel. The central character of the novel is an heiress who, at the insistence of her cruel guardian, plans to wed a villainous man.

The Reformation of Ham (December 25, 1914) Kalem Company. Written, directed and produced by Marshall Neilan. Lloyd V. Hamilton, Richard Coleman, Harry Hoffman. 1 reel. [This film appears on the "Lost Magic of Lloyd Hamilton" DVD collection.] Ham, a burly and harddrinking sailor, gets combative with shipmates while inebriated. His shipmates, determined to stop him from drinking, hide snakes in his bunk to make him think his drinking is causing him bad hallucinations. Later, Ham joins his shipmate Shorty for shore leave in Kulangso, China. At first, the sailors set off fireworks in celebration of a local holiday. Then, they go off to drink at a waterfront saloon. Having had too much drink, Ham and Shorty erupt in loud song, which disturbs a band of Chinese pirates. The pair is able to restrain the pirates with skyrockets and bottles until other shipmates arrive to help them.

Love, Oil and Grease (December 29, 1914) Kalem Company. Written, directed and produced by Marshall Neilan. Marshall Neilan, Ruth Roland, Tim Welsh, Bud Duncan, Lloyd V. Hamilton. 1 reel. [A print of this film is available at La Cineteca del Friuli in Gemona.] Ray is a successful car dealer but is imprudent in the area of romance. He upsets his fiancée, Hazel, by claiming that man is the superior sex. Hazel breaks their engagement and, resolved to surpass Ray, sets out to sell cars. At his car lot, Ray employs Ham and Bud as mechanics. The duo gets off to a poor start — when Ham removes a radiator cap, he unleashes a forceful stream of water that topples several customers. Ray reads a news item about a rotund man who, to enjoy free rides in the country, poses as a prospective car buyer and requests long demonstration drives. Ray presumes that he is confronting the fraudulent customer when a rotund man approaches him for a test spin. Ray is pleased with himself as he deserts the man twenty miles from town. Hazel returns the man to the car lot, at which point he attacks Ray and gives him a brutal beating. Ham and Bud, who have taken a joy ride through town and thoroughly shaken up residents, interrupt the scene with their furious return. The mechanics are so busy shouting at each other that they take their eyes off the road and drive straight into a parked automobile. They proceed to drench each other in petroleum. Then, they hurl brick at one another until they manage to knock each other unconscious. Once the dust settles, the irate customer buys fifteen cars from Hazel. Ray confesses that Hazel is the superior salesperson and Hazel, who has been softened by Ray's admission, consents again to become his wife. Meanwhile, police arrest Ham and Bud and lock them in neighboring cells. Ham is frustrated that he cannot reach Bud through the cell bars. He waves a loaf of bread in front of Bud's face, luring his fellow inmate into extending his head between the bars, and then reaches around and grabs Bud by the hair. Bud howls as the film fades.

A Model Wife (January 26, 1915) Kalem Company. A Marshall Neilan Comedy. Written, directed and produced by Marshall Neilan. Victor Rottman (a sculptor), Marshall Neilan (an artist), Lloyd V. Hamilton (Morton), Ruth Roland (Mrs. Morton), Helen Norman, H.L. Forbes. 5 minutes. (*A Model Wife* shared a reel with *Fatty's Echo*, a comedy starring John E. Brennan and Victor Rottman.) Mrs. Morton loses heavily in a bridge game. Rather than tell her husband of her foolishness, she seeks to recoup her losses by working as an artist's model.

Ham and the Sausage Factory (February 12, 1915) Kalem Company. D: Marshall Neilan (?). Lloyd V. Hamilton, Bud Duncan, Charles Inslee. 1 reel. [A print of this film is available at the Library of Congress. The film also appears on the "Lost Magic of Lloyd Hamilton" DVD collection.] Ham and Bud become employees of a sausage plant. It is Bud's job to collect dogs and deposit them into a chute. Ham, who is positioned at the other end of the chute, is expected to catch the mongrels and convert them into sausage. Ham manages to handle Bud's abductions, but he is disturbed when the sausages follow him around and perform tricks. Ham persists until Bud sends him a mean bulldog who has recently swallowed a stick of dynamite. When the canine goes to bite his leg, Ham strikes the dog with a sledgehammer. This results in an explosion powerful enough to destroy the factory. Sausage links fall from the sky and drape the dazed duo.

A Melodious Mixup (February 19, 1915) D: Chance Ward. Lloyd V. Hamilton, Bud Duncan, Ethel Teare, Gerald Miller. 1 reel. Ham is an orchestra leader in a burlesque troupe. Among his group of musicians is Bud, who is a bass drummer. When a soubrette incites a rivalry between. Ham and Bud, they fight in her dressing room. Bill Jones enters the room and, at the girl's behest, tries to manhandle the pair. For his effort, Jones is severely pummeled. Upon learning that their love is married to Jones, Ham and Bud bid goodbye to the cruel world.

Ham and the Jitney Bus (February 26, 1915) D: Chance Ward. Lloyd V. Hamilton, Bud Duncan. 1 reel. [A print of this film is available at the Library of Congress.] While sitting on a curbstone, Ham and Bud notice a wallet lying on the sidewalk. The tramps simultaneously dive for it and, after a few seconds, arise with twenty dollars. Intending to operate as a nickel bus, Ham and Bud invest the money into the purchase of an automobile.

Ham at the Garbage Gentleman's Ball (March 16, 1915) Sc: Ham and Bud. D: Chance Ward. Lloyd V. Hamilton, Bud Duncan, Marin Sais, Charles Inslee. 1 reel. Ham arrives at the Garbage Gentleman's Ball and produces a slip of paper, which he assumes is his entrance ticket. However, Bud has replaced his partner's pass with a pawn ticket. Ham is barred from the ball while Bud is permitted to stroll inside. As Ham tries entering the ballroom through a back window, an inattentive dishwasher drenches him with a bucket of dirty water. Ham remains determined to attend the ball. He induces the chief bouncer to step outside and then knocks the man unconscious. With the bouncer's badge pinned to his coat, Ham marches into the ballroom. As soon as he locates Bud, he mightily strikes the diminutive dancer on his head. Based on the force of the pounding, Bud imagines a ton of bricks falling on him. The bouncer returns in a rage and searches for Ham. He manages, while tearing through the room, to create a riot. With several male guests in pursuit, Ham and Bud flee to the brickyard, where they initiate a battle of bricks. When the bricks are exhausted, the duo decides to find another way to defend themselves. Each armed with a sledgehammer, the tramps race to a narrow alley formed by brick rows. They position themselves on either side of the alley and efficiently flatten anyone who passes.

Ham Among the Redskins (March 23, 1915) Sc: Ham and Bud. D: Chance Ward. Lloyd V. Hamilton, Bud Duncan, Charles Inslee, Marin Sais. 1 reel. [A print of this film is available at the National Film Archive in London.] When Ham and Bud inadvertently save a woman from Indians, it inspires the twosome to become Indian fighters failing to physically overcome an eight-year old redskin, Ham and Bud figure that they would do better to use their wits. Ham arms himself with a warclub and gives Bud a horn. It is Ham's belief that, when hearing the sound of the horn, an Indian will become distracted long enough to be clubbed. By falling asleep, Bud ruins the initial employment of this scheme. The Indian fighters then exchange items. Ham and Bud encounter another redskin, but Ham feels too tired to blow the horn until Bud is near death. Being unable to rely on each other, the two separate and continue to hunt Indians independently.

Ham in the Harem (March 30, 1915) Sc: Hamilton Smith. D: Chance Ward. Lloyd V. Hamilton, Bud Duncan, Charles E. Inslee, Marin Sais, Martin Kinney. 1 reel. [A print of this film is available with the Film Preservation Associates. The film also appears on the "Lost Magic of Lloyd Hamilton" DVD collection.] Ham and Bud are bootblacks in Egypt. In noticing that passersby are barefoot, they realize that their services are useless and they must find something else to occupy their time. Ham comes across Muslims prostrate to perform their daily prayers. The tramp, assuming the Muslims are bowing down to him, gratefully doffs his hat and waves. The back of one worshiper strikes Ham as a good place to sit down and eat a banana. Soon after, the duo follows a harem girl into the sultan's palace. Ham and Bud are captured while teaching the sultan's wives the Tango, Foxtrot and Maxine. As the sultan prepares to behead the intruders, Ham and Bud engage the sultan in a high-stakes poker game. The team wins all the sultan's possessions, including the sultan's favorite wife. The sultan asks Abdul El Cohen, the royal money-lender, to advance further gambling funds. When El Cohen refuses, the sultan angrily dumps him into a chute that leads to a nearby river. The sultan tries to shove his poker opponents into the chute, but he follows El Cohen himself. Ham and Bud learn that the sultan's favorite has eloped with her lover. Brokenhearted, the tramps kiss each other on the head and then dive headfirst down the chute. [Hamilton remade this film several times. The various versions include *Wurra Wurra, Ham the Explorer, Seaside Romeos, Robinson Crusoe Ltd.*, and *Robinson Crusoe and Son*.]

Ham's Harrowing Duel (April 6, 1915) D: Chance Ward. Lloyd V. Hamilton, Bud Duncan, Marin Sais, Charles Inslee. 1 reel. Tom and Evelina quarrel at breakfast. As Tom departs, Evelina lobs a grapefruit at him. The grapefruit misses Tom, sailing through a window and knocking Ham unconscious. Hoping to make amends for her careless action, Evelina welcomes Ham into her home. She soon gets the idea to use her guest to make her husband jealous. With an inducement of $100, Ham proceeds to act romantically towards her. From a window, Bud observes the money being passed into his partner's hands. To steal the cash, he dresses as an anarchist and grasps a pistol in each hand. The diminutive gunman orders Ham and Tom to stand on their heads, then takes off with the money. While brooding over the loss, Ham reveals Evelina's scheme to Tom. Tom considers staging a mock duel. To procure Ham's cooperation, he reimburses Ham for his stolen money. As Evelina watches, Ham pretends to stab Tom. Evelina throws herself over her husband, who she believes is dead. The deception is revealed by Bud, whose sudden return causes Ham and Tom to frantically set themselves back on their heads.

The Pollywogs Picnic (April 13, 1915) D: Chance Ward. Lloyd V. Hamilton, Bud Duncan, Charles Inslee, Marin Sais, William Planett. 1 reel. The ancient order of Pollywogs organizes a picnic. A general plans to attend the picnic until Ham steals his uniform from a clothesline. Ham, attired in the uniform, is welcomed at the picnic as the guest of honor. At first, Ham ruins the tug of war contest by accidentally setting the rope on fire. Next, he cheats in a pie-eating contest by sneaking pies underneath his shirt. A major competition, which offers a $100 award, sets Ham and Bud after a greased pig. The pig is eventually captured, but the appearance of the real general prompt the pair to flee the grounds without collecting their prize money.

Lotta Coin's Ghost (April 20, 1915) Sc: Ham and Bud. D: Chance Ward. Lloyd V. Hamilton, Bud Duncan, Charles Inslee, Marin Sais. [Prints of this film are available with the John Allen Archives and London's National Film Archive.] Ham and Bud burglarize the Coin home in search of a billion dollar necklace. To frighten away the thieves, Mr. Coin's daughter disguises herself as a ghost.

The Phoney Cannibal (April 27, 1915) Sc: C. Doty Hobart. D: Chance Ward. Lloyd V. Hamilton, Bud Duncan, Charles Inslee, Martin Kinney, Marin Sais. 1 reel. [A print of this film is available at the Museum of Modern Art. The film also appears on the "Lost Magic of Lloyd Hamilton" DVD collection.] A boy hurls a block at his mother, Mrs. Mum, knockings the woman unconscious. In the next room, Ham, sprawled out in bed, is roused from a nap by a ravenous bedbug. He grabs a pistol that lies at his bedside and, balancing the gun across his forearm, he carefully aims at the bug and fires. With the single shot, he succeeds in executing the annoying insect. But then, as he leaves the room, Ham finds Mrs. Mum's still form, which leads him to assume that his shot continued on and struck the woman. Ham, desperate, strangles Bud to eliminate his roommate as a witness. To dispose of Bud's body, he drops it out of the window. The body plummets four stories and slams into the ground. Ham, now remorseful, attempts to hang himself. He ties a rope around his neck and leaps out of the window. As the rope was not properly secured, he hits the ground beside Bud. He rises in a daze and notices that Bud is reawakening. The men casually get to their feet and go for a stroll. During their outing, they notice a street corner reverend displaying a cannibal man to a group of people. The reverend claims that he needs the funds to convert heathens like the cannibal man. Following his speech, he gathers money from the assembly. Inspired by the profitable exhibition, Ham dons clerical attire and has Bud dress as a cannibal. He leads Bud to the street to address the passing crowd. Meanwhile, Mrs. Mum regains consciousness and becomes angry that her boarders Ham and Bud have disappeared without paying their bill. Accompanied by several officers, she eventually discovers her errant boarders. She draws a revolver from her shirtwaist and demands payment. Ham reluctantly surrenders the proceeds of his scam.

Ham's Easy Eats (May 4, 1915) Sc: Hamilton Smith. D: Chance Ward. Lloyd V. Hamilton, Bud Duncan, Hylda Sloman, Agnes Copelin. 1 reel. An assault on a grocery boy provides Ham and Bud with no more than a few potatoes. Disappointed, the pair hurls the spuds at the grocery boy. One of the starchy missiles strikes a cop, but the duo vanishes before the cop sees them. Later, Ham and Bud acquire money by acting as starving beggars. After Bud flees with the alms, Ham is taken in hand by a compassionate woman and her charming daughter and royally entertained at the home of his new benefactors. He tries singing for his kind friends, but hits a variety of unsettling notes. The trio soon embarks on a pleasure drive, but the cop apprehends the malefactor. Ham, in disgrace, is coldly rejected by the mother and daughter. The tramp's spirits aren't lifted until he discovers that his cellmate is Bud. With great speed and violence, he batters his treacherous partner.

Rushing the Lunch Counter (May 11, 1915) D: Chance Ward. Lloyd V. Hamilton, Bud Duncan, Fernandez Galvez, George Drumgold. 1 reel. Ham and Bud come upon the Wayville train station. To get themselves a meal, the two men overrun the lunch room while the owner is absent. The owner is so desperate to keep help that, on his return, he hires Ham and Bud as waiters. Ham and Bud cope with one troublesome patron, a wild westerner, but have greater difficulty when a train unloads a large number of hungry passengers. Because the food is slow in coming, the waiters are eventually chased by the maddened mob. They escape by speeding out of town on a handcar.

The Liberty Party (May 18, 1915) Sc: Harry O. Hoyt. D: Chance Ward. Lloyd V. Hamilton, Bud Duncan, Gus Alexander, Martha Mattox. 1 reel. Posing as paperhangers, escaped convicts Ham and Bud ruin the Smith family's home.

Ham, the Detective (May 25, 1915) Fernandex Galvez, Ethel Teare, Gus Alexander. 1 reel. Guiseppe, the leader of a bandit group, threatens to kill Senor Dedough unless Dedough's daughter becomes his wife. Plucky detectives Ham and Bud are hired to resolve the dilemma. As the sleuths approach Guiseppe's shack, an experimental bomb is tossed out of a window. Bud, caught in the force of the explosion, is blown to a distant location. Ham bravely proceeds alone, but he is soon captured by Guiseppe's gang. Bound and gagged, he expects to be tortured once Guiseppe has killed Dedough. However, Bud returns in time to release Ham, at which point the detectives rush off to stop the villain.

Ham in the Nut Factory (June 1, 1915) D: Chance Ward. Lloyd V. Hamilton, Bud Duncan, George C. Pearce, Fernandez Galvez, Ethel Teare, Martin Kinney, George Drumgold. 1 reel. [A print of this film is available in the John Allen Archives.] Filling in for a vacationing professor, Ham and Bud operate an insane asylum where Ethel, a rich girl, becomes a patient. Ethel's evil guardian, Eclaire, involves Ham and Bud in his scheme to seize Ethel's fortune. Later, a dangerous patient escapes from his cell and chases after Ham and Bud. As the pair are busy outrunning the lunatic, Ethel is able to be rescued by her heroic boyfriend.

Ham at the Fair (June 8, 1915) D: Chance Ward. Lloyd V. Hamilton, Bud Duncan, George Drumgold, Ethel Teare. [This comedy was shot on location at the Panama-Pacific Exposition. The exhibition, which was held in San Francisco, celebrated the opening of the Panama Canal. The British title was *Ham's Giddy Outing*. A print of the film is available at the Library of Congress.] Ham meets a pretty swindler named Goldie. Goldie offers up her lips to Ham, but Ham no sooner leans in to kiss her then she lets out a scream. Ham hands over all his cash to get Goldie to keep quiet. Smarting, Ham guides Bud into Goldie's con. Next, a ferocious-looking westerner approaches the deceitful girl. The outcome of this encounter is decidedly different. Goldie, overwhelmed by the westerner's powerful clasp and passionate kiss, takes out her money and hands it over to the westerner. After being suckered by a con man, Bud uses the same scam on Ham. Ham uses the scam on Goldie, but loses his money again when he tries the scam on the man who introduced it.

Raskey's Road Show (June 15, 1915) D: Chance Ward. Lloyd V. Hamilton, Bud Duncan, Fernandez Galvez, Ethel Teare, Myrtle Sterling, Martin Kinney (Sandough, tragedian and strongman). 1 reel. [A print of this film is available with the Film Preservation Associates. The film also appears in the "Lost Magic of Lloyd Hamilton" DVD collection.] In joining a road show, Ham becomes the senior property man. However, the job involves more than props. First, Ham agrees to assist in the magician's act. He proves to be a lousy helper. Unable to stand the squirming going on underneath his shirt, he brings a rabbit into view minutes before it was scheduled to appear. The act ends when Bud conks Ham with a sandbag. Later, Bud's ill-timed raising of a curtain reveals Ham flirting with the trapeze artist. Ham pursues Bud, but his effort is frustrated when the trapeze girl falls on him. It is expected that, for the road show's closing act, Madame Duffy's lion and tiger will perform tricks. However, the cats ignore the Madame's commands and viciously fight one another. In the heat of the battle, the lion and tiger are revealed to be Ham and Bud in costume.

In High Society (June 22, 1915) Sc: C. Doty Hobart. D: Chance Ward. Lloyd V. Hamilton, Bud Duncan, Walter Reid, Hylda Hollis, Ethel Teare, Fernandes Galvez, Jack W. McDermott. 1 reel. [A print of this film is available at the National Film Archive in London.] Ham dreams that he attends a lavish masquerade ball and tries to rob guests of their jewels.

The Merry Moving Men (June 29, 1915) D: Chance Ward. Lloyd V. Hamilton, Bud Duncan, George Browins, Ethel Teare. 1 reel. [The National Film Archive in London maintains a print of this film under the British title *Tramp On*.] Ham and Bud are not very motivated working as movers. The pair are languid piling furniture onto their truck; they lose a few pieces as they carelessly drive along; eventually, they desert the truck to visit a circus. At nightfall, Ham and Bud unload a bed and bedding to sleep. After an anxious effort to trace their belongings, the Duponts retire on their cottage's cold, hard floor. The next morning, Ham and Bud arrive at the Duponts' country home. To prompt a rapid unloading, Mr. Dupont fires his revolver into the air. Ham and Bud cooperate until the gun's last bullet is discharged. At that point, Ham knocks Dupont to the ground and then marches off with Bud.

Some Romance (July 6, 1915) Sc: Frank Howard Clark. D: Chance Ward. Lloyd V. Hamilton, Bud Duncan, John Brownell, Ethel Teare, John McDermott, Harry DeRoy. 1 reel. [Cole Johnson presented a print of this comedy at the 2008 Manchester Mirthquake festival.] Ham and Bud set aside their duties as streetcleaners to stop Gwen's runaway steed. After Gwen departs, the pair discovers a necklace that the lady lost in the excitement. In expectation of a reward, Ham travels to Gwen's palatial home to return the necklace. The streetcleaner tells Gwen that he is a nobleman in disguise. Gwen, impressed by Ham's revelation, decides it would be insulting to give him a reward. Bud, is tired of waiting for his share of the reward, marches into Gwen's house, which greatly displeases Ham. As soon as he can distract his host's attention, Ham kicks Bud out the door. Gwen's jealous boyfriend directs the streetcleaning inspector to the scene. The inspector immediately returns Ham to his broom. [Plot components of this reel are present in the story line of two later Hamilton Comedies, *Half A Hero* and *Jonah Jones*.]

A Flashlight Flivver (July 13, 1915) D: Chance Ward. Lloyd V. Hamilton, Bud Duncan, Ethel Teare, Margaret Key, Bobbie Turnbill. 1 reel. By replacing a camera lens with a seltzer bottle, Bud causes patrons of Ham's photography studio to be doused with water. Turning the converted camera on Bud, Ham nearly drowns his playful assistant. Next, Ham prepares to photograph a Hook and Ladder company. Prompted by the sound of a firebell, the group breaks their pose and rushes to the exit. On their way out, the rugged firefighters trample Ham and his camera. Seeking revenge for one of Ham's kicks, Bud pours nitroglycerine and gunpowder in a flash pan. When Ham touches a flame to the pan, the studio explodes and Ham is buried beneath wreckage.

The Spook Raisers (July 20, 1915) D: Chance Ward. Lloyd V. Hamilton, Bud Duncan, Harry Griffith, Ethel Teare, Myrtle Sterling, Martin Kinney. 1 reel. [A print of this film is available at the Library of Congress.] While eluding Patrolman Doolittle, Ham and Bud hide in the home of a medium. The pair soon learns that there is money to be made from the spiritualist game. They steal the medium's parapsychic paraphernalia and open "Professor Ham's Ghost Emporium." With Bud acting as his ghost, Ham holds a séance for a group of ladies, one of whom is Mrs. Doolittle. Patrolman Doolittle's arrival quickly ends Ham's spirit summoning.

The Toilers (July 27, 1915) D: Chance Ward. Lloyd V. Hamilton, Bud Duncan, Ethel Teare, Jack Sheehan. [The film is also known as *Ham the Statue*. A print of the film is available at the Library of Congress.] Ham, the senior janitor at a sculptor's studio, becomes enchanted by the beautiful customer he observes purchasing a pair of marble gladiators. To follow the customer home, Ham and Bud take the place of the statue. While maintaining the gladiators' poses, the janitors are delivered to the reception room of the Morton mansion. Nearby, food is set down for upcoming guests. Once the servants have left the room, the "figures" devour the snacks. When the guests finally appear, they don't know what to make of the sculpture as the gladiators' poses seem to keep changing. The sculptor arrives and, seeing the hideous figures that stand in place of his work, attacks the errant janitors. The fast-footed pair manages to elude their pursuers. While leaning against what they think is a statue of a policeman, Ham and Bud chuckle over their escape. Suddenly, the policeman and grabs them by their collars.

The Hypnotic Monkey (August 3, 1915) D: Chance Ward. Lloyd V. Hamilton, Bud Duncan, Fernandez Galvez, Ethel Teare. 1 reel. After eluding a cop, Ham and Bud fall asleep in a quiet spot in a park. Ham is still sleeping when Bud goes walking with an organ grinder's daughter. Meanwhile, Ham has a vivid nightmare. He dreams that, by mimicking a hypnotist's demonstration, he has changed Bud into a monkey. Ham awakens to find the organ grinder's monkey sitting where Bud had been. He starts to cry. When the organ grinder tries to take the monkey away, Ham grabs the monkey and fights off the organ grinder.

The Winning Wash (August 10, 1915) D: Rube Miller. Lloyd V. Hamilton, Bud Duncan, J. Clifford, H. Griffith, Ethel Teare. 1 reel. Ham and Bud work at a Chinese laundry. A vest is left to be cleaned, and within the pocket, they discover a roll of money. For awhile, the two launderers handle the money like two cats playing with a mouse. They are finally begin to count it when the vest's tough owner, who is prepared to tear the laundry apart for the green roll, charges into the store. (The Three Stooges used the identical plot for their 1947 comedy *Sing a Song of Six Pants*.)

Ham at the Beach (August 17, 1915) Sc: Rube Miller. D: Rube Miller. Lloyd V. Hamilton, Bud Duncan, Ethel Teare, H. Griffith, J. Clifford. 1 reel. During a day at the beach, Ham and Bud fight over a tent show soubrette. Later, Ham angers a roulette croupier. He is able to evade the croupier by disguising himself as the showgirl, but his big feet give him away.

Ham and the Experiment (August 24, 1915) D: Rube Miller. Lloyd V. Hamilton, Bud Duncan, Ethel Teare, Betty Teare, Lucille West, Martin Kinney, Fernandez Galvez, Margaret Keys. 1 reel. Ham and Bud are test subjects for scientists seeking to determine if a new chemical will make the subjects irresistible to women. Following the test, Ham and Bud wander through the park. At first, a couple of sisters abandon their suitors and pursue the pair. Then, the sisters are joined by a policewoman, a headmistress, and several girls' school pupils. The females fight to caress Ham and Bud. A policeman tries to arrest the duo for creating a disturbance, but he is soon overwhelmed by their many admirers. Ham and Bud take this opportunity to flee.

Minnie the Tiger (December 7, 1915) Sc: Lloyd Hamilton. D: William Beaudine. Bud Duncan, Charles Inslee, Ethel Teare, Harry Griffith. 1 reel. [Hamilton was sidelined with a broken leg for a number of months. Late in his recovery, he managed to come to the studio on crutches and assist Beaudine in the direction of his unit. In addition, he was credited with having written *Minnie the Tiger* and *Wurra, Wurra*.] Ethel tells Bud and Count De Jalbo, rivals for her hand, that she will wed the one of them who captures an escaped circus tiger. The count boasts about his skills as a hunter, but the first sight of the big cat prompts him to hurry up a tree. The tiger is actually a gentle feline named Minnie. Minnie displays affection for Bud, even more so after Bud plucks a thorn from her paw. Elsewhere, the count tells Ethel that he slew the terrible man-eater. The count's harrowing tale is being concluded when Minnie arrives on the scene. The count, without hesitation, races into the distance. Once he vanishes from view, Ethel lovingly falls into Bud's arms.

Wurra Wurra (February 8, 1916) Sc: Lloyd Hamilton. D: William Beaudine. Bud Duncan, Charles Inslee, Gus Leonard, John McDermott, Ethel Teare. 1 reel.

Ham Takes a Chance (February 15, 1916) D: William Beaudine. Lloyd V. Hamilton, Bud Duncan, Ethel Teare, Gus Leonard, Jack MacDermott. 1 reel. [Prints of this film are available at the National Film Archive in London, the Ceskoslovensky Filmovy Ustav/ Filmovy Archiv in Prague, and the Museum of Modern Art in New York.] Attracted by a delightful dancer, Ham and Bud join a broken-down theatrical troupe. Bud exercises the dancer's pet snakes while Ham acts as the target in a knife-throwing routine. When the becomes ill, Ham decides to take over and induces Bud to become his target.

Ham the Diver (February 22, 1916) Sc: Ham and Bud. D: William Beaudine. Lloyd V. Hamilton, Bud Duncan, Ethel Teare, Jack MacDermott, Juanita Sponsler. 1 reel. Bud assists in lowering novice diver Ham to the ocean floor, but his attraction to Ethel causes him to abandon the irksome task of controlling the air pump. Eventually, Ham manages to re-emerge from the sea. Without pausing to remove his bulky sub-sea suit, he sets out to find his errant assistant and enact revenge. [This comedy was shot in San Diego Bay. Lloyd told writer Stanley Todd that he spent as long as five hours underwater shooting the diving sequence.]

Winning the Widow (February 29, 1916) Sc: Frank Howard Clark. D: William Beaudine. Lloyd V. Hamilton, Bud Duncan, Jack MacDermott, Gus Leonard, Martin Kinney, Adoni Fovier. 1 reel. [The National Film Archive in London maintains a print of this film under the British title *Ham and the Husband*.] Expecting to catch his winsome wife with admirers, a jealous husband pretends that he has been killed. Ham and Bud, who fall for the woman's flirtations, figure that they can win the widow's favor and fortune by setting out to find her spouse's murderer.

Maybe Moonshine (March 7, 1916) Sc: William Beaudine. D: William Beaudine. Lloyd V. Hamilton, Bud Duncan, Adoni Fovier. 1 reel. Ham and Bud appear in a flashback sequence as small boys who are part of rival mountain clans. By manhood, they have become ardent moonshiners and the principal preservers of their families' feud. [Hamilton remade this film as *Moonshine*.]

Ham Agrees with Sherman (March 14, 1916) D: Lloyd Hamilton (?). Lloyd V. Hamilton, Bud Duncan, Porter Strong, Norma Nichols (the spy). 1 reel. Upon hearing news of a foreign foe, Ham assumes command of a motley brigade. The troop consists of soldiers dressed in everything from Mexican guerrilla outfits to Colonial attire. With Bud at his side as a drink mixer, General Ham directs war operations from a hilltop. For a better perspective, Ham perilously flies over the battlefield. His survey ends when enemy guns shoot down his plane. Though he survives the crash, the unpleasant experience convinces Ham to abandon his cause.

For Sweet Charity (March 21, 1916) Sc: Ham and Bud. D: Lloyd Hamilton (?). Lloyd V. Hamilton, Bud Duncan, Porter Strong, Norma Nichols, A. Edmondson, Julia Cruze, Juanita Sponsler, Ed Valentine. 1 reel. Ham and Bud swindle a soap salesman out of a dollar. This money is enough to buy the duo admission into a charity bazaar, but it is not enough to buy them kisses at Ruby Lyps' kissing booth. Undeterred, the duo tries to find ways steal kisses from Ruby. Later, the tramps get kitchen jobs at a seaside restaurant where the specialty is oysters.

Ham and the Hermit's Daughter (March 28, 1916) D: Lloyd Hamilton (?). Lloyd V. Hamilton, Bud Duncan, Porter Strong, Norma Nichols, Julia Cruze, Victor Rottman. 1 reel. Ham and Bud are working in the woods as land surveyors when they encounter a hermit and his daughter. The hermit's daughter, who had never seen a man before other than her father, thinks that Ham is beautiful. Ham is moved by the girl's affection, but he abandons romantic pursuits when he learns that the hermit possesses a large store of gold. The surveyors quickly get together to plan a robbery.

From Altar to Halter (April 4, 1916) D: Lloyd

Hamilton (?). Lloyd V. Hamilton, Bud Duncan, Norma Nichols, Myrtle Sterling. 1 reel. Ham has a nightmare in which he and Bud are married men.

Millionaires by Mistake (April 11, 1916) D: Lloyd Hamilton (?). Lloyd V. Hamilton, Bud Duncan, Norma Nichols. 1 reel. Ham and Bud have recently inherited a million dollars. In celebration of their newfound wealth, the duo visits a grand hotel. Several fortune hunters, including a couple of alluring vamps, are drawn to the rich men. [In 1938, this comedy was remade with the Three Stooges as *Healthy, Wealthy and Dumb*.]

Ham and Preparedness (April 18, 1916) D: Lloyd Hamilton (?). Lloyd V. Hamilton, Bud Duncan, Norma Nichols, Juanita Sponsler. 1 reel. A war disrupts Ham and Bud's visit to Mexico. A shell burst transports Bud far out to sea. After managing to astonishingly sidestep the fire, Ham is welcomed into the home of a regiment captain. Upon glancing into the captain's periscope, Ham notices Bud being received by a charming mermaid. Despite the comfort of his surroundings, Ham becomes consumed with jealousy. Soon after they are reunited, Ham and Bud become involved in the disappearance of important papers. The pair finishes up in the sea, where they tangle with a buoy. As the army, navy and police converge on them, Ham and Bud abandon the buoy and swiftly swim for safer shores.

Ham's Waterloo (April 25, 1916) D: Harry Edwards. Lloyd V. Hamilton, Bud Duncan, Norma Nichols. 1 reel. As the wedding day of Ham and Norma approaches, Ham must deal with opposition from both Bud, who is in love with Norma, and his future father-in-law. At the wedding banquet, Ham secretly intercepts a note that Bud has tried passing to Norma. Ham forwards a reply to Bud. Bud opens the note, which proposes a time and place for a meeting. He arrives at the meeting place only to come within the range of a hosing by Ham.

Ham and the Masked Marvel (May 2, 1916) D: Harry Edwards. Lloyd V. Hamilton, Bud Duncan, Norma Nichols. 1 reel. [A print of this film is available at the Library of Congress.] Though the bout has been rigged in his favor, Ham experiences great difficulty in his match with the Masked Marvel.

The Tank Town Troupe (May 9, 1916) D: Harry Edwards. Lloyd V. Hamilton, Bud Duncan, Norma Nichols, A. Edmondson. 1 reel. Ham and Bud are traveling acrobats called "The Balance Brothers." After entertaining at a sheriff's home, the pair is secretly followed out of town by the lawman's stagestruck daughter. The sheriff, infuriated by his daughter's departure he straps on his gun and, accompanied by a posse of fierce cowboys, swiftly rides in pursuit. Unaware of Ham and Bud's innocence, the lawman plans to shoot down the strolling players.

Ham's Busy Day (May 23, 1916) D: Harry Edwards. Lloyd V. Hamilton, Bud Duncan, Norma Nichols, A. Edmondson. 1 reel. Ham visits Bud at the hospital and meets a flirtatious nurse. On the spot, he decides to join Bud as one of the nurse's patients. Ham and Bud ruin the hospital as they battle to win the woman in white.

A Bunch of Flivvers (May 30, 1916) D: Lloyd Hamilton. Lloyd V. Hamilton, Bud Duncan, A. Edmondson, Norma Nichols. 1 reel. A swami's strange pill endows Ham with supernatural powers. In the meantime, Norma joins Bud for a canoe ride. Ham decides to employ his new powers to disrupt the aquatic outing. By grabbing the handle of a motorized lawn mover, he is magically transported across the lake. The sight of this early jet-ski stuns Bud and Norma. Ham convinces Norma to abandon the canoe and accompany him on a car ride. With pills stolen from the Hindu mystic, Bud also gains unnatural strength. He applies his new power to prevent Ham and Norma's car ride. One by one, he sabotages a series of cheap flivvers. In disguise, he assumes the driver's seat in Ham's final auto. The devious chauffeur gives the couple a wild ride, finally racing the car off a pier.

Midnight at the Old Mill (June 6, 1916) D: Lloyd Hamilton. Lloyd V. Hamilton, Bud Duncan, A. Edmondson. 1 reel. [A print of this film is available at the Library of Congress.] Doc Sawbones receives word that, at midnight, a bundle containing "you know what" will be waiting at the old mill. Anticipating a night of experimentation, the doctor and three colleagues gleefully sharpen their surgical instruments. Ham, the doctor's fearful gardener, sets forth as expressman for the sack. Bud hurries ahead and mischievously slips inside the bag. When Ham places the bundle over his shoulder, Bud tickles his friend in the ribs. Frightened by this, Ham drops his cargo and runs from the scene.

The Alaskan Mouse Hound (June 13, 1916) D: Lloyd Hamilton. Lloyd V. Hamilton, Bud Duncan, A. Edmondson. 1 reel. Planning to surprise his daughter, Mr. Gottrox spends $5000 or an Alaskan mouse hound. Soon after, Agnes the Adventuress steals the new pet and flees. Outside of a department store, Ham and Bud observe that checking shoppers' dogs is a profitable business. Donning messenger caps, the pair undertakes this enterprise. Pursued by the police, Agnes drops the Gottrox pooch into Ham's lap and races into the store. Ham tries to get rid of the hot hound, but the dog continually returns to him. Ham finally persuades Bud to take the hound. He is unaware that, by this time, Bud has been promised $1,000 reward for the pet's return.

The Beggar and His Child (June 20, 1916) Sc: Lloyd Hamilton. D: Lloyd Hamilton. Lloyd V. Hamilton, Bud Duncan, A. Edmondson. 1 reel. Ham, a fiddling beggar, is able to gain the sympathy of passersby by having Bud pose as his young daughter. Lotta Coin is captivated by the beggar's child, who resembles her long-departed Nell. The rich woman adopts Bud and hires Ham as her butler. Ham and Bud's rough battles eventually lead to their exposure.

Ham the Explorer (June 27, 1916) D: Lloyd Hamilton. Lloyd V. Hamilton, Bud Duncan, Eileen

Godsey. 1 reel. [A print of this film is available at the Museum of Modern Art.] A mysterious treasure map leads Ham and Bud on a wild trek to the strange land of Euks. Once there, the pair teaches the dusky tribe members the latest dance steps. The medicine man, who comes upon this scene, calls an end to the dancing and orders Ham beheaded. Ham is able to get the medicine man to roll dice, which allows him to escape death and win the tribal crown. Ham, jealous because the queen likes Bud, orders the executioner to chop off Bud's head. Bud uses his adeptness with dice to gain the crown, but his reign ends abruptly when the followers of the medicine man stage a revolt. The timely arrival of American forces saves the duo from the savage tribe.

The Peach Pickers (July 4, 1916) D: Lloyd Hamilton. Lloyd V. Hamilton, Bud Duncan, A. Edmondson, Eillen Godsey, Freddie Fraelick. 1 reel. A judge cautions Ham and Bud that, if they continue to annoy women, he will put them in prison. Ham and Bud are unaffected by the warning as they flirt with Big Bill's wife. A cop dresses in drag to lure the mashers. He eventually joins Big Bill and, by boat, the pair pursues the malefactors.

The Baggage Smashers (July 11, 1916) D: Lloyd Hamilton. Lloyd V. Hamilton, Bud Duncan, Eileen Godsey, Freddie Fraelick, A. Edmondson. 1 reel. Attracted by a female telegrapher, Ham and Bud abandon their places on a freight car and become baggage men at a train station.

The Great Detective (July 18, 1916) D: Lloyd Hamilton. Lloyd V. Hamilton, Bud Duncan, Eileen Godsey, A. Edmondson. 1 reel. [A print of this film is available at the Library of Congress. The film also appears on the "Lost Magic of Lloyd Hamilton" DVD collection.] Mrs. Worry, questioning her husband's fidelity, employs Ham, celebrated sleuth and master of 999 instant disguises, to spy on her spouse. Trouble starts when Ham notifies Mrs. Worry that her husband has been spotted out with another woman.

Ham's Whirlwind Finish (July 25, 1916) D: Lloyd Hamilton. Lloyd V. Hamilton, Bud Duncan, Ethel Teare, A. Edmondson. 1 reel. [A print of this film is available at the Library of Congress.] Ham and Bud, cooks at a ditch-diggers camp, try to serve up spaghetti and vino at a satisfactory pace. However, the camp's husky crew eventually becomes impatient and attacks the cooks. Using kitchen supplies as ammunition, Ham and Bud manage to withstand the attack. Bambino, a fiery Italian beauty, flirts with Ham. The couple begins to blow kisses at one another. This exchange infuriates Tony, the camp foreman. Tony hurls a bomb at the cooks. Following the explosion, all that remains is Ham's hat and shoes. Clutching these vestiges, Bambino openly sobs.

The Heart Menders (August 1, 1916) D: Lloyd Hamilton. Lloyd V. Hamilton, Bud Duncan, Ethel Teare. 1 reel. [Prints of this film are available at Det Danske Filmmuseum in Copenhagen, Jugoslovenska Kinoteka, and La Cineteca del Friuli in Gemona.] Arriving at a divorce lawyer's office, Ham puts aside his porter duties and impersonates the counselor. Besides collecting fees, the new attorney accepts kisses from grateful female clients. Later, he visits the home of one especially appealing client. Feeling crowded out of the picture, Bud phones the woman's husband and informs him of his wife's objectionable guest.

Good Evening, Judge (August 8, 1916) D: Lloyd Hamilton. Lloyd V. Hamilton, Bud Duncan, Ethel Teare, A. Edmondson. 1 reel. [This film appears on the "Lost Magic of Lloyd Hamilton" DVD collection.] Ham, needing money for a meal, visits a pawnshop to sell an alarm clock. Bud, who is unwilling to part with the clock, pursues Ham into the shop and snatches the clock away from him. While the tramps tussle, a shady character enters the shop and demands money from the owner. The owner is being choked by the robber when Ham grabs the robber by his collar and boots him into the street. The grateful owner asks Ham and Bud to work for him. The tramps are settling into their new jobs when an undercover police detective arrests the owner for fencing. The detective and owner leave the shop just as a pretty young woman arrives looking to pawn stolen goods. The woman tells Ham and Bud that they can make considerable money if they become her partners. That night, Ham and Bud visit the woman at her home and discover that she is married to a sour-faced burglar named Slippery Steve. Slippery Steve is soon able to enlist Ham and Bud's help to rob a home. Before departing, he gives the tramps revolvers to use in case they run into trouble. It doesn't take long for trouble to arise. Bud is so hungry that, while Ham and Slippery Steve are breaking into a safe, he prowls around the kitchen in search of food. Ham and Slippery Steve, hearing Bud making noises, go into the kitchen to investigate. Ham gets angry with Bud and throws dishes at him, which awakens a woman sleeping in a bedroom upstairs. The woman cries out the window for help. A squad of policemen arrives on the scene and is drawn into a shoot-out with the burglars. Ham and Bud keep shooting at the police as they flee the home. The tramps try to elude the police by slipping into a back door, but they find they have in fact entered the police station. They promptly surrender their guns and march voluntarily into a jail cell.

Ham's Strategy (August 15, 1916) D: Lloyd Hamilton. Lloyd V. Hamilton, Bud Duncan, Ethel Teare, A. Edmondson. 1 reel. (Also known as *The Donkey Did It.*) The village flirt urges Ham to buy a cart and a stubborn donkey. Bud becomes jealous when he sees the couple embark on a leisurely ride. He puts on a mask and tries to rob Ham. Ham wants it to look as if he fought before surrendering his boss' money. Obligingly, Bud shoots holes in Ham's coat. After he is asked to do a better job of it, Bud flatly admits that he has run out of bullets. No longer posing a threat, the masked bandit is left in a heap by the roadside. Ham restarts his donkey with a hypodermic needle. The donkey energetically bolts forward, taking the cart and its passengers for a wild ride. When his vigor is exhausted, the donkey stops cold in the path of an oncoming train. Ham struggles to remove the animal from the tracks.

The Star Boarders (August 22, 1916) D: Lloyd Hamilton. Lloyd V. Hamilton, Bud Duncan, Ethel Teare, A. Edmondson, Myrtle Sterling. 1 reel. Ham and Bud are residents of the Grub boardinghouse. The layabouts arrange to sell Mrs. Grub's furniture to a secondhand dealer. First, they spray bug killer through the keyholes. Then, once this emission has put their fellow boarders into a sound sleep, they quickly remove the boarders from the beds to be sold.

Ham in the Drugstore (August 29, 1916) D: Lloyd Hamilton. Lloyd V. Hamilton, Bud Duncan, Ethel Teare, A. Edmondson. 1 reel. Ham and Bud, soda jerks at a drugstore, are put in charge of prescription pick-ups. Ham mixes Wild Bill an indigestion cure that sends Wild Bill on a rampage.

Ham the Fortune Teller (September 5, 1916) D: Lloyd Hamilton. Lloyd V. Hamilton, Bud Duncan, Ethel Teare, A. Edmondson. 1 reel. Ham and Bud wander into a gypsy camp. As the gypsies move to attack, the pair unintentionally gives a mystic sign, which allows them admission into the camp's inner circle. In the meantime, Mr. Lotsacash has a marital squabble and leaves his home. After his car breaks down, Lotsacash arrives at the camp and lets Ham tell his fortune. Ham informs Lotsacash that a dark handsome man is stealing his wife. Warned that he had better be telling the truth, Ham casts Bud in the role of the wife-stealer.

Patented by Ham (September 12, 1916) D: Lloyd Hamilton. Lloyd V. Hamilton, Bud Duncan, A. Edmondson, Ethel Teare. 1 reel. Unaware that Bud is pushing her stalled car, the daughter of an auto manufacturer believes that Ham has found a gasoline substitute. With a thousand dollars to be made, Ham agrees to officially test his product. During the test, Ham does well until his valiant pusher falls through a manhole. Having been exposed, Ham forgets his plans to collect the award and simply races to rescue Bud from the water main.

The Mud Cure (September 19, 1916) D: Lloyd Hamilton. Lloyd V. Hamilton, Bud Duncan, A. Edmondson, Ethel Teare. 1 reel. Ham takes Bud to the dentist. Busy flirting with Ham, Doc Pullem's daughter gives Bud with too much gas. Consequently, Bud dreams that he and Ham are attendants at a health resort, assisting guests in the mud baths.

Bumping the Bumps (September 26, 1916) D: Lloyd Hamilton. Lloyd V. Hamilton, Bud Duncan, Ethel Teare, A. Edmondson. 1 reel. Bud and Ethel become engaged while Ham goes off in search of some other fun. Ham soon meets up with a phrenologist, Professor Fakem. After throwing the professor down a well, Ham dons the professor's flowing robes and takes charge of his business. Bud, who must have his bumps approved for his fiancée's father, pays a visit to the phrenologist.

One Step Too Far (October 3, 1916) D: Lloyd Hamilton. Lloyd V. Hamilton, Bud Duncan, Ethel Teare. 1 reel. A police captain is inspired by Ham's sturdy build. Rather than imprison the tramp for his latest crime, the captain employs Ham as a cop. Saddened that his physique has failed to earn him a similar appointment, Bud joins forces with a clever thief named Adventurous Agnes. Officer Ham finds that it is easy and profitable to relieve collars of half their booty. When he catches Bud and Agnes, he takes the silverware that they have stolen and slips it underneath his coat. Later, as he receives a medal for bravery, the silver load falls to the floor.

The Love Magnet (October 10, 1916) D: Lloyd Hamilton. Lloyd V. Hamilton, Bud Duncan, Ethel Teare, A. Edmondson. 1 reel. [A print of this film is available at the Library of Congress. The film also appears on the "Lost Magic of Lloyd Hamilton" DVD collection.] Bud attracts several pretty females using Professor Bunkem's love magnet. Ham steals his own magnet, but he learns that this particular one only attracts old maids. Ham runs away from his admirers. Bud, who becomes overwhelmed by women, soon runs away, too. They meet up again as their numerous and varied pursuers merge into one big tidal wave of women. [The comedy, a reworking of *Ham and the Experiment*, contains a scene similar to the climax of Buster Keaton's *Seven Chances*, which was released a number of years later.]

A Sauerkraut Symphony (October 17, 1916) D: Lloyd Hamilton. Lloyd V. Hamilton, Bud Duncan, Ethel Teare, Henry Murdoch, A. Edmondson. 1 reel. [A print of this film is available at the Library of Congress. The film also appears on the "Lost Magic of Lloyd Hamilton" DVD collection.] Ham and Bud prepare sauerkraut at Spondolix's Sanitary Sauerkraut factory. The conditions in the factory are, in fact, far from sanitary. Ham is busy chopping up cabbage, bits of which go flying in several directions, while Bud is using a pitchfork to mix sauerkraut in a pair of barrels. At one point, Bud slings soppy sauerkraut from one barrel to the other, causing sauerkraut to splash onto walls and windows. Soon after, Ham climbs inside a barrel and stomps around to help mix the contents. Complicating the preparation of sauerkraut are Krazy Killsky, a bomb-toting anarchist who has vowed the destruction of all sauerkraut factories, and the sudden announcement of a union strike. The factory's safety conditions prove as inadequate as its sanitary conditions when Ham and Bud get into a brawl with one another. The brawl ends with Ham nailing Bud into a barrel and rolling him down a hill.

The Bogus Booking Agents (October 24, 1916) D: Lloyd Hamilton. Lloyd V. Hamilton, Bud Duncan, Ethel Teare, Henry Murdoch. 1 reel. Ham and Bud, aspiring actors arriving at a theatrical agency, find no one available and decide to settle in themselves. Answering the phone, Ham learns that "a girl carrying a small dog" is on her way to the office. The caller explains that the girl, whose name is Stella, is his daughter. He offers Ham $5,000 dollars to dissuade the girl from her acting ambitions. Ham feels he's getting the hang of being an agent when signs Melodramatic Mike to play Mr. Hamlet. Then he is visited by Serena Hatchetface. Ham, who sees Serena holding a dog under her arm, mistakes her for Stella and launches into a tirade against show business. He is unaware that, in the next office, Bud is signing the real Stella to play Mrs. Hamlet.

The Merry Motor Menders (October 31, 1916) D: Lloyd Hamilton. Lloyd V. Hamilton, Bud Duncan, Henry Murdoch, Ethel Teare. 1 reel. Is happiness a warm piston? To bring business into their wayside garage, Ham and Bud use everything from tacks to dynamite. Eventually, Count De Nutte calls on the mechanics to repair his broken-down auto. Trouble develops when Ham starts to flirt with the car's other passenger: De Nutte's bride.

A Desperate Duel (November 7, 1916) D: Lloyd Hamilton. Lloyd V. Hamilton, Bud Duncan, Ethel Teare. 1 reel. Ham duels with a count who has lured Flossie away from him.

The New Salesman (November 14, 1916) D: Lloyd Hamilton. Lloyd V. Hamilton, Bud Duncan, Ethel Teare, Henry Murdoch. 1 reel. Milkmen Ham and Bud put aside their modern methods of delivery to rescue a girl from an apparent masher. What they're actually doing is interrupting the arrest of a shoplifter. Lottie Lightfingers, the shoplifter, rides off with Ham and Bud in the milk wagon while the police officer, Detective Snoop, remains in hot pursuit. Ham and Bud see a "Salesmen Wanted" sign in a department store window and decide it is time for them to find a different profession. Ham is hired to sell shoes, and Bud to sell gloves. Snoop lurks around the store looking for Lottie, and Lottie lurks around looking to steal some merchandise.

Rival Fakers (November 21, 1916) D: Lloyd Hamilton. Lloyd V. Hamilton, Bud Duncan, Ethel Teare, Henry Murdoch. 1 reel. [The DVD collection "The Lost Magic of Lloyd Hamilton" has an unidentified Ham and Bud clip which possibly comes from this comedy.] Ham and Bud become involved with Miss Syrup and Mr. Sap, competitors in the sale of tonic. The valiant tramps eventually make their allegiance to Miss Syrup, who uses their contrasting sizes to illustrate the "before and after" effects of her tonic. Because of this ploy, Miss Syrup ultimately outdoes Mr. Sap.

Dudes for a Day (November 28, 1916) D: Lloyd Hamilton. Lloyd V. Hamilton, Bud Duncan, Henry Murdoch, A. Edmondson, Ethel Teare. 1 reel. (The working title of this comedy was *Fashion Plates*.) As part of their new job, Ham and Bud dress in evening attire and parade the streets with signs publicizing "Klucks Klassy Klothes." Once they walk out of the clothier's view, the two shed their signs and play swells.

Jailbirds (December 5, 1916) D: Lloyd Hamilton. Lloyd V. Hamilton, Bud Duncan, Ethel Teare, Henry Murdoch. 1 reel. Ham and Bud are pleased when Roy L. Flush, a gambler who took all their money, lands in jail. They set out to get revenge against Flush by taking jobs as jailers. Bud, the more vigilant of the guards, cleverly frustrates Flora Flush's attempt to free her father.

The Iceman and the Artist (December 12, 1916) D: Henry Murdoch. Lloyd V. Hamilton, Bud Duncan, Ethel Teare, Henry Murdoch. 1 reel. (On this production, H. Thorpe and R. Curbinson became two of the *Ham* company's supporting players.) Ham and Bud steal an iceman's wagon. While making their unappointed rounds, the pair sees a model robbing her employer's valuables. The pair directs a cop to the scene, but a doctor stops to examine the model and decides that she's a kleptomaniac. The model is forgiven and the cop departs alone. Ham, inspired by what he just saw, comes up with a scheme: He will have Bud rob a house and, if a cop appears, he will pose as a doctor and declare Bud to be a kleptomaniac.

Rival Romeos (January 9, 1917) Sc: S. A. Van Petten. D: Lloyd Hamilton. Lloyd V. Hamilton, Bud Duncan, Ethel Teare, Henry Murdoch. 1 reel. Dissatisfied with their "batching" arrangement, Ham and Bud decide that they need to get wives. Ham is impressed when a marriage broker shows him a picture of a pretty young lady. After Ham pays him a fee, the marriage broker instructs Ham to obtain a marriage license and wait for this woman in the park. Bud shows up at the marriage broker's office, too, and he is shown the same picture. He pays the marriage broker and rushes to the park to meet his bride. Ham and Bud are glad they will both finally have wives. They take turns maintaining an all-night vigil in the park. They are disappointed when no girls appear by morning and they return to the broker's office, where they discover the one girl with whom they both had been matched. Ham grabs the girl and rushes her to Reverend Hookem's cottage. When Ham pulls out a dog license, Bud is quick to take his place at the altar. The ceremony is interrupted by the broker, who proclaims himself to be the bride's lawful husband.

Cupid's Caddies (January 16, 1917) D: Lloyd Hamilton. Lloyd V. Hamilton, Bud Duncan, Henry Murdoch, Ethel Teare. 1 reel. Prince Poppycock offers a huge sum for an American wife of a specified weight. Ham and Bud find themselves a scale and get to work finding this woman. They eventually locate a fair lady who appears to be the appropriate weight. However, plans change when Ham decides to keep this beauty for himself. The prince, with the help of his bodyguards, grabs the woman and carries her away inside a trunk. Later, trying to fool Ham and Bud, the prince takes the woman's place in the trunk.

The Blundering Blacksmith (January 23, 1917) D: Lloyd Hamilton. Lloyd V. Hamilton, Bud Duncan, Ethel Teare, Henry Murdoch. 1 reel. [Prints of this film are available with Film Preservation Associates, the Museum of Modern Art, and La Cineteca del Friuli.] Ham is the blacksmith in a small town. During a church service, the village belle responds favorably to Ham's flirting. Hiram Hardheart says that, unless the belle marries him, he will foreclose on her father's mortgage. Ham frightens Hardheart away, but he realizes that he cannot stop the villain from coming back unless he pays the debt. He puts aside his hammering and challenges "One Punch" Murph for a $1000 purse. The belle, concealed in boy's clothing, sits in Ham's corner and urges her love to win. Ham bounces back from a poor showing in the first round. Then, in a sensational display, the amateur pugilist wins the match and the purse.

The Safety Pin Smugglers (January 30, 1917) D: Lloyd Hamilton. Lloyd V. Hamilton, Bud Duncan, Ethel Teare, Henry Murdoch. 1 reel. [A print of this film is available at the Museum of Modern Art.] After parting from Ham, Bud gets a job at an express office and has many visitors on his first day. Trixie, a smuggler, arrives at the office to conduct some business; a Secret Service agent Sylvester Shush shows up to apprehend Trixie; and Ham makes an appearance to see how his old partner is doing.

Ghost Hounds (February 6, 1917) D: Lloyd Hamilton. Lloyd V. Hamilton, Bud Duncan, Henry Murdoch, Ethel Teare. 1 reel. Silas Shakaleg, Mushroom Manor's fearless sheriff, arrests Ham and Bud for stealing eggs. When a judge declares the pair guilty, a farmer's daughter steps forward and begs for clemency. Rather than throw the pair in jail, the judge sentences them to spend the night in the town's haunted house. The farmer's daughter accompanies the tramps to the haunted house, where threatening ghosts and dancing skeletons create a frightening spectacle. Before the end of their stay, the trio learns that gangsters have been using the house as a rendezvous point and have been manufacturing the apparitions to scare the locals away. [Plump & Runt found themselves in a very similar situation in a 1916 Vim comedy, *The Brave Ones*.]

The Model Janitor (February 13, 1917) D: Lloyd Hamilton. Lloyd V. Hamilton, Bud Duncan, Henry Murdoch, Ethel Teare. 1 reel. [A print of this film is available at the Library of Congress. The film also appears on the "Lost Magic of Lloyd Hamilton" DVD collection.] Ham and Bud, the janitors in an art studio, have the responsibility of sweeping the shavings of renowned sculptor Henry Clay Debris. Debris becomes enraged when he finds his daughter being enticed by his male model. Debris fires the model and decides to use Ham instead. Ham must be persuaded to desert a game of "hide and seek" before he can assume the new job.

A Flyer in Flapjacks (February 20, 1917) D: Lloyd Hamilton. Lloyd V. Hamilton, Bud Duncan, Henry Murdoch, Ethel Teare. 1 reel. [A print of this film is available at the Library of Congress. The film also appears on the "Lost Magic of Lloyd Hamilton" DVD collection.] The pursuit of a relentless patrol cop prevents Ham and Bud from relaxing on a park bench. The tramps manage to elude the lawman by rushing into a pancake house. When confronted by the owner, Pancratius Pancake, they stuff the man into a flour barrel and cover the barrel with a heavy table. After hastily donning aprons, the pair take orders from the eatery's rowdy patrons. Soon, they engage the group in a flapjack-hurling contest.

Efficiency Experts (February 27, 1917) D: Alfred Santell. Lloyd V. Hamilton, Bud Duncan, Henry Murdoch, Ethel Teare. 1 reel. [Prints of this film are available with Film Preservation Associates, Det Danske Filmmuseum, and La Cineteca del Friuli.] With Ham and Bud napping in the driver's seat, a steam-propelled lawnmower puffs about on an unregulated course. Eventually, the contraption shaves the face of Bessie's father. At the same time, an electrician attends to broken wires in the basement. The electrician discovers a note that indicates that jewels are buried underneath a chestnut tree. Rushing to find the precious stones, he carelessly leaves the wires sparking against a water pipe. This reckless act proves dangerous: as Bessie tries to turn the hose on the slumbering lawn-cutters, she is shocked into unconsciousness. Believing that their automower has killed her, Ham and Bud bury Bessie's body beneath the chestnut tree. The treasure-hunting electrician soon unearths Bessie, who reawakens and frightens everyone. While fleeing from this risen dead, Bud accidentally sends a strong electrical current through both himself and Bessie's home.

Bull or Bullets? (March 6, 1917) D: Alfred Santell. Lloyd V. Hamilton, Bud Duncan, Ethel Teare, Henry Murdoch. 1 reel. [A print of this film is available at the Library of Congress.] A band of wild cowpunchers chase Ham and Bud out of the United States. After robbing two bullfighters of their apparel, the duo starts across the desert and finally arrives at a Mexican settlement, where they are mistaken for as renowned bullfighters and entertained by dark-eyed senoritas. Ham, Bud and a great horned bull are eventually set loose inside the local arena. The trio briefly turns the manly spectacle into a merry tango demonstration, but Ham defeats the beast in the end. As Ham readies the death thrust, the bull speaks up to plead for mercy. This phenomenon compels Ham to drop his sword. The arrival of the real bullfighters puts an end to Ham and Bud's charade.

The Bogus Bride (March 13, 1917) D: Alfred Santell. Lloyd V. Hamilton, Bud Duncan, Henry Murdoch. 1 reel. The prospect of wedding gifts makes marriage appear to be a profitable enterprise. It is even better when Pottsville offers a prize for the next local couple to take the matrimonial plunge. Under the circumstances, Ham cannot resist disguising Bud as his young bride.

A Misfit Millionaire (March 20, 1917) D: Alfred Santell. Lloyd V. Hamilton, Bud Duncan, Henry Murdoch. 1 reel. Ham and Bud go their separate ways. Years later, Bud arrives in town on the brake rods of a freight car and sees Ham, dressed finely, leaving a palatial office building and getting into a limousine. Bud discovers that Ham is in charge of the Swell Dishwasher Company and is engaged to the daughter of the local district attorney. Ham keeps Bud from revealing his past by hiring his old friend to be an office boy. Bud soon learns that a Swell dishwasher is simply a sponge that comes to life when it absorbs water. When one of the sponges goes amok in the district attorney's kitchen, Ham must pull out a gun and pump several bullets into the creature. Later, Bud divulges that Ham's recent mining promotion is fraudulent. The police, led by the district attorney, raid the Swell offices. Ham escapes through a secret panel. He opens a suitcase he took along, expecting to find his valuables, but he instead he finds bricks that Bud put in there. At this point, Ham decides, reluctantly, to return to the tramp life.

The Deadly Donut (March 27, 1917) D: Alfred Santell. Lloyd V. Hamilton, Bud Duncan, Henry Murdoch. 1 reel. [A print of this film is available at the Library of Congress. The film also appears on the "Lost Magic of Lloyd Hamilton" DVD collection.] Ham and Bud are hired to care for a bakery while its owner, Mr. Doe, solicits orders for his new "holeless" donut. A villainous rival, the Donut King, kidnaps Doe to steal his recipe. Ham and Bud use explosive biscuits to rescue Doe from a vault.

Doubles and Troubles (April 3, 1917) Sc: Alfred Santell. D: Alfred Santell. Lloyd V. Hamilton, Bud Duncan, Henry Murdoch. 1 reel. Ham and Bud are bouncers at Riley's barroom. After singing for a group of patrons, the pair is invited to attend a society ball. The cabaret queen becomes jealous when a fair member of the ball pays special attention to Bud. To prevent an affair, the cabaret queen has thieves impersonate the bouncers and steal jewels from the ball's guests. Ham and Bud spot their doubles fleeing and succeed in overtaking them.

Hard Times in Hardscrapple (April 17, 1917) D: Alfred Santell. Lloyd V. Hamilton, Bud Duncan, Henry Murdoch. 1 reel. [A print of this film is available at the Museum of Modern Art.] Starvation plagues the frontier town of Hardscrapple. Ham and Bud have several adventures once they arrive in town. At first, the pair has a run-in with some badmen. Next, they open a restaurant with fraudulent gold nuggets. Finally, while visiting the local gambling house, they rob a bankroll from a visiting millionaire. The reprobates soon discover that money is useless to the hungry villagers. They win the villagers' favor by stealing a store of pies from a badman. Though tied to his bed, the badman sprints over mountains and arroyos to reach the pie thieves.

Bandit, Beware (April 24, 1917) D: Alfred Santell. Lloyd V. Hamilton, Bud Duncan, Henry Murdoch. 1 reel. Ham and Bud rescue a wealthy motorist from a robber. Bud stays with the injured victim while Ham hastens to the man's house. On his arrival, Ham makes a hit with the rich man's daughter. While the couple chats, a vacuum cleaner inhales jewelry that the girl has been polishing. The search for the valuables is interrupted by the reappearance of the highway bandit.

A Menagerie Mix-up (May 15, 1917) D: Lloyd Hamilton. Lloyd V. Hamilton, Bud Duncan, John Steppling, Henry Murdoch (I.C. Double), Edythe Sterling. 1 reel. (The short was directed by Hamilton because Santell had fallen ill. The working title was *Bear Facts*.) Ham assists a girl whom he has knocked over while chasing after Bud. The grateful girl invites Ham to a masquerade ball. Ham prepares for the ball by squeezing himself into a bear outfit. In the meantime, Bud finds a job with the Ringworm Circus. In publicizing the circus, he must pose as an escaped bear. In the end, villagers chase the pair of phony bears into a cave. Upon being smoked out of the cave, Ham and Bud dive off a cliff and fall into the gully below.

The Hobo Raid (June 7, 1917) D: Alfred Santell. Lloyd V. Hamilton, Bud Duncan, Henry Murdoch, John Steppling, Edythe Sterling. 1 reel. Armed with a pitchfork, Farmer Cornstalk chases Ham and Bud off his property. Hungry Henry, who has been designated to obtain food for his fellow hobos, is the farm's next visitor. The tough farmer severely pummels Henry and runs him off. Incited by Cornstalk's behavior, the hobo band raids the farmer's home and takes him and his daughter captive. Ham and Bud arrive at the hobo's camp and, included in the division of the band's spoils, are given a diamond ring. Ham recognizes the ring as a possession of Cornstalk's kind daughter. The pair rushes forth to rescue the farmer and his daughter. They take apart the farmer's brick chimney and bombard the hobos with brick missiles. (The plot is similar to the plot of Chaplin's 1915 comedy *The Tramp*.)

A Day Out of Jail (June 28, 1917) D: Alfred Santell (?). Lloyd V. Hamilton, Bud Duncan, Henry Murdoch, John Steppling, Juanita Sponsler. 1 reel. [A print of this film is available at the National Film Archive in London.] Ham, an escaped convict, watches a cop take bananas from a fruit stand without paying for them. In considering this benefit, Ham decides to become a policeman. Bud tags along on the new officer's beat. The pair eventually runs into an old nemesis, a jail guard.

Seaside Romeos (July 5, 1917) D: Alfred Santell (?). Lloyd V. Hamilton, Bud Duncan, John Steppling, Juanita Sponsler, Henry Murdoch. 1 reel. Ham dreams that, in search of treasure, he and Bud arrive on the Island of Silken Seaweed. Soon after their arrival, the pair manages to enrage Professor Lightfoot by interrupting the female students of his aesthetic dancing class. Ham eludes a homely member of the group by hiding his head in the sand. Later, the treasure hunters uncover the loot of a tough robber.

Politics in Pumpkin Center (October 5, 1917) D: Alfred Santell. Lloyd V. Hamilton, Bud Duncan, Juanita Sponsler, John Steppling, Henry Murdoch. 1 reel. [A print of this film is available at the Library of Congress.] In the rural town of Pumpkin Center, Ham is elected to three positions: mayor, judge and fire chief. As his first decree, Ham enacts prohibition in the town. After appearing intoxicated in public, Weary Willie is forced to lead the villagers to his alcohol source. Thanks to Willie's cooperation, cold bottles of the illegal substance are uncovered in

Ham's basement. Ham is so desperate after being fired that he sets his own home on fire to collect on an insurance policy.

The Boot and the Loot (October 12, 1917) Sc: Phil Lang, Frank Howard Clark and Alfred Santell. D: Alfred Santell. Lloyd V. Hamilton, Bud Duncan, Edythe Sterling, John Steppling, Henry Murdoch. 1 reel. [A print of this film is available at the Library of Congress.] While in a uniform "borrowed" from a streetcar conductor, Ham trades a city trolley for a profitable bootblack stand. However, Ham proves to be an incompetent bootblack. One problem is that the sight of a lady's ankles embarrasses him. Later, Ham and Bud learn of a notorious killer whose rubber heels leave a distinctive mark. The bootblacks keep their eyes peeled until they find just the right heel. Their attempt to apprehend the killer leads to an auto chase. The action culminates with several jitneys and the streetcar plunging into a sewer.

A Whirlwind of Whiskers (October 19, 1917) Sc: Phil Lang, Frank Howard Clark and Alfred Santell. D: Alfred Santell. Lloyd V. Hamilton, Bud Duncan, Marin Sais, R. E. Bradbury, Edward Clisbee, Jack Hoxie. 1 reel. [A print of this film is available at the Library of Congress. The film also appears on the "Lost Magic of Lloyd Hamilton" DVD collection.] To escape a cop, Ham and Bud climb up a fire escape and drop into a vacant office, which belongs to the Taik A. Look Detective Agency. The pair is present when an urgent message arrives that the police are on a manhunt for a counterfeiter distinguishable by his long beard. Ham, who thinks he has the investigation skills to track down the counterfeiter, trails clues to a barbershop. Ham, intending to go undercover, pulls a shaggy wig out of his pocket and slaps it on his head before proceeding into the establishment. The wig, unfitted and unstyled, looks like sod sitting on top of his head. Trouble inevitably ensues in a barber shop. The highlight of the comedy is a vertical chase scene—police chasing Ham and Bud down a hill, up a fire escape, down a long flight of stairs, and up a different fire escape. The police, while chasing the sleuthing tramps across several rooftops, end up falling through a skylight and dropping straight down into the room below. Ham and Bud, happy to have been able to escape arrest, hold onto each other as they skip off into the sunset.

The Onion Magnate's Revenge (October 26, 1917) D: Alfred Santell (?). Lloyd V. Hamilton, Bud Duncan. 1 reel. Ham and Bud, "fresh ice farmers," rob a millionaire's source of wealth: a massive stockpile of onions.

The Bathtub Bandit (November 2, 1917) D: Alfred Santell (?). Lloyd V. Hamilton, Bud Duncan, Ethel Teare. 1 reel. [A print of this film is available with the Film Preservation Associates. The film also appears on the "Lost Magic of Lloyd Hamilton" DVD collection.] A thief notorious for purloining bathtubs from wealthy homes employs Ham and Bud to help him with his latest caper.

Roaring Lions and Wedding Bells (November 11, 1917) Fox Sunshine Comedy. Supervised by Henry Lehrman. Sc: Henry Lehrman and Lloyd Hamilton. D: William Campbell and Jack White. Lloyd Hamilton, Mildred Lee, Jimmie Adams (Frank), Charlie Dorety, Jess Welden, Jack H. Richardson, Tom Wilson, Mario Bianchi, two lions, fifty-seven ostriches. 2 reels. "Funny, oh my!"—*Motion Picture Daily*. "Quite worthwhile in its capacity of farce comedy."—*Moving Picture World*. "One of the best laughmakers seen for many a day.... Lloyd Hamilton does splendidly and is responsible for the majority of the laughs."—*Exhibitors Trade Review*. Ham is a farmer who breeds ostriches. Frank is his rival for Mildred's affections. Mildred's father devises a contest: the suitor who retrieves a watch placed inside a lion's cage will receive Mildred as his bride. Goulash, a lion trainer, overhears the plan and chooses to recover the timepiece for himself. Goulash accomplishes the deed, but then loses the watch to Ham. Ham proudly presents the watch for his prize. A wedding is promptly arranged. As revenge, the trainer sends a pair of lions as a gift to the nuptial couple. At the same time, Frank seeks to disrupt the wedding by disguising himself as a lion. Upon the appearance of the lions, the wedding party briskly disintegrates. The guests prove more flightful than Ham's ostriches. In the end, a maniacal police force arrives on the scene to recapture the big cats.

Hungry Lions in a Hospital (February 3, 1918) Fox Sunshine Comedy. Supervised by Henry Lehrman. Sc: Henry Lehrman. D: Jack White. Lloyd Hamilton (Ham Bohn), Mildred Lee (Vera Kosher), Jimmie Adams (a patient), Heinie Conklin (a cop), Tom Wilson, Jess Weldon, Charles Doherty. 2 reels. [Only the second reel is known to exist. The reel was exhibited at Slapsticon 2008.] Ham finds himself under dubious care at the local hospital. The surgeons, who stroll the halls with long, sharp knives, seem eager to cut into wary patients. The hospital administrators maintain close and friendly relations with the local morticians, M. Balmer and Cough Finn, who show up regularly to haul off bodies. The mood lightens briefly when bathing beauties show up at the hospital pool. Elsewhere, a pair of lions gets loose in the hospital. Ham traps one lion in a barrel, but the lion easily manages to escape as the barrel has no bottom. Patients, determined to keep away from the lions, erect a barrier using box springs and mattresses. The lions attack two hospital inspectors. (The inspectors are Weldon and Doherty, who have been dressed and made up to look like Mutt and Jeff.) The police arrive to round up the lions, but one of the big cats gets loose in the squad car while the car is riding across a high bridge. Rather than being mauled to death, the police leap out of the car and plummet into the river below. The unmanned car crashes head-on into an office building.

A Waiter's Wasted Life (April 7, 1918) Fox Sunshine Comedy. Supervised by Henry Lehrman. D: Jack White. Lloyd Hamilton, Eileen Percy, Jimmie Adams, Anita Burrell, Tom Kennedy. 2 reels. (Reissued on August 30, 1920.) "One of the best of the Fox-Lehrman series so far.... It is one of the best comic pictures that I have seen in a long time."—*Moving Picture World*. The comedy revolves around the adventures of the inmates of both a prison and a disorderly neighboring cafe. The latter operation employs Ham as a waiter. The plot thickens when the governor's friends are invited to a prisoner's execution. In anticipation of a grand party, the governor's guests are ecstatic as they get off the train. However, the prisoner escapes and causes problems for Ham.

A Tight Squeeze (July 28, 1918) Fox Sunshine Comedy. Supervised by Henry Lehrman. D: Jack White and William H. Watson. Lloyd Hamilton, Ethel Teare, Jimmie Adams, Charles Dorety, Tom Kennedy, Dave Morris, Frank Coleman, Fritz Schade, Frank Hays, Hazel Dean, Mae Eccleston. 2 reels. [A print of this film is available at the Ceskoslovensky Filmovy Ustav/ Filmovy Archiv in Prague.] A farm boy contends with several violent animals.

Roaring Lions on the Midnight Express (September 22, 1918) Fox Sunshine Comedy. Supervised by Henry Lehrman. D: Henry Lehrman. Hugh Fay, Sylvia Day, Billie Ritchie, Jimmie Adams, Monty Banks, Dave Morris, Frank Coleman, Slim Summerville, Jack Cooper, Mae Eccleston, Charles Dudley. 2 reels. [A print of this film is available at the Ceskoslovensky Filmovy Ustav/ Filmovy Archiv in Prague.] Lions get loose on a train. Amidst the subsequent commotion, one of the large cats chases several passengers across the top of the moving cars. [Lloyd wore blackface for a brief appearance as a Negro chef.]

Mongrels (November 17, 1918) Fox Sunshine Comedy. Supervised by Henry Lehrman. D: Jack White. Lloyd Hamilton, Gertrude Selby, Jimmie Adams, Charles Dorety, Dave Morris, a fox terrier. 2 reels. The opening sequence features three dogs representing the Allied forces. The dogs include a bulldog (England), a poodle (France) and a terrier (the United States). Dastardly Germany, which is signified by a dachshund in a Hun helmet, gains the upper hand by spraying poison gas from his mouth. Despite this assault, the alley pooches ultimately thwart their foe. Later, Lloyd battles Hun spies in a munitions factory. Jimmie Adams, the leader of the spies, ends up hanging from a flagpole.

The Son of a Hun (December 29, 1918) Fox Sunshine Comedy. Supervised by Henry Lehrman. D: Jack White. Lloyd Hamilton, Gertrude Selby, Dave Morris, Charles Dorety, Jimmie Adams. 2 reels. "Many laughable stunts are performed."—*Moving Picture World*. On his wedding day, Lloyd is forced to contend with German spies. The ceremony ultimately gives way to a farcical battle. At the height of the conflict, a tank demolishes the house that holds the wedding party.

His Musical Sneeze (February 23, 1919) Fox Sunshine Comedy. Supervised by Henry Lehrman. D: Jack White. Lloyd Hamilton (Woodrow Butts), Virginia Rappe, Glen Cavender, Vera Steadman, Frank Coleman, Jimmie Adams, Charlie Dorety, a musical skunk. 2 reels. [A copy of this comedy was discovered in the Film Archive of The Danish Film Institute in the summer of 2008.] Lodgers at a mountain inn include an overzealous hunting party willing to use dynamite and heavy artillery to slay rabbits. Confusion arises later, during a fox hunt, when hunter Woodrow Butts expels a musical sneeze that is mistaken for a fox hunting horn. Eventually, the fox hunt entangles one of the inept sportsmen with a polecat. Woodrow returns from a fox hunt in a horse-drawn coach. He reaches into a sack thinking he has captured a fox, but he pulls out a skunk instead. The horse immediately faints from the skunk's odor. [This final gag was reworked by Jack White in 1936 for the Three Stooges comedy *Ants in the Pantry*.]

Unfinished Sunshine Comedy: Title Unknown (produced in December, 1918) Fox Sunshine Comedy. Supervised by Henry Lehrman. D: Jack White. Lloyd Hamilton, Ethel Teare, Jack Cooper, Hugh Fay, Billie Ritchie, Dave Morris. Before embarking towards foreign shores, a pirate sea captain chooses to add Ham's girlfriend to his contraband cargo. This cargo already includes (what else?) several lions. As the ship is preparing to leave port, Ham sneaks aboard. In his rescue effort, he sinks the craft. The comedy closes on crew members vigorously swimming to put distance between themselves and the liberated lions. [Hamilton remade this comedy under the title *April Fool*.]

A Twilight Baby (December 22, 1919) A Henry Lehrman Comedy. Produced by Henry Lehrman. Released through First National Corp. D: Jack White. Lloyd Hamilton, Virginia Rappe, Billie Ritchie, Harry McCoy, Harry Todd, Lige Conley, Charles Dorety. Three-reel and four-reel versions were released. [A print of this film is available at the Museum of Modern Art.] While caring for her new litter of puppies, a farm dog notices an abandoned baby. The dog quickly drags the helpless infant to a cow and stands guard while he suckles. The babe grows to be an awkward, cowardly youth whom the farm animals must constantly rescue from trouble. The animals are unable to rescue the young man when, for violation of moonshine laws, he is sent to jail. Later in the story, the lad learns that he is the offspring of nobility.

Duck Inn (August, 1920) A Mermaid Comedy ("Mermaids for Merriment"). Produced by Astra Film. Distributed by Educational Pictures. Supervised by Jack White. D: Gilbert Pratt. Lloyd Hamilton, Marvel Rea, Monte Banks. 2 reels. "One of the best comedies of the season."—*Moving Picture World*. "High class nonsense-comedy, ranking with the best."—*Film Daily*. Lloyd sets out to meet his sweetheart, Marvel. To reach his destination, he copes with a fickled rainstorm and drives through a windy desert. Lloyd finally greets his girlfriend, but she has bad news. She wants to marry Lloyd but her father wants her to marry rival suitor Monte. Marvel explains that her father has chosen to settle their differences with a contest — the one who is able to slay the elusive Whiffinpoof duck will win Marvel's hand in marriage. Accepting the challenge, Lloyd places a rifle over his shoulder and commences in search of the Whiffinpoof. His hunt, however, turns into a fiasco. At the outset, he experiences difficulty with his pointer dog and decoy duck. Monte, who presents a dead duck that he secretly obtained at a market, is declared the winner. But Marvel balks at the results of the contest and throws herself into Lloyd's arms. Before the fadeout, Lloyd must contend with the intrusive rainstorm for one last time.

Occasionally Yours (September 29, 1920) Lew Cody Films Corporation/L.J. Gasnier Productions. Sc: H. Tipten Steck. St: Elmer Forst. Ph: Joseph A. DuBray. D: James Horne. Lew Cody, Betty Blythe, J. Barney Sherry, Elinor Fair, Yvonne Gardelle, Cleo Ridgley, Lloyd Hamilton. 5 reels. [The film is also known as *The Mischief Man.*] Lovers match and mismatch in this romantic comedy involving a practical joke.

Dynamite (October, 1920) A Mermaid Comedy. Produced by Astra Film. Distributed by Educational Pictures. Supervised by Jack White. D: Gilbert Pratt. Lloyd Hamilton, Iva Brown. 2 reels. [This film reuses story material from *A Sauerkraut Symphony* and *Mongrels*. A print is available in the David Wyatt Collection.] On the apparent death of his father, Ben Zeen (Hamilton) becomes the foreman of his father's power plant. The plant, a normally dangerous place, is made even more perilous by an anarchist and a delegation of union agitators. Ben learns that the anarchist is secretly holding his sister and father captive. In the climactic scene, an explosion tears off all Ben's clothes except for his underwear and darkens his skin so that he looks like something out of a minstrel show.

The Simp (December, 1920) A Mermaid Comedy. Produced by Astra Film. Distributed by Educational Pictures. Supervised by Jack White. D: Owen Evans and Arthur Roche. Lloyd Hamilton, Marvel Rea, Otto Fries, Jess Weldon. 2 reels. [Prints of this film are available with the National Film Archive in London and the David Wyatt Collection.] "Ingenuity and invention.... discretion of director who never outstretches the antics. Much high mark that more of his contemporaries should follow."— Motion Picture News. When Lloyd arrives home late, he tries not to wake his parents. To muffle his footsteps, he ties pillows to his feet. However, he makes noise in an encounter with the family cat. Roused from sleep, Lloyd's father races down the stairs. Lloyd hides behind a chair and meows. His father, who sees his reflection in a mirror, kicks him in the backside. After his father exiles him from home, Lloyd spends the night on a park bench. He is awakened the next morning when a sprinkler comes on underneath the bench. Nearby, a girl walks her small dog by a pond. When a fish grabs the dog and drags him across the pond, Lloyd comes to the rescue. He squeezes the dog's tail to wring him out and he is startled when the tail spurts a prolonged stream of water. Lloyd learns that the girl is a mission worker. She invites him to attend a religious revival at the mission.

April Fool (February, 1921) A Mermaid Comedy. Produced by Astra Film. Distributed by Educational Pictures. Supervised by Jack White. D: Charley Chase (under the name Charles Parrott). Lloyd Hamilton, Beatrice Monson, Otto Fries. 2 reels. [A print of this comedy is available with the David Wyatt Collection. A fragment of the film is included on the "Lost Magic of Lloyd Hamilton" DVD Collection.] While dumping freight into the hold of a steamer, a derrick inadvertently shanghais Lloyd. At sea, Lloyd becomes a cabin boy. The ship's intimidating first mate forces the new seaman to perform heavy chores. Though nauseated by the tossing of the vessel, Lloyd tries to properly fill the role of sailor. In his eagerness, he consistently endeavors to salute his superiors at the appropriate times. He also befriends Beatrice, who is a missionary's daughter, and intervenes when the winsome girl resists the captain's rough advances. Lloyd recounts the ship's voyage in a letter to his mother. He writes the letter so intensely that he is unaware that a leak is causing sea water to slowly fill his cabin. During a mutiny, the first mate attacks Lloyd. Lloyd barricades himself inside the ship's magazine, where he inadvertently ignites gunpowder and causes the vessel to explode. Lloyd isn't immediately aware of the explosion or its effects as he is adrift on the wreckage of the storeroom, still pressed against the standing door to keep out the first mate. He refuses to open the door when he hears a knock, but he soon learns that it is Beatrice on the other side. She assures him that no one else is on this wreckage except for her, Lloyd and a parrot.

Moonshine (April, 1921) A Mermaid Comedy. Produced by Astra Film. Distributed by Educational Pictures. Supervised by Jack White. D: Charley Chase (under the name Charles Parrott). Lloyd Hamilton, Beatrice Monson, Otto Fries. 2 reels. [A print of this comedy is available with the David Wyatt Collection.] "First rate."— Film Daily. Lloyd is born while revenue agents besiege his parents' mountain home. Upon coming of age, he must join his family in their moonshine trade. His mother worries about her son, but he cleverly combats revenue men and an unkempt rival for Beatrice's affections. In the end, the law enforcers accomplish a major rout of the moonshiners.

The Greenhorn (June, 1921) A Mermaid Comedy. Produced by Astra Film. Distributed by Educational Pictures. Supervised by Jack White. Sc: Chuck Reisner. D: Chuck Reisner. Lloyd Hamilton, Kathleen Myers. 2 reels. "One of— if not *the*—best."— Film Daily. "Generally good fun ... somewhat out of the ordinary."— Moving Picture World. "A delight to witness."— Motion Picture News. Lloyd travels to America to collect his father's fortune. An Ellis Island doctor, having stolen a cablegram, is aware that a large sum of money will become available if Lloyd dies. The doctor schemes to become the immigrant's beneficiary and cause his demise. Lloyd, however, proves to be smarter than the doctor thought. After acquiring the aid of a nurse, he thwarts the doctor's various devices. At one point, he escapes detection by disguising in drag. Later, he avoids station officials by smearing on blackface. Much of the film is a long, relentless chase, during which Lloyd runs into a variety of complications. But Lloyd remains unstoppable, even when he falls through a trap door and tumbles down a chute.

A Game Lady (June 28, 1921) A Henry Lehrman Comedy. Produced by Henry Lehrman. Released through First National Corp. D: Noel Smith. Lloyd Hamilton, Phil Dunham. 2 reels. While in engaging in their favorite pastime, a group of frenetic duck hunters create great commotion. The activity culminates in a merry chase involving autos and wild geese.

The Misfit Pair (August 15, 1921) A Universal Star Comedy. 1 reel. Lloyd, a grocery store clerk, is wrapping up a fish when the fish escapes and drops down his pants. Later, Lloyd witnesses a worker accidentally kick away a ladder while climbing down from a roof. Lloyd grabs the ladder to rescue the man, who is dangling helplessly from the building, but he then hears the cries of a man who has fallen into a lake and is drowning. Lloyd dashes back and forth between the two men in a desperate effort to rescue both of them. [This comedy was reviewed in a trade magazine without cast credits. Researcher Karel Caslavsky has associated the film with Hamilton as the lead character is named Lloyd and the character gets a fish down his pants as Hamilton did in other films. This is a reasonable assumption. In fact, the climax of the film features just the type of desperately unmanageable situation that plagued Lloyd's awkward hero. Hamilton pal Charles Reisner wrote, directed and acted in at least nine short comedies for Universal in 1920 and 1921. It is possible that Reisner arranged for Hamilton to guest star in this comedy. Reisner may have also played the grocery clerk's romantic rival, whose name in the film is Charles.]

Robinson Crusoe Ltd. (August, 1921) A Mermaid Comedy. Produced by Hamilton-White Comedies, Inc. Distributed by Educational Pictures. Supervised by Jack White. Sc: Archie Mayo. D: Jack White. Lloyd Hamilton, Irene Dalton. 2 reels. "The comedian indulges in every trick on the calendar."—Motion Picture News. On board an ocean liner, Lloyd enjoys the atmosphere until he is overcome by seasickness. While in this disoriented state, Lloyd mistakes a floating mine for a whale. He hurls a harpoon at the mine, causing an explosion that rips a hole in the side of the liner. The passengers and crew scramble to abandon ship. Lloyd opens the lifebelt manual. He is so methodical about following the instructions correctly that he is still reading the book after the liner has sunk and he is standing underwater. When he reappears, Lloyd is calmly smoking a cigarette and sitting in a tin washtub being driven ashore by a poodle. Lloyd joins Irene and her guardian on Crusoe's tropical isle. In a crap game with a cannibal chieftain, he wins sovereignty over the island community. He pompously leads the chief to the chopping block that was already prepared for his own head. The chief, though, escapes being executed and regains control of his tribe. Lloyd discovers exploding eggs, the product of an ostrich who consumed blasting powder. Riding the ostrich and tossing the volatile spheres, Lloyd rescues his companions. As the group escapes atop the ostrich, the sequence dissolves into a more placid and mundane scene: a cozy living room where Lloyd, as a young boy, sits in his father's lap and listens to his father tell him the end of the far-fetched tale. [The sequence where Lloyd harpooned a mine, sunk his ship and was driven to shore by a poodle was reworked by Jack White in the Three Stooges' *Back from the Front*. Another Stooges comedy, *Some More of Samoa*, recalled Lloyd's island adventure when Curly, emerging from a native hut wearing a top hat, leopard sarong and seashell necklace, explains to his partners that he has won his flamboyant new outfit by engaging the native king in a game of craps.]

The Vagrant (October, 1921) A Mermaid Comedy. Produced by Hamilton-White Comedies, Inc. Distributed by Educational Pictures. Supervised by Jack White. Sc: Archie Mayo. D: Hugh Fay and Jack White. Lloyd Hamilton, Irene Dalton, Tom Wilson, Lige Conley, Hugh Fay, Frank Coleman. 2 reels. [Prints of this film are available at the Museum of Modern Art and Prague's Ceskoslovensky Filmovy Ustav/ Filmovy Archiv.] "Earnest attempt to bring in new hokum ... practically one long chase, with all variations known to comedymakers thrown in."—Motion Picture News. A hard-hearted cop forces Lloyd to stop loafing with his fellow tramps. The cop stands by while the youth secures a position at a bootblack stand. When the cop becomes his first customer, Lloyd securely ties the lawman's feet to the stilts of the booth. Before the cop can untangle himself, Lloyd makes a quick getaway. Lloyd encounters Irene, whose demonstrations of corn salve is failing to attract buyers. To channel business to Irene, Lloyd situates himself at a basement window and hammers the feet of passersby. The cop returns and chases the young tramp into Chinatown. Lloyd goes on the roof of a building, unaware that police are raiding an opium den on the floor below. The cop corners Lloyd on the roof just as the opium den attendants discard opium into the fireplace. Lloyd and the cop, who are both near the chimney, become veiled in one big opium cloud and become light-headed. Lloyd, looking down from the rooftop, sees the street as a sparkling pool filled with alluring bathing beauties. He eagerly dives off the rooftop, but the pool suddenly disappears and he slams into the asphalt.

The Advisor (December) A Mermaid Comedy. Produced by Hamilton-White Comedies, Inc. Distributed by Educational Pictures. Supervised by Jack White. D: Hugh Fay. Lloyd Hamilton, Irene Dalton. 2 reels. Lloyd is initially seen in a sober conference with President Wilson and William Jennings Bryan, but a dissolve reveals the scene to have only been a dream. Lloyd, an inept lawyer, loses his first case. When his client escapes from prison, all he can think about is wreaking vengeance on Lloyd. Any resemblance to *Cape Fear* is merely coincidental.

Rolling Stones (January, 1922) A Mermaid Comedy. Produced by Hamilton-White Comedies, Inc. Distributed by Educational Pictures. Supervised by Jack White. Sc: Archie Mayo. D: Hugh Fay. Lloyd Hamilton, Robert DeVilbiss, Irene Dalton, Jack Lloyd, Otto Fries, Juanita Archer. 2 reels. [The working title of this comedy was *Distress*.] Lloyd and his kid brother, Bobby, are destitute orphans. At the start of the day, they duck the usual army of bill collectors. Later, they see Irene working in a men's hat shop. When they learn that Irene works on commission, they decide to do something to increase her sales. Perched atop an awning, Bobby knocks the hats of male passersby into the path of Lloyd's borrowed steamroller. Since their efforts make Bobby hungry, Lloyd must scheme to get food. He uses a belt to suspend his sibling from his waist, then dons a spacious overcoat to conceal the boy. Lloyd then enters a cafeteria and pretends to eye the fare, giving Bobby the opportunity to reach out and grab dishes. The boy eventually drops plates, which brings his big brother to the manager's attention.

The Rainmaker (March 12, 1922) A Mermaid Comedy. Produced by Hamilton-White Comedies, Inc. Distributed by Educational Pictures. Supervised by Jack White. D: Hugh Fay. Lloyd Hamilton, Irene Dalton. 2 reels. Lloyd boards a westbound train and settles in a Pullman car. When a rainmaker is mistakenly left at a side-station, Lloyd appropriates the professor's high hat and assumes his identity. In this disguise, the lad is welcomed at a drought-stricken town. The town is so parched that it is shown (via slow motion) to be moving at a snail's pace. The villagers, who expect their first downpour in years, are wearing bathing suits when they attend Lloyd's rain ceremony. But Lloyd incorrectly launches the rainmaker's skyrockets and causes the town to be buried in snow.

Poor Boy (June 18, 1922) A Mermaid Comedy. Produced by Hamilton-White Comedies, Inc. Distributed by Educational Pictures. Supervised by Jack White. Sc: Archie Mayo. D: Hugh Fay. Lloyd Hamilton, Irene Dalton. 2 reels. A tramp, accompanied by his dog, travels to town by stowing away on a freight train. A kindhearted cop who catches the tramp stealing a ride is hesitant to arrest him, instead persuading the tramp to work. The tramp visits the local mission, where he makes himself useful by singing in the choir and passing the collection plate. The young man, who has squeezed himself into a stiff suit for church service, finds himself struggling with a choking collar. Later, he plays a violin in accompaniment of the choir. He is so preoccupied with playing that he doesn't notice that a bird has landed on his bow until he pulls the bow under his nose. In the end, he kneels in prayer on the carpet that runs down the center aisle. A mischievous boy ties the end of the carpet to a horse-drawn carriage and whips the horse to get it going. Still kneeling, the tramp is dragged through the streets and eventually passes an open fire hydrant, which washes him down into the sewer.

The Speeder (September 24, 1922) A Lloyd Hamilton Comedy. Produced by Lloyd Hamilton Corporation. Distributed by Educational Pictures. Sc: Archie Mayo. D: Lloyd Bacon. Lloyd Hamilton, Ruth Hiatt, Tom Kennedy. 2 reels. Lloyd is proud of his new car, but he has trouble driving around town. At first, he has problems parking. Later, he engages in a fierce rivalry with the "Sheik of Avenue B."

The Educator (November 12, 1922) A Lloyd Hamilton Comedy. Produced by Lloyd Hamilton Corporation. Distributed by Educational Pictures. Sc: Archie Mayo. D: Lloyd Bacon. Lloyd Hamilton, Ruth Hiatt, Otto Fries, Josephine Adair, Orral Humphrey, F.B. Phillips. 2 reels. Lloyd, his mother's pride, is a reputable young professor in Boston. In search of new worlds to conquer, he accepts an assignment in Angelville, a Wild West town that violently opposes education. Lloyd patiently awaits the stagecoach that will deliver him to his new post. During the wait, he observes the arrival of several stretchers. The men bound in the stretchers introduce themselves as his predecessors. Though he faces an Indian attack en route, Lloyd manages to make it to Angelville. At the town square, he stands in front of a crowd and delivers salutations. His earnest speech convinces the townsfolk to get rid of the new educator as quick as possible. Production stills show Lloyd filled with great admiration as he shakes hands with Abraham Lincoln.

No Luck (January 14, 1923) A Lloyd Hamilton Comedy. Produced by Lloyd Hamilton Corporation. Distributed by Educational Pictures. Sc: Archie Mayo. D: Lloyd Bacon. Lloyd Hamilton, Ruth Hiatt, Bobbie DeVilbiss, Coy Watson, Jr., Lloyd Bacon, Tom Kennedy, Tom McGuire. 2 reels. Lloyd is knocked unconscious from smoking a cigar for the first time. While in this state, he dreams that he attends a fashionable ballroom reception. The dream concludes with a violent storm destroying the posh gathering.

Extra! Extra! (February 25, 1923) A Lloyd Hamilton Comedy. Produced by Lloyd Hamilton Corporation. Distributed by Educational Pictures. D: Lloyd Bacon. Lloyd Hamilton, Ruth Hiatt, Bobbie DeVilbiss. 2 reels. Lloyd is a poor but kindhearted New York City lad who aspires to become a reporter. He uses his trusty typewriter and camera to document his experiences in the big city. The police search for a mysterious dynamiter. Because the criminal's only identifiable item of clothing is a checkered cap, Lloyd is briefly held as a suspect. On Lloyd's release, a reporter hires him as his photographer. Lloyd shadows a cop who is on the criminal's trail. When the lawman finally catches up to the dynamiter, Lloyd quickly sets up his camera, unaware that he is positioned on an elevator shaft, and he keeps being lowered whenever he is about to take a picture. Fortunately, Lloyd obtains an incriminating shot before the dynamiter escapes.

Uneasy Feet (March 25, 1923) A Lloyd Hamilton Comedy. Produced by Lloyd Hamilton Corporation. Distributed by Educational Pictures. D: Lloyd Bacon. Lloyd Hamilton, Ruth Hiatt. 2 reels. Lloyd, a country boy, is introduced to the big city. In their effort to claim a fare, several cabbies tear off most of his clothing. A cop threatens to arrest Lloyd unless he visits a clothing store and gets something to wear. Lloyd, despite difficulty in the store, finally manages to re-outfit himself. Just then, he gets caught in the rain and his new suit shrinks. Delight Evans, who interviewed Lloyd for *Screenland* magazine, expressed a fondness for this film, particularly a scene where Lloyd is trying on shoes. Evans wrote, "[Every time] a clerk asks him if he likes a pair, the feather in the hat of the lady sitting behind him tickles his ear and he shakes his head." The clerk ends up piling up hundreds of shoes in his effort to find a pair that Lloyd likes.

F.O.B. (May 13, 1923) A Lloyd Hamilton Comedy. Produced by Lloyd Hamilton Corporation. Distributed by Educational Pictures. Sc: Archie Mayo. D: Lloyd Bacon and Hugh Fay. Lloyd Hamilton, Ruth Hiatt, Ed Kennedy, Lew Morrison, C. L. Davidson, Eddie Flaif, Buddy (Lloyd's dog). 2 reels. After outraging the citizens of Philyburg, Lloyd and Buddy are expelled from town. Aboard a freight car, the pair joins a small band of hobos.

Hollywood (August 19, 1923) Distributor: Paramount. Produced by Famous Players-Lasky Corp. Presented by Jesse L. Lasky. Adapted from a Frank Condon story by Thomas J. Geraghty. D: James Cruze. Hope Drown (Angela Whitaker), Luke Cosgrove (Joel Whitaker), George K. Arthur (Lem Lefferts), Ruby Lafayette (Grandmother Whitaker), Harris Gordon (Dr. Luke Morrison), Bess Flowers (Hortense Towers), Eleanor Lawson (Margaret Whitaker), King Zany (Horace Pringle), Roscoe Arbuckle (man in casting director's office). 8 reels. Friends convince young Angela that she is pretty enough to be a movie star. In the company of her grandfather, an ailing old man who hopes to benefit from a sunny climate, Angela departs for Hollywood. On the pair's visit to a film studio, it is grandfather who is given a vital role in a movie. Numerous Hollywood celebrities play themselves in the film. Hamilton is among the comedy stars to appear. Other comedy stars include Charles Chaplin, Snitz Edwards, James Finlayson, Gale Henry, Walter Hiers, Hank Mann, Kalla Pasha, Chuck Riesner, Will Rogers, Ford Sterling and Ben Turpin.

The Optimist (September 9, 1923) A Lloyd Hamilton Comedy. Produced by Lloyd Hamilton Corporation. Distributed by Educational Pictures. Sc: Lloyd Bacon, Lloyd Hamilton and Hank Mann. D: Gilbert Pratt. Lloyd Hamilton, Ruth Hiatt, Del Lorice, Andrew Arbuckle, Percy Hildebrand, Lloyd Bacon, Hank Mann. 2 reels. [A print of this film is available at the Filmmuseum in Amsterdam.] "Emphasizes Hamilton's unique ability."—Moving Picture World. Lloyd seeks to spread an optimistic outlook on life. In addressing a destitute family, he explains that a sunny day exists outside of their squalid living quarters. To illustrate his point, he opens a window and extends a hand to outdoors. In reaching for sunshine, he unintentionally catches a silver piece that a pair of gamblers has tossed from the street below. Lloyd doesn't pay much attention to the coin as he has to wrest a whiskey bottle from the family's drunken father. When he tosses the bottle out of the window, it falls into the hands of the gamblers. The duo takes the whiskey as compensation for their coin and depart without another word. Soon after, the gamblers return with more than two dozen friends. A sudden downpour of glimmering coins follows. To capture the coins, Lloyd holds a basket outside of the window. When the basket is filled, he hands it to the stunned family. A flashback shift the focus of the film to the Pilgrims of early America. During this episode, Lloyd's philosophy of good will inadvertently triggers an Indian attack on the Pilgrim settlement.

My Friend (January 13, 1924) A Lloyd Hamilton Comedy. Produced by Lloyd Hamilton Corporation. Distributed by Educational Pictures. Supervised by Jack White. D: Fred Hibbard. Lloyd Hamilton, Ruth Hiatt. 2 reels. "Hamilton has never been funnier."—Motion Picture News. "Hamilton at his best."—Exhibitor's World. "Don't miss this one. The gags are not new but they are put over so well ... Hamilton is funnier than he has been in some time."—Film Daily. Pursued by the neighborhood's canine population, Lloyd ducks into his car and attempts to drive away. His mongrel pursuers clamber through the auto's windows, doors and roof. Even a driving rainstorm fails to stop them. Later, while searching for a job, Lloyd meets up with a man whose life he saved during the war. The old friend, a member of high society, invites Lloyd to attend an elaborate party at his home.

Lonesome (February 24, 1924) A Lloyd Hamilton Comedy. Produced by Lloyd Hamilton Corporation. Distributed by Educational Pictures. Supervised by Jack White. D: Gilbert Pratt. Lloyd Hamilton, Ruth Hiatt. 2 reels. Lloyd leaves home to set the world on fire, but he ends up penniless and is too proud to return home. An affable stranger tells him that he is looking for a dinner companion. After dinner, the fellow informs Lloyd that he must hurry to keep an appointment. He gives the lad a dollar to pay the bill and then rushes out of the restaurant. When the dollar proves to be counterfeit, Lloyd is violently ejected from the premises. Lloyd's sister, in disguise searching for her lost brother, decides to duck inside a drug store to avoid getting wet in a storm. She happens to pass her brother outside the store but neither one recognizes the other. In the end, though, the sister locates Lloyd and convinces him to come home.

His Darker Self (March 16, 1924) A G & H Picture distributed by W.W. Hodkinson Corp. presented by Albert L. Grey. Titles: Ralph Spence. Based on "Mammy's Boy," an original story by Arthur Caesar. D: John Noble. Lloyd Hamilton (Claude Sappington), Tom Wilson (Bill Jackson), Tom O'Malley (Uncle Eph), Irma Harrison (Darktown's Cleopatra), Edna May Sperl (Jackson's girl), Sally Long (Claude's girl, the governor's daughter), Kate Bruce (Claude's mother), Warren Cook (the governor), Lucille LaVerne. 5 reels. [A print of the two-reel version is retained at the Library of Congress. This truncated version appears on the DVD collection "The Lost Magic of Lloyd Hamilton."] "Full advantage taken of every comic situation. It is all good fun, plus good melodrama with fights and thrills, and while on a whole it cannot be taken seriously, it will provide smiles and laughs for the most hardened."—The Moving Picture World. "If one is feeling listless and does not desire to have his eyes or imagination taxed too severely, it may prove to be amusing."—The New York Times. "Hamilton is the highlight.... He possesses sufficient individuality of expression to fulfill the demands of the role. His keen sense of burlesque inspires him to squeeze every ounce of comedy from the part."—Laurence Reid, Motion Picture News. Uncle Eph, a longtime servant of the Sappington family, is moonlighting to earn extra money. In his spare time, he delivers cartons to the Black Cat, a cafe "For culled folks 'sclusively." He is told that the boxes contain bananas, but his nightly hauls in fact consist of contraband liquor. When Uncle Eph is framed for a murder committed by Bill Jackson, the cafe's owner and the leader of the bootleggers, Claude Sappington, a young mystery writer, sets forth to prove the servant's innocence. At first, Claude shows nothing but ineptitude. For instance, a tall collection of parcels piled up in his arms obscures his view and causes him to fall into a sidewalk's elevator shaft. But he has the ingenuity to blacken his face with burnt cork and convince the Black Cat to hire him as a busboy. During his effort to penetrate the bootleggers' inner circle, Claude finds himself the target in a knife-throwing contest. Later, he tries to elude an irate bootlegger by concealing himself in a riverside gathering. After being dunked in the water as part of a solemn baptismal ritual, he reemerges completely white. This not only shocks the crowd, but brings Claude to the bootleggers' attention. Claude survives all this adversity with the aid of his sweetheart, the governor's daughter. Overhearing Jackson arguing with his girlfriend, Claude discovers that Jackson is the real murderer. The young sleuth scuffles with Jackson, but the bootlegger gets away and leads Claude on a speedboat chase. Claude soon captures Jackson and brings him to the state capitol. By presenting proof that Jackson is the murderer, Claude saves Uncle Eph from hanging. The governor is scandalized to find his daughter embracing a Negro. However, his daughter explains that she is only hugging Claude. Relieved, the governor gives the couple his permission to wed.

Killing Time (April 6, 1924) A Lloyd Hamilton Comedy. Produced by Lloyd Hamilton Corporation. Distributed by Educational Pictures. Supervised by Jack White. D: Fred Hibbard. Ruth Hiatt, Dick Sutherland, Julia Malone, Lloyd Bacon. After completing his milk delivery rounds, Lloyd arrives at a restaurant and meets a millionaire who says that he was a sheepherder until he recently discovered oil underneath his grazing fields. Upon Lloyd's successful demonstration of how one should eat in public, the new oil magnate engages the milkman as his etiquette tutor.

Going East (May 11, 1924) A Lloyd Hamilton Comedy. Produced by Lloyd Hamilton Corporation. Distributed by Educational Pictures. Supervised by Jack White. D: Fred Hibbard. Lloyd Hamilton, Ruth Hiatt, Dick Sutherland. 2 reels. Unable to befriend his father's new bull, Lloyd informs his father that either he or the bull must leave their farm. When the $50 bull is chosen over him, Lloyd packs his belongings and sets out into the world. He is followed by his faithful dog. Riding an eastbound train, Lloyd joins the company of a sheriff who is escorting two convicts to Sing-Sing. When the sheriff needs to momentarily step away, Lloyd is deputized and left in charge of the criminal pair. A commotion ensues. Later, Lloyd must adjust to his first night in a Pullman sleeper. During this experience, he allows a woman's four small children to sleep with him. Before long, he is removing crumbs and toys from his bed. Due to a runny-nosed bedmate, Lloyd is fighting a cold by morning. Despite his illness, the young traveler rushes to retrieve a stripped fur-piece that has blown out of a window. When Lloyd ignorantly returns with a skunk, fellow passengers abandon the car and unbolt it from the rest of the train.

Good Morning (June 8, 1924) A Lloyd Hamilton Comedy. Produced by Lloyd Hamilton Corporation. Distributed by Educational Pictures. Supervised by Jack White. D: Lloyd Bacon. Lloyd Hamilton, Dick Sutherland, Ruth Hiatt, June Marlowe. 2 reels. Because he views his master's newsboy duties as a game, Lloyd's dog retrieves newspapers as fast as Lloyd delivers them. Lloyd starts for home, pausing to help needy neighbors on his way. Though well intentioned, these efforts invariably end in disaster.

A Self-Made Failure (June 29, 1924) Distribution: Associated First National Pictures. A J.K. McDonald Production. St: J.K. McDonald. Sc: Violet Clarke, Tex Neal and John Grey. D: William Beaudine. Lloyd Hamilton (Breezy), Benny Alexander (Sonny), Matt Moore (John Steele), Patsy Ruth Miller (Alice Neal), Mary Carr (Grandma Neal), Sam DeGrasse (Cyrus Cruishank), Chuck Riesner (Spike Malone), Victor Potel (Pokey Jones), Dan Mason (Dan), Harry Todd (the constable), Alta Allen (Mrs. Spike Malone), Doris Duane (the waitress), Priscilla Moran (Alice Neal, age 4), Joel McCrea (Verman),

Cameo (herself, a dog). 8 reels. The script indicates that incidental roles were written for Dot Farley and Monte Collins. A trailer for *A Self-Made Failure* is in the archives at the Library of Congress. The trailer was shown at the Pordenone Film Festival. "Pleasing and amusing.... [Hamilton's] excellent performance extracts every bit out of the situations. Sympathy-tugging."—Moving Picture World. Breezy, a kindly, easygoing tramp, takes care of an orphan boy.

Jonah Jones (September 21, 1924) A Lloyd Hamilton Comedy. Produced by Lloyd Hamilton Corporation. Distributed by Educational Pictures. Sc: Fred Hibbard. D: Fred Hibbard. Lloyd Hamilton (Jonah Jones), Babe London, Dorothy Seastrom, Dick Sutherland. 2 reels. [The film appears on the "Lost Magic of Lloyd Hamilton" DVD collection.] Jonah Jones, a young backwoods farmer, prepares to drive his sweetheart Babe to his cow pasture. Realizing that it is a habit of Jonah's dilapidated auto to strand its passengers, Babe slips into a pair of roller skates before boarding the vehicle. At the pasture, Jonah sits down between a pair of cows and gets to work milking, but he is unable to get the job done as the cows' swishing tails keep hitting him in the face. Jonah is soon distracted by a motorist with flat tire. The motorist, a lovely city girl named Margaret Morgan, tells Jonah that the police are after her for speeding. Jonah quickly patches the tire to help Margaret escape. The farmer contentedly leans against a fence to watch Margaret drive off. Margaret recklessly speeds away, hitting the fence as he swerves to get back on the road. The fence posts collapse like a row of dominoes, causing Jonah to fall back into a pool of mud. Later, Jonah discovers that Margaret left behind her purse. The chivalrous lad, determined to return the purse, journeys to the big city, where he finds Margaret's home elaborately decorated for a wedding ceremony. Though he is kicked, shoved and bodily thrown out of the home, the farmer uses perseverance and wit to reach Margaret. Margaret, dressed in a bridal gown, is in tears. She tells Jonah that her family is forcing her to marry a brutish foreign count. Jonah decides to help Margaret to get away. Babe arrives in time to see Jonah standing a ladder under Margaret's bedroom window and she assumes that Jonah is getting ready to elope with Margaret. She follows Jonah up the ladder and her added weight causes the ladder to sink steadily into the wet lawn. When the ladder breaks apart, Jonah uses a detached side piece to pole-vault into Margaret's window. Margaret grabs hold of Jonah and the two of them vault out of the window. Jonah places Margaret inside his car to whisk her away, but his car is wedged in a parking space between two other cars. Margaret's father comes charging towards them. Jonah, coming up with an idea, throws a banana in the man's path. The father slips on the banana, topples forward, and drives his outstretched arms into the car, propelling the vehicle perfectly out onto the road. Jonah races away, provoking a wild automobile chase. The father manages to finally catch up with Jonah. Jonah runs for his life when the father threatens him with a gun. One good shot sends the cap flying off of Jonah's head. The cap sails steadily through the air, with Jonah in close pursuit. Jonah, who isn't watching where he going, follows the cap over a cliff and falls into the ocean. Babe jumps into the water to rescue him. [Leonard Smith, the director of photography, went on to receive four Oscar nominations. He won an Oscar for his last film, *The Yearling*. Smith, who was acclaimed for his work in *The Yearling*, *National Velvet* and *Lassie Come Home*, certainly knew how to capture the beauty of an animal. This is probably the reason those cows look exceptionally beautiful as they swing their tails into Hamilton's face.]

Hello, 'Frisco (September 29, 1924) Universal Pictures. D: Slim Summerville. 1 reel. Slim Summerville, James Rolph Jr., William Duncan, Bobby Dunn, Antonio Moreno, Norman Kerry, Hoot Gibson, William Desmond, Hobart Bosworth, Jack Hoxie, Rin Tin Tin, William S. Hart, Jackie Coogan, Bebe Daniels, Anna Q. Nilsson, Syd Chaplin, J. Warren Kerrigan, Lloyd Hamilton, Bull Montana, Barbara La Marr, Lew Cody, Fred Niblo, Belle Bennett, Ralph Lewis, Elliott Dexter.

Crushed (November 23, 1924) A Lloyd Hamilton Comedy. Produced by Lloyd Hamilton Corporation. Distributed by Educational Pictures. Ph: Francis Corby. Sc: Fred Hibbard. D: Fred Hibbard. Lloyd Hamilton, Dorothy Seastrom, Blanche Payson, Fenwick Oliver, William Dyer. 2 reels. [Prints of this film are available at the Museum of Modern Art and Ceskoslovensky Filmovy Ustav/ Filmovy Archiv. The film also appears on the "Lost Magic of Lloyd Hamilton" DVD collection.] Lloyd will not earn a fortune for his "mosquito-proof" walking suit, which is easily penetrated by a swarm of insects. A telegram notifies Lloyd that, if he arrives in New York City and weds by noon, he will receive a hefty inheritance. The executor of the will promises that, for a share of the inheritance, he will arrange for Lloyd to marry his daughter, Dorothy. Upon arriving in New York City, Lloyd boards a subway car for the first time. He withstands impatient and violent commuters, who push and slam him from side to side, only to find that he has boarded the wrong train. At the next station, he encounters further mishaps while attempting to change trains. He finally manages to reach the uptown courthouse before noon, but a misunderstanding causes Dorothy to storm out of the building. Out of desperation, Lloyd marries a woman who needs a husband to support her and her five fat kids. At his new family's home, visitors show up unexpectedly. A terrible storm rises and his wife invites the visitors to spend the night. A shortage of beds forces Lloyd to sleep on the floor. In the middle of the night, Lloyd is awakened by a leak in the roof. He is up on the roof, repairing the leak, when a strong gust comes along and carries him back to his hometown.

Hooked (February 8, 1925) A Lloyd Hamilton Comedy. Produced by Lloyd Hamilton Corporation. Distributed by Educational Pictures. Sc: Fred Hibbard. D: Fred Hibbard. Lloyd Hamilton, Dorothy Seastrom, Kewpie Morgan, Dick Sutherland (tough guy). 2 reels. [A five-minute fragment obtained from George Eastman House was included on "The Lost Magic of Lloyd Hamilton" DVD collection.] Lloyd tries hard to catch a fat fish for Dorothy, but he fails to snare even a guppy. Dorothy doesn't care that Lloyd shows up empty-handed, and gives him the warmest of welcomes. The couple sits closely together underneath a tree. This is a pleasant spot until a squirrel pursues a nut that has dropped down Lloyd's neck. Captain Kewpie, whom Dorothy's parents prefer as their daughter's suitor, invites Dorothy on a trip aboard his ocean liner. Lloyd makes himself useful by carrying Dorothy's baggage to the wharf. He is carrying the baggage aboard the liner when Kewpie tells him that his help is no longer needed. Lloyd tries unsuccessfully to steal aboard the ship. He is sitting at a dockside lunch wagon when the wagon becomes fastened onto Kewpie's liner. As the ship pulls away, it brings along the wagon and everyone inside it. One by one, the diners fall from the wagon the ocean. Lloyd manages to grab onto a porthole which gives him a clear view into Dorothy's cabin. Dorothy, happy to see Lloyd, helps him to get on board.

Half a Hero (March 8, 1925) A Lloyd Hamilton Comedy. Produced by Lloyd Hamilton Corporation. Distributed by Educational Pictures. Sc: Fred Hibbard. D: Fred Hibbard. Lloyd Hamilton, William Horn, Dorothy Seastrom, Babe London. 2 reels. [An incomplete print of this film may be available at The New Zealand Film Archive.] It looks as if Lloyd is comfortably riding in a limousine, but the camera moves back and reveals the lad to be purloining a ride on a freight train. While eluding a brakeman, Lloyd runs into a group under police escort and is marched with them into a patrol wagon. At the station house, the men are made to stand in a line as uniforms are handed out to them. Lloyd is surprised that the uniforms do not have black and white stripes. This is because these men are not prisoners, as Lloyd thought, but the latest batch of rookie cops. Lloyd is assigned to traffic duty.

Hello, Hollywood (March 15, 1925) A Mermaid Comedy. Distributed by Educational Pictures. P: Jack White. Sc: Norman Taurog. D: Norman Taurog. Lige Conley, Lee Moran, Cliff Bowes, Virginia Vance. Special guest star: Lloyd Hamilton. 2 reels. Planning to earn big money as a film actor, Lige cranks up the old family flivver and leaves his country home for Hollywood. Days later, he arrives inside a grand studio. As a mob extra, he is battered and tangles with comedian Lloyd Hamilton. While acting as the prop boy, he stumbles around a battlefield stage and blows up the entire picture plant.

King Cotton (May 3, 1925) A Lloyd Hamilton Comedy. Produced by Lloyd Hamilton Corporation. Distributed by Educational Pictures. D: Hugh Fay. Lloyd Hamilton, Dorothy Seastrom, William Dwyer, Glen Cavender. 2 reels. [A print of this film is available at the Ceskoslovensky Filmovy Ustav/ Filmovy Archiv in Prague.] Lloyd, a cotton harvester, gets sprayed by a skunk while working in the fields. He sets out to remove the skunk's stench by removing his clothing and cleaning himself off in an irrigation ditch. The ditch quickly empties just as Lloyd sees his sweetheart Dorothy coming his way. Lloyd is desperate that she not see him naked. He is trying to figure what to do when the ditch is reflooded and the water carries him off. Lloyd ends up several miles away. His priority as he climbs out of the ditch is to find something he can use to cover his body. To his relief, he is able to borrow a housedress and apron from a clothesline. So that he won't attract undue attention in this outfit, he blackens his face to look like a mammy. As he starts for home, he is mistaken for a domestic servant and made to cook dinner.

Waiting (July 19, 1925) A Lloyd Hamilton Comedy. Produced by Lloyd Hamilton Corporation. Distributed by Educational Pictures. Sc: Fred Hibbard. D: Stephen Roberts. Lloyd Hamilton, Ruth Hiatt, Glen Cavender, Otto Fries, Bill Blaisdell. 2 reels. [Prints of this film are available at the Ceskoslovensky Filmovy Ustav/ Filmovy Archiv and the Museum of Modern Art.] Lloyd is distressed when Ruth agrees to go to a restaurant with Glen. To keep an eye on the couple, Lloyd becomes a waiter and tries to maintain an air of dignity, but everything he does goes wrong. Even before attending to his first customer, he fumbles with trays and smashes a stack of dishes. Later, he pours soup down a patron's neck; he drops a pie in someone's lap; and he sets fire to himself while trying to serve rarebit. While fleeing from his boss and other waiters, Lloyd finds Ruth and Glen in a private dining room. Fortunately, he is just in time to save Ruth from Glen's unwelcome advances.

The Movies (October 4, 1925) A Lloyd Hamilton Comedy. Produced by Lloyd Hamilton Corporation. Distributed by Educational Pictures. D: William Goodrich (Roscoe Arbuckle). Lloyd Hamilton, Marcella Daly, Arthur Thalasso, Frank Jonnasson, Glen Cavender. 2 reels. [The film appears on the "Forgotten Films of Roscoe 'Fatty' Arbuckle" DVD collection presented by Laughsmith Entertainment.] Lloyd is prepared to make his fortune in Hollywood. After promising his aged parents that he will adhere to their instructions, the lad departs his family's vine-covered cottage. He turns from the gate, takes one step away, and he is *in* the big city, as if the city has come directly to the cottage. Lloyd, bewildered by the fast pace of city traffic, creates a traffic jam trying to get across the street. Looking for a way out of his predicament, he pretends to be blind so that a police officer will help him. This ruse seems to have worked out fine until Lloyd trips up in his blind act and reveals to the officer that he really can see. Lloyd breaks into a run and crashes into a burly man, who drops his groceries all over the sidewalk. The man, not in a forgiving mood, turns a deaf ear to Lloyd's apologies and tries to pick a fight. Lloyd manages to avoid a pummeling by tricking a police officer into arresting the man. Further up the street, Lloyd follows some enticing bathing beauties into Montmarie, a famed cafe where film actors congregate for lunch. The country boy is confused seeing some of these actors in costume. He is in awe meeting three actors dressed as Abraham Lincoln, George Washington and Teddy Roosevelt. He interrupts the men's lunch to tell them how much he admires them. He takes a tomahawk from an Indian at another table and asks Washington to chop down a cherry tree. Lincoln, accompanied by the solemn chords of "Glory, Glory Hallelujah," rises from his chair, rests a hand on Lloyd's shoulder and delivers a forceful speech. According to the title card, his message to Lloyd is, essentially, "Leave quietly and cause us no further annoyance." Lloyd Hamilton, famed film comedian, is relying on a cane as he limps into the restaurant. His director (the guy with the giant megaphone) is at his side saying that it's too bad he's hurt his leg and they are unable to finish his latest picture. The men are sitting down for lunch when they notice Lloyd at a nearby table. The director, struck by the boy's resemblance to Hamilton, is convinced that they could use him to double for Hamilton. Lloyd is hesitant to go along with the plan as he promised his parents he'd stay away from the movies, but he changes his mind once he meets Hamilton's alluring leading lady. At the studio, Lloyd dresses in a Roman toga for a love scene with the leading lady. He is supposed to take her in his arms and kiss her, but he finds this all silly and can't stop laughing. Another actor, Bull, comes on the set. Bull is the man Lloyd had arrested earlier. He lunges after Lloyd, who dashes out the nearest exit. The film ends with the disaster-prone youth racing back home. After embracing his mother, father and little brother on the front porch, Lloyd happily follows his family back into their cozy cottage.

Framed (December 6, 1925) A Lloyd Hamilton Comedy. Produced by Lloyd Hamilton Corporation. Distributed by Educational Pictures. D: Stephen Roberts. Lloyd Hamilton, James Kelly, Virginia Vance, Ruth Hiatt, Otto Fries, Peg O'Neill. 2 reels. In a photographer's packed waiting room, a mad scramble occurs whenever the next patron is summoned. Lloyd manages to overcome this first obstacle, but he still fails to have his picture taken. Later, Lloyd attends a party at his girlfriend's home. He is chosen as the subject of a magician's levitation act, which proves disastrous. After discovering that a gang of thieves is using the magician as an "inside man," Lloyd hastens to foil the illusionist and his accomplices.

Careful Please (February, 1926) A Lloyd Hamilton Comedy. Produced by Lloyd Hamilton Corporation. Distributed by Educational Pictures. Sc: Norman Taurog. D: Norman Taurog. Lloyd Hamilton, Marcella Daly, Dick Sutherland, Louise Carver, Eddie Boland, Stanley Blystone, Lester Sutherland. 2 reels. [The film appears on the "Lost Magic of Lloyd Hamilton" DVD collection.] Lloyd works as a bill collector in the city's meanest district. As he proceeds down Tough Street, he notices that the surrounding activity is becoming progressively rougher. He finally arrives at the last house. The lady of the house batters Lloyd with her rolling pin while her bratty kids kick him. The lad reciprocates by throwing the woman's furniture into the street. Dick, the man of the house, is leading a nasty bunch of hoodlums as he arrives on the scene. The tough guy is in time to find the bill collector in possession of his furniture. At first, Lloyd carries furniture back into the house to avoid trouble, but this fails to appease Dick, and Lloyd soon finds himself under attack. Lloyd, through pluck and luck, manages in the end to flatten the gang. Later in that day, Lloyd's car becomes tangled in hoisting tackle. The car is raised eight floors. Via a strong gust, the auto is carried into the apartment of a vamp. The vamp's guardian becomes furious and pulls out a gun. Fearing for his life, Lloyd urgently drives down the eight flights leading to the street.

Nobody's Business (April, 1926) A Lloyd Hamilton Comedy. Produced by Lloyd Hamilton Corporation. Distributed by Educational Pictures. Sc: Norman Taurog. D: Norman Taurog. Lloyd Hamilton, Dick Sutherland, Stanley Blystone, Eddie Boland, Helen McNair, James Kelly. 2 reels. [A print of this film is available at the George Eastman House in Rochester, New York. The film also appears on the "Lost Magic of Lloyd Hamilton" DVD collection.] Lloyd, a serious businessman, carefully attires himself for work. As moths have gotten into his closet, he must try five suits before finding one that will stay together. After a difficult ride on a streetcar, he arrives at his business: a hot dog wagon on the beach. This day, a drunken patron avoids arrest by dropping his bottle into Lloyd's coffee urn. Lloyd is astonished to discover his patrons singing and slurping repeated cups of coffee. A sudden windstorm blows Lloyd, his wagon and his customers along the street. The wind deposits the wagon on roller coaster tracks. Throughout all this wild activity, the singing and drinking continues unabated. [In the opening scene, Lloyd walks down the street unaware that a rolling clothes rack is attached to his coat. Dick Van Dyke later used this same gag sequence for his tribute to silent comedy, *The Comic*.]

Here Comes Charlie (June, 1926) A Lloyd Hamilton Comedy. Produced by Lloyd Hamilton Corporation. Distributed by Educational Pictures. Sc: Norman Taurog. D: Norman Taurog. Lloyd Hamilton, Stanley Blystone, Virginia Vance, Glen Cavender. 2 reels. Lloyd hopes to marry his girlfriend Virginia but the affluence of her family makes him feel unworthy. He becomes ambitious when he learns that a grand department store is opening. He submits an employment application and is soon hired as a floorwalker. Encouraged by his new position, Lloyd raises sufficient confidence to propose to Virginia. Virginia accepts, but her father refuses to give his consent. Upon entering his new workplace, Lloyd is trampled by a rush of early shoppers. Undeterred, he returns to his feet and immediately attends to his duties. The floorwalker eagerly assists busy clerks, directs shoppers, holds babies, and cares for lost children. He is also placed in charge of a one-hour sale, during which he is overrun by bargain-hunting women who pull hair and slug in the clinches.

Move Along (July, 1926) A Lloyd Hamilton Comedy. Produced by Lloyd Hamilton Corporation. Distributed by Educational Pictures. Sc: Norman Taurog. D: Norman Taurog. Lloyd Hamilton, Helen Foster, Glen Cavender, Jack Lloyd, Otto Fries, Anita Garvin. 2 reels. [This film appears on the "Lost Magic of Lloyd Hamilton" DVD collection.] Though he is hungry and broke, Lloyd gives Helen his place in the unemployment line. This act of good will causes Lloyd to lose the last available job. Because he is unable to pay his rent, his hardened landlady throws him out of her rooming house. With his trunk and rolling bed, Lloyd eventually settles in a poorer quarter of town. He pushes his bed under a streetlamp. When it begins to rain, he unfolds a store awning as a roof. The hard storm rapidly fills the awning to the lip. Under the strain, the awning collapses and the collected water drenches his impromptu home. The rain later turns to snow. Helen comes along cold and wet, and Lloyd takes in the young lady. The couple's cramped shelter gradually becomes enclosed by the relentless snow. In the end, it revealed that the whole thing was a dream. Lloyd wakes when a cop prods him with a nightstick and orders him to "move along."

Jolly Tars (August, 1926) A Lloyd Hamilton Comedy. Produced by Lloyd Hamilton Corporation. Distributed by Educational Pictures. Sc: Norman Taurog. D: Norman Taurog. Lloyd Hamilton, Grace Dalton, Dick Sutherland, Phil Dunham, Henry Murdock. 2 reels. [A print of this film was discovered in 2009 by German museum Deutsche Kinemathek. The print has the German title *Amerikanische Marine-Groteske*.] Though Grace does not want to be separated from Lloyd, she fails to dissuade her father from sending her to Europe. Grace asks Lloyd to see her off at the pier. On his way to the dock, Lloyd gets on the wrong bus and mistakenly enlists for five years in the navy. As a sailor, Lloyd has difficulty with everyone from the cook to the admiral. He even has a hard time trying to settle in his hammock. During the crew's big gun practice, the rookie seaman is dispatched to repair the ship's target. While attending to the task, he becomes more occupied with dodging shells and sharks. He finally jumps onto a passing torpedo. Riding the missile as well as a western hero riding a horse, he seems hopeful that he is heading for calmer waters.

Nothing Matters (September, 1926) A Lloyd Hamilton Comedy. Produced by Lloyd Hamilton Corporation. Distributed by Educational Pictures. Sc: Norman Taurog. D: Norman Taurog. Lloyd Hamilton, Anita Garvin, Stanley Blystone. 2 reels. [A print of this film is available at the George Eastman House. The film also appears on the "Lost Magic of Lloyd Hamilton" DVD collection.] Lloyd, a correspondent school sleuth, is the pride of his village. When the townspeople are swindled out of a large amount of cash, he trails the con men to the big city. A clue soon leads him to a mysterious opium den. [The climax of *The Vagrant* is reworked in this film.]

Teacher, Teacher (October, 1926) A Lloyd Hamilton Comedy. Produced by Lloyd Hamilton Corporation. Distributed by Educational Pictures. Sc: Norman Taurog. D: Norman Taurog. Lloyd Hamilton, Bobby Burns, Aileen Lopez, Henry Murdock, Johnny Sinclair. 2 reels. Lloyd is a night school teacher. The educator normally naps during the day, but because an annoying bird has perched outside his window, sleep is unattainable on this particular morning. Later, the dignified instructor experiences even more difficulty at school as class truants constantly disturb his lecture. Embarrassing mishaps occur during a visit from the principal and school board. In the end, the classroom is invaded by dogs.

Goose Flesh (November, 1926) A Lloyd Hamilton Comedy. Produced by Lloyd Hamilton Corporation. Distributed by Educational Pictures. Sc: Norman Taurog. D: Norman Taurog. Lloyd Hamilton, Fred Spencer, Al Thompson, Estelle Bradley, Richard Carter. 2 reels. Scarface, a mysterious criminal, threatens to steal a necklace belonging to a millionaire's daughter. Determined to protect the valuable chain, Detective Lloyd arrives at the Bixby mansion. For the remainder of the story, Lloyd encounters trite "haunted house" comedy devices: secret exits in the walls, strange noises, and a man dressed in a gorilla suit.

One Sunday Morning (December 12, 1926) A Lloyd Hamilton Comedy. Produced by Lloyd Hamilton Corporation. Distributed by Educational Pictures. Sc: William Goodrich (Roscoe Arbuckle). D: William Goodrich (Roscoe Arbuckle). Lloyd Hamilton, Estelle Bradley, Stanley Blystone. 2 reels. For a Sunday outing, Lloyd loads his wife, two kids and dog into the family's Ford. The outing begins badly when the engine fails to start. To fix his car, Lloyd crawls beneath the vehicle; a neighbor washing her car causes water to flow down the gutter and seep under Lloyd's car. As a result, Lloyd reemerges soaked. Lloyd lowers the car top for his wife, nearly breaking one of his legs in the process, and then returns to the driver's seat. His car still won't start. A boy stops to watch Lloyd's repair efforts. The boy distracts Lloyd by suddenly playing his ukulele. Eventually, Lloyd's wife and kids desert the scene and attend church service.

Unidentified Newsreel (1926) Hamilton and a woman are seen arriving at the grand opening of Grauman's Chinese Theatre. Roscoe Arbuckle also appears. This footage is included in *Memories of Silent Stars, Part 2*, a compilation assembled by Blackhawk Films.

Peaceful Oscar (January 30, 1927) A Lloyd Hamilton Comedy. Produced by Lloyd Hamilton

Corporation. Distributed by Educational Pictures. D: William Goodrich (Roscoe Arbuckle). Lloyd Hamilton, Blanche Payson, Billy Hampton, Toy Gallagher, Henry Murdock, Chick Collins. 2 reels. Oscar is henpecked by Blanche, his heavyweight spouse. Blanche's domination does not prevent Oscar from eyeing his pretty maid, Toy. The chef and butcher boy battle over the servant girl. Toy sends Oscar into the kitchen to break up the fight. The sight of the rough row deters Oscar from becoming involved. Blanche, who can no longer take the noise, marches into the room and tosses out the combatants. Blanche's action prompts a sudden rise of bravery in Oscar, who steps outside to run the duo off his property. The cowardly Oscar is chased back into this house for his effort. Toy, who is found with Oscar comforting her, is the next one expelled by Blanche. Since Blanche his scheduled to host an afternoon reception, Oscar must remove his smoking jacket and alternately don the apparel of maid and chef. Oscar bumbles through his duties. After dinner is done, Oscar suffers listening to one of his wife's guests sing opera. Afterwards, he takes his small son to the beach, where he gets into a fight with his former chef.

Somebody's Fault (March, 1927) A Lloyd Hamilton Comedy. Produced by Lloyd Hamilton Corporation. Distributed by Educational Pictures. Sc: Norman Taurog. D: Norman Norman Taurog. Lloyd Hamilton, Bob Kortman, Estelle Bradley, Al Thompson. 2 reels. [A print of this film is with Film Preservation Associates.] Lloyd is an electrician's inept helper who upsets the operation of his employer's shop. On a call, he mistakenly connects a high-voltage line into a simple household circuit. This one mistake causes numerous disruptions. The suction of a vacuum cleaner increases. A radio swells and bursts. A player piano runs so rapidly that it fires all of its keys and strings.

Breezing Along (May, 1927) A Lloyd Hamilton Comedy. Produced by Lloyd Hamilton Corporation. Distributed by Educational Pictures. Sc: Norman Taurog. D: Norman Norman Taurog. Lloyd Hamilton, Al Thompson, Eva Thatcher, Estelle Bradley, Vincent Cullen. 2 reels. [Prints of this film are available with Film Preservation Associates, the Museum of Modern Art, and La Cineteca del Friuli.] At an employment bureau, Lloyd overhears a woman expressing her need for a chauffeur. The lad eagerly informs the woman that he is a wonderful driver. The woman's husband and daughter look him over and everyone agrees to hire him. Lloyd takes the family on a rocky ride back to their palatial estate. The auto crashes into a portico column before it comes to a complete stop, and the room supported by the column comes crashing down. The accident compels Lloyd to confess that he cannot drive. Still, he insists, he is a good butler. Within hours, he manages to disprove this claim beyond any shadow of a doubt.

His Better Half (August, 1927) A Lloyd Hamilton Comedy. Produced by Lloyd Hamilton Corporation. Distributed by Educational Pictures. Sc: Norman Taurog. D: Norman Taurog. Lloyd Hamilton, Estelle Bradley, Glen Cavender, Al Thompson, Blanche Payson, Henry Murdock. 2 reels. [A print of this film is available at the Museum of Modern Art and the Ceskoslovensky Filmovy Ustav/ Filmovy Archiv.] Glen recalls little of the previous night's party, but a wire from his parents suggests he made a call to tell them he was getting married. His parents are eager to meet his new bride and plan to give the newlyweds $50,000 as a wedding present. Despite an exhaustive search, Lloyd fails to produce a wife for his roommate. Desperately, Lloyd dresses in drag and pretends to be the bride. Due to his disguise, Lloyd receives unwelcome attention from Glen's jealous brother and frisky father. The situation becomes more complicated when Lloyd becomes attracted to Glen's sister.

At Ease (September, 1927) A Lloyd Hamilton Comedy. Produced by Lloyd Hamilton Corporation. Distributed by Educational Pictures. Sc: Norman Taurog. D: Norman Taurog. Lloyd Hamilton, Stanley Blystone, Glen Cavender, Estelle Bradley. 2 reels. [A print of this film is available at the Library of Congress.] Upon being admitted into a civilian training camp company, Lloyd is placed in the hands of a tough top sergeant. While the rookie is marched along a walkway, his clothes are snatched from his body and replaced by an ill-fitting uniform. Next he is given a gun and assigned to the camp's misfit squad. Upon joining the unit, Lloyd fumbles with the manual of arms exercise. Afterwards, Lloyd joins a general inside a plane. As a consequence of his clumsiness, the plane executes an unscheduled take-off. As neither passenger knows how to pilot the craft, the general frantically buckles on a parachute and bails out. Lloyd jumps out of the plane without a parachute and is fortunate enough to land on top of the general's open chute.

New Wrinkles (November, 1927) A Lloyd Hamilton Comedy. Produced by Lloyd Hamilton Corporation. Distributed by Educational Pictures. Sc: Norman Taurog. D: Norman Taurog. Lloyd Hamilton, Henry Murdock, Al Thompson, Toy Gallagher, Phil Dunham, Elfie Fay, Glen Cavender, Blanche Payson, Jack Lloyd. 2 reels. [A print of this film is available at the Library of Congress.] A sudden gust carries Lloyd's cap into the thick of traffic. Despite his extensive recovery effort, the cap is destroyed. Lloyd buys a new cap in a hat shop. This and another headpiece are ruined as well. To have the pleasure of a fourth cap's destruction, Lloyd tosses the item away. However, this cap returns to him like a boomerang. The trick so impresses Lloyd that he attempts to share it with a police officer. Again, he tosses his cap and it comes back to him. He then borrows the officer's hat and throws it hard, expecting it to come back as well, but instead it lands in a fire. Lloyd, seeing that the officer is furious, can see no way to make up for this other than to hand his own cap to the officer and leave the scene as quickly as possible. Lloyd next secures a position in a beauty shop, but he manages to create several problems and must soon put up his scissors and move on.

Movieland (November 28, 1927) A Lupino Lane Comedy. Educational Film Exchanges, Inc. Sc: Norman Taurog. D: Norman Taurog. Lupino Lane (Nip), Kathryn McGuire, Wallace Lupino, Glen Cavender, Tom O'Grady, Lloyd Hamilton (man starting car). 2 reels. [A print of this film is in the collection of Patrick Stansbury.] Nip tries to sneak into a movie studio to see his girlfriend.

Papa's Boy (December, 1927) A Lloyd Hamilton Comedy. Produced by Lloyd Hamilton Corporation. Distributed by Educational Pictures. Sc: Norman Taurog. D: Norman Taurog. Lloyd Hamilton, Robert Graves, Glen Cavender, Betty Boyd, Al Thompson. 2 reels. (The working title of this comedy was *Who's Kidding Who?*) Lloyd, a bespectacled bugologist, is preoccupied with catching a rare butterfly. A tattoo resembling the butterfly is displayed on a woman's calf. Lloyd, who fails to recognize the image as a tattoo, carefully follows the woman. When he descends on the mock butterfly, he knocks the woman to the ground. The woman whacks him with an umbrella, which becomes tightly wrapped around his neck. Lloyd's father, a manager of a lumber operation, is disturbed by his son's peculiar interests. Determined to toughen the lad, he has his foreman take Lloyd camping in the woods. The mismatched pair joins a vacationing millionaire and his daughter. Whenever his colorful prey appears, Lloyd sets forth with his net. With this constant pursuit, he causes much trouble for his wilderness companions. At one point, Lloyd sets a tent on fire. He dutifully runs to the river bank, lowers his face into the current, and fills his mouth with water. Then he races back to the fire and, with all his might, sprays the mouthful of water at the raging blaze. Later, Lloyd mistakes a snoozing crocodile for a log. He leisurely reclines on the reposed reptile and cracks open a book. As he becomes absorbed in reading, the crocodile carries him into a nearby river.

Life in Hollywood No. 2 (1927) Grace Darmond, Carmelita Geraghty, Gaston Glass, Lloyd Hamilton, Ruth Hiatt, Ben Lyon, Colleen Moore, Herbert Rawlinson, George Siegmann, Al St. John, Maurice Tourneur. 2 reels.

Rose Marie (1927) Metro-Goldwyn-Mayer. D: William Nigh. Renee Adoree, Ralph Forbes, Creighton Hale, Harry Carey, Lloyd Hamilton. This feature was not completed, but stills of the production exist. Hamilton appears in the stills as a bearded trapper named Fuzzy.

Always a Gentleman (February 5, 1928) A Lloyd Hamilton Comedy. Produced by Lloyd Hamilton Corporation. Distributed by Educational Pictures. Sc: Norman Taurog. D: Norman Taurog. Lloyd Hamilton, Stanley Blystone, Edna Gregory, Al Thompson, Jack Miller. 2 reels. [A print of this film is available at the Ceskoslovensky Filmovy Ustav/ Filmovy Archiv in Prague.] Though inexperienced at golf, Lloyd agrees to play in a foursome match. First, Lloyd tees up with an umbrella. The umbrella opens as he swings and a breeze carries him off the tee. Lloyd then swats numerous balls off the fairway. One of these balls sails into the head of Dr. Frank, who runs the local sanitarium. When the game ends, Lloyd's friends board a chauffeured car that has come to take them home. Unaware that his new friends reside at the sanitarium, Lloyd gladly agrees to join them. At the sanitarium, Lloyd is puzzled by everyone's bizarre behavior. A girl begs Lloyd to help her escape, but forcibly kicks him every time his back is turned. Eventually, Dr. Frank arrives and orders that Lloyd be restrained in a straitjacket. Before attendants tighten the jacket's straps, a mouse secretly crawls into the back of the garment. Lloyd begins to feel something moving on his body. He frantically tears his outfit to pieces. While fleeing the doctor and the attendants, Lloyd encounters a mad genius who has built a self-propelled airship. Lloyd, looking to escape the asylum, boards the airship and goes on a bumpy ride.

Between Jobs (March 18, 1928) A Lloyd Hamilton Comedy. Produced by Lloyd Hamilton Corporation. Distributed by Educational Pictures. Sc: Norman Taurog. D: Norman Taurog. Lloyd Hamilton, Marjorie Moore, Al Thompson, Stanley Blystone, Jack Miller. 2 reels. In a park, Lloyd observes an attractive girl drop her purse. He hurries to return the item, but the girl assumes that he's a wolf and calls the police to arrest him. After discovering the lad's true intent, the girl offers him a job helping to build her father's new home. Though he initially chooses to avoid work, Lloyd later shows up to accept the offer. The story advances twenty years. Through incompetent workmanship, Lloyd has created a home that stands at a sharp slant. The girl and her father arrive to inspect the home. When Lloyd taps in the final nail, the residence completely collapses.

Blazing Away (April 22, 1928) A Lloyd Hamilton Comedy. Produced by Lloyd Hamilton Corporation. Distributed by Educational Pictures. Sc: Norman Taurog. D: Norman Taurog. Lloyd Hamilton, Kewpie Morgan, Lucille Hutton, Al Thompson. 2 reels. Lloyd and Kewpie, cab drivers in a rough town, are all-around rivals. Besides competing for fares, each man is romantically interested in Lucille and each man heads his company's football team. In the morning, several cabbies arrive at the local train depot. By employing football tactics, they get visiting salesmen as passengers. Though meek, Lloyd picks up a few fares and survives opposition from truckers on the road. At the close of the work week, Lloyd and Kewpie lead their football teams into a tough "no substitutions" game. Kewpie's tacklers hit Lloyd so hard that their fallen bodies create a deep impression in the field. A derrick arrives to hoist the players out of the imprint. Upon regaining possession of the ball, Lloyd is again faced by a formidable line of tacklers. This time, he climbs into his faithful taxi and stomps on the gas pedal. Kewpie's men tackle the cab. The cab, helpless under this hard-pressed weight, quickly falls to pieces.

A Homemade Man (June 17, 1928) A Lloyd Hamilton Comedy. Produced by Lloyd Hamilton Corporation. Distributed by Educational Pictures. Sc: Norman Taurog. D: Norman Taurog. Lloyd Hamilton, Lucille Hutton, Kewpie Morgan. 2 reels. Kewpie is the owner of a businessman's gymnasium-cafe. When he discovers that none of his gym workers can mix a soda, Kewpie hires Lloyd as a counterman. Lloyd tries to mimic the artful style of his co-workers, but he only succeeds in spilling a drink and producing a misshapen stuffed tomato. To save his counter from total ruin, Kewpie assigns Lloyd to lead Indian club exercises. Lloyd's error in instructions causes his pupils to knock each other unconscious. Prompted by this blunder, Kewpie engages Lloyd in a gruff boxing lesson.

Listen Children (July 22, 1928) A Lloyd Hamilton Comedy. Produced by Lloyd Hamilton Corporation. Distributed by Educational Pictures. Sc: Norman Taurog. D: Norman Taurog. Lloyd Hamilton, Jack Miller, Al Thompson, Jackie Levine. 2 reels. Lloyd, whose car has suffered a series of tire blowouts, is forced to walk to his job at a boys' military academy. He enters the school just as the flag attendant, who has become tangled in hoisting ropes, puts himself at half-mast. Once Lloyd is dressed in his instructor's uniform, he raises his sleeping cadets and carefully follows them through their morning routine.

No Sale (October 24, 1928) A Smitty Comedy. Van Burean Corporation/ Pathe. The *Smitty* series was based on a comic strip by Walter Burns. P: James J. Tynan. D: George Marshall. Donald Haines, Jackie Combs, Maude Truax, Joseph Belmont. The *Smitty* series depicted the humorous domestic life of an average American family. John T. Weaver noted in his book *Twenty Years of Silents* that Lloyd made an appearance in the series' *No Sale* installment, in which the Smith family tries to sell their house. Rob Farr believes that Lloyd may have had a cameo as a prospective buyer. This cannot be confirmed as no copies of the film are known to exist.

Black Waters (April 14, 1929) A British and Dominions Film. Distribution: Sono Art World Wide Pictures, Inc. Producer: Herbert Wilcox. Sc: John Willard (based on his play "Fog"). D: Marshall Neilan. James Kirkwood (Tiger Larabee/ the Rev. Kelly), Mary Brian (Eunice), John Loder (Charles), Hallam Cooley (Elmer Chester), Frank Reicher (Randall), Lloyd Hamilton (Temple), Robert Ames (Jimmy Darcy), Ben Hendricks (Olaf, an old watchman), Noble Johnson (Jeelo). 90 minutes, U.S. version; 81 minutes, British version. Summoned to attend a houseboat party, six people board a mysterious fogbound schooner: a young couple named Eunice and Charles; playboy Elmer Chester and his valet Temple; a bitter man named Randall; and a grotesque wandering evangelist. Increasing the group's number to seven is Darcy, a newspaper reporter who has been captured while snooping around the vessel. Tiger Larabee, the ship's unseen captain, announces over the address system that he has arranged the gathering in order to kill his guests. As the ship drifts out to sea, guests are inexplicably murdered and thrown over the side.

His Big Minute (May 5, 1929) A Lloyd Hamilton Talking Comedy. Educational Film Exchanges. Lloyd Hamilton Productions, Inc. Recording by Western Electric. Supervised by Harry D. Edwards. Sc: Gilbert Pratt. D: William Watson. Lloyd Hamilton (Vernon), Gladys McConnel, Bert Woodruf, Ivan Christy, Fred Peters. 2 reels. Vernon, a trusting tenderfoot, arrives in a wild west town named Bloody Gulch. He enters the local saloon, where the year's biggest poker game is in progress. Bad Joe and his equally bad brother, Hank are players. When the lad kindly informs Bad Joe that he has dropped a couple of cards in his boot, he has some words whispered to him that literally cause his ears to burn. When the stakes grow beyond his ready funds, Joe asks Vernon to watch his hand while he attends to business. On the next draw, Vernon shatters Hank's full house by discarding three aces. Shushing Hank on his return, Vernon shows him his new hand and whispers that the cards add up to 21; "...then there's the ten of diamonds —*big casing*," he explains. The gunslinging brothers are enraged. As they menacingly approach Vernon, the lad simply tells them that he does not choose to fight and races out of the saloon. With the grizzled pair in close pursuit, the tenderfoot rushes into a general store with sufficient force to frustrate a robbery attempt. The grateful shopkeeper's daughter invites Vernon to dinner. At her home, the girl introduces Vernon to her kid brothers: Joe and Hank. The boys instantly draw their pistols, but then they remember having promised their late "maw" to never shed blood in the house. Hank and Joe put away their guns and anxiously await Vernon's departure. Under the circumstances, Vernon is glad when his gracious hostess asks him to spend the night. He is less happy when the girl's sleeping arrangements place him in a bed between her angry brothers.

Don't Be Nervous (July 7, 1929) A Lloyd Hamilton Talking Comedy. Educational Film Exchanges. Lloyd Hamilton Productions, Inc. Recording by Western Electric. Supervised by Harry D. Edwards. St: Gilbert Pratt. D: William Watson. Lloyd Hamilton (Vernon Snodgrass), Rita LaRoy, Mahlon Hamilton. 2 reels. [This film appears in the "Lost Magic of Lloyd Hamilton" DVD collection.] Nick the Sheik, a gang leader, is released from prison. This event rouses the district attorney and various underworld figures. As he physically resembles Nick, Vernon Snodgrass soon becomes entangled in the situation. Vernon, pursued by a police stakeout team, climbs up a fire escape and randomly jumps inside a room. The room is occupied by several gangsters, who enthusiastically welcome home "their chieftain." However, the real Nick soon appears and proves that Vernon is an imposter. A threatening note from Nick's successor prompts Nick to release Vernon. The innocent lookalike is told that a car is waiting to "take him for a ride." Saving Vernon from the lethal ride is Nick's passionate sweetheart, who suddenly pulls Vernon into a passing cab. The girl takes Vernon to her apartment. The serenity of the scene is broken when rival gangsters converge inside the apartment. During a riotous battle, Vernon uncovers an arsenal inside a closet. Jumbled by a rap on his head, he begins to perform a spring dance, dropping tear gas bombs as he gingerly prances among the battling mobsters. The gas subdues the mobsters long enough for the police to arrive.

His Baby Daze (August 18, 1929) A Lloyd Hamilton Talking Comedy. Educational Film Exchanges. Lloyd Hamilton Productions, Inc. Recording by Western Electric. Supervised by Harry D. Edwards. St: George Bentley. D: Gilbert Pratt. Lloyd Hamilton (Vernon), Little Billy, Eddie Barry, Glen Cavender, Martie Martell, Jimmie Hertz. 2 reels. [A print of this film is available in the David Wyatt Collection.] Vernon is both secretary and butler to Mr. Marshall, an eccentric millionaire uncle. On a whim, Mr. Marshall advertises that he is interested in adopting a young boy. Slick, a thief, persuades a midget accomplice to answer the ad so that the two of them can burglarize the millionaire's home. Impressed with the "child," Mr. Marshall places him in Vernon's care. Besides struggling with Vernon over being given a bath, the midget must suffer through Vernon's bedtime reading of "Mother Goose" rhymes.

Peaceful Alley (September 29, 1929) A Lloyd Hamilton Talking Comedy. Educational Film Exchanges. Lloyd Hamilton Productions, Inc. Recording by Western Electric. Supervised by Harry D. Edwards. D: Alf Goulding. Lloyd Hamilton, Douglas Scott, Adrienne Dore. 2 reels. Pinky is a three-year-old street waif. To obtain a nickel for ice cream, he takes a newspaper from the trash and mimics the shouting newsboys. He makes his first sale, but the customer is upset to find the paper is printed in Chinese and helps himself to a refund. Pinky encounters Lloyd, who is also penniless and homeless. Lloyd, concerned for the child's welfare, agrees to look after him. Pinky, who is grateful, promises his new guardian to get them money. Pinky sits down and pretends to cry. As soon as he attracts a passing girl, he tells her that he lost a nickel down a nearby grating. To soothe the forlorn moppet, the passerby gives the child a nickel. Trying to impress morals on Pinky, Lloyd scolds the child and sends him to return the coin. The girl, who has overheard Lloyd's admonishment, invites the pair to a mission meeting.

Toot Sweet (November 10, 1929) A Lloyd Hamilton Talking Comedy. Educational Film Exchanges. Lloyd Hamilton Productions, Inc. Recording by Western Electric. Supervised by Harry D. Edwards. Sc: Vernon Smith. D: Alf Goulding. Lloyd Hamilton, Lena Malena, Will Hays. 2 reels. [This film appears on the "Lost Magic of Lloyd Hamilton" DVD collection.] Lloyd shops for a good car to impress a girl. When he confides his motive to a used-car salesman, the dealer offers to personally help the bashful lad to win his girl. The dealer offers to pretend to accost the girl, and will allow Lloyd to rush to her rescue. Lloyd, who is waiting in his car, watches the dealer approach the girl. As the dealer begins to do his part, Lloyd discovers that the car door is jammed. The delay permits another man to flatten the annoying flirt. This action prompts an argument between the heroic man and his jealous wife. After finally freeing himself, Lloyd races to the scene. In the confusion, he mistakenly kicks the jealous woman's spouse. Soon after, Lloyd meets the girl again on a street corner. Though dismayed to learn that she can hardly speak English, he arranges a date with her. That evening, they meet at an elegant cafe. By ordering an extravagant meal and accidentally breaking a glass, the girl causes staggering figures to be tallied by an omnipresent waiter. The girl's eyes burn with rage as she observes the Apache dancer, who is a former lover. She becomes so enraged seeing the dancer kiss his gorgeous partner that she breaks a lot more tableware. Lloyd snatches an expensive lamp from the girl's path, then ruins it himself. In the end, the bill is for as much money as Lloyd has in his wallet. Lloyd pays the bill as his date blissfully leaves with the Apache dancer.

Tanned Legs (November 10, 1929) An RKO Production. Assistant director: Ray McCarey. D: Marshall Neilan. June Clyde (Peggy Reynolds), Arthur Lake (Bill), Sally Blane (Janet Reynolds), Allen Kearns (Roger), Albert Gran (Mr. Reynolds), Edmund Burns (Clinton Darrow), Dorothy Revier (Mrs. Lyons-King), Ann Pendington (Tootie), Lincoln Stedman (Pudgy), Lloyd Hamilton (the detective). 71 minutes. [Hamilton is not in prints currently in cable television distribution. Cole Johnson, a film historian, speculates that Hamilton appeared in an alternate silent version of the film. The fact that not all theatres were set up for sound in 1929 prompted studios to produce these alternate silent versions. As it turned out, the silent versions sometimes had different scenes and different actors. Mack Swain appears as an American general in the silent version of Marion Davies' *Marianne*, but another actor, Robert Edeson, shows up as the general in the sound version. Edgar Kennedy appears briefly as a desk sergeant in the silent version of Harold Lloyd's *Welcome Danger*, but the desk sergeant is nowhere to be seen in the scenes reshot with sound.] The comedy-melodrama is set at a fashionable resort. Rich scions engage in scandalous affairs from which complications arise.

The Show of Shows (November 21, 1929) A Warner Brothers Production. Sound: Vitaphone. supervised by Darryl Francis Zanuck. D: John G. Adolfi. Starring a cast of 77 performers of stage and screen including: Frank Fay (the master of ceremonies), Johnny Arthur, John Barrymore, Richard Barthelmess, Noah Beery, Sally Blane, Monte Blue, Irene Bordini, Hobart Bosworth, George Carpentier, Betty Compson, Chester Conklin, Heinie Conklin, Dolores Costello, Helene Costello, Viola Dana,

Douglas Fairbanks Jr., Louise Fazenda, Lloyd Hamilton, Lupino Lane, Lila Lee, Ted Lewis, Winnie Lightner, Beatrice Lillie, Myrna Loy, Tully Marshall, Patsy Ruth Miller, Bull Montana, Lee Moran, Chester Morris, Jack Mulhall, Sally O'Neil, Marion Nixon, Kalla Pasha, Rin Tin Tin, Bert Roach, Sid Silvers, Ben Turpin, Loretta Young. 128 minutes. In 1929, Warner Brothers produced this revue movie to demonstrate their new sound and Technicolor processes. Hamilton appears as one of the forgotten Floradora Boys chorus. The group also includes Ben Turpin, Lupino Lane, Heinie Conklin, Lee Moran, and Bert Roach. In the number, each of the comics takes a turn to musically recount their unfortunate fate since the Floradora show ended. Turpin punctuates his song of plight with his famed "108" fall. Lane treats viewers to his classic "jack-knife split" and "spring-return" stunts. This requires Lane to move his legs apart until he slides to the floor with his legs parallel to the surface; he then suddenly springs back into a standing position. Hamilton, who wears an undersized top hat and long black coat, steps absurdly into the center of the frame and proceeds to sing about his unpleasant duties driving a cab. Hamilton later joins Frank Fay, Beatrice Lillie and Louise Fazenda for a poetry recital. The scene is simple but funny. It possesses a self-assuredness lacking in the rest of the film. In the show's "Execution Number," Hamilton, Fay, Lee Moran, Noah Beery, Kalla Pasha, and Tully Marshall play members of a firing squad that has been assigned to shoot Monte Blue. Performing before painted flats meant to depict Mexico's badlands, Commander Fay and his corps march Blue to a wall and prepare for the execution. The scene that follows is made funny only by Fay's remarks. At one point, a pleading moan bursts loose from Blue. Startled by the sudden outburst, the soldiers toss their guns aside and run for cover. The soldiers calm down once they realize the noise came from Blue. Fay is turning around to retrieve his rifle when he realizes that the gun has slid across the stage and now lies far out of his reach. Another member of the squad employs his own gun to golf the errant weapon back to Fay. "Clever boy," declares Fay, "remind me to make you a colonel." William K. Everson has said that *The Show of Shows* is "very disappointing." I will go beyond that assessment. With its dull and awkwardly choreographed musical numbers, the film is often painful to watch and seems to just go on and on forever. The revue has a few bright spots, but these are stifled by the bigger and noisier surrounding segments. The best moments come when Fay's performance as host is interrupted. In the role of master of ceremonies, Fay is uncertain, pretentious and unfriendly. With each disparaging intrusion, he discharges a squall of snide remarks. At one point, Fazenda appears as a bold and defensive chorus girl. She demands to speak to Fay, and is not deterred when she learns that Fay is in the midst of dressing. With his pants hanging below his knees, Fay arrives on stage to confront Fazenda. Fazenda communicates various complaints but finds Fay less than receptive. The chorus girl begins to shove Fay, hindering the man's effort to pull up his pants.

Grass Skirts (December 22, 1929) A Lloyd Hamilton Talking Comedy. Educational Film Exchanges. Lloyd Hamilton Productions, Inc. Recording by Western Electric. Supervised by Harry D. Edwards. St: Will King. D: Alf Goulding. Lloyd Hamilton, Ruth Hiatt, Fred Peters, Beatrice Blinn, Will Hays. 2 reels. Lloyd arrives on the tropical beach of Waikiki suffering from seasickness. Also present on the island is Ruth, a young society debutante who seeks to join the exclusive "Jolly Widows" club. A cruel and unscrupulous doctor accepts $5000 to arrange for a dying patient to become Ruth's groom. The doctor, who mistakenly diagnoses Lloyd's seasickness as a deathly disease, convinces the queasy man to marry Ruth. Ruth proves to be a most indifferent bride and goes away on a solo honeymoon. In the meantime, Lloyd enjoys lively ukulele strumming and native hula girls. To Ruth's dismay, he has fully recovered by the time she gets back.

Reel # 1/First Series (December, 1929) Voice of Hollywood. Tiffany Productions. Lloyd Hamilton (host), Dorothy Burgess, Leatrice Joy, Ruth Hiatt, Carlotta King, Walter Hiers. 1 reel. [A print of the film is available with Film Preservation Associates.] The Voice of Hollywood series was set at the fictitious Hollywood radio station STAR. In this installment, Hiers tells jokes about his cars and King sings "The Song of Siberia."

Camera Shy (February 9, 1930) A Lloyd Hamilton Talking Comedy. Educational Film Exchanges. Lloyd Hamilton Productions, Inc. Recording by Western Electric. Supervised by Harry D. Edwards. St: George Bentley. D: Gilbert Pratt. Lloyd Hamilton, Ruth Hiatt, Harry Woods, Natalie Joyce, Will Hays. 2 reels. Trying to sell a far-fetched scenario, Lloyd disrupts a movie company on location. [W.C. Fields used a similar premise in *The Bank Dick* and *Never Give a Sucker an Even Break*.]

Polished Ivory (March 16, 1930) A Lloyd Hamilton Talking Comedy. Educational Film Exchanges. Lloyd Hamilton Productions, Inc. Recording by Western Electric. Supervised by Harry D. Edwards. Sc: Alf Goulding. D: Alf Goulding. Lloyd Hamilton, Tom Kennedy, Stella Adams, Billy Engle. 2 reels. At a music house, the shipping clerk seeks to amend an order's delay with a rush delivery. He desperately flags down a small truck, the Bear Cat Transfer. The truck drivers, Lloyd and Tom, are directed to deliver a grand piano to Mrs. Dowling's elaborate reception. As the truck starts off, the weight of the piano bends its rear wheels out of shape. The truck runs in a pitching motion that makes Lloyd contemplate Dramamine. Finally, the truck breaks down. Blinded by oil in his repair, Lloyd nearly dismantles someone else's vehicle by mistake. Back on the road, Lloyd drives up to a light signal that is being tested. Lloyd, who is confused by the way the signal keeps changing, is uncertain whether to stop or go and soon manages to tangle up traffic. Soon after this problem is resolved, the truck is scrambled by an express train. When the movers arrive at the reception, the shipping clerk and the distinguished pianist are fighting over some heated words that were exchanged on the phone. Lloyd locates Mrs. Dowling. Hoping that they will be of some use, he hands her a pedal and unidentifiable remnants of the smashed piano.

Follow the Swallow (April 27, 1930) A Lloyd Hamilton Talking Comedy. Educational Film Exchanges. Lloyd Hamilton Productions, Inc. Recording by Western Electric. Supervised by Harry D. Edwards. St: Vernon Smith. D: Alf Goulding. Lloyd Hamilton, Ruth Hiatt, Billy Barty, Will Hays. 2 reels. Accompanied by his wife and two-year-old son, Lloyd spends a Sunday outing at a seashore amusement resort. A fast-talking sideshow barker claims he can magically pass a handkerchief through a large cake of ice. Unfortunately, the barker has Lloyd hold the rapidly melting ice block while he engages in a lengthy discourse. Later, Lloyd's son runs off with a raffle token. To retrieve the token, Lloyd must chase his son through the park's crazy house, which is filled with many unpleasant surprises. Just as Lloyd hears his number called at the raffle drawing, his baby son regains the token and swallows it.

Good Morning, Sheriff (May 25, 1930) A Lloyd Hamilton Talking Comedy. Educational Film Exchanges. Lloyd Hamilton Productions, Inc. Recording by Western Electric. Supervised by Harry D. Edwards. St: Robert Stewart, Adaptation and dialogue: Jack Preston. D: Alf Goulding. Lloyd Hamilton, John C. Fowler, Ruth Hiatt, Eddie Baker, Lige Conley. 2 reels. [This film appears on the "Lost Magic of Lloyd Hamilton" DVD collection.] Rather than face Black Jack, the sheriff of Bloody Gulch turns in his badge. Disgusted that no one is willing to claim the badge, the mayor states that he will pin it on the next man to enter his office. Enter Lloyd. No one possesses confidence in the new lawman except for the mayor's daughter. Upon learning that Black Jack has harassed the citizenry, Lloyd boldly rides off after the bandit. The badmen are delighted to shoot to pieces the cute compact auto in which Lloyd is riding.

Honk Your Horn (June 29, 1930) A Lloyd Hamilton Talking Comedy. Educational Film Exchanges. Lloyd Hamilton Productions, Inc. Recording by Western Electric. Supervised by Harry D. Edwards. D: Alf Goulding. Lloyd Hamilton (Oswald), Lige Conley, Alyce McCormack, Eddie Baker. 2 reels. (Oswald's fleas are billed as "Oscar, Herman, Ignatz and Fatima.") Destitute garage proprietor Lige and his wife nearly expire from joy when a potential customer, Oswald, comes crashing into their garage. Sadly, the garage man's skills prove useless to Oswald, whose old flivver fails to survive the collision. Oswald introduces himself as the owner of a flea circus. Lige tells Oswald of his deplorable financial state. To help, Oswald obtains a handful of tacks and scatters them on the nearby highway. He remains on hand and recommends Lige's garage to drivers who suffer sudden blowouts. To relieve Lige of the monotony of repairing flats, Oswald also hurls rocks to break windshields. As one last way to increase Lige's workload, the showman wildly cavorts on the highway to prompt collisions. During this performance, he causes the wreck of an auto speeding away from a bank robbery. The police, grateful for the bank robber's capture, declare Oswald a hero. [Hamilton was actually struck by a car soon after this film was released. Seven years later, Lige Conley died as the result of being hit by an automobile.]

Service Wins Again (July, 1930) Richfield Oil/Electrical Research Products, Inc. Eddie Baker. An industrial film.

Prize Puppies (August 3, 1930) A Lloyd Hamilton Talking Comedy. Educational Film Exchanges. Lloyd Hamilton Productions, Inc. Recording by Western Electric. Supervised by Harry D. Edwards. D: Alf Goulding. Lloyd Hamilton, Stella Adams, Henry Fenwick, Will Hays. 2 reels. [A print of the film is available with Film Preservation Associates.] Lloyd is constantly annoyed by noisy tenants, including an opera singer, tap dancer and tuba player. Lloyd sets out to silence this raucous concert, but his efforts manage to attract his landlady's attention. As Lloyd cannot produce his rent money, the landlady seizes his trunk and has the local cop toss him out. Lloyd, accompanied by a tramp, sneaks back in to regain his trunk, but he is caught in the act by the landlady. Lloyd, after thinking quickly, explains that he is simply helping his companion to move *into* his old room. Indignantly, the landlady orders the men to remove the trunk from her house. Seeking greener pastures, Lloyd travels to a new and distant city. On his arrival, he is mistaken for an official who is expected to judge the town's big dog show.

Won by a Neck (October 5, 1930) A Lloyd Hamilton Talking Comedy. Educational Film Exchanges. Lloyd Hamilton Productions, Inc. Recording by Western Electric. Supervised by Harry D. Edwards. D: William Goodrich (Roscoe Arbuckle). St: Tom Whitely. Sc: Harry McCoy and Walter DeLeon. Lloyd Hamilton (Percy), Ruth Hiatt, Addie McPhail, Ed Brady, Dan Wolheim, William McCall, Glen Cavender (cafe owner). 2 reels. "One Shot" Louie's recent crime wave has depleted the city's detective ranks. Desperate, the police force allows Percy to join them. Percy is prepared for action. Before he leaves, his trainers test his bulletproof vest by shooting him with a machine gun. Percy is sent to the tough cafe where Louie and his pals lounge. A customer wearing a badge is promptly shot, but it's found out afterwards that the tin piece was not police issue. The cafe owner remains suspicious. He insists that he senses the presence of a lawman. He starts to vigorously search his establishment. Worried, Percy sits perfectly still. He remains that way until the draft from an open window becomes unbearable. He reaches over to shut the window, but a hard-looking gangster demands that he leave it open. When Percy's trousers are torn, his badge is revealed pinned to the tail of his shirt. At this point, the rookie cop frantically escapes from the cafe. Percy discovers that the draft caused his neck to stiffen. On his way to a doctor's office, he enters "One Shot" Louie's apartment by mistake. The occupants of the apartment mistake Percy for Red Hogan, Louie's murderous rival. The gang pounces on Percy and bends him out of shape. Percy, assuming that this is part of a medical treatment, does nothing to stop them.

Are You There? (November 30, 1930) Produced by the Fox Film Corp. Sound: Movietone. Songs by Grace Henry and Morris Hamilton. D: Hamilton MacFadden. Beatrice Lillie (Shirley Travis), John Garrack (Geoffrey), Olga Baclanova (Countess Helenka), George Grossmith (Duke of St. Pancras), Roger Davis (barber), Jillian Sand (Barbara Blythe), Gustav von Seyffertitz (barber), Nicholas Soussanin (barber), Richard Alexander, Henry Victor (international crooks), Lloyd Hamilton (hostler), Paula Langlen (page). 6 reels. Geoffrey employs a detective, Shirley Travis, to stop his nobleman father from marrying a crooked countess. While visiting the family castle under the guise of Lady Diana Drummond, Shirley exposes the countess and wins the duke's love. *Are You There?* is historically significant for being one of the earliest movie musicals and for featuring a rare film performance by revue star Beatrice Lillie. Fox gave *Are You There?* a limited release in 1930. The film didn't have an official New York City premiere until 1971, when it was shown as part of a Museum of Modern Art retrospective. The audience, by all accounts, responded well. Roger Greenspun, a *New York Times* critic, begrudgingly admitted to being entertained by much of the film. He wrote, "The tacky production pieces, the labored comedy routines, the generally helpless acting, even the California hills rising behind the portals of Castle Troon — gain from mellowness what they never have had in style.... [T]he changes of 40 years furnish a patina that in the popular arts inevitably encourages a kind of silly, forgiving nostalgia." Mr. Greenspun wrote, as his one complaint, "A good part of [Ms. Lillie's] time is wasted with a dreadful comedian named Lloyd Hamilton, feeding him material for slapstick clowning." Hamilton did, in fact, have some funny moments in the film. In his main scene, he teaches Lillie how to ride a horse. Later, he brings out a pack of hounds for a fox hunt, but the hounds take off abruptly and drag him across the estate.

Up a Tree (November 30, 1930) A Lloyd Hamilton Talking Comedy. Educational Film Exchanges. Lloyd Hamilton Productions, Inc. Recording by Western Electric. Supervised by Harry D. Edwards. D: William Goodrich (Roscoe Arbuckle). St: William Goodrich (Roscoe Arbuckle). Sc: Harry McCoy and Jimmy Starr. Lloyd Hamilton, Addie McPhail, Del Henderson. 2 reels. Elmer Doolittle (Hamilton) infuriates his wife, Addie, with his latest muddle. To get away from Addie, Elmer races out of his house and climbs a tree in his backyard. Feeling secure in the tree, Elmer refuses to come down until Addie is in a better mood. Present during the domestic dispute is Del, a promoter who gets publicity for people challenging endurance records. Del convinces Elmer to remain where he is in order to break the tree-sitting record. Addie becomes enthusiastic that her lackadaisical spouse will finally be accomplishing something. Through spring and summer, Elmer stays in the tree. In the meantime, Addie competes in a dance marathon. One of Del's other candidates, an endurance flier, regularly buzzes over Elmer's head. Elmer manages to cope with the aid of various necessities filling his lofty perch. Elmer, Addie and the aviator come within minutes of breaking their respective endurance records. First, Addie wins the dance contest. But then, as Addie is congratulated on her victory, the aviator allows himself to get cocky and makes a careless mistake while refueling. The aviator drenches Elmer's tree with the last of his gasoline. The tree quickly catches fire, but Del pleads with Elmer to linger for just a little while longer. Ending any further exhorting, the plane crashes through the treehouse. Emerging from the wreckage, Elmer discovers that both endurance records were broken.

Wedding Belles (1930 or 1931) Cavalcade Film Corporation. D: Sam Newfield. Ph: Otto Him. Sound: Hans Weeren. Sonophone Sound System. Lloyd Hamilton, Jack del Rio, Eddie Gribbon, Arthur Houseman, Gertrude Astor. 2 reels. [A print of this film is available at the Museum of Modern Art.] Lloyd stows away on a ship to be near his girlfriend.

Marriage Rows (January 18, 1931) A Lloyd Hamilton Talking Comedy. Educational Film Exchanges. Lloyd Hamilton Productions, Inc. Recording by Western Electric. Supervised by Harry D. Edwards. St: William Goodrich (Roscoe Arbuckle). Sc: Walter Reed. D: William Goodrich (Roscoe Arbuckle). Lloyd Hamilton (Elmer), Al St. John, Addie McPhail, Doris Deane, Al Thompson, Edna Marion. 2 reels. Jealous when his wife Winnie is visited by an old flame, Elmer decides to test her fidelity by arranging for her ex, Al, to make a pass at her. With the trap set, Elmer pretends to leave his house. Winnie, who has overheard her spouse's scheme, responds passionately to Al's advances. [Arbuckle had used the same basic premise in the memorable 1916 Keystone comedy *He Did and He Didn't*.]

Reel # 25 / Second Series (January, 1931) Voice of Hollywood. Tiffany Productions. Seben 'N' Leben (hosts), John Boles, Lloyd Hamilton, Noah Beery, Carmel Myers, Maureen O'Sullivan. One reel. "Fine." — *Motion Picture Daily*. "Interesting stuff for fans." — *Motion Picture Herald*. A trade journal summed it up as follows: "Boles sings and Hamilton clowns."

Ex-Plumber (March 8, 1931) A Lloyd Hamilton Talking Comedy. Educational Film Exchanges. Lloyd Hamilton Productions, Inc. Recording by Western Electric. Supervised by Harry D. Edwards. Sc: William Goodrich (Roscoe Arbuckle). Sc: Walter

Reid. Assistant director: Ralph Nelson. D: William Goodrich (Roscoe Arbuckle). Lloyd Hamilton, Addie McPhail, Amber Norman, Mitchell Lewis, Stanley Blystone, Polly Christy. 2 reels. Addie receives a call from a former suitor, a fanatical Russian duke who recently pursued her all over Europe. Addie explains that, when she arrived back in America, she fell in love with a man and got married. Enraged by this revelation, the Russian tells Addie that he will immediately visit her to see that she is telling the truth. He threatens that, if he finds that she is lying, he will murder her. The problem: Addie's new husband has just left town on a business trip. Addie must work quickly. She persuades Elmer Swift (Hamilton), a plumber who lives next door, to temporarily substitute for her absent spouse. The duke and plumber meet and engage in a lively chat. The nobleman simply interprets Elmer's slips as examples of his American sense of humor. Unfortunately, Elmer's luck does not hold out. Addie's husband, who has missed his train, arrives home. Elmer's wife also appears at the apartment. Elmer tries to escape the predicament, but both the duke and Addie's husband lunge at him. A pipe is broken in the process. Being a plumber at heart, Elmer automatically begins fixing the pipe while steam obscures the chaotic scene.

No Privacy (April, 1931) A Lloyd Hamilton Comedy. Universal Pictures Corporation. D: Harry Edwards. St: Francis J. Martin and James Mulhauser. Continuity: Henry R. Symonds. Lloyd Hamilton, John Ince, Tom O'Brien, Sheila Bromley (credited as Sheila Manners), Harry Wilson, Cliff Saum, Harry Tenbrook, Andy White, Charles Sullivan, George Magrill, Joe Torillo, Robert L. Stephenson, Jack "Tiny" Lipson, George R. Raymond. 2 reels. "Slow and lifeless ... most audiences will look for the end."—*Motion Picture Herald*. "Fair... not so original, but the comedian's original style of humor gets it over for laughs."—*Film Daily*. Lloyd nervously prepares to meet his girlfriend's father, who is a respectable banker. For the occasion, Lloyd charges a new hat and suit to his father's account, unaware that his father will no longer accept his bills. While Lloyd awaits the banker, creditors arrive to retrieve the clothing. Left in his underwear, Lloyd fails to make a good impression on the banker.

Hello Napoleon (May, 1931) A Lloyd Hamilton Comedy. Universal Pictures Corporation. D: Harry Edwards. St: Francis J. Martin and James Mulhauser. Lloyd Hamilton, Dell Henderson, Marion Shockley (the nurse), Arthur Hoyt, Eddie Baker (the home owner), Anne Shirley (the little girl), Billy Franey (the doctor). 2 reels. "A rather disjointed two-reeler.... It is all very flat and repetitious."—*Film Daily*. "The antics are so puerile and lacking in humor that one wonders who okayed such a script."—*Motion Picture Daily*. Harold (Hamilton), a gardener, hurts his nose while employing various methods to catch some elusive rabbits. Seeking to have the injury treated, he mistakenly enters an insane asylum and receives rough medical attention from four lunatics posing as doctors.

Howdy Mate (June, 1931) A Lloyd Hamilton Comedy. Universal Pictures Corporation. St: Johnny Grey, Sidney Levee and Mitchel Rhein. D: Harry Edwards. Lloyd Hamilton, Anne Shirley (credited as Dawn O'Day), Billy Franey, Al Thompson, Alona Marlowe. 2 reels. "This one has a barrel full of laughs.... Hamilton walks off with the honors."—*Motion Picture Daily*

An Apple a Day (September 30, 1931) A Lloyd Hamilton Comedy. Universal Pictures Corporation. St: Francis J. Martin and James Mulhauser. D: Harry Edwards. 2 reels. Lloyd, an apple-seller, infuriates a jealous husband.

Reel # 11/ Third Series (November 22, 1931) Voice of Hollywood. Tiffany Productions. Marjorie White (host), Lloyd Hamilton, Joan Crawford, Douglas Fairbanks, Jr., Gloria Swanson, Buster Keaton, Norma and Natalie Talmadge, Al Jolson, Ruby Keeler, Lionel Barrymore, Billie Dove, William Haines, Gilbert Roland, Gloria Swanson's poodle, others. 1 reel. During a helicopter ride over Hollywood, White introduces us to the several celebrities and sights that she spies below her airborne vehicle. Spotted are Marion Davies' home, the Hollywood Bowl and a star-studded beach. White eventually comes across Lloyd Hamilton, who appears to be making a daring solo flight. This is disproven when the cameraman pulls back, revealing that Lloyd's craft is a quarter ride.

Robinson Crusoe and Son (February 24, 1932) A Lloyd Hamilton Comedy. Universal Pictures Corporation. D: Harry Edwards. St: Frances J. Martin and Sidney Levee. Lloyd Hamilton. 14 1/2 minutes. [The only known copy of this film, which is available at the Library of Congress, lacks a soundtrack.] "[A goofy tale] that is gagged up very originally and contains some good laughs ... kidding stuff down with a snap."—*Film Daily*. While his adopted son listens intently, Lloyd recounts his wild adventures as a shipwrecked voyager on a cannibal island.

False Impressions (November 4, 1932) A Mack Sennett Comedy. Paramount Publix. D: Leslie Pearce. Lloyd Hamilton, Marjorie Beebe, Edmund Burns, Dorothy Granger, Marvin Loback, William McCall, Bud Jamison, George Gray, Herman Bing, Lorena Carr, Estella Essex, Pat Hanna, Ted Stroback, Marion Weldon. 2 reels. [A print of this film is available at the Jugoslovenska Kinoteka.] Lloyd works in the toy department of a large department store. Marjorie, a co-worker, is trying on a fur in the fur department when she meets a rich bachelor, Windy Windemere. Marjorie pretends to be a rich customer to impress Windy, who responds by inviting her to a party at his estate. Lloyd, who decides to go along with Marjorie, crashes the party disguised as a butler.

Doubling in the Quickies (December 16, 1932) A Mack Sennett Comedy. Paramount Publix. D: Babe Stafford. Lloyd Hamilton, Marjorie Beebe, Bud

Jamison, Aggie Herring, Ted Strobach. 2 reels. [The film is also known as *A Hollywood Double*. Prints of the film are available with Film Preservation Associates and the Jugoslovenska Kinoteka.] Aspiring to be a movie star, Marjorie leaves Piperville and travels to Hollywood. Joe Ditz (Hamilton), a grocer who intended to marry Marjorie, is left heartbroken. After giving the matter some thought, he resolves to pursue his beloved and win her back. Meanwhile, Marjorie's auditions provoke no more than derisive laughter. Unknowingly, Marjorie accepts a job as a stunt woman.

The Lion and the House (December 23, 1932) A Mack Sennett Comedy. Paramount Publix. D: Babe Stafford. Lloyd Hamilton, Arthur Stone, Babe Kane, Aggie Herring. 2 reels. [The film is also known as *Hokey Honeymoon*. A print is available at the Jugoslovenska Kinoteka.] A lion parachutes into Lloyd's newly redecorated house.

Too Many Highballs (February 10, 1933) A Mack Sennett Comedy. Paramount Publix. Sc: Clyde Bruckman. D: Clyde Bruckman. Lloyd Hamilton, Marjorie Beebe, Tom Dugan, Aggie Herring, Bud Jamison, Joe Bordeaux, Tom Kennedy, George Gray, William McCall, Dave Morris. 2 reels. [The film is also known as *His Perfect Day*. A print is available at the Jugoslovenska Kinoteka.] Henry Hobbs (Hamilton) figures to get a break from his wife's disagreeable mother and brother by sneaking off to a wrestling match. To be excused from work, he lies to his boss that his brother-in-law has just died. On his way to the match, Henry struggles to squeeze his car into a parking space between two other cars. A policeman approaches Henry to give him a ticket for parking in a "no parking" zone. Based on Henry's clumsy maneuvering to get out of the space, the officer decides that Henry has been drinking and arrests him for drunk driving. In the meantime, Henry's brother-in-law becomes sick from castor oil that Henry slipped into his whiskey as a prank. The brother-in-law is such a bad state that he passes out. It is at this time that Henry's boss calls Mrs. Hobbs to offer condolences about her brother's sudden passing. The family assumes that Henry expected his brother-in-law to die because he had, in fact, poisoned him. [W. C. Fields was an uncredited writer on this short. Two years later, Fields and Bruckman would expand the script for a feature film, *The Man on the Flying Trapeze*. The film, including Fields' recreation of the parking sequence, is generally regarded as one of the great comedy classics.]

Hollywood on Parade A-2 (September 9, 1933) Paramount Pictures. P: Louis Lewyn. Buster Crabbe, Mae West, Cecil B. DeMille, Lloyd Hamilton, Groucho, Chico and Harpo Marx. 1 reel. Hamilton travels around Hollywood to try out a camera sent to him by a fan. His misadventures are largely an excuse to introduce newsreel footage of Hollywood celebrities. In the opening scene, Hamilton joins Crabbe at Paramount's "Search for Beauty" contest. He later attends the premiere of Mae West's *I'm No Angel*, where he snaps pictures of celebrities walking down the red carpet. In the closing scene, Hamilton appears dressed as Baby Leroy. The comedian strutting forward in a toddler's outfit and brandishing a baby bottle, is surrounded by several pretty nursemaids.

Pop's Pal (December 29, 1933) A Mermaid Comedy. Educational Pictures, Inc. Ph: Dwight Warren. Sc: Ernest Pagano, Ewart Adamson and C. Edward Roberts. D: Harry J. Edwards. Billy Bevan, George Bickel, John Harron, Lloyd Hamilton, Josephine Hull. 2 reels. John is visited by his father and his father's friend. At first, the two visiting men tenderly hug, deliver salutations, and pat each on the back. Later, the affectionate clasping shifts to violent clutching. After fiercely seizing one another, the men tumble down a long staircase together. Lloyd, a businessman who intends to hire John, arrives in the midst of the fray and falls victim to a stray blow. Frightened, he quickly flees the scene. The men, eager to apologize, chase after the businessman. Lloyd, fearing the deranged pair will pummel him, pedals away on a bicycle. The chase quickly escalates, with Lloyd using first a wagon and then a horse to escape.

An Old Gypsy Custom (January 12, 1934) An Andy Clyde Comedy. Educational Pictures, Inc. D: Harry Edwards. Andy Clyde, John Sheehan, Lloyd Hamilton, Addie McPhail, Cecilia Parker, Fern Emmett, Spec O'Donnell, Betty Boyd, Chiquita de Montes. 2 reels. "With Lloyd Hamilton and Addie McPhail among his supporting cast, Andy Clyde's latest is a generally enjoyable affair.... Hamilton plays the role of a cop in his familiar old-time style that is still good for laughs."— Film Daily. Storeowner Andy is enamored of a gypsy girl, but he experiences many difficulties with her gypsy kinsmen. Lloyd, playing a lawman, is dressed up in his well-known outfit, but he has a sheriff's star pinned to his lapel and a pair of handcuffs locked around his belt. In a search of pig thieves, he prowls the neighborhood with a shotgun. Being quick on the trigger, he nearly ventilates poor Andy. In the final scene, Andy resolves his problems with the gypsies and both parties decide to go home. Lloyd is left alone in the scene. After a moment of reflection, he turns on his heel and employs his trademark gait to exit the frame.

Star Night at Cocoanut Grove (January 31, 1935) An MGM Colortone Musical. P: Louis Lewyn. Leo Carrillo, El Brendel, Mary Pickford, Bing Crosby, Gary Cooper, Toby Wing, Raquel Torres, Johnny Mack Brown, Candy Candido, Lloyd Hamilton. 2 reels.

The Fox-Sunshine Comedies Without Lloyd Hamilton

The First Season (1917–1918)

A Milk-fed Vamp (November 25, 1917) Supervised by Henry Lehrman. Sc: Henry Lehrman. D: David Kirkland. Dot Farley, Jimmie Adams, Victor Potel, Joe the Monk. 2 reels. A simple farmer's daughter, who enjoys her ability to charm the opposite sex, transforms herself into a vamp. The extravagant farm girl elopes with a city youth named Cobble Stonio. In the city, the girl meets another of Cobble's wives, a woman who works as an organ grinder to support herself and her three children.

His Smashing Career (December 9, 1917) Supervised by Henry Lehrman. Sc: Henry Lehrman. D: Henry Lehrman. Billie Ritchie, Gertrude Selby, Billy Bevan (father), Victor Potel. 2 reels. Gertrude, an athletic and shapely lass, steps out of the simming pool to greet her father. She gives Dad an affectinate uppercut, which sends him into his rocking chair with enough force to cause the chair's collapse. Gertrude's maids apparently possess equal might. One of the maids subdues a forward male servant by tossing the fellow into the pool. Gertrude is enmeshed in a troubled love affair with a valorous auto racer, Hundred Horsepower Harry. Harry must face the numerous dastardly villains set after him by Gertrude's disapproving father. The vile group tries everything possible to prevent Harry from winning his race, but the driver escapes their obstructions with an amazing repertoire of auto tricks. Unbeknownst to Harry, the judge of the race is a romantic rival. As flivvers break apart on the course, the judge plots relentlessly for Harry to lose the race. The judge seems assured of success until the last few minutes of the race. It is during this time that the father's henchmen tie a rope from Harry's auto to the racing stand on which the judge is perched. The auto pulls out the support beams from the stand and the judge is forcibly brought to earth. Moments later, Harry emerges victorious.

Damaged—No Goods (December 23, 1917) Supervised by Henry Lehrman. D: Jay Howe and Jack White. Mark Davidson, Gertrude Selby, Mildred Lee. 2 reels. Before he can wed Gertrude, Mark must get the consent of Gertrude's father. The father instead forbids Mark to ever see his daughter again. Mark disguises himself as a woman in order to gain access to Gertrude's house and get her to elope with him. Once inside the house, the skirted beau flirts with Gertrude's father, who proves to be rascally. A count who also wants to marry Gertrude mistakes Mark for Gertrude and carries him away. A considerable amount of roughhouse and frantic activity follow. During a car chase, a Ford interferes with traffic and passengers spill off the back of a sightseeing bus. In the end, the count is captured and the couple is given Dad's permission to wed.

Shadows of Her Past (January 6, 1918) Supervised by Henry Lehrman. D: Henry Lehrman. Dot Farley, Victor Potel. 2 reels.

Son of a Gun (January 20, 1918) Supervised by Henry Lehrman. Sc: Henry Lehrman. D: Richard Jones. Billie Ritchie, Winifred Westover, Hugh Fay, Sid Smith. 2 reels. A young couple elopes to Mexico, where the bride becomes the captive of a local general. To rescue her, the groom enlists the aid of an American ambassador and his hometown police force. In the end, the young lady is freed and the Mexican general is punished.

Are Married Policemen Safe? (February 17, 1918) Supervised by Henry Lehrman. Sc: Henry Lehrman. D: Richard Jones. Hugh Fay, Billie Ritchie, Charles Conklin. 2 reels. A moral crusade is undertaken to enforce laws forbidding brief public apparel. As a result, several young women are arrested for wearing leg-baring bathing suits at the beach. The women imprison their jailers as an act of protest. While the situation is being resolved, an angry Mexican inmate is able to make an escape. The Lehrman police trail the escaped convict to a Mexican city, where they find the convict works as the chief of police.

Her Husband's Wife (March 3, 1918) Supervised by Henry Lehrman. D: David Kirkland. Winifred Westover, Jimmie Adams, Hugh Fay. 2 reels.

A Self-Made Lady (March 24, 1918) Supervised by Henry Lehrman. Sc: Henry Lehrman. D: Henry Lehrman. Dot Farley, Bobby Vernon, Ed Kennedy, John Rand. 2 reels. A lady shoplifter is sentenced to seven days in prison, but a clerical error has her serve seven *years*. After her release, the ex-inmate plans to go straight. [Stills indicate that the Lehrman police force played a large role in this comedy. The cops race autos off a cliff and, while wading up to their chests in water, pursue a canine through a sewer system. When the comedy was reissued in the summer, the exhibitor material listed David Kirkland as director.]

A Neighbor's Keyhole (May 5, 1918) Supervised by Henry Lehrman. D: Henry Lehrman. Winifred Westover, Hugh Fay, The Sunshine Bathing Beauties. 2 reels. (The film was partially shot at Coronado Beach in Los Angeles.) Some excitement results when Mr. Adam Sapple (a fellow in possession of a large, bobbing neck projection) is made matron of a girls' seminary. Early on, Adam saves a bottle with an associate. To insure the bottle's safekeeping, the associate ties a bell around Adam's distinctive larynx so that an alarm will sound if Adam gulps down the bottle's contents. Adam and his friend subsequently become rivals for Winifred, a situation seeming to require the delicate placement of a second bell. Also involved are the Lehrman cops, an obstinate swan and a belligerent ram. The story concludes with a race involving a large variety of outlandishly designed automobiles. These super funny-cars can ford streams, mend punctures underwater, and spew frogs and fish from their radiators.

Wild Women and Tame Lions (June 2, 1918) Supervised by Henry Lehrman. D: William Campbell. Ford Sterling, Jimmie Adams, Ethel Teare, lions, alligators, apes, elephants, kangaroos. 2 reels. After being accidentally tied up in a laundry bag, a lion winds up getting loose in a boudoir.

Who's Your Father? (July 7, 1918) Supervised by Henry Lehrman. D: Tom Mix. Tom Mix, Gertrude Selby, Victor Potel. 2 reels.

The Diver's Last Kiss (August 25, 1918) Supervised by Henry Lehrman. D: Noel Smith. Slim Summerville, Frank J. Coleman, Bobby Dunn. 2 reels. (The film was also known as *A Highdiver's Last Kiss*.) The film climaxes with Slim becoming trapped out on an airplane wing. [George Axelrod, a noted screenwriter whose credits include *Breakfast at Tiffany's* and *The Manchurian Candidate*, talked about his mother, Betty Carpenter, appearing in this film as one of the bathing beauties. Axelrod said, "[S]he was a high diver on a diving board, and [Summerville] comes along in an autogiro ... and her bathing suit gets all tangled up in the blades."]

The Second Season (1918–1919)

Choose Your Exit (October 20, 1918) 2 reels. Though released as a Sunshine comedy, it is likely that this short was a reissued *Foxfilm* comedy.

The Fatal Marriage (December 15, 1918) Supervised by Henry Lehrman. D: William Campbell. Billie Ritchie, Hugh Fay, Sylvia Day, Betty Carpenter. 2 reels.

Oh, What a Knight! (January 26, 1919) Supervised by Henry Lehrman. D: Fred Fishback. Mack Swain, Ethel Teare, Jack Cooper, Glen Cavendar. 2 reels. Swain plays a well-fed sheriff in this frantic western satire, a remake of *His Bitter Pill* (a comedy that Fishback and Swain had made at Keystone). This popular film was later reissued under the titles *The Sheriff's Moustache* and *Cowboy Ambrose*.

Money Talks (March 23, 1919) Supervised by Henry Lehrman. D: Fred Fishback. Mark Swain, Jack Cooper, Gertrude Selby, Hazel Deane. (Bobby Dunn may have also appeared in this film.) 2 reels.

The House of Terrible Scandals (April 20, 1919) Supervised by Henry Lehrman. Sc: Henry Lehrman. D: Henry Lehrman. Dot Farley, Billie Ritchie. 3 reels. [Originally released as a *Foxfilm* comedy in February, 1917.]

A Lady Bellhop's Secret (May 4, 1919) Supervised by Henry Lehrman. D: William Campbell. Betty Carpentier, Hugh Fay. 2 reels. At a lavish hotel, a lady bellhop and the hotel proprietor's son intend to elope, but a leaking pipe interferes with their plans. At first, water trickles into an upper suite. Ultimately, the drip causes a severe flood to rush through the hotel. Blamed for having caused the deluge, the bellhop is imprisoned. Once the bellhop escapes from jail, she returns to the hotel by plane and snatches her love from an eighty-foot ladder. Friends of the boy's father fly after the bellhop's plane and employ dogfight maneuvers to stop the pair from getting away. At one point, a pilot bails out of his plane and parachutes into an open cage of lions. In the end, the young couple is able to make it to the justice of the peace.

Virtuous Husbands (May 25, 1919) Supervised by Henry Lehrman (?). D: J.G. Blystone. Jack Cooper, Slim Summerville. 2 reels.

The Merry Jailbirds (July 6, 1919) Supervised by Henry Lehrman (?). D: Fred Fishback. Glen Cavender, Jack Cooper. 2 reels. (The working title of this comedy was *High Life in Jail*.)

Third Season (1919–20)

Her First Kiss (August 31, 1919) Supervised by Hampton Del Ruth. D: Frank Griffin. Ethel Teare, Slim Summerville (Dave Morris may have also appeared in this film). 2 reels.

Dabbling in Society (September 14, 1919) Supervised by Hampton Del Ruth. D: Reggie Morris. Glen Cavender, Jack Cooper. 2 reels.

His Naughty Wife (September 28, 1919) Supervised by Hampton Del Ruth. D: Victor Heerman. Harry Gribbon, Bobby Dunn, Harry McCoy. 2 reels.

Wild Waves and Women (October 12, 1919) Supervised by Hampton Del Ruth. D: Frank Griffin. Slim Summerville, Ethel Teare, Virginia Warwick, Polly Moran, Dave Morris, Bartine Burkett, The Beauty Brigade. 2 reels.

The Yellow Dog Catcher (October 26, 1919) Supervised by Hampton Del Ruth. D: Jack Blystone. Jack Cooper, Glen Cavender, Billy Franey. 2 reels.

Back to Nature Girls (November 9, 1919) Supervised by Hampton Del Ruth. D: Jack Blystone. Chester Conklin, Harry McCoy, Dorothy Lee, Tom Kennedy. 2 reels.

Footlight Maids (November 23, 1919) Supervised by Hampton Del Ruth. D: Jack G. Blystone. Tom Kennedy, Jack Cooper, Glen Cavender, Mary Emory. 2 reels.

A Schoolhouse Scandal (December 7, 1919) Supervised by Hampton Del Ruth. D: Eddie Cline. Polly Moran, Slim Summerville, Jack Cooper. 2 reels.

The Roaming Bathtub (December 21, 1919) Supervised by Hampton Del Ruth. D: Frank Griffin. Ethel Teare, Billy Franey, Ed Kennedy, Jack Cooper. 2 reels.

Chicken ala Cabaret (January 4, 1920) Supervised by Hampton Del Ruth. D: Victor Heerman. Chester Conklin, Dorothy Lee, Billy Armstrong, Harry Booker. 2 reels.

Hungry Lions and Tender Hearts (January 18, 1920) Supervised by Hampton Del Ruth. D: Roy Del Ruth and Mal St. Clair. Jack Cooper, Glen Cavender, Marvel Rea. 2 reels.

Sheriff Nell's Comeback (February 1, 1920) Supervised by Hampton Del Ruth. D: Eddie Cline. Polly Moran. 2 reels.

Her Naughty Wink (February 15, 1920) Supervised by Hampton Del Ruth. D: Jack G. Blystone. Billy Franey, Ethel Teare, Ed Kennedy. 2 reels.

The Heart Snatcher (March 1, 1920) Supervised

by Hampton Del Ruth. D: Roy Del Ruth. Jack Cooper, Marvel Rea, Harry Booker, Bobby Dunn, Kewpie Morgan, Joseph Swickard, Joe Murphy, Blanche Payson, Glen Cavender, Frank J. Coleman. 2 reels.

Her Private Husband (March 15, 1920) Supervised by Hampton Del Ruth. D: Frank Griffin. Chester Conklin, Alice Davenport. 2 reels.

A Lightweight Lover (March 29, 1920) Supervised by Hampton Del Ruth. D: Roy Del Ruth. Jack Cooper, Ed Kennedy, Marvel Rea. 2 reels.

Training for Husbands (April 12, 1920) Supervised by Hampton Del Ruth. D: Eddie Cline. Slim Summerville, Polly Moran, Dave Morris. 2 reels.

The Great Nickel Robbery (April 26, 1920) Supervised by Hampton Del Ruth. D: Jack G. Blystone. Chester Conklin, Dorothy Lee. 2 reels.

Dangerous Eyes (May 10, 1920) Supervised by Hampton Del Ruth. D: Jack G. Blystone. Chester Conklin, Dorothy Lee, Ed Kennedy, Gus Pixley, Laura LaVarnie. 2 reels.

Should Dummies Wed? (May 24, 1920) Supervised by Hampton Del Ruth. D: Roy Del Ruth. Ethel Teare. 2 reels.

Monkey Business (June 7, 1920) Supervised by Hampton Del Ruth. D: Eddie Cline. Ethel Teare, Dave Morris, Harry Booker. 2 reels.

The Jazz Bandits (June 21, 1920) Supervised by Hampton Del Ruth. D: Roy Del Ruth. Glen Cavender, Dave Morris, Ethel Teare. 2 reels.

Through the Keyhole (July 5, 1920) Supervised by Hampton Del Ruth. D: Roy Del Ruth. Dave Morris, Glen Cavender, Ed Kennedy. 2 reels.

10 Nights Without a Barroom (July 19, 1920) Supervised by Hampton Del Ruth. D: Eddie Cline. Slim Summerville, Ethel Teare, Tom Kennedy, Ford West, Harry Gribbon, Harry McCoy. 2 reels.

Slippery Feet (August 2, 1920) Supervised by Hampton Del Ruth. D: Jack G. Blystone. Harry Gibbon, Gladys Walton, Gus Pixley, Bobby Dunn. 2 reels.

Mary's Little Lobster (August 16, 1920) Supervised by Hampton Del Ruth. D: Eddie Cline. Slim Summerville, Bobby Dunn, Gus Pixley, Lois Boyd, Tom Kennedy. 2 reels. Other Sunshine players for the season included Alta Allen, Hyman Binensky, Bert Gillespie, Rosa Gore and Blanche Payson. Assistant directors included Frank Beal, Vin Moore and Travis Vale. Hampton Del Ruth left the Sunshine company at the end of the season. Del Ruth announced that he was forming his own company, but the new company never materialized.

Fourth Season (1920–21)

Farmyard Follies (September 13, 1920) D: Roy Del Ruth. 2 reels.

Chase Me (September 27, 1920) D: Roy Del Ruth. Glen Cavender, Olive Dale, Dave Morris, Ed Kennedy. 2 reels.

An Elephant's Nightmare (October 11, 1920) D: Vin Moore. Jack Cooper, Larry Bowes. 2 reels.

His Noisy Still (October 25, 1920) D: Roy Del Ruth. Glen Cavender, Dave Morris, Olive Dale, Kewpie Morgan. 2 reels.

Hold Me Tight (November 8, 1920) Slim Summerville, Harry Booker, Ethel Teare. 2 reels.

Pretty Lady (November 22, 1920) D: Jack G. Blystone. Slim Summerville, Ethel Teare, Bobby Dunn, Marion Aye, Kewpie Morgan. 2 reels.

She Loves Me, She Loves Me Not (November 29, 1920) D: Al St John. Al St. John. 2 reels.

A Doggone Wedding (December 6, 1920) D: Harry Williams. Dave Morris. 2 reels. (The working title of this film was *His Wife's Caller*.)

Pals and Petticoats (December 20, 1920) D: Melville W. Brown and Delmar Lord. Harry McCoy. 2 reels.

The Slicker (January 3, 1921) D: Al St. John. Al St. John, Polly Moran (Little Nell, the country maid). 2 reels.

The Baby (January 17, 1921) D: Harry Williams. Gus Pixley, Ethel Teare, Tom Kennedy, Ernie Adams. 2 reels.

His Unlucky Job (January 31, 1921) D: Ray Enright and Melville Brown. 2 reels.

Roaring Lions on Parade (February 14, 1921) D: Harry Williams. Tom Kennedy, Ethel Teare. 2 reels.

His Fiery Beat (February 28, 1921) Bobby Dunn (police chief and fire chief), Olive Dale, Larry Bowes. 2 reels.

The Simp (March 13, 1921) D: Ferris Hartman. Al St. John. 2 reels.

The Big Secret (March 27, 1921) D: Ferris Hartman. Al St. John, Larry Bowes. 2 reels.

The Janitors (April 10, 1921) D: Delmar Lord. 2 reels.

Verse and Worse (April 24, 1921) D: Ray Enright and George Gray. Chester Conklin. 2 reels.

His Meal Ticket (May 8) D: Ferris Hartman. Bobby Dunn, Joe Roberts. 2 reels.

The Night Before (May 22, 1921) D: Malcolm St. Clair. 2 reels.

The Hayseed (June 5, 1921) Al St. John, Alice Davenport. 2 reels.

Three Good Pals (June 19, 1921) St: Lew Seiler. D: Nate Watt. 2 reels.

Who's Who (July 3, 1921) Bobby Dunn, Joe Roberts. 2 reels.

The Singer Midget Scandal (July 17, 1921) D: Eddie Cline. Slim Summerville, the Singer Midgets. 2 reels.

Ain't Love Grand? (August 14, 1921) D: Al St John. Al St. John. 2 reels.

A Devilish Romeo (August 28, 1921) D: Frank Griffin. Hallam Cooley, Ford West, Joe Roberts, Bobby Dunn. 2 reels. This season, the Sunshine company also released:

Skirts (April 10, 1921) Sc: Hampton Del Ruth. D: Hampton Del Ruth. Assisting in the direction: Jack G. Blystone, Eddie Cline, Roy Del Ruth, Mal St. Clair, Vin Moore, Frank Griffin, and a peaked chihuahua. Clyde Cook, The Singer Midgets (with their complete bantam circus), Slim Summerville, Tom Kennedy, Mutt Murphy, Blanche Payson, Tiny Ward, Bert Gillespie, Alta Allen, Chester Conklin, Harry Booker, Jack Cooper, Laura LaVarnie, Ethel Teare, Alice Davenport, Glen Cavender, Bobby Dunn, Ed Kennedy, Dave Morris, Jim Donnelly, Harry Gribbon, Dorothy Lee. 5 reels (4,950 ft.). This feature, billed as a "hippodromic comedy spectacle," was made over a period of five months in early 1920. Also included in its cast were several circus animals and numerous bathing beauties. The studio unbelievably promised in newspaper ads that the film featured 3,000 bathing beauties, "the most bewildering array of beauties ever shown on the screen."

Fifth Season (1921–22)

Say It with Flowers (September 11, 1921) D: Al Herman. Jimmy Savo. 2 reels.

The Book Agent (September 25, 1921) 2 reels.

Singer Midgets' Sideshow (October 9, 1921) D: Eddie Cline. The Singer Midgets. 2 reels.

One Moment Please (October 23, 1921) D: Slim Summerville. 2 reels.

A Perfect Villain (November 6, 1921) D: Erle Kenton. Chester Conklin. 2 reels.

Love and War (November 20, 1921) D: Al Herman. 2 reels.

Business Is Business (December 4, 1921) 2 reels.

Try and Get It (December 18, 1921) 2 reels.

Pardon Me (January 1, 1922) Jimmy Savo. 2 reels.

Hold That Line (January 15, 1922) D: Slim Summerville. Jimmy Savo. Lois Scott, Bert Roach, Glen Cavender. 2 reels.

False Alarm (January 29, 1922) Chester Conklin. 2 reels.

Please Be Careful (February 12, 1922) Charles Doherty, Ethel Teare, Joe Murphy, Jimmy Finlayson. 2 reels.

West is West (February 26, 1922) D: George Marshall. Harry Depp. 2 reels.

Laughing Gas (March 12, 1922) D: Erle Kenton. Chester Conklin. 2 reels.

The Barnstormers (March 26, 1922) D: Slim Summerville and Del Lord. Vernon Dent, Billy Armstrong, James C. Morton. 2 reels.

The Piper (April 9, 1922) D: Erle Kenton. 2 reels.

His Wife's Son (April 23, 1922) D: Ed Kennedy. Chester Conklin. 2 reels.

Excuse Me, Sheriff (May 7, 1922) D: John McDermott. 2 reels.

The Wise Duck (May 21, 1922) D: Tom Buckingham. Charles Conklin, Jimmy Finlayson. 2 reels.

The Landlord (June 4, 1922) D: Erle Kenton. 2 reels.

Safe in the Safe (June 18, 1922) D: Ed Kennedy. Charles Conklin. 2 reels.

Sixth Season (1922–23)

Splitting Hairs (August 20, 1922) D: Erle Kenton. 2 reels.

Puppy Love (September 3, 1922) D: Tom Buckingham. 2 reels.

The Tin Bronco (September 17, 1922) D: John McDermott. 2 reels.

Dandy Dan — He's a Detective Man (October 1, 1922) D: Noel Smith. Sid Smith. 2 reels.

Step Lively Please (October 15, 1922) D: Ed Kennedy. Chester Conklin, Charles Conklin. 2 reels.

The Haunted House (October 29, 1922) D: Erle Kenton. 2 reels.

The Ranch Romeo (November 12, 1922) D: Slim Summerville. Gilbert Holmes. 2 reels.

Cupid's Elephant (November 26, 1922) D: Noel Smith. 2 reels.

The Fresh Heir (December 10, 1922) D: Ed Kennedy. Chester Conklin. 2 reels.

A Poor Fish (December 24, 1922) D: Erle Kenton. 2 reels.

Rides and Slides (January 7, 1923) D: Herman C. Raymaker. 2 reels.

The Five-Fifteen (January 21, 1923) D: Slim Summerville. 2 reels.

The Wise Cracker (February 4, 1923) D: Erle Kenton. 2 reels.

Hello, Pardner (February 18, 1923) D: Herman C Raymaker. Peewee Holmes, Buster Gardner. 2 reels.

Clothes and Oil (March 4, 1923) D: Erle Kenton. Chester Conklin. 2 reels.

The Four-flusher (March 18, 1923) D: Norman Taurog. Joe Roberts. 2 reels.

The Mummy (April 1, 1923) D: Norman Taurog. 2 reels.

The Three-Gun Man (April 15, 1923) D: Erle Kenton. 2 reels.

Where There's a Will (April 29, 1923) D: Jack G. Blystone. 2 reels.

Roaring Lions on a Steamship (May 13, 1923) D: Tom Buckingham. Harry Sweet, Charles Conklin. 2 reels.

Circus Pals (May 27, 1923) D: William Campbell and Lew Seiler. 2 reels.

Applesauce (June 10, 1923) D: Noel Smith. 2 reels.

Seventh Season (1923–24)

Jungle Pals (August 26, 1923) D: Lew Seiler. Jack Duffy, trio of humanzees. 2 reels.

The Explorers (September 9, 1923) D: Tom Buckingham. Charles Conklin. 2 reels.

Unreal Newsreel (September 23, 1923) D: George Somerville (Slim Summerville). 2 reels. This was a clip compilation of previous Fox comedies, including the Sunshine comedies, Clyde Cook comedies and Al St. John comedies.

Dance or Die (October 7, 1923) D: Erle Kenton. 2 reels. (The working title of this comedy was *The Marathon Dancers*.)

The Roaring Lion (October 21, 1923) D: Erle Kenton. 2 reels. (The working title of this comedy was *Nobody Home*.)
Somebody Lied (November 4, 1923) D: Stephen Roberts and Bryan Foy. 2 reels.
Rough Sailing (November 18, 1923) D: George Somerville. 2 reels.
The Income Tax Collector (December 2, 1923) D: Erle Kenton. Lew Brice (brother of Fanny Brice). 2 reels.
The Riding Master (December 16, 1923) D: George Somerville. 2 reels.
Spring Fever (December 30, 1923) D: Archie Mayo. Harry Sweet, Al St. John, Jean Arthur. 2 reels.
School Pals (January 13, 1924) 2 reels.
Jazz Newsreel (January 27, 1924) 2 reels.
The Weakling (February 10, 1924) D: Noel Smith. Henry Murdoch. 2 reels.
Etiquette (February 24, 1924) D: Tom Buckingham. 2 reels.
Unreal Newsreel No. 2 (March 9, 1924) This was a clip compilation. 2 reels.
The Jazz Weekly (March 23, 1924) Arranger: Ralph Spence. 2 reels.
When Wise Ducks Meet (May 4, 1924) D: Ben Stoloff and Clyde Carruth. 2 reels.
Sad but True (May 25, 1924) D: George Somerville. Chester Conklin. 2 reels.
Unreal Newsreel No. 3 (June 8, 1924) D: George Somerville. This was a clip compilation. 2 reels.
Children Wanted (June 22, 1924) D: Henry Lehrman. Victoria Louise Kenner. 2 reels.
Scenario School (July 6, 1924) Edited and titled by Ralph Spence. 2 reels.
Pain as You Enter (July 20, 1924) D: Norman Taurog. Lee Moran, Paul Parrott, Ruth Hiatt, Frank "Fatty" Alexander. 2 reels.

Eighth Season: The Lion in Winter (1924–25)
Stretching the Truth (August 24, 1924) D: Benjamin Stoloff. 2 reels.
Unreal Newsreel No. 4 (September 7, 1924) D: George Somerville. This was a clip compilation. 2 reels.

The Diving Fool (September 21, 1924) D: Charles Lamont. 2 reels.
The Electric Elopement (October 5, 1924) D: Albert Ray. 2 reels.
The Radio Riot (October 19, 1924) Editor: Ralph Spence. 2 reels.
The Nickel-Plated West (November 2, 1924) D: Al Herman. 2 reels.
The Masked Marvel (November 16, 1924) D: Roy Del Ruth. Paul Parrott. 2 reels.
A Movie Mad Maid (November 30, 1924) D: Al Herman. 2 reels.
The Milk Bottle Bandit (December 14, 1924) Sc: Harry Sweet. D: Harry Sweet. 2 reels.
Dangerous Curves (December 28, 1924) D: William Campbell. 2 reels.
Up on the Farm (January 11, 1925) Lee Moran. 2 reels.
Nobody Works But Father (January 25, 1925) D: Al Herman. 2 reels.
The Mysterious Stranger (February 8, 1925) D: Roy Del Ruth. 2 reels.
Head Over Heels (February 22, 1925) D: Roy Del Ruth. 2 reels.
The Butterfly Man (March 8, 1925) St: Andrew Bennison. D: Lew Seiler. Sid Smith. 2 reels.
Stop, Look and Whistle (March 22, 1925) D: Al Herman. 2 reels.
Neptune's Stepdaughter (April 5, 1925) D: Max Gold. Babe Hardy. 2 reels.
The Brainless Horseman (April 19, 1925) 2 reels.
When Dumbbells Ring (May 3, 1925) D: George Somerville. 2 reels.
A Scientific Husband (May 17, 1925) St: Murray Roth. D: Bryan Foy. 2 reels.
The Honeymoon Limited (May 31, 1925) D: Robert Kerr. Lee Moran. 2 reels.
Love and Lions, an *Imperial* comedy, was released in the fall of 1925. This production was proof that, beyond the close of the Sunshine series, the spirit of the Sunshine would endure at Fox. In addition, the studio debuted, as part of their 1926–27 program, the *Fox Animal Comedies*.

Chapter Notes

Chapter 1

1. Walter Kerr, *The Silent Clowns* (New York: Alfred A. Knopf, 1975).
2. Robert Louis Stevenson, *The Strange Case of Dr. Jekyll and Mr. Hyde* (New York: Scribner, 1886).
3. Federal Writers' Project, *Michigan: A Guide to the Wolverine State* (Reprint. New York: Somerset, 1981 [orig. 1941]).
4. Richard Koszarski, *The Man You Loved to Hate: Erich von Stroheim and Hollywood* (New York: Oxford University Press, 1983).
5. Malcolm E. Barker, *More San Francisco Memoirs 1852-1899 The Ripening Years* (San Francisco: Londonborn Publications, 1996), p. 178.
6. Frank Trippett, "First the Shaking, Then the Flames." *Time Magazine*, October 30, 1989.
7. Rudyard Kipling, "How I got to San Francisco and took tea with the natives here" (1889).
8. Benjamin Estelle Lloyd, *Lights and Shades of San Francisco* (San Francisco: A.L. Bancroft, 1876), p. 79.
9. Lloyd, p. 494.
10. Lloyd, p. 86.
11. Barker, p. 46.
12. Barker, p. 199.
13. Lloyd, p. 488.
14. Barker, p. 266.
15. Barker, p. 268.
16. Barker, p. 251.
17. Barker, p. 252.
18. Barker, p. 178.
19. Lloyd, p. 350.
20. Barker, p. 107.
21. Barker, p. 242.
22. Lloyd, p. 122.
23. Barker, p. 274.
24. Lloyd, p. 124.
25. Lloyd, p. 299.
26. Herbert Ashbury, *The Barbary Coast: An Informal History of the San Francisco Underworld* (New York: Alfred A. Knopf, Inc., 1933), p. 30.
27. Barker, p. 230.
28. Ashbury, p. 133.
29. Lloyd, p. 351.
30. Doris Muscatine, *Old San Francisco: The Biography of a City from Early Days to the Earthquake* (New York: G.P. Putnam's Sons, 1975), p. 415.
31. Charles Reynolds Brown, *My Own Yesterdays* (New York: The Century Company, 1931), p. 89.
32. Brown, p. 92.
33. Brown, p. 115.
34. Charles Reynolds Brown, *Where Do You Live?* (New Haven: Yale University Press, 1926), p. 17.
35. Charles Reynolds Brown, *The Art of Preaching* (New York: The MacMillan Company, 1922), p. 56.
36. *Oakland Tribune* (March 18, 1917).
37. Richard Schickel, *Harold Lloyd: The Shape of Laughter* (New York: Graphic Society, 1974).
38. John McCabe, *The Comedy World of Stan Laurel* (Golden City, New York: Doubleday, 1974).
39. Allan Buckingham, "Just 'Ham and Bud.'" *Photoplay Vogue* (August 20, 1915).
40. H. Ames, "Ham and Bud." *Motion Picture Classic*, 2:41 March, 1916.
41. Frank Capron, "He Who Gets 'Soaked': Lloyd Hamilton Is Still Taking Falls and Ducking Custard Pies, But Has Hopes of Tossing His Checkered Cap at Bigger Targets." *Motion Picture Classic*, 24:62, February, 1927.
42. W. M. Henry, "Ham and Bud." *Photoplay*, 10– 3:95, August, 1916.
43. *The College Star* (Southwest Texas State) (June 19, 1929). Editorial in campus student newspaper.
44. Ames.
45. Charleson Gray, "His Comeback." *Motion Picture Classic*, 30:39, November, 1929.
46. Robin Williams, *An Evening with Robin Williams* (1982). New York: HBO.
47. Lloyd, p. 150.
48. Lloyd, p. 151.
49. London, Jack. *The Valley of the Moon*. New York: The Macmillan Company, 1914. p. 228.
50. Lloyd, p. 124.

Chapter 2

1. Charles Augustus Keeler, *San Francisco and Thereabout* (San Francisco: A. M. Robinson/The California Promotion Committee of San Francisco, 1906).
2. Muscatine, p. 168–69, 425.
3. Rudi Blesh, *Keaton* (New York: Macmillan Publishing Company, January, 1966).
4. William Dorward, Alfred Santell interview. Transcript provided by Kevin Brownlow.
5. "Ham, Kalem comedian, started in Heavy Parts." *Motion Picture News* (October 9, 1915).
6. Ibid.
7. Press sheet for the Hamilton Comedy *Breezing Along* (May, 1927).
8. Bo Berglund, *Lloyd Hamilton: His Film Beginnings* (Griffithiana, September, 1992).

Chapter 3

1. Gloria Swanson, *Swanson on Swanson* (New York: Random House, 1980), p. 165.
2. Swanson, p. 193.
3. Joe E. Brown and Ralph Hancock, *Laughter Is a Wonderful Thing*

(New Haven: A. S. Barnes & Company, 1956), p. 185.
 4. Gray.
 5. Ibid.
 6. Stanley W. Todd, "Our Versatile Comedians: Film Comedy of Every Trade and Profession as Exemplified by Ham and Bud." *Motion Picture Magazine*, March, 1917.
 7. Kalton C. Lahue, *World of Laughter: The Motion Picture Comedy Short (1910–1930)* (Norman, OK: University of Oklahoma Press, 1966).
 8. Todd.
 9. Hal Erickson, All Movie Guide. www.allmovie.com.
 10. Kerr.
 11. Kalton C. Lahue and Samuel A. Gill, *Clown Princes and Court Jesters* (South Brunswick and New York/London: Barnes & Co., 1970).
 12. Todd.
 13. Rob Stone & David Wyatt, *Laurel or Hardy: The Solo Films of Stan Laurel and Oliver "Babe" Hardy* (Temecula, CA: Split-Reel Publishers, 1996).

Chapter 4

 1. Ames.
 2. Allan Buckingham, "Just 'Ham and Bud.'" *Photoplay Vogue* (August 20, 1915).
 3. "Hamilton Sees Art in Making Comedies." Press sheet for the Hamilton Comedy *Moonshine* (December, 1920).
 4. Ames.
 5. Dee Monroe, phone interview conducted by the author, 1978.
 6. Henry.
 7. Charles Chaplin, *My Autobiography* (London: Bodley Head, 1964).
 8. Max Weber, *The Protestant Ethic and the Spirit of Capitalism* (New York: Charles Scribner's Sons, 1930).
 9. Kevin Brownlow, *The Silent Films of William Beaudine*, Research Dossier of American Film Institute, October, 1972.
 10. Ibid.
 11. Ibid.
 12. *Moving Picture World* (October 30, 1915).
 13. Ibid.
 14. *Motion Picture News* (November 20, 1915).
 15. Brownlow, *The Silent Films of William Beaudine*.

Chapter 5

 1. *Moving Picture World* (December 18, 1915).
 2. Brownlow, *The Silent Films of William Beaudine*.
 3. Preston Sturges, *Preston Sturges by Preston Sturges: His Life in His Words* (New York: Simon & Schuster, 1990).
 4. David N. Bruskin, *The White Brothers: Jack, Jules, & Sam White* (Metuchen, NJ: The Directors Guild of America and the Scarecrow Press, 1990).
 5. Lloyd Hamilton, "Harder to Get a Laugh" (February 2, 1918). A clipping of this article was found in the Locke clippings collection at New York's Library of the Performing Arts. The newspaper name, as handwritten on the clipping, is hard to read. It is most likely either the *St. Louis Star-Times* or the *St. Louis Post-Dispatch*.
 6. Ibid.
 7. Gene Fowler, *Father Goose* (New York: Covici, Friede, 1934).
 8. Lloyd Hamilton, "Why Comedians Don't Marry." *The Cleveland Leader* (December 10, 1916).
 9. Ibid.
 10. Ibid.
 11. Ibid.

Chapter 6

 1. Dorward.
 2. Ibid.
 3. Todd.
 4. Ibid.
 5. Ibid.

Chapter 7

 1. Lahue and Gill.
 2. Fowler.
 3. Richard Roberts, alt.movies.silent forum. August 3, 2006. http://groups.google.com/group/alt. movies.silent/browse_thread/f0708a9a967d0fcf/c29777e65420f5b7?lnk=gst&q=henry+Lehrman#c29777e65420f5b7
 4. *Moving Picture World* (January 6, 1917).
 5. "Billie Ritchie Stuck in the Mud" (September 10, 1916). Locke Collection Clippings, Envelope 1910, New York Public Library for the Performing Arts.
 6. *Moving Picture Weekly* (July 8, 1916)
 7. Bruskin.
 8. Ibid.
 9. Ibid.
 10. Ibid.
 11. Ibid.

Chapter 8

 1. David A. Yallop, *The Day the Laughter Stopped* (New York: St. Martin's Press, 1976).
 2. Hamilton, "Harder to Get a Laugh."
 3. Ibid.
 4. Capron.
 5. Ibid.
 6. Kerr.
 7. "Lack of Make-up Makes Comedy-making Harder." Press sheet for the Mermaid Comedy *Moonshine* (December, 1920).
 8. Lloyd Hamilton, "Comedy Ideas at a Premium." *Photoplay* (August, 1918).
 9. Hamilton. "Harder to Get a Laugh."
 10. Ibid.
 11. "Hamilton So Serious They Won't Believe Him a Comedian." Press sheet for the Hamilton Comedy *The Greenhorn* (June, 1921).
 12. Hamilton, "Harder to Get a Laugh."
 13. Hamilton, "Comedy Ideas at a Premium."
 14. Georgina Hale interview, *Unknown Chaplin*, eds. Kevin Brownlow and David Gill. London: Thames Television, 1986.
 15. Hamilton, "Comedy Ideas at a Premium."
 16. Erwin Bauer, *The Duck Hunter's Bible* (Garden City, NY: Doubleday, 1965).
 17. Ibid.
 18. Ibid.
 19. Fox Exhibitors' Bulletin (July, 1918).
 20. "Being Serious Is Big Element in Comedies." Press sheet for the Mermaid Comedy *Dynamite* (October, 1920).
 21. Ibid.
 22. Blesh.
 23. Joe Franklin, interview with the author, 1978.
 24. Bruskin.
 25. Ibid.
 26. *Oakland Tribune* (December 1, 1918).
 27. The story was covered in the *New York Sun* and the *New York Evening Post*.
 28. *Los Angeles Times* (January 19, 1919) p. IV12.
 29. Bruskin.
 30. "Mack Sennett and Hamilton Speak Again." *Oakland Tribune* (October 17, 1932).
 31. *The Oregonian* (May 19, 1919), Volume LVIII, issue 18247, p. 8.
 32. Bruskin.

Chapter 9

 1. Yallop.
 2. Press sheet for the Hamilton Comedy *Nothing Matters* (June, 1926).
 3. *Moving Picture World* (April 23, 1927).

4. *New York Tribune* (July 19, 1920)
5. Richard M. Roberts, Robert Farr, Joe Moore, "Lloyd Hamilton: Silent Comedy's Poor Soul." Griffithiana, September, 1992.

Chapter 10

1. Bruskin.
2. Ibid.
3. Ibid.
4. Ibid.
5. Ibid.
6. *Photoplay* (July, 1923). p. 45.
7. Bruskin.
8. "Veteran Film Star Finds Ideal Comedy." Press sheet for the Mermaid Comedy *Duck Inn* (August, 1920).
9. Ibid.
10. John McCabe, Al Kilgore and Richard Bann, *Laurel and Hardy* (New York: E. P. Dutton, 1975).
11. "Cutting Means Much in Comedy's Success." Press sheet for the Mermaid Comedy *Dynamite* (October, 1920).
12. Ibid.
13. "Funny Situations and Action Invented Step by Step." Press sheet for the Hamilton Comedy *Hooked* (February, 1925).
14. Kerr.
15. Ibid.
16. "Being Serious Is Big Element in Comedies." Press sheet for the Mermaid Comedy *Dynamite* (October, 1920).
17. Capron.
18. Leonard Maltin, *The Great Movie Comedians: From Charlie Chaplin to Woody Allen* (New York: Crown Publishers, 1978).
19. Robert and Joan Franklin, Columbia Oral History Project. A. Edward Sutherland interview. Transcript provided by Kevin Brownlow.
20. Ibid.
21. Recorded interview with Edward Dryhurst, as reported by Kevin Brownlow.
22. Individuality Is Greatest Asset, Says Lloyd Hamilton." Press sheet for the Hamilton Comedy *Good Morning* (June, 1924).
23. Ibid.
24. Maltin, *The Great Movie Comedians*.
25. "Individuality Is Greatest Asset, Says Lloyd Hamilton." Press sheet for the Hamilton Comedy *Good Morning* (June, 1924).
26. Ibid.
27. Capron.
28. "Veteran Film Star Finds Ideal Comedy." Press sheet for the Mermaid Comedy *Duck Inn* (August, 1920).
29. Kerr.
30. Maltin, *The Great Movie Comedians*.
31. Ibid.

Chapter 11

1. Press sheet for the Mermaid Comedy *The Simp*.
2. Bruskin.
3. Brian Anthony and Anthony Edmonds, *Smile When the Raindrops Fall: The Story of Charley Chase* (Lanham, MD: The Scarecrow Press, 1998).
4. Ibid.
5. Bruskin.
6. Stuart Oderman, *Roscoe "Fatty" Arbuckle: A Biography of the Silent Film Comedian, 1887–1933* (Jefferson, NC: McFarland, 1994).
7. Jeanine Basinger, *Silent Stars* (Wesleyan University Press, 2000), p. 95.
8. "Lew Cody in Cleveland." *Cleveland Press* (March 1, 1922).
9. Marilyn Slater, "Mabel Normand and Her Hal Roach Years." http://looking-for-mabel.webs.com/halroachstudios.htm.
10. Betty Harper Fussell, *Mabel: Hollywood's First I-Don't-Care Girl* (New Haven: Ticknor & Fields, 1982), pg. 225.
11. "Making of Comedies a Serious Business." Press sheet for the Hamilton Comedy *April Fool* (November, 1920).
12. Bruskin.
13. Blesh.
14. "Hamilton So Serious They Won't Believe Him a Comedian." Press sheet for the Hamilton Comedy *The Greenhorn* (June, 1921).
15. Bruskin.
16. Ibid.
17. Capron.
18. Kerr.
19. Yallop.
20. Press sheet for the Hamilton Comedy *Poor Boy* (June, 1922).
21. Ibid.
22. Ibid.
23. Capron.
24. Bruskin.
25. Ibid.
26. "Hamilton Would Play Darkface Role After Two Experiences." Press sheet for the Mermaid Comedy *The Greenhorn* (June, 1921).
27. *Oakland Tribune* (May, 1922).

Chapter 12

1. George E. Turner and Michael H. Price, *Forgotten Horrors: Early Talkie Chillers from Poverty Row* (South Brunswick & New York: A.S. Barnes; London: Thomas Yoseloff, 1979).
2. Fussell, p. 126.
3. Maltin, *The Great Movie Comedians*.
4. "Individuality Is Greatest Asset, Says Lloyd Hamilton." Press sheet for the Hamilton Comedy *Good Morning* (June, 1924).
5. Buster Keaton, interview with Herbert Feinstein. *Massachusetts Review*, Winter, 1963.
6. Kevin Brownlow, email correspondence with author (March 15, 2008).
7. Keaton, interview with Herbert Feinstein.

Chapter 13

1. Capron.
2. Delight Evans, "A Flyer in the Art." *Screenland*, November, 1923.
3. Charleson Gray, "His Comeback." *Motion Picture Classic*, 30:39, November, 1929.
4. "Hamilton Appears in Garb of Woman in His Latest Comedy." Press sheet for the Hamilton Comedy *His Better Half* (July, 1927).
5. Harold Lloyd and Wesley W. Stout, *An American Comedy* (New York: B. Blom, 1928).
6. Chaplin.
7. Marion Meade, *Buster Keaton: Cut to the Chase* (New York: Da Capo Press, 1997), p. 213.
8. J.K. McDonald, Letter attachment to the *Sulphur Springs* script. First National Pictures, 1924.
9. Kerr.
10. Buster Keaton, *A Hard Act to Follow*, Episode One. Thames Television. Editors Brownlow and Gill, 1987.
11. Capron.
12. McDonald.

Chapter 14

1. "Popular Star to Continue in Short Fun Films." Press sheet for the Hamilton Comedy *Jonah Jones* (September, 1924).
2. Oderman, p. 211.
3. "'Comedy Will Soon Crowd Dramas Out,' Says Lloyd Hamilton." Press sheet for the Hamilton Comedy *Here Comes Charlie* (June, 1926).
4. "Comedian's Yearnings Lose Wife." *Los Angeles Times* (October 21, 1925), p. A5.
5. Ibid.
6. *Moving Picture World* (June 5, 1926).

Chapter 15

1. Gray.
2. William K. Everson, *American Silent Film* (New York: Oxford University Press, 1978).
3. Kerr.
4. "Well-Known Cap and Tie Laid Aside for Soldier Garb." Press sheet for the Hamilton Comedy *At Ease* (September, 1927).
5. Capron.
6. Ibid.
7. Ibid.
8. Ibid.

Chapter 16

1. "Owens Divorce Up Today." *Los Angeles Times* (February 16, 1925), p. 6.

Chapter 17

1. Kerr.
2. Maltin. *The Great Movie Comedians*.
3. Ibid.
4. Joseph McBride, *Frank Capra: The Catastrophe of Success* (New York: Simon & Schuster, 1992), p. 174.
5. "Hamilton Appears in Garb of Woman in His Latest Comedy." Press sheet for the Hamilton Comedy *His Better Half* (July, 1927).
6. Bruskin.
7. Ibid.
8. Brownlow, email correspondence.

9. Charles Lamont, interview with the author (1980).
10. Press sheet for the Hamilton Comedy *Listen Children* (July, 1928).
11. Gray.
12. Jules White, correspondence with the author (1979).

Chapter 18

1. Kerr.
2. Edward Watz, *Wheeler & Woolsey: The Vaudeville Comic Duo and Their Films, 1929–1937* (Jefferson, NC: McFarland, 1994).
3. Gray.
4. Ibid.
5. Ibid.
6. Blesh.
7. Gloria Swanson, *Swanson on Swanson*, p. 218.

Chapter 19

1. Studs Terkel, *Working* (New York: The New Press, 1974).
2. Kerr.

Chapter 20

1. Hamilton v. Hamilton, Superior Court County of Los Angeles, Case Number D39620.
2. *The Piqua Daily Call* (January 13, 1932).
3. Maltin. *The Great Movie Comedians*.
4. W.C. Fields, *W. C. Fields By Himself: His Intended Autobiography* (Upper Saddle River, NJ: Prentice-Hall, 1973).
5. Anthony and Edmonds.
6. Brown, p. 310.
7. Bruskin.
8. Meade, p. 211.
9. Bruskin.
10. *The Fresno Bee* (January 19, 1935).
11. Anthony and Edmonds.
12. Meade, p. 213.
13. Wes D. Gehring, *Joe E. Brown: Film Comedian and Baseball Buffoon* (McFarland, 2006, p. 125).
14. Leonard Maltin, *The Great Movie Shorts* (New York: Crown Publishers, 1972).
15. Kerr.
16. Ibid.
17. Martin Scorsese, Letter from The Film Foundation. March, 1993.
18. Franklin.
19. Karin Adir, *The Great Clowns of American Television* (McFarland, 2001), p. 130.
20. Jackie Gleason, correspondence received by the author from Gleason's secretary, 1980.
21. Buster Keaton, interview with Christopher Bishop. Film Quarterly, Fall, 1958.
22. Maltin, *The Great Movie Shorts*.
23. Dorward.
24. Bruskin.
25. Ibid.
26. Ibid.
27. Ibid.
28. Ibid.
29. Ibid.
30. McBride, p. 276.
31. White.

Bibliography

Periodicals

Educational pressbooks
Exhibitor's Herald (1918–1920)
Film Daily (1920–1931)
Fox Exhibitor Bulletin
The Kalem Kalender (1914–1917)
The Kalem Klip Sheet (1915–1917)
The Lubin Bulletin (1914)
The Motion Picture Almanac (1929–1933)
Motion Picture Daily (1916–1931)
Motion Picture Herald (1928–1934)
Motion Picture News (1915–1930)
Motion Picture Studio Directory and Trade Annual (1918–1924)
The Moving Picture World (1914–1927)
Photoplay (1915–1918)
Standard Casting Directory (1923–1933)
Sunshine Comedy Special (1919)

Newspapers

Cleveland Leader
Los Angeles Examiner
Los Angeles Times
New York Evening Post
New York Herald Tribune
New York Sun
New York Times
Oakland Tribune
San Francisco Chronicle

Books

Anthony, Brian, and Anthony Edmonds. *Smile When the Raindrops Fall: The Story of Charley Chase*. Lanham, MD: Scarecrow Press, 1998.
Blesh, Rudi. *Keaton*. New York: Macmillan, 1966.
Bruskin, David N. *The White Brothers: Jack, Jules, & Sam White*. Metuchen, NJ: Directors Guild of America and Scarecrow Press, 1990.
Chaplin, Charles. *My Autobiography*. London: Bodley Head, 1964.
Everson, William K. *American Silent Film*. New York: Oxford University Press, 1978.
Fields, W. C. *W. C. Fields By Himself: His Intended Autobiography*. Upper Saddle River, NJ: Prentice-Hall, 1973.
Fowler, Gene. *Father Goose*. New York: Covici, Friede, 1934.
Keaton, Buster. *My Wonderful World of Slapstick*. New York: Doubleday, 1960.
Kerr, Walter. *The Silent Clowns*. Alfred A. Knopf, 1975.
Lahue, Kalton C. *World of Laughter: The Motion Picture Comedy Short (1910–1930)*. Norman: University of Oklahoma Press, 1966.
_____, and Samuel A. Gill. *Clown Princes and Court Jesters*. South Brunswick, NJ: A.S. Barnes, 1970.
Maltin, Leonard. *The Great Movie Comedians: From Charlie Chaplin to Woody Allen*. New York: Crown, 1978.
Maltin, Leonard. *The Great Movie Shorts*. New York: Crown, 1972.
Marshall, Wendy L. *William Beaudine: From Silents to Television*. Metuchen, NJ: Scarecrow Press, 2004.
McBride, Joseph. *Frank Capra: The Catastrophe of Success*. New York: Simon & Schuster, 1992.
Oderman, Stuart. *Roscoe "Fatty" Arbuckle: A Biography of the Silent Film Comedian 1887–1933*. Jefferson, NC: McFarland, 1994.
Okuda, Ted, and Edward Watz. *The Columbia Comedy Shorts*. Jefferson, NC: McFarland, 1987.
Ragan, David. *Who's Who in Hollywood, 1900–1976*. New York: Arlington House, 1976.
Schickel, Richard. *Harold Lloyd: The Shape of Laughter*. Norwalk, CT: New York Graphic Society, 1974.
Schuster, Mel. *Motion Picture Performers: A Bibliography of Magazine and Periodical Articles, Supplement No. 1, 1970–1974*. Metuchen, NJ: Scarecrow Press, 1976.

Stone, Rob, and David Wyatt. *Laurel or Hardy: The Solo Films of Stan Laurel and Oliver "Babe" Hardy*. Temecula, CA: Split-Reel Publishers, 1996.

Turconi, David. *Mack Sennett Filmography*. Paris: Seguers, 1961.

Turner, George E., and Michael H. Price. *Forgotten Horrors: Early Talkie Chillers from Poverty Row*. South Brunswick, NJ: A.S. Barnes; London: Thomas Yoseloff, 1979.

Walker, Mickey, and Joe Reichler. *Mickey Walker: The Toy Bulldog and His Times*. New York: Random House, 1961.

Watz, Edward. *Wheeler and Woolsey: The Vaudeville Comic Duo and Their Films, 1929–1937*. Jefferson, NC: McFarland, 1994.

Weaver, John T. *Twenty Years of Silents*. Metuchen, NJ: Scarecrow Press, 1971.

Woods, Leslie. *The Romance of the Movies*. London: W. Heinemann, 1937.

Yallop, David A. *The Day the Laughter Stopped*. New York: St. Martin's Press, 1976.

Index

Numbers in ***bold italics*** indicate pages with photographs.

Abbott & Costello 57
Across Swiftcurrent Pass (1913) 21
Adair, Josephine 97, ***105***
Adams, Jimmie 61–62, ***63***, 82
The Adventures of Stingaree 43, 56–57
The Alcazar Theatre 16, 147
Alexander, Ben 112, ***114***, ***118***, ***120***
Alexander, Gus 11
Alexander, Richard ***158***
Allen, Woody 86–87
The America Theatre 18
Andy Gump 135
April Fool (1920) 85, 93
Arbuckle, Roscoe (William Goodrich) 1, 38, 41, 77, 91, 93–94, 98–99, 102, 129, 135, 164, 182
Are You There? (1930) ***158***, 159, ***159***, ***160***
Asher, Max 19
At Ease (1927) 134
Aubrey, Jimmy 35

Bacon, Lloyd 16, 46, 82, 105, 176
Banks, Monte 83
Bara, Theda 59–60, 64
The Barbary Coast 6
Bassinger, Jeanine 92
bathing beauties 61, 83, 117, 122
The Bathtub Bandit (1917) 57
Beaudine, William 42–45, 113, 122–123
Bechdolt, Fred 52
Beebe, Marjorie 168
The Beggar and His Child (1916) 50
Ben-Hur 23
Between Jobs (1928) 144
Bevan, Billy 122, 172–173
Big Boy 132, 143, 145
The Bingville Fire Department (1914) 25
Biograph 57
Bishop, John 172, 175
Bishop, Richard 2–3, 5, 171–172, 176

Black Waters (1929) ***148***, 149
Blackwell, Carlyle 23, 39, 43
Boardman, True 42, 44, 51, 52, 57
Bow, Clara 125
Boy of Mine (1923) 112
Bradley, Estelle 145
Breezing Along (1927) 133, 182
Brennan, John E. 24, 26
The Broadway Theatre 13
Brooks, Louise 129
Brown, Rev. Charles Reynolds 9–10, 171
Brown, Joe E. 147, 150, 157, 175
Bruckman, Clyde 170
Burgess, Earl 71
Burns, Neal 38
Burns, Robert 39
Busch, Mae 60

Cameo the Wonder Dog 122
Campbell, William 62, 67, 74
Cantor, Eddie 83, 108, 110
Capra, Frank 120
Capron, Frank 12
Carney, Augustus 71
Cavendor, Glen ***161***
Century Comedies 74
Chaplin, Charles 1, 5, 38, 41–42, 47, 58–59, 68, 74–75, 78, 97, 100, 114, 127, 129, 132, 148, 168, 182, 184
Chaplin, Sydney 37–38
Chase, Charley 59, 89, 91, 147, 157, 167, 175
Christie, Al 19, 36, 70, 83, 100, 144, 150, 157, 180
"The Cinnamon Bear" radio show 178–179
Clark, Violet 122
Clyde, Andy 174
Coaley, Hallom ***148***
Cody, Lew 92–93, 147, 157, 175
"Cohen & Kelly" series 165
Coleman, Frank 86

Conklin, Charles (Heinie Conklin) 62, 95
Conklin, Chester 39, 142
Conley, Lige 80, 82, 127
Coogan, Jackie 99, 112
Cooley, Frank 18
Cooper, Georgia 13–14
Cooper, Jack 74
Corr, Mary ***114***
The Count of Monte Cristo 14
Courtot, Marqueritte 43, 45
Crushed (1924) 85, 126
The Cure (1917) 148

Dale, Olive 409, 411
Dalton, Irene 3, 96, ***96***, ***99***, 100, 137–139, 142, 144–145
Dana, Viola 91
Darkfeather, Mona 23
Davenport, Dorothy 148
The Deadly Battle of Hicksville (1914) 26
De Grosse, Sam ***118***
Del Ruth, Hampton 74
Detroit 5
DeVilbiss, Bobby 97
DeVito, Danny 29
Diggins, Eddie 137–141
Diver's Last Kiss (1918) 71
Dix, Richard 147
Dr. Jekyll and Mr. Hyde 10–11, 67
Don't Be Nervous (1929) 153, ***153***
Doubling in the Quickies (1932) 168
dress extras 63
Duck Inn (1920) ***82***, 83, 88, 89
Duck Soup (1933) 127
Duncan, Bud 18–19, 29–41, ***32***, ***34***, ***38***, 43–44, 46–51, ***47***, ***48***, ***50***, 89, 171, 178–180
Dynamite (1920) 85, 89, 101

Edison 21, 35, 52
Educational Film Corporation 132
The Educator (1922) ***104***, ***105***, 106, ***107***

249

Edwards, Harry 46
Elleford, W.J. 16–17
Evans, Owen 43
Everson, William K. 132
Extra! Extra! (1923) 85

False Impressions (1932) 168
Farley, Dot 21, 60–61
Farnum, William 64
Fay, Frank 184
Fay, Hugh 67, 70, **71**, 73, 82, 102–104, 175
Felix the Cat 144
Fields, W.C. 169–170
First National Pictures 75–76, 115
Fishback, Fred (Fred Hibbard) 73, 125, 127
A Flyer in Flapjacks (1917) 97
Fovieri, Adoni **50**
Fox, William 59
The Fox Film Corporation 59–60
Foxfilm Comedies 60
Framed (1925) 130–131
Franz, Joseph J. 21
A Fresh Start (1920) 80, 83, 89
From Manger to Cross (1912) 23
Frontier Motion Picture Company 20–22

Gasnier, Louis 80
General Film 19, 51
Gibson, Helen 43, 56
Gibson, Hoot 43
Gibsone, E.M.E. 12
Gilbert, Billy 90
Gill, Sam 145
The Girl from Frisco (1916) 51–52
Girl Shy (1924) 121
Gleason, Jackie 184
Going East (1924) 85
Good Evening, Judge (1916) 49
Good Morning 87
Goose Flesh (1927) 134
Graff, Herb 1
Granger, Dorothy 168
Grant, Police Reporter (1916) 51, 56
The Greenhorn (1921) **91**, **92**, 93, **98**
Grey, John 122, 126, 179
Grey, Zane 64–65
Gribbon, Eddie 165
Griffith, D.W. 75, 100, 109–112
Griffith, Raymond 60, 182

Hackett, James K. 17, 19
Hale, Georgina 69
Hall, Huntz 184
Ham Agrees with Sherman **46**
Ham Among the Redskins (1915) 57
Ham and the Jitney Bus (1915) 35, **38**
Ham and the Villain Factory **28**
Ham in a Harem (1915) 32–**34**, 50
Ham Takes a Chance (1916) 45
Ham the Detective **32**
Ham the Diver (1916) 45
Ham the Explorer (1916) 50, 57
Ham the Iceman (1914) 26–**27**
Ham the Lineman **28**
Hamilton, Ethel (first wife) 20, 49, 99–101, 128–129, 155–157, 164, 168, 174
Hamilton, Mary (mother) 5–9, 12–13, 105, 167, 171, 175–177
Hamilton, William (father) 5–6, 8, 11, 105, 176
Hamilton-White Comedies, Inc. 94–97
Hammons, E.W. 80–81, 95, 134, 150, 177
Hanford, Ray 162
Hardy, Oliver 35
The Hash-House Count (1913) 24
Hawksley, Virginia 2–3, 9, 73, 106, 171, 172
The Hays Office 132
The Hazards of Helen 30, 51
Hello, Hollywood (1925) 127
Here Comes Charlie (1926) 134
Hiatt, Ruth 105, 112, 125, 127, 151, 154
Hiers, Walter 112
Hill, Terrence 86
His Big Minute (1929) 152
His Darker Self (1924) (*Black and White*) **109**, 109–112, 114, 127
His Musical Sneeze (1919) 73
His Smashing Career (1917) 60–61
Hochberg, Charles 73–74
Holmes, Helen 43
A Homemade Man (1928) 85, 144
Horn, Clarence W. 156–157, 164, 167, 169–170
Horton, Edward Everett 155
Hot Water (1924) 126
Houseman, Arthur 35
Howard, Curly 184
Howard, Edward 169, 174
Humphrey, Orral 13, 19, 106
Hungry Lions in a Hospital (1918) 67
The Hypnotic Monkey **40**
Hypnotic Nell (1912) 24

Ince, Thomas 127
Inslee, Charles 30, 43

The Jans Corporation 77
The Jazz Singer (1927) 146
Johnson, Noble **148**
Jolly Tars (1926) 132
Jolson, Al 109
Jonah Jones (1924) 126
Joyce, Alice 23, 30, 42–43

Kalem Corporation 23–25, 29–31, 36, 39, 42–46, 49–52, **53**, 55–57
Keaton, Buster 1, 5, 91, 93, 97, 100, 105, 107–108, 110, 113, 120, 129, 149, 153, 177, 182, 185
Keller, Al S. 156–158, 163, 165–166
Kendall, Douglas 162
Kendig, Walter 35
Kennedy, Edgar 179
Kerr, Walter 1, 31, 33, 67, 84, 133, 146, 153, 183
Keystone Cops 64
Keystone Film Company 21, 24, 25, 39, 58, 70

A Kick in the High Life (1920) 95
The Kid (1921) 93, 97, 154, 184
King Cotton (1925) **126**, 128
Kleine, George 23
Kolb and Dill 19

A Lady Bellhop's Secret (1918) 73
Lahue, Kalton 33
LaMarr, Barbara 102
Lamont, Charles 145
Lane, Lupino 108
Langdon, Harry 1, 5, 129, 135, 142, 153, 177
Larkin, George 24
La Roy, Rita **153**
Laurel, Stan 11, 86, 184
Laurel & Hardy 54, 88
Lease, Rex 167
Lee, Dorothy 4/2
Lee, Mildred 62
Lehrman, Henry 42, 57–60, 62, 64–66, 73–77, 95, 157
Leonard, Gus 44–45, **50**
Leone, Sergio 86
"The Lesson Story" (script) 75
Lewis, Jerry 87
Lillie, Beatrice 154, 159, **160**
Linder, Max 182
The Lion and the House (1932) 168
lion comedies 69, 75
Lizzie the Lifesaver (1914) 29
L-KO Comedies 60–61, 70, 74
Lloyd, Harold 1, 5, 11, 87, 100, 105, 113, 120–121, 124, 126, 179, 182, 184
Lloyd Hamilton Talking Comedies 150, 153, 164
Lonesome (1924) 111, **123**
The Los Angeles Athletic Club 41–42, 46, 70, 144, 147–148, 151, 157, 185
Love, Oil and Grease 30
Lowe, Edmund 16, 147
Lubin 19–20
Lyons, Eddie 36

MacDermott, Jack 44–45
Maggie Pepper 1
Maltin, Leonard 86, 142
Mann, Hank 38, 60, 108, 109, 142
The Mann Act 137
Mansfield, Richard 11
Marion, Frank 23, 51–52, 55–57
Marriage Rows (1931) **162**, 164
Martin, John V. 137, 141
Mayo, Archie 82, 155
McBride's Bride (1914) 26
McCall, William **161**
McDonald, J.K. 112–113, 115, 122
McGuire, Paddy 60
McPhail, Addie **162**, 164
Meehan, Charles 137–141
Melville, Rose 45
The Merry Motor Menders (1916) 51
Millarde, Harry 45
Miller, Jack 31
Miller, Patsy Ruth **114**
Miller, Rube 42
Minnie the Tiger (1915) 44

Index

Mix, Tom 60, 64
Monroe, Dee 40
Monson, Beatrice **90**
Moonshine (1920) 85, 90, **90**
Moore, Grace 160
Moran, Lee 19, 36
Morehouse, Pierce 73
Morgan, Kewpie 57
Morosco, Walter 91
Morris, Dave 43, 70
Morris, Lee 60
Motion Picture Classic (magazine) 13, 67, 111
Motion Picture News (magazine) 52, 65, 97
Move Along (1926) 131
The Movies (1925) 85, 129
Moving Picture World (magazine) 50, 55, 57, 59, 61, 72, 79, 87–89, 108
Mulgro, Charles 43
Murdock, Henry 51, 54, 132
Murray, Charles 38, 41
My Friend (1924) 111
Myers, Kathleen **92**

Neal, Lex 122
Neilan, Marshall 24–26, **25**, 29–30, 75, 149–150, 154, 177–178
Nelson, J. Arthur 21
New Moon (1930) 159–161
New York City 65, 94–95, 97, 101, 104
Nichols, Norma **46**
No Luck (1923) 85
Noble, John 82
Nobody's Business (1926) 134
Normand, Mabel 38, 41, 51, 92–93, 102

Oakland 3, 7–9, 19–20, 185
Oakland Polytechnic High School 12
The Oakland Tribune 12, 20, 73, 167
O'Malley, Tom **109**
One Exciting Night (1922) 101
Oofty Goofty 7, 38
The Optimist (1923) 109, 111
Oscar & Conrad 35
ostriches 78–79
"Oswald the Rabbit" cartoons 165
Ouelette, Charles Ray 149–150, 155–156, 158
Owen, Claudia 2

Pardon My Sarong (1942) 57
Patented by Ham **53**
Pathé 57
pathos 79, 112, 119–121
Peaceful Alley (1929) 153–154
Penrod and Sam (1923) 112, 113, 122
Photoplay (magazine) 135
Pickford, Mary 30, 75, 150, 177
Plump & Runt 35
Pokes & Jabs 39
Pollard, Daphne 165
Poor Boy (1922) 100, 154–155
Poor Soul 184
Pordenone Silent Film Festival 185
Porterville 3

Potel, Victor 31, 113
Pratt, Gilbert **82**, 83–84, 152, 154
Pretzel Captures the Smugglers **20**
Princess of the Nile (1954) 179
Private Snuffy Smith (1941) 179

Quillan, Eddie 146

The Rainmaker (1922) 86, **99**, 100
Rand, John 43
Rappe, Virginia 60, 98, 125
Ray, Al 95
Rea, Marvel 82–83, 112
Red Wing 23
Reed, Walter C. 60
The Reformation of Ham (1914) 29
Reid, Wallace 102, 148
Rin Tin Tin 75
Ritchie, Billie 58, 61, 78–79, 95
Roach, Bert 165
Roach, Hal 9, 150
Roaring Lions and Wedding Bells (1917) 61–64, **63**
Roaring Lions on the Midnight Express (1918) 72
Roberts, Stephen 180
Robinson Crusoe and Son (1932) 167
Robinson Crusoe, Ltd. (1921) 96, 106, 155, 166, 174
Rodgers, Walter L. 21
Roland, Ruth 23–24, **25**, **27**, 30, 51, 151
Rolling Stones (1922) 97
Rose Marie (1928) **140**, 142
Rosson, Dick 2
Rottman, Victor 25, **25**, **28**
Rubens, Alma 102–103
Ruge, Billy 35
Russell, Harry 25

Safety Pin Smugglers (1917) 52
St. John, Al 112, **162**, 164
Sais, Marin 30, 42, 44, 51
San Francisco, California 6–8, 14, 16, 185
Sandrich, Mark 180
Santell, Alfred 2, 52–56
A School House Scandal (1919) 74
Schwarzenegger, Arnold 29
Seastrom, Dorothy 127, 135
Selby, Gertrude 73
A Self-Made Failure (1924) 114–124, **114**, **118**, **120**, 126
Selig 31
Sellers, Peter 133
Semon, Larry 130, 135, 142, 182
Sennett, Mack 39, 41, 49, 75, 79, 95, 129, 150, 167, 169–170, 183
Service Wins Again (1930) 159
Seyffertiz, Gustav von **158**
Sherlock Bonehead (1914) 26
Sherlock, Jr. (1924) 120–121
Show of Shows (1929) 154, 159
Shy, Gus 160–161
Silk Hose and High Pressure (1915) 61
The Simp (1920) 13, 85, 89
Sis Hopkins 45, 51

The Slavery of Foxicus (1914) **25**, 27
Slim 21
Smith, Hamilton 45
Somebody's Fault (1927) 134
Soussanin, Nicholas **158**
The Speeder (1922) 105–106
Star Night at the Cocoanut Grove (1934) **173**, 174
Sterling, Ford 21–22, 26, 49, 60, 142
Stern, Abe 59
Stevens, Lander 13
Stevenson, Robert Lewis 8, 10
Strongheart 4
Strongheart (dog star) 75
Stull, Walter H. 39
Summerville, Slim 38, 41, 66, 71, 142, 165
Sunshine Comedies 60–61, 64–66, 73, 130
Sutherland, A. Edward 86, 103–104
Sutherland, Dick 125, 127
Swain, Mack 38, 39, 73, 142
Swanson, Gloria 24

Tanned Legs (1929) 154
Tati, Jacques 87
The Tattered Duke (1914) 27
Taurog, Norman 88, 127, 130–131, 135
Taylor, Sam 45
Taylor, William Desmond 99
Teare, Ethel 39, 42–45, 62, **69**, 70, 73, **107**
The Three Stooges 177, 180, 184
Tibbett, Lawrence 160
A Tight Squeeze (1918) **69**–71
Tomlin, Pinky 178
Too Many Highballs (1933) 170
Toots and Casper 178
Turpin, Ben 75, 88, 108
A Twilight Baby (1920) 77–79, 90, 93
Twins (1988) 29

Uneasy Feet (1923) 85
Universal Series **164**

The Vagrant (1921) **96**, 97
Venice, California 91
The Ventures of Marguerite (1915) 43
Vernon, Bobby 112, 132
Victor, Henry **158**
Vidor, King 112
Vitagraph 31, 57, 132, 135
"Voice of Hollywood" series 154, 174
von Seyffertiz, Gustav **158**

Waddy & Arty 35
Wadsworth, William 35
A Waiter's Wasted Life (1918) 70, 72
Waiting (1925) 127
Walker, Mickey 134
Walsh, Raoul 64
Ward, Chance E. 30, 42
Watson, William 152

Weber, Lois 57
Wedding Belles (1930) 165
Weldon, Jess 103
Welheim, Dan *161*
We're in the Navy Now (1926) 132
Wet and Warmer (1920) 95
Wheeler, Bert 146
White, Jack 2, 62–64, 72, 76, 80, 82, 91, 94, 100, 110, 130, 132, 145, 155, 166, 172, 180–181
White, Jules 145, 181
White, Pearl 51
Wide Open (1930) 165
Winning a Widow (1916) *50*
Won by a Neck (1930) *161*
Word, Chance *28*

Ye Liberty Theatre 12–13
Young, Roland 161

www.ingramcontent.com/pod-product-compliance
Lightning Source LLC
Chambersburg PA
CBHW081548300426
44116CB00015B/2802